THE ONE YEAR
DEVOS
FOR GIRLS

TYNDALE

Tyndale House Publishers, Inc.
Carol Stream, Illinois

Visit Tyndale's exciting Web site at www.tyndale.com.

TYNDALE and Tyndale's quill logo are registered trademarks of Tyndale House Publishers, Inc.

The One Year is a registered trademark of Tyndale House Publishers, Inc.

The One Year Devos for Girls

Copyright © 2000 by Children's Bible Hour. All rights reserved.

Previously published as The One Year Book of Devotions for Girls by Tyndale House Publishers, Inc.

Cover background artwork © by Kristy Pargeter/iStockphoto. All rights reserved.

Cover artwork of girl jumping © by Pavel Losevsky/iStockphoto. All rights reserved.

Designed by Jacqueline L. Nuñez

Edited by Debbie Bible and Betty Free

Stories written by Katherine R. Adams, Darlene Anderson, Philip J. Anderson, Sandra L. Ardoin, Esther M. Bailey, Melissa M. Bamberg, Brenda Benedict, Trula H. Bensinger, Ruth E. Blount, Karen L. Blumhagen, Gail D. Brown, Wanda E. Brunstetter, Teddie Bryant, Robert Byers, Karen E. Cogan, Kim Cogan, V. Louise Cunningham, Brenda D. Decker, Harriett A. Durrell, Bethany R. Elms, M. Tanya Ferdinandusz, Stephanie E. Frantz, Cathy L. Garnaat, Rose Gobel, Dianne V. Godbold, Jorlyn A. Grasser, Ruth M. Hamel, Jan L. Hansen, Mary G. Houlgate, Ruth Hryshkanych, Cindy Huff, Vera M. Hutchcroft, Ruth I. Jay, Gail L. Jenner, Victoria Johnson, Dean Kelley, Beverly Kenniston, Nance E. Keyes, Sharon King, Phyllis I. Klomparens, Sherry L. Kuyt, Jacqueline J. Leaycraft, Suzanne M. Lima, Agnes G. Livezey, Karen R. Locklear, Richard S. Maffeo, Deborah S. Marett, Hazel W. Marett, Lorna B. Marlowe, Tanya K. Marshall, Anne Martin, Beverly McClain, Susi McCord, Nancy I. Merical, Martha A. Mitchell, Gloria D. Morrison, Sara L. Nelson, Violet E. Nesdoly, Jan Nieland, Sharyl Noelle, Matilda H. Nordtvedt, Mary Rose Pearson, Carolyn A. Penner, Raelene E. Phillips, Connie I. Rainbolt, Sharon K. Regehr, Victoria L. Reinhardt, Lynn Stamm Rex, L. Gail Rhodes, Barbara Riegier, Phyllis Robinson, Deana L. Rogers, Lucinda J. Rollings, Catherine Runyon, A. J. Schut, Marilyn J. Senterfitt, Rhonda S. Sherrill, L. Anne Siegrist, Patricia C. Singletary, Irene C. Strobel, Heather M. Tekavec, Emily I. Thompson, Nancy A. Thompson, Harry C. Trover, Charles VanderMeer, Trudy M. VanderVeen, Janet K. VanDyke, Sandra K. Vaughn, Geri Walcott, Linda M. Weddle, Barbara J. Westberg, Jane Weverink, Cathy J. Wilt, Lois A. Witmer, Carolyn E. Yost. (The author's initials appear at the end of each story.)

All stories are taken from issues of Keys for Kids, published bimonthly by the Children's Bible Hour, PO Box 1, Grand Rapids, Michigan 49501.

Unless otherwise indicated, all Scripture quotations are taken from the Holy Bible, New Living Translation, copyright © 1996 by Tyndale House Foundation. Used by permission of Tyndale House Publishers, Inc., Carol Stream, Illinois 60188. All rights reserved.

Scripture quotations marked NKJV are taken from the New King James Version.® Copyright © 1982 by Thomas Nelson, Inc. Used by permission. All rights reserved. NKJV is a trademark of Thomas Nelson, Inc.

Scripture quotations marked NIV are taken from the Holy Bible, New International Version,® NIV.® Copyright © 1973, 1978, 1984 by Biblica, Inc.™ Used by permission of Zondervan. All rights reserved worldwide. www.zondervan.com.

For manufacturing information regarding this product, please call 1-800-323-9400.

The Library of Congress has cataloged the previous edition as follows:

One year book of devotions for girls.
    p. cm.
   Includes index.
   ISBN 978-0-8423-3619-2 (pbk.)
   1. Girls—Prayer-books and devotions—English.   2. Devotional calendars—Juvenile literature. [1. Prayer books and devotions.   2. Devotional calendars.] I. Title: Devotions for girls.   II. Tyndale House Publishers.

BV4860 .O54 2000
242′.62—dc21   00-029915

Printed in the United States of America

15   14   13   12   11
18   17   16   15   14

TABLE OF CONTENTS

DECEMBER

INDEX OF TOPICS

INDEX OF SCRIPTURE READINGS

INDEX OF MEMORY VERSES

INTRODUCTION FOR PARENTS

For many years Children's Bible Hour has published *Keys for Kids,* a bimonthly devotional magazine for kids. Parents and children have appreciated their fine ministry over the years, and Tyndale House is proud to present this new collection of stories from *Keys for Kids.*

The One Year Devos for Girls has a full year's worth of stories that girls will find especially interesting. Each story illustrates a Scripture reading for the day, and following each one is a "How about You?" section. This asks girls to apply the story to their lives.

There is also a memory verse for each day, often taken from the Scripture reading. Unless otherwise noted, memory verses are quoted from the *New Living Translation.* Verses marked NIV are from the *New International Version,* while those marked NKJV are from the *New King James Version.* You may want to encourage your girls to memorize each verse as it appears, or you can have them use the Bible translation your family prefers.

Each devotion ends with a key phrase at the bottom of the page. This three- to five-word phrase summarizes the lesson and helps girls know how to respond to it.

The stories in this devotional are geared toward girls between the ages of six and ten. Your daughters can enjoy these stories by themselves as they develop their own daily quiet time. (You can supervise that time as much or as little as you wish.) Or the stories can be used as part of your family devotions. Like stories from the Bible, the stories here speak not only to children but also to adults. They are simple, direct, and concrete. And they speak to everyone in understandable terms, just as Jesus' parables do.

This book contains Scripture indexes of daily readings and of memory verses, as well as a topical index. The Scripture indexes are helpful for locating a story or verse related to a passage that you want to discuss. The topical index is useful for dealing with concerns that arise in any family, such as health, relationships, telling the truth, and trusting God.

We hope you'll use this book every day, but don't feel locked into any one format. Please use any story any time you feel it relates to a special situation in your family.

CRITICISM VERSUS LOVE

(Read Mark 12:28-33)

As the family car swung away from the curb, little Annie waved to Mrs. Shrively, who was climbing her porch steps. Sarah leaned forward and rested her arms on the back of the front seat. "Whew! I'm glad Mrs. Shrively's gone," she said. "She was about to drive me crazy."

Her brother Rob agreed. "And she looks funny, too."

"And her dresses . . . ," Sarah giggled. "They're worse than bags. They're tents!"

"Kids!" Mother's voice showed her disapproval. "You both know you're not to talk like that! Mrs. Shrively is a wonderful Christian woman."

"But she bosses me around all the time," said Rob, "and then she quotes Scripture to back it up. I wish she'd just leave me alone."

"She embarrasses me in front of my friends," complained Sarah.

Dad joined the conversation. "But she is just the kind of person that Jesus would have befriended. He loves everyone, including the Mrs. Shrivelys of the world."

"And I doubt that Jesus would make fun of her," answered Sarah.

Dad nodded.

"But it sure will be hard not to make fun of her," said Rob.

"I'm sure God will help you," said Mother.

"Let's all ask God to help us," suggested Dad. "If we hold up one another in prayer, God will help us to do what is right." *RG*

HOW ABOUT YOU?

Maybe there's someone you really have trouble liking—someone who dresses differently or acts strangely or just bugs you. Don't join the kids at school if they pick on one of your classmates. Whenever you're tempted to be critical or unkind, remember that God made the person you're criticizing, and God loves that person just as much as he loves you.

**LOVE OTHERS
AS JESUS DOES**

MEMORIZE:

"But God showed his great love for us by sending Christ to die for us while we were still sinners." Romans 5:8

JANUARY 2

SINCERELY WRONG

(Read Isaiah 64:6-8)

Dana and Dan were spending the week with their uncle and aunt, and one day they got into a discussion on how to get to heaven. "The Bible says that only people who admit they're sinners and accept Jesus will go to heaven," Uncle Scott told them.

"But we know lots of really good people," argued Dan. "They go to all different kinds of churches and probably believe all different kinds of things. But they're all sincere."

"Yeah," agreed Dana. "How can anybody say they're not going to heaven?"

That night, Dana heard a groaning sound coming from Dan's room. She went to investigate. "O-o-oh," moaned Dan, "my stomach! What can I do?"

"You ate too much tonight," scolded Dana. "But I saw some pink stuff in the medicine cabinet—stuff like we use at home. That should make you feel better. It's on the top shelf in a white bottle."

Dan headed for the bathroom and took the medicine. Then he tried to sleep again but soon gave up. He called his sister. "If anything, that medicine made me worse," he told her.

"Did you take the pink stuff?" Dana asked.

"Pink stuff?" Dan groaned. "I thought you said the white stuff in the pink bottle!"

Quickly, Dana called Aunt Sue and explained what had happened. Aunt Sue checked, and she saw that what Dan had believed to be something that would help his stomach was actually hand lotion. "I don't think it will hurt you," she said, "but we'll check with the doctor to make sure." She headed for the telephone and soon found out what to do.

"It really is silly to think it doesn't matter what you believe as long as you're sincere about it, isn't it?" Dan said when Uncle Scott talked with him. "I sure was sincere when I took that stuff last night. Now I know what you meant about people being sincere but still being wrong and missing the way to heaven."

Uncle Scott nodded. "I'm glad you realize that now," he said. "It was bad enough to be wrong about the medicine, but it's much worse to be wrong about the way to heaven. Jesus is the one and only way." *HCT*

HOW ABOUT YOU?

Do you think it doesn't matter so much what religion you follow? Do you believe everyone who sincerely does his best will go to heaven? That isn't true. Did you notice what God says about your good works, sincere though you may be? He compares them to filthy rags! Quit doing things your own way and come to Jesus.

MEMORIZE:

"All our righteous acts are like filthy rags." Isaiah 64:6, NIV

YOU CAN BE SINCERE— BUT WRONG

THE GREATEST MIRACLE

(Read Romans 6:4-11)

Greg's eyes lit up as he listened to Aunt Karen on the phone. "Thank you for praying for Maria," she said. "The infection in her eye has completely cleared up."

"That's really a miracle!" exclaimed Greg as he thought back over the past months. His little cousin had been taking various medications to clear up an eye infection, but the doctor thought he'd have to send Maria to an eye specialist for possible surgery. Greg and his family had been praying every day that God would heal Maria's eye.

"Tonya!" called Greg. "Guess what? Aunt Karen says that Maria's eye is better!"

"Really? Oh, great!" cheered Tonya. "Mom, come and hear about our miracle!"

Mother hurried into the room to see what all the commotion was about. "What happened?" she asked. Tonya and Greg told her about their Aunt Karen's call. "Isn't that neat!" exclaimed Tonya. Then she added thoughtfully, "God answered our prayers, didn't he? I wish he'd do a miracle in my life, too."

Mother smiled. "Actually, he has," she said. "As a matter of fact, God has performed a wonderful miracle in each of your lives."

"I can't remember him healing me," protested Tonya.

"What miracle are you talking about, Mom?" Greg wanted to know.

"I'm talking about the day that each of you received Jesus as Savior," Mother explained. "He healed you on the inside by changing you from children who wanted to do wrong into children who want to do right. That is really the greatest miracle of all." *DLR*

HOW ABOUT YOU?

Has Jesus done a miracle in your life? Would you like him to? Many people today are looking for miracles to prove that God's power is real, but they fail to recognize the greatest miracle of all—a changed life. If you've experienced this miracle, thank God for demonstrating his saving power in your life. If you haven't yet experienced this, talk with a trusted friend or adult.

MEMORIZE:

"What this means is that those who become Christians become new persons. They are not the same anymore, for the old life is gone. A new life has begun!"

2 Corinthians 5:17

SALVATION IS A MIRACLE

JANUARY
4

A SACRIFICIAL GIFT

(Read 2 Corinthians 9:6-9)

"I wonder if that missionary will get the money he needs to go to the mission field," said Russ after the service one Sunday. "Too bad Mr. Gaylord wasn't there. He always manages to miss the sermons on giving. I bet he's never given a sacrificial gift in all his life!" Russ was referring to a rich old man who lived not far from their home and who attended their church.

Connie agreed. "Remember how the missionary spoke about 'giving till it hurts'?" she asked. "I'll bet just the thought of giving hurts Mr. Gaylord." Both children laughed.

"Now, wait a minute, you two," protested Mother. "Have either of you ever given a sacrificial gift?"

Connie was surprised. "But it's different with us!" she exclaimed. "We've got nothing to sacrifice or we would."

"Sure we would!" agreed Russ. "If I have anything the Lord wants, I'll give it."

"Be careful," warned Mother. "If you make a promise to the Lord, he expects you to keep it."

That afternoon the children were playing with their dog, Taffy, when Mr. Gaylord came by. To their surprise, he offered to buy Taffy for ten dollars. "No way!" said Russ.

"Not enough money, eh?" grunted Mr. Gaylord. "Well, all right—I'll give you $25 for him, and that's my final offer."

Again the children shook their heads. "We wouldn't sacrifice Taffy for any . . . ," began Connie. She stopped, startled. The word "sacrifice" reminded her of their earlier conversation. Russ and Connie looked at each other. They knew what they needed to do. With tears in their eyes, they sold Taffy to a very surprised Mr. Gaylord.

Later Mr. Gaylord talked with their mother and learned why they had sold Taffy. "That dog meant all the world to those children," he exclaimed when he had heard the story, "yet they were willing to give him up for the Lord!" He shook his head in amazement. "This is the most powerful sermon I've ever had preached to me," he added. "If they can give $25, I can give a thousand. And from now on, I'm going to start giving the way those children have taught me to give." *HCT*

HOW ABOUT YOU?

Sometimes God asks us to give sacrificially. Ask him what he would have you do, and then do it. After all he has done for you, no sacrifice is too great to make for him!

MEMORIZE:

"God loves the person who gives cheerfully." 2 Corinthians 9:7

GIVE SACRIFICIALLY

KEEP GROWING

(Read 1 Peter 2:1-3)

"Did I really wear this?" asked Michelle. She held up the tiny, knitted bonnet.

Mother smiled. "Yes," she said. "Isn't it amazing how little we are at first and how much we grow?" She picked up a pair of baby shoes. "You wore these when you were about a year old and had just started walking." Mother rubbed the soft leather. "Before long, you were running everywhere and were ready for a larger pair of shoes."

Michelle grinned, and they continued to dig through the box of memories. Michelle picked up a small scrapbook and opened it. "You wrote in this, Mom. It says, 'Michelle's drawings from ages three to six.'" She examined the pages. "At least my drawings got better each year," she said.

"Yes, they did," agreed Mother. "The bigger you grew, the more you learned about how to draw houses, trees, and people." She picked up a sheet of paper. "Look. Here's a list of questions you asked when you were in second grade."

"Really? That was the year I asked Jesus into my heart," said Michelle. She looked at the list. "Listen to these, Mom. 'Are clouds made out of cotton candy?' 'Is God in all places?' 'Why did Jesus have to die?'"

"All good questions," said Mother. "Do you know the answers now?"

"Sure," said Michelle. "I've learned a lot since then."

Mother nodded. "Good," she said. "You grew physically and mentally, and you grew spiritually, too. That's as it should be."

Michelle smiled. "We grow physically and mentally by eating food and studying, and we grow spiritually through things like Bible reading and church, right?" she asked.

"Those things certainly help," agreed Mother. "And don't forget that we must not only read but obey God's Word."

Michelle held up the scrapbook. "It's like these drawings," she said. "The more I grew, the better I drew. And the more I . . . ah . . ." She laughed. "Oops! I can't think of a rhyme to tell how I grew spiritually." *SLA*

HOW ABOUT YOU?

You don't wear the same clothes you wore a few years ago, do you? You're able to solve harder problems and do better at sports, right? Have you also grown spiritually? Do you know more about Jesus? Memorizing Bible verses, faithful attendance in church and Sunday school, and studying God's Word will help you grow spiritually.

MEMORIZE:

"But grow in the special favor and knowledge of our Lord and Savior Jesus Christ." 2 Peter 3:18

GROW SPIRITUALLY

TWICE ADOPTED

(Read Galatians 4:4-7)

Brenda, the adopted daughter of Rev. and Mrs. Marsh, never got tired of hearing the story about when her parents took her home from the adoption agency. "It happened when you were only six weeks old," her father told her one evening when she begged to hear the story again. "Since the ride home was a long one, they sent a bottle along with us so we could feed you on the way home. But you kept falling asleep when you were supposed to be drinking your bottle."

Brenda giggled. "So you kept blowing the horn to try to keep me awake, right?"

"Right," said Dad. "And I'll never forget when the agency first called me at work and told me they had a baby for us. I was so excited, I forgot to ask if it was a boy or a girl." Everyone laughed as the family recalled the happy event.

"What does the word *adopt* mean?" asked Brenda.

"I looked it up once," said Mother. "The dictionary says it means to voluntarily take a child of other parents as one's own child." Mother gave Brenda a hug. "We gladly took you as our own. We're so thankful the Lord brought you to us."

"You know, Brenda," added Dad, "the same thing is true of our relationship to God. The Bible tells us that when we trust the Lord Jesus Christ, God accepts us as his own children. We're adopted into the family of God."

"Then I've been adopted twice," said Brenda happily. "I was adopted into your family when I was a baby, and I was adopted into God's family when I became a Christian. Now I belong to you, and I belong to God. I like being adopted!" *CVm*

HOW ABOUT YOU?

Have you been adopted into God's family? He wants you to be a part of his family. But first, you need to accept Jesus as your Savior. If you have questions, ask a trusted friend or adult.

MEMORIZE:

"But to all who believed him and accepted him, he gave the right to become children of God." John 1:12

GOD WANTS TO ADOPT YOU

HANDLE WITH CARE

(Read Luke 12:16-21)

Crash! The sound of shattering glass echoed through the house. Both Randy and his mother ran into the kitchen. "Oh, Jennifer, you didn't!" Mother exclaimed when they saw the little girl looking in dismay at pieces of a crystal vase scattered all over the floor. "I told you not to touch that! You've broken my new vase!"

"I didn't mean to," Jennifer sobbed. "I just wanted to hold it."

Mother nodded. "I see that," she said. "Right now I want you to go wait in your room before you get cut on this glass. I'll be there to talk to you in a minute, but first I need to get this picked up. Randy, would you get out the vacuum for me, please?"

As they worked, Randy shook his head. "Jennifer should have known better than to pick up the vase," he said. "But since she did pick it up, she should have hung on tight!"

"That's true," agreed Mother. She looked thoughtful. "I can't help but think of something else that we all are holding in our hands—something people often let slip away," she added. Randy looked at his empty hands in bewilderment. "Our souls are in our hands," continued Mother. "The soul is the most valuable thing we possess, yet people play with it so carelessly. Many are like the rich fool Jesus talked about—interested only in having enough to eat, having a good time, and being popular. Remember, Son, you need to handle your soul with care." *BJW*

HOW ABOUT YOU?

Are you being careless with your soul? It's that special something inside your body that will live forever. It's worth more than the whole world! Your soul is in your care. It's up to you to decide if your soul will go to heaven. To find out more, ask a trusted friend or adult.

YOUR SOUL IS VALUABLE

MEMORIZE:
"And how do you benefit if you gain the whole world but lose your own soul in the process?" Mark 8:36

JANUARY
8

MORE THAN MILK

(Read Hebrews 5:12-14)

"Lindy, have you memorized your Bible verse for church?" asked Mom.

"Yeah, but church isn't fun anymore," grumbled Lindy.

"Why not?" asked Mom, spooning mashed carrot into baby Robyn's mouth.

"Things are just different," replied Lindy. "Now we have to read right from the Bible and memorize verses and . . ." She paused as baby Robyn made a gagging sound. "What's the matter, Robyn?" asked Lindy as she tapped a spoon on the high chair, trying to distract her baby sister.

"She's so used to milk and cereal and juices that she's finding it a bit difficult to handle lumps," explained Mom.

"Poor Robyn," said Lindy sympathetically. She turned to her mother. "Why not just let her have milk then?"

"Because she's no longer a tiny baby," said Mom. "Robyn has to get used to taking solid food if she's to grow and be healthy."

"Oh," said Lindy. She stroked her sister's cheek. "Eat up, Robyn. You've got to get big and strong soon so you can play with me!"

Mom again held the spoon to the baby's mouth. "You're having the same kind of trouble as Robyn," she observed.

"Me!" exclaimed Lindy indignantly. "I have no problem swallowing my food!"

"Not your physical food," agreed Mom, "but how about your spiritual food? When you were a baby in the faith, you were fed 'milk'—cute little songs, simple Bible stories, fun-to-do drawings and handwork. Now that you're growing up, milk alone isn't enough, and you need solid food—things like more difficult Bible verses to study and memorize." *MTF*

HOW ABOUT YOU?

Are you having trouble with the "lumps" in your spiritual diet? Do you feel like the Bible is too hard to understand, like church lasts too long, or like it's more fun to play than to learn Bible verses? Remember, God wants you to grow up on the inside and the outside.

MEMORIZE:

"Brothers, stop thinking like children.
In regard to evil be infants, but
in your thinking be adults."
1 Corinthians 14:20, NIV

GROW IN THE LORD

IT'S A FACT

(Read 1 John 5:9-13)

Sherri sat in her science class, nibbling the end of her pencil, but her mind was still on the message she had heard in church the day before. It was about how all have sinned and need Jesus as Savior. Sherri sighed. *I know I'm a sinner, and I have asked Jesus to forgive me,* she thought. *I know the Bible says he will, but I wonder if I should ask him to forgive me again. I really don't feel like I'm a Christian.* Actually, Sherri often didn't feel like she was a Christian, so several times before, she had confessed her sin and told Jesus she trusted him to forgive her.

Suddenly Sherri's thoughts were interrupted as she heard her teacher, Mr. Shanks, saying, "Did you know you're spinning right now? Like a top, the earth spins on its axis, making a complete rotation every 24 hours. The axis is an imaginary line that connects the North Pole and the South Pole. The earth also travels around the sun at an average speed of 66,600 miles an hour. It takes 365 days to make the 595 million-mile circuit. Those are the facts. So even though we don't feel it, we're not only moving, we're spinning!"

Wow! thought Sherri. She was impressed. Suddenly another thought struck her. *Even though I don't feel like I'm spinning, scientists say that I am. And even though I don't feel like I'm a Christian, the Bible says I am! And the Bible is more accurate than science.*

That evening Dad finished family devotions by asking Sherri to read several verses from 1 John (see today's Scripture). After reading the verses, Sherri smiled and told her family what she had learned about the earth in science class. "I believe what the scientists say about the earth moving and spinning, and I believe what God says about salvation," she told them. "It's a fact that the earth is spinning even though I can't feel it, and it's also a fact that I've accepted Jesus as my Savior—so I'm a Christian even though I might not always feel like I am. It doesn't depend on my feelings at all." *NAT*

HOW ABOUT YOU?

Do you know you have eternal life? You can be sure of it. The Bible says you have eternal life if you've trusted in Jesus Christ to be your Savior. Rely on the fact of God's Word, not on your feelings.

BELIEVE GOD'S WORD

NO EXCUSE

(Read Romans 3:19-23)

"Come on, Shannon!" Nicole urged her older sister. "You can make the light."

Shannon grinned. "OK. Hang on!" With a burst of speed, they went through the traffic light just after it turned red.

Shannon groaned as she noticed a police car in the rearview mirror. Nicole turned, and she saw it, too. She felt guilty as she remembered how she had urged Shannon to go through the changing light. They pulled to the side of the road in response to the flashing police signal, and the officer approached their car. Soon the policeman was driving away, leaving the girls staring at the traffic ticket Shannon held in her hand.

When the girls' parents learned about the ticket, Shannon made excuses. "I don't see why that policeman couldn't have just overlooked it," she said. "If the light was red, it had only just turned! Besides, all I did is go through that one little red light when no cars were coming anyway! It's not like I robbed a bank or murdered somebody."

Mom shook her head. "It was foolish and dangerous and wrong to go through a changing light," she said. "You broke the law, and now you have to pay."

"That's right," agreed Dad as he looked at the ticket. "Your excuses remind me of people who think they aren't bad enough to miss heaven. They think they don't need to be saved from their sins. But everyone who is honest has to admit he's done at least one wrong thing. So he's a lawbreaker, and the fine must be paid." Dad handed the ticket back to Shannon. "You'll have to pay this fine your-self—but, thank God, Jesus already has paid the fine for your sins." *PR*

HOW ABOUT YOU?

Do you think you can get into heaven just because you haven't done very many wrong things? Have you ever told one lie? Disobeyed just once? Had a bad thought? Done just one wrong thing? Then God says you're guilty—you've broken his law. Only Jesus could pay the "fine." He did this on the cross. Talk to a trusted friend or adult if you have more questions about what having a relationship with Jesus means.

MEMORIZE:

"And the person who keeps all of the laws except one is as guilty as the person who has broken all of God's laws." James 2:10

ONE WRONG BRINGS GUILT

MOST EXCITING LAUNCH

(Read 1 Thessalonians 4:15-18)

Jana was glad when her father was transferred to a town only 25 miles from the Kennedy Space Center. She was excited one night when a launch was to take place, because her father had promised to wake her shortly before the liftoff time. Jana could think of nothing else as she went to bed, but she finally drifted off to sleep.

The next thing Jana knew, Dad was bending over her and calling her name. Jana sat up quickly. Then, putting on her robe, she followed her father outside to a spot where they'd be able to see the bright light from the launch pad.

"I'm glad they're doing a night launch!" exclaimed Jana. "And just think how great it would be to go up—that would really be exciting!" As she spoke, a yellow light appeared, suddenly brightening the entire sky. "Is that it?" Jana wanted to know, just a little disappointed that it wasn't more striking.

Dad shook his head. "No, just keep looking in that . . ."

Before her father could finish what he was saying, Jana called out, "There she is, Dad! Just like a big ball of fire!" They stood watching as long as the red spot was in view. When it disappeared into the clouds, they returned to the house. "Wow! I wouldn't have wanted to miss that for anything," said Jana.

"I'm glad you got to see it, too," agreed Dad. He put an arm around Jana's shoulder as he added, "Being out here and watching the sky reminds me of another, even more exciting launch I don't want either one of us to miss."

"The next launch?" Jana asked. "Will that one be more exciting?"

Dad smiled. "It could be the next one or it could happen later than that," he said. "I'm thinking of the time when Jesus will come and take those who love him to be with him in heaven. Will you be ready for that event?" Dad asked.

Jana slowly shook her head. "I'm not sure," she admitted, "but I don't want to miss it either." Together Jana and her father talked about how to prepare for eternity, and Jana was glad she had already asked Christ to be her Savior. *RIJ*

HOW ABOUT YOU?

Are you ready for that "most exciting launch" when all those who have believed in Jesus will rise to meet him in the air? If you have questions about how you can be ready, ask a trusted friend or adult.

BE READY FOR ETERNITY

JANUARY
12

THE NAME CRAZE (PART 1)

(Read Revelation 20:12-15; 21:2, 27)

Kendra used to like having a name that was different from any other in school, but not anymore. Some of the girls had pencils with their names on them. Julia had a notebook with her name printed on it, and Susan even had shoestrings with her name on them. Kendra wanted something with her name printed on it, too, but she couldn't find anything at all. "You might as well give up looking, Kendra," advised Mother after one shopping trip. "I'm afraid you won't find your name on anything."

Kendra sighed. "What does my name mean, Mom?" she asked. "Jan's name means 'beloved of God.' I'd like to at least know what my name means."

"I don't know, honey. We just liked the name, so we gave it to you."

"Well, I wish I had a normal name," complained Kendra. "I'd love a notebook with my name on it like Julia has."

"I guess it would be nice to have a notebook with your name printed on it," Mother agreed. "But there's another book—a much more important one—with your name in it."

Kendra looked at Mother in surprise. "There is?"

Mother smiled. "You've accepted Jesus as your Savior, haven't you?" Kendra nodded, and Mother continued. "Then your name is written in heaven, in the Lamb's Book of Life," she said. "And that's important because only those whose names are written in that Book will go to live in heaven."

Kendra looked thoughtful. Then she grinned. "Yeah," she said, "and that's better than having my name on things like notebooks or shoestrings, isn't it? Those things will wear out, but having my name in the Book of Life is forever!" *REP*

HOW ABOUT YOU?

Can you find your name on notebooks, stickers, or other things? These things are fun, but they're not forever things. It's much more important to have your name in the Book of Life. You can do this by becoming a Christian.

MEMORIZE:

"Rejoice because your names are registered as citizens of heaven."
Luke 10:20

HAVE YOUR NAME WRITTEN IN HEAVEN

THE NAME CRAZE (PART 2)

(Read Isaiah 43:1; John 10:3; Revelation 3:5)

As Kendra waited for the morning church service to start, she nudged her mother. "Look!" She pointed to the church bulletin. Mother smiled as she saw the title of the evening sermon—"The Name Craze."

That evening, Kendra smiled and nodded when Pastor Davis began his message by pointing out that it's important to have your name written in the Book of Life. She was so glad her name was there. *I still wish I knew what the meaning of my name was, though,* she thought.

Suddenly Kendra realized that Pastor Davis was talking about that very thing. "Maybe your name doesn't seem to have a meaning like Bible names did, but what does your name mean to God?" asked Pastor Davis. "When God thinks of you, what comes to his mind? Does he think 'patience' or 'my faithful servant'? Or does he think 'complainer' or 'grouchy'?"

Hey, thought Kendra, *I'm going to quit fussing about not having an earthly meaning for my name. Instead, I'll work on living the way God wants me to. What he thinks of me is what's really important. REP*

HOW ABOUT YOU?

As you read today's Scripture, did you notice that God knows you by name—that you're not just one of the crowd? Do you know what your name means? If so, maybe you'll want to live up to its meaning. But perhaps you have a "different" name, one that has no meaning. No matter. Your name can be a good name as you choose to love God and live as he wants you to live.

**YOU CAN HAVE
A GOOD NAME**

MEMORIZE:
"Choose a good reputation over great riches, for being held in high esteem is better than having silver or gold."
Proverbs 22:1

JANUARY
14

FAMILY PORTRAIT

(Read 1 Corinthians 12:12-14)

Maya waited as Miss Hamilton passed out drawing paper. "Take out your crayons," said Miss Hamilton. "I want each of you to draw a picture of your family."

Some of the children groaned in protest, but Maya thought it sounded like fun. She knew just what to draw. She first drew her parents, her brother and sister, and herself. Then she added their cat, Princess. But she didn't stop there. She drew girls, boys, men, and women. Blondes, brunettes, redheads, and baldheads. She used peach, tan, light brown, darker brown, yellow, and pink crayons to draw the faces. She drew some people with glasses, braces, casts, and crutches. She was drawing a boy in a wheelchair when Miss Hamilton asked, "Who would like to share your picture with us?"

Randi raised her hand. She waved her paper proudly. "Here's me, my parents and brother, and all my grandparents, aunts, uncles, and cousins," she said.

"Aunts and uncles and cousins?" asked Benji. "I thought we were supposed to just draw our parents and brothers and sisters."

"I said 'family' so that can be whoever you want to include," said Miss Hamilton. She stopped at Maya's chair. "Maya, please tell us about your picture," she said.

Maya held up her picture. "Here's me, Valerie and Rick, our parents, and our cat. And here are some of you and some other people from all over the world."

"We're not your family," said Benji, "and I don't think those other people you drew are either."

"Last week our church memory verse was about everyone who's a Christian being part of God's family. Well, I'm part of God's family, so all kinds of people are in my family, too." She stopped, unsure of what her classmates and her teacher would think of that.

"I like it!" Randi said, sketching a few extra figures into her picture.

"So do I," said Miss Hamilton. "It's nice to think of all of us as one big family." *SN*

HOW ABOUT YOU?

Who fits your definition of "family"? Your relatives? Your fellow Sunday school and church members? People you might not like right now? Christians in other countries? If you're part of God's family, then everyone who loves him—even people you don't like or don't know—are part of your family.

MEMORIZE:

"Whenever we have the opportunity, we should do good to everyone, especially to our Christian brothers and sisters." Galatians 6:10

ALL CHRISTIANS ARE GOD'S FAMILY

DIFFERENT WAY TO TALK

(Read 1 Corinthians 9:19-23)

Julie walked into the kitchen and took a deep breath. "Oh, boy! Homemade bread!" she exclaimed.

Her dad looked up from his work. "That's right, honey. But this loaf isn't for us. I'm taking it next door to our new neighbors." He paused briefly. "Did you know they have a girl just about your age?" he asked. "You should meet her."

Julie shook her head. "I already did, but she's no fun. She doesn't talk or anything."

"Maybe she's just a little shy," suggested Dad. "It takes some people longer to adjust than others."

"No," said Julie. "You don't understand. She doesn't . . . I mean, she *can't* talk. She can't say anything, and she can't hear either. So there's no point in going over there."

"I see," said Dad thoughtfully. "Well, if she can't talk the way you do, maybe you should learn to talk her way. I'll learn, too, OK?"

Julie looked at Dad in surprise. "Her way? You mean learn sign language?" she asked. "Why should I bother to do that? I'm sure she already has friends."

"Perhaps," said Dad. "But who knows . . . maybe the Lord sent her here for us to witness to her."

"But, Dad," protested Julie. "He wouldn't really expect us to learn sign language, would he? That's a lot of work."

"True," agreed Dad, "but think about it. When your brother went to Bangladesh as a missionary, what was the first thing he had to do?"

"Go to language school," replied Julie reluctantly.

Dad nodded. "Do you think our neighbors might be *our* mission field?" he asked. "If learning sign language would help us to tell them about Jesus, that wouldn't be too much to ask, would it?" *RIJ*

HOW ABOUT YOU?

Did you know that the apostle Paul said he became 'all things to all men' in order to win some? Are you willing to go out of your way to tell someone about Jesus? Maybe you need to become a friend to someone, help someone with schoolwork, or do extra chores at home. What special thing can you do?

GO OUT OF YOUR WAY TO WIN OTHERS

MEMORIZE:
"Yes, I try to find common ground with everyone so that I might bring them to Christ." 1 Corinthians 9:22

JANUARY
16

After Grandma's funeral, Amy sat on her bed with a photo album on her lap. Tears blurred her vision as she looked at pictures of a teenage Grandma standing by a 1940s automobile, and then at more recent pictures of Grandma in her flower garden.

Amy heard talking and laughter downstairs. Everyone was having a good time. Everyone but her. *How can they talk and eat and laugh like nothing's happened?* she wondered. Amy had noticed that even at the funeral most people—her mom included—did not behave as though they were sorry Grandma had died.

After a while, Amy's mother came looking for her. "Are you all right, honey?" asked Mom. "You've been so quiet today."

Anger bubbled up in Amy. "I won't be happy about Grandma's death like everyone else," she said. "It sounds like one big party downstairs—I hear you all laughing."

Her mother sat on the bed beside her. "We've been remembering the good times we had with Grandma," she said. "We will miss Grandma very much." She took Amy's hands. "Grandma suffered because of her illness these last few years, but that's over now. Remember that we talked about how she has a new life in heaven with no more pain?"

Amy sighed. "Well . . . yes, but . . ." She wiped her eyes.

"Do you remember the time we gave your dog, Max, to the Johnsons?" asked Mom. "You missed him a lot, but he was too big for our apartment and he was miserable cooped up like that. Max lives a better life on their farm than we could give him here. You wouldn't want to bring him back now, would you?"

"No. He's happier there with all the room he has to run and play," admitted Amy. She thought a moment then smiled a little. "I know Grandma must be happier in heaven with Jesus than she was in the nursing home. Even though I miss her, I *am* glad she's living in a better place." She stood up. "I'll come downstairs now." *SLA*

HOW ABOUT YOU?

Has someone you loved died? It's natural to be sad and to miss that person. But if your loved one was a Christian, he or she has begun a better life with Jesus in heaven. And you will see that person again someday.

MEMORIZE:

"For to me, living is for Christ, and dying is even better."
Philippians 1:21

BELIEVERS HAVE ETERNAL LIFE

GROWING

(Read James 1:22-25)

Jessie picked up the tiny crab and placed it in her palm. "You're still living in the same small shell," she said. "Why haven't you moved into the bigger one?"

Both Jessie and her sister Kelsey had received a little hermit crab for Christmas, along with an extra shell for the crab to live in. "The pet store owner explained that these crabs live in shells abandoned by snails," Dad had told the girls. "As they grow, they must move into bigger shells. Since he said these were just about ready to move, we got larger shells, too, so that they'll be ready for them." Sure enough, a few days later, Kelsey's crab had moved into its new shell. But although Jessie thought her crab should move, too, it had not yet done so.

As Jessie was studying in her room after supper, her mother came to the door. "Jessie, Mr. Hanks called while you were at school," said Mother. "He wants you to come to the church activity on Saturday."

"Oh, Mom, I don't want to go," said Jessie. "They're going to hand out tracts at the mall and invite people to our church. I'm too young . . . I can't speak to strangers about Jesus." She plopped onto her bed.

Mother walked over to the aquarium and looked at Jessie's crab. "He's really growing, isn't he?" she said.

"He changed shells!" exclaimed Jessie. "I thought he was afraid to leave his old one."

Mother smiled. "Maybe he was," she said, "but part of growing is taking new steps." She gave Jessie a hug. "Maybe you've been a little afraid to grow," she suggested. "If you'll try helping on Saturday, maybe you'll find you can handle it after all." Jessie looked at her mother, then back at her little crab. "Why don't you call Mr. Hanks and tell him you'll be there," encouraged Mother.

Jessie hesitated. Then she nodded. "OK," she agreed. "I guess it's time to break out of *my* shell, too." *SLA*

HOW ABOUT YOU?

Have you been growing as a Christian this past year? Have you put away your fear and become stronger in your faith by serving the Lord in different ways?

MEMORIZE:

"And remember, it is a message to obey, not just to listen to. If you don't obey, you are only fooling yourself."
James 1:22

GROWTH TAKES ACTION

MIRIAM BABYSITS MOSES

(Read Exodus 2:1-10)

"Bethany," said Mother, "please entertain Josh for a little while."

Bethany frowned as she glanced at her baby brother. "But, Mom, I'm reading!" she whined, turning her attention back to her book.

"Reading will have to wait," said Mother. "Isn't Stacy coming over today? I thought maybe the two of you could take Josh for a walk."

"Stacy had to babysit," Bethany said. "I feel sorry for her. She has to take care of her little sister all the time."

"She doesn't seem to mind," Mother replied. "She seems happy, and it's a good thing to help your mother."

Bethany squirmed. She tried to change the subject. "Stacy's mother calls her 'Little Miriam,' Mom. Why does she do that?"

Mother smiled. "Do you remember the Bible story about Moses?" she asked. "The King of Egypt was afraid the Israelite slaves would outnumber his people and take over his kingdom. He commanded all the boy babies to be thrown into the river. But Miriam's mother trusted God to save baby Moses."

Bethany nodded. "She put him in a little basket in the river, didn't she? And his sister Miriam watched to see what would happen."

"Right," said Mother. "And when the king's daughter found Moses, Miriam got his own mother to take care of him."

"So that's why Stacy's mother calls her 'Little Miriam,'" said Bethany. "It's because Stacy helps her mom take care of her baby sister just like Miriam helped her mother."

"That's right," agreed Mother. "And when Moses grew up to lead God's people out of slavery in Egypt, I'm sure Miriam was really glad she had a part in taking care of him."

Bethany looked over at Josh, who was sleeping soundly now. "Mom, I'm sorry about grumbling when you ask me to help," she said. She smiled. "Who knows—maybe Josh will grow up to be somebody famous, too."

Mother smiled. "Thank you, Miriam," she said. *NIM*

HOW ABOUT YOU?

Do you appreciate how much your parents do for you? Do you grumble when they ask for your help? Remember this—when you help your parents, you're obeying Jesus.

MEMORIZE:

"You children must always obey your parents, for this is what pleases the Lord." Colossians 3:20

BE A WILLING HELPER

WHOLESOME DIETS

(Read Philippians 4:8-9)

Lauren rushed up the steps and opened the door with her key. Since Mom started working, Lauren liked the freedom of being on her own for an hour before Mom got home. She poured herself a glass of milk, grabbed a chocolate cookie, and sat down to watch her favorite program on TV. The first few times Lauren had watched the program, she felt somewhat guilty. But now she watched and even listened to the off-color jokes without feeling any sense of guilt. In fact, she was laughing so hard she didn't hear her mother's car pull into the driveway.

When Mom entered the room, Lauren jumped up in surprise. "Mom, you're home early!" she exclaimed.

Mom looked at the TV screen. "I don't think you should be watching that," she said.

"I watch it for the good part and don't pay attention to the bad part," replied Lauren.

Mom frowned. "We'll have tacos tonight. Please go shred the lettuce and cheese," she said. Glad to end the discussion about TV, Lauren quickly headed for the kitchen.

Soon Mother came in. She went to the refrigerator and took out some hamburger. She also pulled out a plastic container and opened it. She wrinkled her nose as she looked at the contents. Then she put the cover back on. "Oh, look," she said as she handed it to Lauren. "Here's the leftover turkey casserole. Since you like it so much, why don't you heat it up and finish it tonight. I know you like it even better than tacos."

"Oh, good!" exclaimed Lauren. But when she opened the container, she made a face. "Mom!" she exclaimed. "This is moldy! It's gross!"

"Well, don't eat the bad part," said Mom. "Just eat the good part."

"It's all mixed up. I can't eat just the good part."

"Exactly," said Mom.

Lauren slowly shook her head. "I see what you're saying. From now on I'll find something better to watch after school."

"Wise decision," Mom said as she took the container of spoiled food and threw it out. *EMB*

HOW ABOUT YOU?

Are you careful about what goes into your mind? Or do you think you can remain pure even when you allow offensive language or immoral behavior to fill your mind? Be careful! When you no longer notice the bad part, you're in trouble! Ask God to cleanse your mind and help you to keep it clean.

MEMORIZE:

"Keep away from every kind of evil."
1 Thessalonians 5:22

AVOID BAD INFLUENCES

IS ANYONE LOOKING?

(Read Jeremiah 32:17-19)

"Oh, cool! I wish I could get this," said Hannah when she and Beth were at a toy store one day. She glanced around as she held up a miniature doll. "I'm gonna take it," she said. She was about to put it in her pocket when Beth pointed to a nearby sign that read, "Someone is watching you."

Hannah shrugged. "They just put those signs up to scare kids," she said as she pocketed the toy. "Come on, let's get going." She held out another doll. "Don't you want one?"

"No," replied Beth. "It's wrong to steal. I'm leaving." She turned and walked away. Hannah just shrugged and laughed.

As the two girls were about to leave the store, an employee walked up to Hannah. "You'll have to come with me," he said. Beth watched as Hannah was taken to the manager's office.

"Sit down, young lady," said the manager. "I've got something I want you to see." He pressed a button and the whole scene of Hannah stealing the doll flashed up on a TV screen. After sternly questioning Hannah, the manager called her parents. Hannah nervously stared at the floor in shame. A time of judgment was ahead!

When her parents arrived, Hannah was too ashamed to look them in the eye. "Since this is the girl's first offense, I'll release her to you," the manager said. Hannah was relieved to hear that, but she knew she would still be punished.

"You thought no one saw what you did," said her dad as they drove home. "You need to remember that Someone always sees. Even if the manager hadn't found out what you did, someone would have known. God says our every deed is recorded. He'll reward or discipline us as we deserve." *PR*

HOW ABOUT YOU?

Are you comfortable with the thought that God sees all you do? Or are there things you do in secret that you wouldn't want anybody to see? Whenever you're tempted to do something wrong, remember that God is watching you. He loves you very much. He wants to reward you for doing the things that please him, but he must also discipline when you do wrong. Don't forget—he sees all!

MEMORIZE:

"You have all wisdom and do great and mighty miracles. You are very aware of the conduct of all people, and you reward them according to their deeds." Jeremiah 32:19

GOD IS WATCHING YOU

ACCORDING TO THE LABEL

(Read 1 Peter 2:9-12)

Amy wanted a new pair of jeans, but she wouldn't settle for just any kind. "They have to be one of the popular name brands, or I don't want them!" she declared.

"Let's look in Conrad's," Mother suggested. "They have nice jeans, and they're reasonably priced, too."

"I don't want to go in there! Nobody wears those jeans," stormed Amy.

"Someone must wear them or they wouldn't be selling," Mother said. "I'm sorry, but it's either Conrad's or you'll have to buy the name brands yourself." Amy didn't want to buy jeans with her own money, but Mother was firm. So Amy reluctantly spent most of her savings on a pair of name-brand jeans.

Amy gloried in the many compliments she received when she wore her new jeans. But after they were washed, they didn't look the same! "Mom, what happened to my jeans?" gasped Amy. "Just look at them! They're all limp and baggy looking! I paid a lot for these. They should have lived up to their name and lasted a long time."

"I know. I followed the washing instructions carefully," Mother said, "but they just didn't hold up well. Maybe if you take them back to the store, they'll be able to make some adjustment. In any case, I hope you've learned something from this experience."

"Like what?" Amy said, pouting.

"Things don't always live up to their label," answered Mother. "People don't either."

"People? What do they have to do with this?" asked Amy.

"We who are Christians need to live up to our name and act Christlike and loving toward others," Mother explained.

Amy felt guilty. Just that morning she had whispered unkind things about a classmate who was wearing new jeans from Conrad's. "It's easy to want the label of popularity," added Mother. "But with God's help we can live up to our 'name brand'—Christian!" *JLH*

HOW ABOUT YOU?

If you have accepted Jesus as your Savior, you are called a Christian. Are you living up to that name?

MEMORIZE:

"It was there at Antioch that the believers were first called Christians."

Acts 11:26

LIVE LIKE A CHRISTIAN

JANUARY
22

BETTY'S DECISION

(Read Ephesians 6:1-3)

Betty thought her parents were too strict, and she made it a point to tell them how she felt. "Being 'grounded' for two days is too big a penalty for coming in late," she told them. "And I know I was kinda . . . ah . . . sassy to Mom one time last week, but . . . well, I don't think it was so bad that I should have part of my allowance taken away. None of the other kids in the neighborhood get such hard punishments."

"God didn't put me in charge of the neighborhood children," Dad replied, "but he has given me that responsibility with you. Mom and I are trying to bring you up the way we think is right. To do that, sometimes we have to punish you."

"I wish you'd let me decide my own punishment," Betty snapped.

"All right," her father replied. "After this, every time Mom or I correct you for something, you go to your room and write down how you think you would have handled it if you were the parent. We'll talk over your ideas. OK?"

"OK!" agreed Betty, smiling broadly.

The first time Betty didn't like the way she was punished, it was easy to write down what she thought was a better idea. But as the days passed, she wrote less and less. She really didn't know what to write. Besides, when she was honest about it, she had to admit that it was right for her parents to punish or correct her. After all, they were older and wiser than she was—and didn't the Bible say that parents were to be in charge of their kids, and that the kids were to obey their parents? She thought about it over and over again—and she often prayed, asking God to forgive her for the way she had acted.

"Well, shall we go over your list?" Dad asked one day.

Betty shook her head. "I don't have a list, Dad," she said. "I started one, but I found out it wasn't so easy." *RIJ*

HOW ABOUT YOU?

Are you ready to accept the fact that God has put your parents in charge of you? Can you thank him for it? Do that, and then listen to them and obey them.

MEMORIZE:

"Honor your father and mother. Then you will live a long, full life in the land the Lord your God will give you."
Exodus 20:12

HONOR YOUR PARENTS

LIGHT IN THE DARKNESS

(Read Psalm 119:11-16)

Robin sat in the old porch swing with her grandmother and watched the first stars appear in the sky. "I love spending the weekend with you," said Robin.

"I'm glad you do," Grandma said. "In a while we'll go in for a Bible story."

Robin frowned. "I like the Bible stories you read. But I don't like memorizing Bible verses. Mom makes me say them for her every Wednesday afternoon before I go to Bible class. What's the point of learning so many verses?"

"Oh," said Grandma, "when you know verses, they remind you of how you should think and live."

Robin sighed. "I still think it takes too much time," she insisted.

After Grandma and Robin had hot cocoa and a story, Robin settled into bed. She thought about what her grandmother had said about Bible verses. *Maybe they're important to Grandma and Mom, but I don't see how they do me any good,* she thought. She soon drifted off to sleep, but before long, she woke up again. Muffy, Grandmother's cat, was crying at the front door. *I guess Muffy wasn't around when Grandma went to bed,* thought Robin. *I'll go let him in.* Robin crept quietly out of bed and into the dark hall. She felt her way along the wall toward the front door and was nearly there when she stubbed her toe hard on the coat rack. "Ouch!" she exclaimed loudly.

Robin was still holding her toe when Grandma's door opened and Grandma turned on the light. "Why are you walking in the dark?" asked Grandma.

"Muffy's crying to come in and I didn't want to wake you," replied Robin.

"Thanks, honey, but next time turn on the light so you don't get hurt," said Grandma.

After breakfast the next morning, Grandma picked up her Bible. "We're going to learn a verse today," she announced with a twinkle in her eye. "Your experience last night reminds me that Bible verses are like lights that help us through dark times in our life—times when we're upset or confused." She turned to Psalm 119. "Maybe you already know this verse, but it will be good to review it anyway."

Robin rubbed her sore toe. "OK, Grandma," she agreed. She grinned. "From now on, I'll try hard to let my memory verses help light my way." *KC*

HOW ABOUT YOU?

Do you memorize Bible verses? Time spent doing that is never wasted. The verses you know will help you when temptation comes your way. They will comfort you through trouble. They will remind you of how you can please God in your daily life.

MEMORIZE GOD'S WORD

MEMORIZE:

"Your word is a lamp for my feet and a light for my path." Psalm 119:105

JANUARY
24

"Did you deposit your money in the bank today?" asked Mother as Sherry helped make a salad for supper.

Sherry nodded. "I sure did, Mom," she replied. "I put in twenty dollars today. My bank account is really growing!"

"Why did you give your money to the bank?" asked Sherry's little sister, Pam. She had been busy setting the table and was listening to the conversation. "Didn't you want to keep it? I wouldn't give my money to the bank!"

Sherry smiled at Pam. "I didn't give it to the bank to keep for themselves. I just gave it to them to take care of for me," she explained. "The money is still mine, and I can get it back when I need it. Right, Mom?"

Mother nodded. "That's right. The bank is only keeping your money safe for you."

"Hey," said Sherry, "that's kind of like something my Sunday school teacher said. She said God made everything so he really owns it all. But he gives us things to use, and he expects us to take good care of them."

"What things?" asked little Pam.

"Lots of things," replied Sherry. "Things like your bike and all your toys, and my money and books and trumpet . . . to name a few."

"And Waggles?" asked Pam, looking at the puppy sleeping on his bed in the corner.

"Right," agreed Mother. "The bank takes good care of our money, and we should remember to do the same with all the things God has given us to use, whether they're things in nature, talents, houses, toys, or money. All that we have really belongs to God, and we should be using it wisely." *WEB*

HOW ABOUT YOU?
Are you taking good care of all the things that God has given you? Everything you have is really just loaned to you from God, so it's important to do your best to take very good care of those things.

MEMORIZE:
"He created everything there is.
Nothing exists that he didn't make."
John 1:3

TAKE CARE OF THINGS

THE EASY ROUTE

(Read Psalm 143:8-10)

Chris frowned as she looked at the stack of church bulletins lying on the table. The youth pastor had asked the kids to choose jobs to help out at church. *I should probably help rake the yard,* Chris had thought, *but that's such hard work. I'll just offer to fold bulletins instead.* Now she began to fold the bulletins as fast as she could, trying not to feel guilty about getting out of raking. But she did feel guilty, especially when she saw that there still was a lot of raking to be done when she left for home.

When she got home, Chris found her little brother, Andy, in his room. Andy grinned at Chris. "I owed you a chore, remember? So I took out your trash."

Chris scowled. "The wastebasket wasn't even full," she complained. "You should have asked me. I wanted you to clean out my closet."

"Well, taking out the trash was easier," retorted Andy.

Chris had just opened her mouth to reply when Mom walked into the room. "How did your work at church go?" she asked.

Chris swallowed hard. She realized that she felt disappointed when Andy took an easy job instead of asking what needed to be done. She felt more guilty than before. "I . . . I took an easy job instead of what I really thought I should do," she admitted.

"We call that taking the 'easy route,'" said Mom. "What did you think you really should do?"

"Rake the church yard," murmured Chris. "I wish I had done that instead of folding bulletins."

Mom put her arm around Chris's shoulder. "First of all," Mom said, "I want to be sure you realize that folding bulletins is serving God, too. But if raking the yard is what you felt God really wanted you to do, folding bulletins is not enough. Why don't you ask Mr. Miller if you can help with both jobs next week?"

Chris nodded, feeling relieved. "OK," she said. "Or if the raking is all done, I'll offer to help mow the church lawn this summer." *KEC*

HOW ABOUT YOU?

Do you try to learn what God wants you to do instead of choosing tasks you think would be easiest or what sounds like fun? Don't seek your own way. You will find happiness not in going the "easy route" but in doing what God wants you to do.

MEMORIZE:
"I take joy in doing your will, my God,
for your law is written on my heart."
Psalm 40:8

SEEK GOD'S WILL

JANUARY
26

SOUND OF THE TRUMPET

(Read 1 Thessalonians 4:13-18)

Stephanie was propped up against her pillows as Mother came into her room, Bible in hand. They always read together before Stephanie settled down to go to sleep. Tonight Mother read from 1 Thessalonians. "Mother," said Stephanie when they had finished reading. "There are lots of things in the Bible I don't understand—like what you just read. What does it mean, about trumpets sounding and dead people rising in the air?"

Mother smiled. "That's what we call the 'rapture' of the church," she said. "It will happen when Jesus comes to take all Christians to heaven."

"What about the dead coming out of the graves? Will Mrs. Evans come out of her grave, too?" asked Stephanie. "It all sounds so strange."

Mother smiled. "It's going to be a wonderful day!" she said.

Stephanie shuddered. "Brrrr . . . doesn't sound wonderful to me! Sounds spooky and scary! I hope it doesn't happen for a long, long time," she said anxiously.

"Why does that make you so afraid, honey?" asked Mother.

"Because it's spooky!" exclaimed Stephanie, pulling the blankets close around her. "It gives me the creeps to think of seeing the Lord suddenly in the middle of the night!"

"Stephanie, tell me," said Mother, "will you be afraid to see your friend Mrs. Evans again?"

"Afraid to see Mrs. Evans?" echoed Stephanie. "I can't wait to see her! I loved her, and I know she loved me."

Mother spoke quickly. "You're not afraid to see Mrs. Evans because you loved one another. It is the same with Jesus."

Stephanie looked thoughtful. "I guess so," she admitted.

"You see," said Mother, "for those who love Jesus with all their hearts, there's nothing scary, or spooky, about his coming." *HCT*

HOW ABOUT YOU?

Will you be ready if Jesus comes today? He may come at any moment—morning, noon, or night. Only those who have given their hearts and lives to Jesus will rise to meet him. Talk to a trusted friend or adult to find out more.

MEMORIZE:

"You also must be ready all the time. For the Son of Man will come when least expected." Matthew 24:44

BE READY FOR JESUS' RETURN

THROUGH IT ALL

(Read Isaiah 43:1-3)

Stunned, Briana stared at her grandfather. She had just learned that Grandpa Jackson had a terminal disease, and the doctor could not even promise that surgery would help. "You're not really going to die, are you?" she whispered.

Briana's grandfather didn't answer immediately. "That's something only God knows for sure," he managed at last. "Cancer of this type is usually fatal, but whatever is God's will is what will take place."

"But, Grandpa," Briana protested, "that's not fair. Grandma needs you. We all need you, and . . ." Her voice trailed off.

"Your grandma and I have come to the place where we just want God's will to be done, whatever it is," said Grandpa. "We're hoping you can come to that place, too."

"I'm not sure I can," Briana said honestly. "It seems all wrong."

Briana's grandfather shook his head. "No, honey. God never makes any mistakes. I love you very much, yet it may be God's will for me to leave you." Grandpa smiled at Briana. "Whenever it seems to be more than you can handle, remember that God loves you even more than I do, and he will be with you forever."

Briana looked away, thinking about her grandfather's words. Sure, she knew God was in control of everything. And she knew God never made any mistakes, but . . .

Suddenly Briana stopped. What had Grandpa said? "God loves you and will be with you forever." With determination in her heart, Briana spoke silently to the Lord. "Help me to trust you for the outcome, no matter what." *RIJ*

HOW ABOUT YOU?

How do you react when really hard things come into your life—perhaps loss of a loved one through death or divorce, perhaps an illness of your own? Do you get bitter and angry? Or do you remember that God has promised to go with his children through every difficult time? Trust him to keep you—you're not alone! And remember that he never makes mistakes.

MEMORIZE:

"When you go through deep waters and great trouble, I will be with you. When you go through rivers of difficulty, you will not drown! When you walk through the fire of oppression, you will not be burned up; the flames will not consume you."

Isaiah 43:2

GOD IS WITH YOU

JANUARY
28

GOD'S MAGIC SLATE

(Read Psalm 51:1-12)

"See what I bought, Mother," said Megan excitedly as she took a magic slate out of a sack. She began scribbling on it as they drove home. "Now look," she said as she lifted the top plastic sheet. "The writing is all gone." As she talked, her brother Andy simply stared out the window. He wasn't hearing the conversation or seeing the scenery.

"Andy!" Mother raised her voice. "This is the third time I've called your name. Is something wrong?"

"No." Andy lapsed into silence again.

And now you've told another lie, his conscience said. *That makes two.*

Andy sighed deeply. *But it was a little lie,* he argued with his conscience.

"I know something is bothering you, Andy," insisted Mother. "Want to talk?"

"I told Dad a lie yesterday," Andy blurted out.

Mother was silent for a moment. Then she nodded. "He knows that," she said softly, "but he is waiting for you to admit it."

Megan, busy with her magic slate, paid no attention to the conversation. She chuckled as she said, "I made a stupid mistake! I put a long tail on a rabbit! Oh, well! I'll just erase it and start over." Again she lifted the top plastic sheet, and like magic, the picture disappeared.

Mother smiled. "When you sin, Andy, it's something like writing the wrong thing on a magic slate," she said. "If you don't do anything about it, it remains there. But if you repent of your sins and admit them to God, he will erase them. Tell both your dad and the Lord what you told me. Let them know you're sorry, and the slate will be clean."

Megan smoothed the plastic sheet on her slate. "This time I'm going to do it right," she announced.

"Me, too, Megan," echoed Andy. "Me, too." *BJW*

HOW ABOUT YOU?

Have you told a lie? Disobeyed? Been sassy? Cheated? Right now, admit to God whatever sin you are aware of in your life and let him wipe the slate clean.

MEMORIZE:

"The high and lofty one who inhabits eternity, the Holy One, says this: 'I live in that high and holy place with those whose spirits are contrite and humble. I refresh the humble and give new courage to those with repentant hearts.' " Isaiah 57:15

CONFESS YOUR SIN

SPECIAL IDENTITY (PART 1)

(Read Acts 17:24-28)

Carla dashed into the house, waving a paper. "Please, Mom, may I go?" she asked. Her mother read the notice. On Saturday the shopping mall was conducting a free fingerprinting clinic for all children accompanied by a parent. "My teacher says it's real important," Carla said, "in case I need to be identified some time."

"We already know who you are," teased Carla's older brother, David.

Carla ignored him. "May I have it done, Mom?"

"Sure, it's a good idea," said Mother with a smile. "No one else in all the world has fingerprints just like you, Carla. You're one of a kind."

"Whew! That's a relief," laughed David, and then he got serious. "When I did a report on abortion for health class, I found out that a person's fingerprint pattern appears on the fingers four or five months before he's even born."

"That shows how special a baby is to God," said Mother. "Even before we are born, he forms every little detail in just the way that's best for us. It's sad that so many people regard the life of an unborn baby so lightly that they feel they have the right to end that life—just because having a baby would be inconvenient for them."

Carla nodded. "Mrs. Weaver, my Sunday school teacher, is going to have a baby any day now. She told us that the doctors were afraid there might be something wrong. They wanted her to have some tests and then have an abortion if the tests showed the baby would be deformed. But she wouldn't do it. She says God knows just what kind of baby she needs, and whatever he sends will be perfect for her."

"That's great," Mother exclaimed. "To take a life is never right, even if it's a life that is yet unborn and even if we fear it may have some defect. Life and death must be left in the hands of God." *JLH*

HOW ABOUT YOU?

Have you heard that the mother of an unborn child should be allowed to decide whether or not to have her baby? The decision should not be up to the mother. It should be up to God. Abortion—the killing of an unborn baby—is wrong.

ABORTION IS WRONG

SPECIAL IDENTITY (PART 2)

(Read Jeremiah 1:5-10)

Carla was very excited as she and her mother headed for the fingerprinting clinic in a nearby mall. Just the day before, her Sunday school teacher had given birth to a healthy baby girl—a perfect baby. "Just think," squealed Carla, "Mrs. Weaver named her baby Carlotta—almost the same as my name! I wonder what she'll be when she grows up."

"I don't know," Mother said, "but God does. He knows who we are before we are born. He has a special plan for our life. Even before they were born, the Lord chose Jeremiah to be a prophet, Samson to be a strong man, and John the Baptist to be a preacher."

"That's really neat," said Carla. "Mom, can we buy a gift for the baby?"

Mother agreed, so after the fingerprinting session, Carla and her mother went shopping for a gift. They chose a pastel colored planter shaped like a building block. Carla carried it as they went to pick out a plant to put in it. She idly turned it over. "Mom, look at this," she said, pointing to a mark on the bottom of the planter. "Is this a defect?"

Mother examined the planter closely. "That's the artist's initials, Carla," she said. "It identifies its creator."

"Like my fingerprints identify me?" asked Carla.

"Something like that," agreed Mother. "God made you in his image, Carla, and gave you a special identity. He has a wonderful plan for your life." *JLH*

HOW ABOUT YOU?

Did you know that you are a "designer's special"? God made you as you are for a particular purpose. He has a wonderful plan for your life.

MEMORIZE:

"I knew you before I formed you in your mother's womb. Before you were born I set you apart and appointed you as my spokesman to the world." Jeremiah 1:5

GOD HAS A PLAN FOR YOU

WHY SO SNAPPY?

(Read 1 Peter 3:8-12)

Erin slammed the door behind her. "Oh, that Trina is so hateful!" A tear slipped down her cheek.

Mother looked surprised. "I thought Trina was your best friend," she said.

"She used to be," choked Erin, "but lately she's so touchy. Nothing I do pleases her."

"That's too bad," sympathized Mother, "but try to be patient with her. She hasn't been a Christian very long."

"I know, but I'm getting sick of it." Erin sighed. "I haven't done anything about it yet, but if she doesn't stop snapping at me, I'm going to . . ." The squeal of tires and the loud yipping of a dog sent Erin and her mother running out to the yard. "Oh, Mother! It's Buffy. Someone left the gate open, and he got into the street!" Erin ran to the curb where a young man was bending over the puppy.

"I'm so sorry," he told them. "The dog just ran right out in front of me."

Mother knelt beside the whimpering puppy. As she started to touch him, Buffy snapped at her hand. "It's OK, Buffy. You're going to be all right," she said softly. Once more she reached for him, and again Buffy snapped. "Erin, can you hold his jaws shut?" asked Mother. "I want to see how badly he's hurt before we move him."

Several hours later, they returned from the vet with a stiff and sore puppy. "I'm so thankful Buffy wasn't killed," Erin told her father, who had arrived home from work. "But he sure is snappy."

"That's because he's hurting," Dad told her. He looked up over the top of his newspaper. "Say, do you know the names of Trina's parents? Aren't they Phillip and Lisa?"

"Yes," Erin replied. "Why?"

"Because they are getting a divorce," replied Dad. "Did you know that, Erin?"

"Oh no!" Erin took a deep breath. "Oh, poor Trina! No wonder she's been so snappy lately. She's hurting! I'm so glad I didn't snap back at her." *BJW*

HOW ABOUT YOU?

When someone snaps at you, do you snap back? Or do you stop to consider why he or she might be acting that way? Before you snap back, ask yourself, "Is she hurting?" If so, she needs your love and kindness to ease the pain. She needs your patience and your prayers.

HELP THOSE WHO HURT

MEMORIZE:
"Do not repay evil with evil or insult with insult, but with blessing."
1 Peter 3:9, NIV

JUST LIKE A BABY

(Read 1 Peter 2:1-3)

"What a beautiful baby," Mom said as she looked through the nursery window.

"Hold me up so I can see," begged Samantha. Robby had been born the day before, and his cousin, Samantha, was eager to see him. "How soon will Robby be able to play ball with me?" she asked doubtfully.

Mom laughed. "I think it may take him a while to get the hang of baseball," she said. "Robby will have to grow quite a bit before he can play catch with you. We have to be patient with babies and give them time to grow, like God planned it.

"Did you know that it takes human babies longer to grow up than almost any of the animals God made?" Mom asked. "Colts can run just a few hours after they're born. And remember the puppies Ginger had last year? They were old enough to leave their mother in a few weeks. God made babies to need their parents in a special way," she added. "And did you know that a baby Christian also needs time to grow?"

"What's a baby Christian?" asked Samantha.

"It's someone who hasn't been a Christian very long and doesn't know very much about God and the Bible," answered Mom. "When you asked Jesus to save you last year, you were a newborn Christian, Samantha, just like Robby is a newborn baby."

"Am I a growed-up Christian now?" questioned Samantha.

"Not quite yet," Mom replied. "It takes quite a while for baby Christians to grow. They need someone to teach them. That's where I come in, along with your Sunday school teachers and Pastor James," added Mom. "God has given us the privilege and responsibility to teach you as you grow in him." *RB*

HOW ABOUT YOU?

Are you growing up as a Christian? Do you know more about God and do you love and obey him more now than you did when you first became a Christian? Spend time in the Bible and in prayer. Learn from your teachers, pastor, and Christian parents, and your spirit will grow right along with your body.

MEMORIZE:
"But grow in the special favor and knowledge of our Lord and Savior Jesus Christ." 2 Peter 3:18

GROW AS A CHRISTIAN

A CALL FOR HELP

(Read Psalm 139:1-12)

"Yip! Yip!" The small terrier yelped and fled across the yard to the back door.

"Trixie!" screamed Ann. "Something's happened to Trixie." She and her brother, Carl, ran to their pet. The little dog snuggled in her arms, trembling and whining. "Oh, Carl, she's hurt!"

"Where?" asked Carl.

"I don't know, but she's scared," answered Ann. "You can tell by the way she sounds."

"Let's check her over," suggested Mother, who had come to see what was going on. Gently Trixie was lowered to the floor where all three intently examined her. "Her legs are all right," observed Mother.

"And she's not bleeding," said Carl. "There's not a spot on her."

Both children stroked the sleek head. "Whatever it was, it sure scared her," said Ann.

"Yeah," said Carl. "I've never seen her run so fast."

"She's not the only one who moved fast," said Mother. "I hope she appreciated her two protectors!"

Carl chuckled. "Our Sunday school lesson last week was about how God is our Protector. Does he come running like this when we call for help?"

"Interesting question," said Mother. "Do you think God needs to run?"

"I don't think so," said Ann. "God is everywhere."

"Right," agreed Carl, "and it would be pretty difficult to run somewhere when you're already there."

Ann hugged her pet. "I'm glad God's everywhere and I don't have to wait for him to come when I'm in trouble." She laughed as Trixie tried to lick her face.

The others laughed with her. "We need to appreciate our Protector, too," observed Mother. *RG*

HOW ABOUT YOU?

Are you confident that God is willing to help you whenever you need him? Have you been aware of his presence when you were hurt or lonely? Have you thanked him for what he's done for you? Be sure to do that, and tell someone else about it, too.

MEMORIZE:

"God is our refuge and strength, always ready to help in times of trouble." Psalm 46:1

GOD CARES FOR YOU

THE RIGHT ANSWER

(Read Titus 3:4-7)

On their way home from school, Debra and Siew Choo were in the middle of an argument when they met Debra's Sunday school teacher. "Oh, Mr. Brown," said Debra, "maybe you can settle this for us. We had a quiz in math today—only two problems. My answers were way off, but Siew Choo just had a couple of numbers turned around."

"Yeah." Siew Choo nodded. "Our teacher gave us both a big red zero. That wasn't fair, was it? My answers were much closer to being right than Debra's. I think I should have gotten a better grade than she did."

"And I say it makes no difference," put in Debra. "So who's right?"

"Well, this reminds me of scientists who are working on a cure for cancer," said Mr. Brown. "Some have come very close to solving the problem, but people continue to die of cancer."

"So . . . you're saying there are times when you've got to have the exact answer," said Siew Choo thoughtfully. "And you're telling me this is one of them, aren't you?"

Mr. Brown nodded. "I'm sorry, but if I were grading this paper, I'm afraid I'd give you a zero, too. You were close, but you were wrong. Now, before you go, kids, I'd like to ask you another question. You must have the exact answer to this one, too. The question is this—how can you get to heaven?"

"Well . . . by being good and doing our best and going to church and Sunday school," suggested Debra. "And by giving money for the poor and needy and helping others."

"No," disagreed Siew Choo. "It's by accepting Jesus as Savior."

Debra looked thoughtful as Mr. Brown nodded. "You're right, Siew Choo," he said. He turned to Debra as he said, "Perhaps we can talk about this some more."
HCT

HOW ABOUT YOU?

Did you have the right answer to Mr. Brown's question? None of the good things you do can ever get you to heaven. It may seem that you're closer to being right than someone who leads a very wicked life, but being close will do you no good. The Bible says only those who believe in Jesus will go to heaven. Talk to a trusted friend or adult if you have more questions.

MEMORIZE:

"He saved us, not because of the good things we did, but because of his mercy." Titus 3:5

GOOD WORKS CAN'T SAVE

FEBRUARY 4

INSTANT ANSWERS

(Read Lamentations 3:25-27)

"I don't really see the use of praying about things," remarked Cynthia, peeking in the fridge one morning. "I've prayed and prayed, but God doesn't seem to be hearing. . . ."

"Mom!" Ben yelled out from the living room, "the remote's not working again. It's such a nuisance," he grumbled.

"That's the second time that thing's been broken in two weeks," said Cynthia. "I hate having to get up to switch channels." She closed the fridge. "No orange juice," she complained.

"I bought some fresh oranges yesterday," said Mom. "You can squeeze some."

"Aw, Mom," whined Cynthia, "why didn't you get a carton of juice?" She sighed. "It's too much work to squeeze oranges."

"Cynthia, it sounds like you and Ben are both developing an 'instant' mentality," said Mom. She eyed Cynthia thoughtfully. "And judging from what you said a few minutes ago, I'm afraid that attitude seems to be creeping into your prayer life, too!"

"What do you mean?" asked Cynthia indignantly.

"Well, you're so used to having things quickly, conveniently, instantly, that you can't tolerate even small delays—like getting up to switch channels or taking a few minutes to squeeze an orange," explained Mom. "And you apparently expect God to answer instantly, too."

Cynthia squirmed uneasily as she thought about it. "Maybe," she admitted reluctantly. "But we're supposed to expect answers, aren't we?"

"Yes, but prayer is not like turning on a faucet and expecting the water to come gushing out, you know," said Mom, ruffling her daughter's blonde curls. "God's timing doesn't always match ours, and we must learn to wait and not expect instant answers." *MTF*

HOW ABOUT YOU?

Are you developing an "instant" mentality? Do you always want things now? There's nothing wrong with owning or using time-saving, labor-saving conveniences like dishwashers or microwaves or even remote controls and canned juices! But guard against getting so used to having everything instantly that you expect God's answers to be instant, too. Sometimes God says, "Wait!"

MEMORIZE:

"But you must not forget, dear friends, that a day is like a thousand years to the Lord, and a thousand years is like a day. The Lord isn't really being slow about his promise to return, as some people think. No, he is being patient for your sake." 2 Peter 3:8-9

WAIT ON THE LORD

WARNING WORDS

(Read James 3:8-12)

"How was your day?" asked Mom as Stacey jumped into the car after school one Friday afternoon.

"Horrible!" Stacey slammed the door. "Lindsey asked Jessica to go shopping with her tomorrow and never asked me." She scowled. "Jessica's my best friend," she declared. "Not Lindsey's. I hate Lindsey."

"Whoa!" said Mom. "Words of hate coming from the mouth of a Christian mean that something's wrong."

Stacey sat glum and silent on the drive home until she noticed a red light in the dashboard panel. "What does that light mean?" she asked.

Mom looked down. "I don't know," she said. "It says, 'Check Engine Soon.' I better call the mechanic when we get home. He may be able to tell me if there's a problem."

When they got home, Stacey had a snack and then started on her homework. But her thoughts went back to Lindsey and Jessica. She was in the middle of imagining what she'd say to Lindsey the next time they met when Mom popped her head in the doorway. "The mechanic said to bring the car right in," said Mom. "I'll be back soon." After Mom left, Stacey forced herself back to homework, but she still couldn't forget her anger.

When Mom had been gone for over an hour, the phone rang. It was Mom calling. "They found the problem with the car," said Mom, "but it's taking a little longer to fix than they expected. I decided to call so you wouldn't be wondering what happened to me. It's a good thing I paid attention to that light."

As Stacey hung up, she thought about the light as a warning of something wrong. *Mom said the words I used about hating Lindsey were also a warning of something wrong,* she thought. *Maybe I better pay attention to them, too. VEN*

HOW ABOUT YOU?

What kinds of words come out of your mouth? The Bible says our words show what's going on in our hearts. Bitter, angry, and hateful words are a warning that something is wrong. If you're having a problem with them, ask God to show you what's at the root of those words. Find and deal with the problem.

PAY ATTENTION TO YOUR WORDS

MEMORIZE:
"And so blessing and cursing come pouring out of the same mouth. Surely, my brothers and sisters, this is not right!" James 3:10

FEBRUARY
6

ONE-WAY COMMUNICATION

(Read Psalm 143:5-8)

Mom put down the receiver and let out a long sigh. "Phew! Mrs. Willis is a kind, good-hearted old lady, and she's an expert at talking nonstop!"

Melissa chuckled. "Poor Mom! I only heard you say 'Mmm' and 'Aha' occasionally! Didn't she even ask if your broken arm was better?"

"She did," said Mom, "but before I could reply, she started talking about something else; and when she finished, she hung up so fast I could hardly squeeze in a good-bye."

Melissa giggled again. "Jane's a bit like that, too," she said. "She talks and talks and we have to practically scream for her to stop before any of us can get a word in. She seems to forget that communication is a two-way thing!"

Dad laughed. "I guess we're all like that sometimes."

Melissa shook her head. "Not me!" she cried indignantly.

"What about the way we talk to God?" asked Dad. "Don't we spend most, if not all, of our prayer time telling God what's going on in our life, pouring out our problems, and asking him for things we need? And perhaps occasionally remembering to say thank you for his blessings?"

"But, Dad, that's part of prayer," protested Melissa.

"Oh, I agree," said Dad, "but so is being quiet and listening to what God has to say to us. For instance, if you pray that God will reveal his will for your life, shouldn't you stop and listen for his answer instead of rushing on to the next item?"

"I guess so," said Melissa thoughtfully. "But does God actually talk to us?"

"Indeed he does," said Dad, "though not in a voice such as mine. But he often quietly impresses on our heart the things he wants us to know or do."

"Dad's right," said Mom. "At other times God talks to us through his Word or through parents or teachers. Our conversations with other people shouldn't be one-sided, one-way communication, and neither should our prayer times with God." *MTF*

HOW ABOUT YOU?

Do you have a daily "quiet time" with the Lord? How do you spend this time? Do you spend the full time pouring out all your problems and worries? Telling God your needs and asking him to give you this, that, and the other? Praying for your family and friends? All those are important parts of prayer, but don't forget that listening to God is equally important.

MEMORIZE:

"Be silent, and know that I am God!"
Psalm 46:10

LISTEN TO GOD

PEN PALS

(Read John 20:24-31)

"My English teacher gave each of us the name of someone in another state, and we're supposed to exchange letters with them," Marsha excitedly reported one day. "My pen pal's name is Jenny Parker."

Marsha sat down that evening and wrote her first letter to Jenny. She told all about herself, her church, and her family. Soon a reply came from Jenny. It contained a picture and told about Jenny's big family and their house in the country. Jenny also said that her family didn't go to church.

During the next several months, Marsha and Jenny wrote many letters. The more Marsha knew about Jenny, the more she wanted to meet her. One afternoon, Marsha came running into the kitchen, holding a letter in her hand. "Mom! Mom!" she shouted. "Jenny's dad is coming to our state on business, and he said Jenny could stay with us that weekend! Can she, Mom? Can she?"

Mother laughed. "Calm down!" she said. "I'm sure it'll be OK."

Jenny did come to Marsha's house, and the two girls had so much fun talking and getting to know each other better! After supper, Mom read from the Bible about Abraham, who was called the "friend of God."

"Mrs. Davis," said Jenny, "I don't understand. How could Abraham be God's friend? We can't see God, so how can we know him?"

"Tell me, Jenny, how did you get to know Marsha?" asked Mom.

"Marsha wrote letters, telling me all about herself," replied Jenny.

Mom nodded. "God has written us a letter, too," she said. "It's the Bible! It tells us what God is like, and that he loved us so much he sent Jesus to die for our sins. It says that by receiving Christ as Savior, we can know him in a personal way, even though we can't see him."

Jenny thought it over. Suddenly she smiled and looked at Marsha. "Well, I'm sure glad I got to know Marsha," she said. "I think I'd like to find out more about this Jesus, too." *JLH*

HOW ABOUT YOU?

Have you "met" God? Even though you can't see him, you can meet him and get to know him by reading the Bible—God's "letter" to you.

MEMORIZE:

"You love him even though you have never seen him. Though you do not see him, you trust him; and even now you are happy with a glorious, inexpressible joy." 1 Peter 1:8

KNOW GOD BY FAITH

FEBRUARY 8

A WAY TO WITNESS

(Read Acts 5:17-18, 26-29)

Mother was taking chocolate chip cookies out of the oven when Suzanne came home from school. Suzanne picked up a cookie, and Mother poured a glass of milk for her. "How was school?" Mother asked.

"OK," Suzanne answered, "except we have to do an oral book report in two weeks. I hate oral reports. I don't see why we can't do a written one instead. It's scary standing up in front of the class."

"I know. But it's not so bad if you prepare ahead of time," advised Mother. "What book are you reading?"

"*Pilgrim's Progress for Children*," Suzanne answered.

"*Pilgrim's Progress* is an excellent book," Mother said, "and the author is almost as interesting as the book."

"Why do you say that?" asked Suzanne.

"John Bunyan was a preacher in England," explained Mother. "At that time they only allowed preaching in one main church, but Bunyan believed everyone should hear the gospel. He preached even though he was arrested several times."

Suzanne bit into her cookie. "What did he do then?"

"Preached inside the jail," Mother said. "That frustrated the jailers. They offered to let him go if he would promise not to preach anymore, but of course he couldn't promise that. He said, 'God called me to preach, and preach I must.' "

"Wow!" exclaimed Suzanne. "He was brave, wasn't he?"

"Yes, he was," Mother replied. "His enemies kept him in jail about 12 years to stop his preaching. During that time, he wrote many tracts and books—including *Pilgrim's Progress*. That book was written more than 300 years ago. Bunyan preached to a greater audience through his books than he did in person."

"Maybe I'll pretend I'm him when I give my report," said Suzanne with a chuckle. "Just think—in a way he'll be 'preaching' again!" *JLH*

HOW ABOUT YOU?

Have you been watching for an opportunity to witness in your school or classroom? Maybe you can make a report on a Christian topic or book. Be sure to prepare well so that you can do a good job in sharing the good news of Jesus with your classmates.

MEMORIZE:

"And every day, in the Temple and in their homes, they continued to teach and preach this message: 'The Messiah you are looking for is Jesus.' " Acts 5:42

SPEAK UP FOR JESUS

THE ROCK

(Read Deuteronomy 32:16-21, 36-37)

"A new girl came to school today," Kristen told her mother. "Her name is LaTonda. She's really nice, and I invited her to come to church with me."

"How nice!" exclaimed Mom. "Will she come?"

Kristen shook her head. "No. She goes to a church already, but it sounds odd to me. She says they can believe whatever way they want to—that God is really a part of each one of us, and that we're all sort of gods in ourselves. I don't really get it, but she has a quartz rock that she says has power. She's going to show it to me tomorrow."

"Good," Mom said. "Then you can tell her about Jesus—the Rock with true power."

"Yeah, I guess so," murmured Kristen, "but I don't think she'll be impressed. She thinks everybody is OK and will go to heaven."

"But that's not what God says, is it?" asked Mom.

"No," answered Kristen, "The Bible says we need to have Jesus in our heart in order to go to heaven. But LaTonda is such a nice person."

"Do you remember when we visited the Niagara Falls?" asked Mother, a sober expression on her face. "Remember when we were at the lake above the giant waterfall and we saw a little duckling swimming in the lake?"

Kristen nodded. "Yeah! And the water current was pulling it toward the falls," she said. "I was scared it was going to go over the falls and be crushed. But then that fisherman came along and saved it! I'm glad he could get to it in time!"

"So am I," said Mom. "And though LaTonda is nice, too, she is like that little duck—she is being pulled away from what is right."

Kristen thought about that. Then she nodded. "Tomorrow when LaTonda shows me her rock, I'll tell her about the greatest Rock of all," she decided. "If she doesn't believe me at first, I'll keep praying for her."

"Good," said Mom. "Let's all pray that she will believe." *PCS*

HOW ABOUT YOU?

Do you have friends who are being pulled in the wrong direction and are clinging to false hope? Do they believe there is power in such things as crystals or in their own human abilities? They may be very nice people, but they need to know that Jesus is the true Rock and only he is to be trusted and worshiped. Tell your friends about Jesus.

JESUS IS THE TRUE ROCK

MEMORIZE:
"But the rock of our enemies is not like our Rock, as even they recognize." Deuteronomy 32:31

FEBRUARY
10

TOO EMBARRASSED!

(Read Mark 8:34-38)

"Hurry, Dana," called Mom, "Marcy's mother will be here soon."

Dana rushed down the stairs and looked out the window. "Poor Marcy," she said. "Marcy's always in a bad mood when her mother drives the car pool."

"Why would that put her in a bad mood?" asked Mom.

"Well, sometimes her mother acts silly in the car," replied Dana. "She's really funny, actually, but it embarrasses Marcy."

"I see," Mom said thoughtfully. "I hope you're not embarrassed by me when I drive."

Dana chuckled. "Only when you wear your orange jogging suit," she teased. "But don't worry. The kids think you're neat."

"And that's important to you?" asked Mom.

"Sure," said Dana. "I don't want them to think you're weird like Marcy's mom."

"I thought you told me once that Marcy's mom is really a lot of fun to be with," Mom reminded her. "And you just said she's funny."

Dana nodded. "She is. But Marcy spends so much time apologizing for her and saying how weird she is, that the kids are starting to believe her. Once Marcy even hid in the bathroom when her mom showed up with her lunch."

Mom shook her head thoughtfully. "It's too bad Marcy's ashamed of her mom," she said. "And it's even worse that Marcy makes her mom look bad to others." After a moment she added, "The saddest thing of all, though, is that people do the same thing to Jesus."

"You mean when he was on earth?" asked Dana.

"I mean now," said Mom. "Many Christians act ashamed of him. Maybe they're afraid that if people know they belong to Jesus, they won't be accepted anymore. They may not come right out and say 'Jesus is weird,' but they laugh along when people joke about things in the Bible or about Jesus."

"I guess I need to remember that," added Dana. *HMT*

HOW ABOUT YOU?

Do you worry about what other people will think of you if they know you love Jesus? What they think may be affected by what you say or don't say. If you show that you're happy to know Jesus, he will look much better to them than if you're ashamed of him.

MEMORIZE:

"For I am not ashamed of this Good News about Christ. It is the power of God at work, saving everyone who believes—Jews first and also Gentiles." Romans 1:16

DON'T BE ASHAMED OF JESUS

FIFTY-MILE BIBLE

(Read Psalm 19:7-11)

"Hi, Grandpa!" said Abby as she entered her grandfather's living room. "Mother says to come home with me for dinner." She tossed her Sunday school book and Bible on the arm of a chair and walked to the bookcase. "Got any books I could read this afternoon?"

Abby saw Grandpa frown as her Bible slid to the floor. He said nothing about it, however, but joined her as she continued to scan the book titles. "Here's one you might like," he suggested, drawing out a thin volume. "Now, pick up your things, and we'll be going."

That afternoon, Abby read the book Grandpa had chosen. It was the story of Mary Jones, a little girl who lived in England in the 1700s. When Mary was ten years old, her most earnest prayer was that she might have a Bible and be able to read it. God soon began answering her prayer by making it possible for her to attend school, where she learned to read. Then she was often allowed to read from the Bible of a wealthy neighbor. Still, she longed for a Bible of her own. When Mary was 16, she heard of a pastor who had Bibles for sale. He lived in a town 25 miles away, and with her parents' permission, Mary decided to take all the money she had saved and walk to that town to buy a Bible. This she did! The 25-mile return trip seemed short as she proudly carried her Bible home.

Twenty-five miles to the town, and then another 25 miles back—she walked 50 miles for a Bible, Abby whispered to herself as she closed the book. She looked at her own Bible lying on the dresser. How often she had carelessly handled it! How often she failed to read it! *I'm sure I know why Grandpa chose this book for me,* she thought. *From now on I'll read and appreciate my Bible a lot more. EIT*

HOW ABOUT YOU?

How careful are you when handling your Bible? How often do you read it? Whenever you're tempted to take it for granted, remember that even today there are people in some countries who do not have the privilege of owning a copy of the Word of God. Thank God that he has provided it for you. Care for it and use it.

CARE FOR YOUR BIBLE

MEMORIZE:
"Let the words of Christ, in all their richness, live in your hearts and make you wise. Use his words to teach and counsel each other." Colossians 3:16

DEBBIE'S RING

(Read Mark 10:29-31)

Debbie and her daddy had a special daily habit. She would sit on his knee when he came home from work, and he would say, "Debbie, do you love me?" Debbie would say, "I love you, Daddy." Then she would reach into his coat pocket and find a little gift. It might be a quarter, or a piece of gum, or candy—just a little treat.

One day Debbie's daddy said, as usual, "Debbie, do you love me?"

As usual, Debbie answered, "I love you, Daddy." Reaching into his pocket she found a little ring he had bought at a discount store. "Oh, Daddy," exclaimed Debbie, "it's just beautiful! I'm going to wear it and wear it and never take it off." And after that, Debbie wore that ring everywhere. She wore it even though it made a green mark on her finger.

When Debbie's daddy realized just how much the ring meant to his little girl, he decided to buy her a real gold one. And that afternoon, as always, Debbie sat on her daddy's knee. "Debbie, do you love me?" he asked.

"I love you, Daddy," answered Debbie.

"Then give me your ring," her father said with a twinkle in his eye.

But Debbie didn't notice the twinkle. "Oh, Daddy, please," she protested. "I love my ring. Why do you want it?"

"Just give me the ring," Daddy insisted.

When Debbie saw that he meant it, tears came to her eyes. "Oh, Daddy, I do love you, but please let me keep my ring," she pleaded. Daddy still held out his hand. As Debbie gave him the ring, she was trying not to cry.

"Now reach into my pocket," said Daddy with a smile.

Debbie could hardly believe her eyes when she pulled out the shiny gold ring. "Oh, Daddy," she exclaimed. "It's so much prettier than the other one. If I had only known, I'd have given you that one right away." *PR*

HOW ABOUT YOU?

Do you give Jesus whatever he asks—your life, your time, and your talents? Or do you say, "Jesus, I love you," and then hold things back from him? Give him all of you. In return, he will give you a far more beautiful life than you'll have if you go your own way.

MEMORIZE:

"The Lord will indeed give what is good." Psalm 85:12, NIV

GIVE ALL TO GOD

IMITATE ME

(Read 1 Peter 2:21-24)

"Mom, tell Kevin to stop," said Susan as she came in the back door with her little brother following her.

"Kevin, are you teasing your sister again?" Mother asked, as she picked up the phone to order pizza.

"No," said Kevin with his thumb in his mouth.

"He is too," insisted Susan. "Every time I move, he moves the same way I do. He repeats almost everything I say, too. I can't do anything without having him copy me. It's so irritating!"

"I'm sorry it bothers you, honey," said Mother. "I don't think he does that to tease you, though. I think he loves you so much that he wants to be like you."

Susan looked at little Kevin. "He does?" she asked.

Mother nodded. "Actually, it should please you," she said.

"Well . . . ," Susan hesitated. "I suppose so."

Mother smiled. "Did you know that there is Someone who wants you to imitate him, too?" she asked.

"Who?" asked Susan. She couldn't imagine who that could be.

"Jesus does," Mother told her. "He set an example for you and asked that you follow him and do as he did. It's in following his example in serving and loving others that we show him we love him." Mom smiled at Susan. "Read the four Gospels—Matthew, Mark, Luke, and John," she suggested. "As you read, write down various characteristics of Jesus so that you can practice them."

"Sounds like a lot of work," said Susan.

"Yes, but you may find you enjoy it," replied Mom. "You probably already know many of Jesus' characteristics. Can you think of some?"

"Well . . . he loves everyone," began Susan. "He helped people a lot. He forgave them, too."

"Good start," approved Mom, "and I'm sure you'll find lots more. Maybe you'd like to pick one of them and especially practice that one for a week or two. It should soon become a habit for you. Then you could pick another to work on." *JJL*

HOW ABOUT YOU?

Do you follow Jesus' example? That's the way to be truly happy. It's a way to show that you really love him. Which characteristic of Jesus will you work on first?

MEMORIZE:

"I have given you an example to follow. Do as I have done to you."

John 13:15

IMITATE JESUS

FEBRUARY
14

THE CHOCOLATE BOX

(Read Titus 3:3-7)

"Mom, I asked my friend Renee if she's a Christian, and she said, 'Sure. I go to church all the time.' I told her that didn't make her a Christian, but she didn't believe me."

Mom nodded. "It's often hard to convince people that, although it's true that Christians generally do go to church, going to church doesn't make a person a Christian," she said. "But don't give up."

Sarah's little sister toddled up to them, with a pretty chocolate box clutched tightly in her hands. "Mommy, here's a chocolate for you," squealed Jane. She held out the box.

"Thank you, sweetie," said Mom, taking something from the box.

"You can have one, too," Jane told her big sister, passing her the box.

Sarah stretched out her hand eagerly, but withdrew it when she saw what was in the box. "Those aren't chocolates," she protested. "They're stones!"

"No! Chocolates!" insisted Jane. "Look, Sarah!" With a grubby little finger, she pointed to the pictures of big creamy-looking chocolates on the cover of the box.

Sarah laughed. "Oh, Jane! That's just a picture," she said. "Putting stones inside a chocolate box doesn't make them turn into chocolates!"

"Just like putting a person inside a church doesn't make her a Christian!" said Mom quickly. "Maybe you should tell Renee about Jane's chocolates."

"Good idea!" agreed Sarah. "Maybe that would help her understand that being in church doesn't make her a Christian. She needs to trust in Jesus." *MTF*

HOW ABOUT YOU?

Are you a Christian? If you answered "yes," are you saying yes because you go to church? Or is it because you have trusted Jesus? Going to church is a good thing, but the Bible says any good things we do, do not save us. Good deeds do not make a Christian. A Christian is someone who has accepted Jesus as Savior.

MEMORIZE:

"He saved us, not because of the good things we did, but because of his mercy. He washed away our sins and gave us a new life through the Holy Spirit." Titus 3:5

CHURCH DOESN'T SAVE: JESUS DOES

THE PLANT

(Read Ephesians 3:14-19)

Kim was looking at the planter hanging from the ceiling. "What's the matter with your plant, Mom?" she asked.

"Oh, dear!" exclaimed Mother. "I've been so busy with all our company that I forgot to water it! I'll do it right now."

A few days later, Kim noticed the plant again. This time it looked bright, and the leaves weren't drooping. It looked like a healthy plant once more. "Mom, look at your plant now!" she exclaimed. "I guess it just needed to be watered. Or did you do something else to it?"

"I gave it water that had plant food in it," explained Mom, smiling, "and when it got the nourishment it needed, it perked right up." She looked fondly at her plant. "Plants are something like Christians," she observed.

Kim raised her eyebrows. "How are we like plants?"

"The Bible tells us that we're to be rooted and grounded in Jesus," explained Mother. "We need to get spiritual nourishment from his Word, from Christian fellowship, and from spending time in prayer. You saw what happened when the plant wasn't faithfully watered and fed."

"Do you think others can tell when we aren't being spiritually fed?" asked Kim.

"I believe they often can," answered Mother. "When we lose touch with God's Word and his people, our life may lose the evidence that God is in control. Many times we're unhappy and impatient." She looked at the plant. "If we see this plant drooping again, maybe it will remind us that we must not let that happen in our spiritual life." *BR*

HOW ABOUT YOU?

Do you feel "droopy" when it comes to spiritual things? Think about your life—is it a shining testimony for Christ? Maybe it's been too long since you received spiritual nourishment. Spend time with other Christians, enjoying their fellowship and learning from them. Read the Bible daily, and spend time in prayer. Become well established in your Christian life.

MEMORIZE:

"Let your roots grow down into him and draw up nourishment from him, so you will grow in faith, strong and vigorous in the truth you were taught." Colossians 2:7

SEEK SPIRITUAL FOOD

FEBRUARY
16

THE OLD DESK

(Read Psalm 51:10-13)

Annette looked in dismay at the old desk her mother had bought at an auction. *Does Mom really expect me to put that ugly, old piece of junk in my bedroom?* she wondered. Mother saw the worried look on Annette's face and laughed. "Oh, Annette, we won't use it this way," Mother assured her. "We're going to restore this old desk to the thing of beauty it once was." Annette breathed a sigh of relief.

When they began the work on the desk, Annette found the process fascinating. First, they removed layer after layer of paint. The desk had evidently been painted light green, then blue, and then yellow—and each layer of paint was embedded with dirt and grime. Next they sanded, stained, and finally added the finishing coat. "There you are," said Mother. "This beautiful, solid oak desk was hiding under all that paint and grime. It was fun restoring its beauty to it, wasn't it?"

Annette nodded. She loved the way the desk looked now, and she was thrilled when it was put into her room. She sat down at it. Her Bible was lying there, so she thought she'd read it—something she rarely had time for anymore. She opened to Psalms and began reading Psalm 51.

As Annette read, the Holy Spirit worked in her heart. The word *restore* caught her eye, and she stopped and read it again. *We restored this old desk,* she thought, *and this verse talks about restoring the joy of salvation! I wonder what that means.* Then Annette remembered that right after she was first saved, she had enjoyed Bible reading and learning about God. Lately she'd been taking such things for granted. *I guess I need to be restored, too,* she thought. *Just like we removed all the old paint and dirt from the desk, I need bad attitudes and habits removed. I bet that's what this verse means. REP*

HOW ABOUT YOU?

Do you still find a great deal of joy and happiness in your salvation and in serving God? If not, ask the Lord to renew your spirit and restore the joy you can have in him.

MEMORIZE:

"Restore to me again the joy of your salvation, and make me willing to obey you." Psalm 51:12

FIND JOY IN SALVATION

A PERFECT CREATION

(Read Job 38:1-11)

"Science is really fascinating," said Karla, as she painted a model fish to use for her science fair project. "Did you know that fish can live in deep water because the pressure inside their bodies is as strong as the pressure of all that water?"

"That *is* incredible," Dad agreed.

"My teacher calls it a wonder of nature," said Karla.

"It is a great part of nature," Dad said, "and it is a wonder, though not in the way your teacher probably meant it. God, the creator of nature, carefully planned it that way." He paused. "Maybe you can demonstrate that as your project."

"How would I do that?" asked Karla.

Dad thought for a moment, then picked up a bucket of blocks from the floor and handed it to Karla. "Here," he said, "dump these out."

Karla looked at the blocks. "Dump out Patsy's blocks?" she asked. She shrugged. "Well, OK." Karla dumped them into a messy pile.

Dad looked at the blocks on the floor. "No good," he said, putting them back into the bucket. "Do it again."

Karla frowned, but she did it again . . . and again . . . and again. Karla started to laugh. "How long are we going to do this?" she asked at last.

Dad smiled. "I want them to land in a perfect castle," he said.

"Dad!" protested Karla. "Count me out on that project. It's never gonna happen."

"Why not?" Dad asked.

"It just couldn't," said Karla. "It's impossible."

Dad smiled. "You're right, of course," he said. "Now . . . since it would take careful planning to make a block castle, just think how much planning must have gone into making the whole world . . . the stars . . . and the rivers . . . and the . . ."

". . . and the oceans and the fish, right?" asked Karla with a grin. "Can I take these blocks to school tomorrow?" she asked. "I have a new idea for the science fair." *HMT*

HOW ABOUT YOU?

Does your school teach things that don't match up with the Bible? Do you have a teacher or friends who believe everything in nature just evolved? There is a lot of evidence to contradict evolution. Find some, so that you can share the truth with others.

MEMORIZE:

"From the time the world was created, people have seen the earth and sky and all that God made. They can clearly see his invisible qualities—his eternal power and divine nature. So they have no excuse whatsoever for not knowing God." Romans 1:20

GOD IS THE CREATOR

FEBRUARY
18

RASCAL'S SONG

(Read Psalm 68:3-4, 32-35)

Jo's parents agreed that she could have either a bird or a guinea pig if she'd care for it properly. In a way she wanted a bird. *It would be neat to have a pet that sings,* she thought, *but I could hold and pet a guinea pig.* Finally, she decided on the guinea pig and named it Rascal.

Each day, Jo checked Rascal's food and water and spent time petting him. Soon Rascal scrambled to her whenever she set him on the floor. Rascal liked little nooks and would crawl under Jo's leg if she held it up a bit.

One morning Jo rushed into the kitchen. "Mom! Come to my room," she exclaimed. "There's something you've got to see!" Setting the frying pan to one side, Mom followed Jo to her room. "Listen!" said Jo as Rascal began making chirping and whistling sounds. "He's singing! What do you think of that?"

"I didn't know guinea pigs could sing!" Mom declared. "What a sweet sound!" She smiled at Jo. "Why do you think Rascal sings?"

"I don't know." Jo shrugged. "I guess he's happy!"

"He sounds happy to me," Mom agreed, "and I noticed that he began singing when you stepped into the room. Do you think he's singing to thank you for your care and to express affection in his own way?"

Jo's eyes lit up with the thought. "Yeah, I guess," she replied, pleased with the idea.

"It makes you feel pretty good, doesn't it, to think you're taking care of all his needs, and he's happy and content and showing his gratitude." Jo nodded. "I believe God is pleased when we sing praises to him, too," continued Mom. "David did that with God, and God called David a man after his own heart." *RSS*

HOW ABOUT YOU?

Do you appreciate—or even notice—all the care God gives you? Do you thank him for what he's provided—food, clothes, toys, family, friends, and protection? Even more important, do you thank him for forgiveness, new life, a sure future in heaven? Sing a song to God in the morning, even right out loud! Love him. He loves you and likes to hear you sing his praises.

MEMORIZE:

"But as for me, I will sing about your power. I will shout with joy each morning because of your unfailing love." Psalm 59:16

SING PRAISES TO GOD

ESCAPED

(Read Psalm 124)

Mom's just not with it, Dottie thought to herself. *She'll never let me play rock music like all the other kids do. I don't see why I can't listen to what I want.*

On the way to her grandparents farm one evening, Dottie sang softly to herself. "Sing louder," suggested Mother, "so we can hear the words." But Dottie was obviously embarrassed and said she didn't know the song well enough. "Dottie, if you don't want to repeat those words to us, do you think it's good for you to be repeating them to yourself?" asked Mother.

Dad spoke up. "Grandpa and I plan to work on some traps tonight," he said. "Do you know that Satan has traps, too? Some kinds of rock music can be one of them. At first you seem to be in control over it, but soon the beat and words get a grip on your mind."

"That's right," agreed Mother. "Just tonight the paper had an article about the need for police control at rock concerts. That music seems to make people act crazy. I've also heard that the performers are often high on drugs."

Dottie scowled. "You surely don't think I get high on music, do you?" she asked.

"Not yet," replied Mother as they reached the farm. "But you must admit that it has a hold on you. You have to be told four or five times to shut it off and do other things. You think about this. Break loose from the trap while you can."

Several days later, Dottie was helping Mother. Soft music played in the background. "May I ask you something?" said Mother. "You seem to have changed your listening habits—I haven't had to tell you to shut off rock music for some time. What happened?"

"It was the night at Grandpa's farm," answered Dottie. "I went along to inspect the traps, and we found one where a coyote had been caught. He had fought to get loose—and he did, but he had hurt himself fighting! It still makes me sick. I remembered what you said about Satan's trap, and I wanted to get away before I got hurt." *BJW*

HOW ABOUT YOU?

Do you listen only to songs with words that honor God? Or does the wrong kind of rock music have you in its grip? Don't allow Satan to trap you through your sense of hearing. Don't let the beat and rhythm of the music control your actions. Seek God's help in choosing good music.

MEMORIZE:

"We escaped like a bird from a hunter's trap. The trap is broken, and we are free! Our help is from the Lord, who made the heavens and the earth." Psalm 124:7-8

DON'T BE TRAPPED

FEBRUARY 20

AFRAID OF CLOUDY DAYS?

(Read 1 Thessalonians 4:13-17)

"What did you learn today, girls?" asked Dad as they sat around the Sunday dinner table.

"Well, ah . . . we learned that Jesus is coming," said Corey.

"Yeah, and he'll take all those who believe in him to heaven," added Jamie. "It could be today." She grinned. "Mr. Shaw read a verse that says Jesus is coming with clouds, and today is a cloudy day."

Dad laughed. "That's true, but I'm sure you know it doesn't have to be a cloudy day for Jesus to come," he said. "He's coming with 'the clouds of heaven,' but it could happen on a bright, sunny day, too. The important thing is to be ready. Only those who are Christians will go to be with him."

"Our teacher said it will happen really fast." Tina joined the conversation. "It will happen faster than you can blink. An angel will shout and a trumpet will sound, and . . ."

". . . and 'all the Christians who have died will rise from their graves,'" interrupted Jamie. "'Then, together with them, we who are still alive and remain on the earth will be caught up in the clouds to meet the Lord in the air and remain with him forever.' That was our memory verse."

Jamie and Tina went on to describe more of what their teacher had said. Only Corey failed to join the discussion.

The next day, Corey hurried home from school. *The clouds look really weird—kind of scary,* she thought. *I wonder if Jesus might come today? I think I better find out more about how to become a Christian so I can go to heaven when he comes. LJR*

HOW ABOUT YOU?

Will you be ready if Jesus comes today? Have you asked him to forgive your sins and to be your Savior? If not, talk with a trusted friend or adult.

MEMORIZE:
"Look! He comes with the clouds of heaven." Revelation 1:7

**BE READY WHEN
JESUS COMES**

HERE'S MY GIFT

(Read 1 Chronicles 28:9, 20)

Christa enjoyed occasionally playing the piano for the opening exercises in Sunday school. But then Ken asked her to accompany his trumpet solo at Bible club. "I suppose I can," she agreed reluctantly. Ken suggested times when they could practice, but she found she was either busy or unwilling to give up her free time. Finally she agreed to run over the piece just before the program.

During the next few months, Mother noticed that Christa was often invited to play for various groups. She usually agreed to play, but she did so without much enthusiasm. "Is it really so bad?" Mother asked.

Christa scowled. "You always tell me I should use my gift of music for the Lord, but now that I'm using it, you're still not satisfied." She sighed impatiently and left the room.

That evening Christa spoke to her older brother, Bill, as he left the dinner table. "Would you help me with my math? I just don't understand it."

"I've got things to do," Bill replied.

"But I have a test tomorrow. Please help me," pleaded Christa.

"Call one of your friends to help you," protested Bill.

"I'm sure you can take a little time to help your sister," suggested Mother.

"Oh, all right," Bill growled. "I'll be in my room. Call when you need me."

"Oh, Mother!" wailed Christa. "When he's so grouchy about it, I don't even feel like having him help me. But I do need help. Why can't he be pleasant about it?"

"Are you always pleasant when people ask you to do something?" asked Mother.

Christa blushed as she remembered how unhappily she had promised to play for someone just that afternoon. "I know what you mean," she admitted. "I guess playing the piano unwillingly isn't really using my gift for the Lord at all, is it? I'm going to do it more cheerfully from now on!" *HWM*

HOW ABOUT YOU?

Are you grumpy when you are asked to serve in some way? Solomon was told to serve God with a "perfect heart and with a willing mind." That's good advice for Christians, too. You should be happy to serve the Lord who has done so much for you.

SERVE GOD CHEERFULLY

MEMORIZE:
"Worship the Lord with gladness."
Psalm 100:2

FEBRUARY
22

A VERY IMPORTANT LETTER

(Read Philippians 1:3-7)

Sandy-haired JC chewed the end of her pencil as she tried to think of something to write next. "Whatcha doin'?" asked her brother, Josh. "Is that your home-work?"

JC shook her head. "No, I'm writing a letter to Mr. Sandborn," she said. "He's the missionary who came and spoke at our church last fall."

"He probably doesn't even remember you," said Josh.

"I know," replied JC, "but I thought he might like to get a letter since he's not married and works all alone in that village."

Some days later, in a small, run-down hut, a missionary sighed in the swel-tering heat and sat down at the table. He was tired and discouraged. The work progressed so slowly, and sometimes it seemed that he might just as well go back home and give up his missionary work. He looked at the mail in his hand. Letters were scarce, and he especially wondered about the long envelope addressed in a child's unfamiliar handwriting.

He smoothed out the letter and began to read. "Dear Mr. Sandborn," it said. "I just wanted to tell you we're all thinking of you and praying for you. I liked it when you came to our church last fall. I hope you're having a good time there." The missionary smiled as he continued reading. "I remember the things you told us about having faith in God. I will try to have more faith. Because of you, I think I would like to be a missionary someday. Thank you for your help. Love, JC Watson."

Mr. Sandborn sat for a few moments, and then he whispered a prayer of thanks for the encouragement of that simple letter. *Perhaps this is God's way of letting me know he intends to use my ministry here,* he thought. *Maybe I need more faith, too.*

He smiled as he looked out the window at the village children playing in the sand. Then he took out a piece of paper. He had to write a thank-you letter to a very important person. *SLK*

HOW ABOUT YOU?

Have you thought about ways you could encourage the missionaries you know? Even a child can write a simple letter to a missionary. You may never know just how much it means to some-one far away. Why not write one this week?

MEMORIZE:

"Good news from far away is like cold water to the thirsty." Proverbs 25:25

WRITE TO MISSIONARIES

FOX AND GEESE

(Read 1 Corinthians 10:12-14)

Amy and Carl had invited their friends to come over and play fox and geese. The children shuffled their feet into the snow to make a huge pie-face design. It looked like a giant wheel with eight spokes running through it.

Ken volunteered to be the first fox. "Remember, the center is the safety spot," Carl instructed. "Run into it, and you are safe. But you have to use the escape spokes to get there. If the fox catches you, you're it."

The children romped in the snow until Amy and Carl were called in for lunch. "You seemed to be having a good time out there," observed Mother. "But why didn't you take turns being the fox?"

"We did," Amy said.

Mother looked surprised. "But every time I looked out, Bryan was it," she said.

Carl laughed. "That was Bryan's own fault. He always tried to get just as close to the fox as possible before he'd run. Then he got caught."

"And he never used the escape routes until it was too late," Amy added.

Mother nodded. "You know," she said, "many people do the same thing in the game of life."

"The game of life?" asked Carl.

"We face trials and temptations, but Jesus has given us escape routes," explained Mother. "We can run to him for safety. But sometimes we try to get so close to sin before we run away that we get caught by that sin."

"Like the time I sat with the older kids at the assembly even though I knew they were troublemakers," Amy said.

"That's right," agreed Mother.

"And the time I listened to those bad jokes instead of walking away," Carl said. "Those bad thoughts hung in my mind for days."

"You've got the right idea," Mother said with a smile. *JLH*

HOW ABOUT YOU?

Do you run away from sin before you get involved? Ask Jesus for help. He will show you the way to escape.

MEMORIZE:

"But remember that the temptations that come into your life are no different from what others experience. And God is faithful. He will keep the temptation from becoming so strong that you can't stand up against it. When you are tempted, he will show you a way out so that you will not give in to it." 1 Corinthians 10:13

ESCAPE FROM SIN

FEBRUARY
24

OLD AND HONORABLE

(Read 1 Timothy 5:1-4)

"Anne, you look very thoughtful," commented Mother. "What's on your mind?"

"Oh, I was just reading the strangest story in this book," Anne answered. "It's about a man and his wife. The man's father lived with them. He was old and kind of sick, and his hands shook. When he ate, sometimes he knocked things over, so the wife told her husband to make a wooden bowl for him so he wouldn't break the good dishes. After that, the man got tired of seeing his father spill food at the table, and he made his father take the wooden bowl and sit on a stool in the corner behind the stove to eat."

"Does sound strange," agreed Mother.

"Here's the strangest part of the story," Anne continued. "The couple had a boy, and one day they saw him making two stools. The father asked what he was doing, and the little boy said, 'I'm making stools so they will be ready for you when you're old and come to live with me.'" Anne paused a moment. "Do you think that's a true story?" she asked.

"It's probably not true," answered her mother, "but I know there are many people who don't respect or care for their parents."

Anne nodded. "Rachel's grandmother lives with them, and the poor old woman isn't allowed to come out of her room when they have company. Rachel says it's because she's had a stroke and talks real funny."

"That really is sad," said Mother. "The Bible instructs children to honor their parents, no matter how old they might be. It's important to start showing them respect and honor when you're young. Then it will become a habit, and it will be natural for you to show them love and care when they get old, too." *CR*

HOW ABOUT YOU?

Do you honor your parents? Do you show respect to your grandparents? To all old people? Do you treat them the way you want to be treated when you grow old? God says you are to respect and honor your parents. You are to do that all your life. Start while you're young, and it will be easier to do when you're older.

MEMORIZE:

"But if she has children or grandchildren, their first responsibility is to show godliness at home and repay their parents by taking care of them. This is something that pleases God very much." 1 Timothy 5:4

RESPECT YOUR PARENTS

ON THIN ICE

(Read Proverbs 4:14-23)

"I don't see why I can't go. It seems like a fair exchange," Connie told her mother. "Since Karen is willing to come to church tomorrow if I go with her this afternoon, I think I should."

Mother shook her head. "She wants you to go to a horror movie and then to Peyton's to eat and play electronic games, right? I've explained before why I don't think going to either of those places is the way to win your friend to the Lord."

"But, Mother!" protested Connie. "It will get Karen to come . . ."

"I said no, Connie," Mother stated firmly.

Later, with Mother's permission, Connie spent the afternoon figure skating with some friends at Horn's Lake. When she returned home, she was bursting with excitement. "You know Jack Wolter? He almost drowned! He zipped right past the danger sign toward the middle of the lake. But the ice didn't hold him. One leg went right through into freezing water. I screamed for help!"

Mother was concerned. "Is he all right?"

Connie nodded. "He was hanging onto the ice, half in and half out of the water. He's just lucky the men on duty got there in time."

"Oh, good!" said Mother. "But why didn't you skate out and rescue him yourself? You took that lifesaving swim class last summer."

Connie looked at her mother in disbelief. "You've gotta be kidding! The men used boards and ropes and stuff to crawl out and reach Jack. If anybody had skated out there, it would have broken more of the ice and made it worse!"

Mother nodded. "I'm glad you had the good sense to know that," she said. "Now think about this—when you see someone in sin, you don't rescue him by joining him. If you do, you might both get trapped in sin."

As Connie heard Mother's words, she remembered their conversation that morning. She would have to find some other way to help Karen. *HWM*

HOW ABOUT YOU?

In order to win a friend to Jesus, are you sometimes tempted to go someplace you should not go or to do something you know is wrong? If you yield to that temptation, you're just fooling yourself—you're not winning your friend. The way to win others to Jesus is through living a pure life before them. Pray for them.

WITNESS BY YOUR LIFE

MEMORIZE:
"Do not participate in the sins of others. Keep yourself pure."
1 Timothy 5:22

FEBRUARY
26

THE MISSING SWEATER

(Read Leviticus 19:15-18)

"Mom, I can't find my purple sweater," wailed Phyllis.

"When was the last time you wore it?" Mother asked.

Phyllis wrinkled her brow. "Last Sunday."

"Maybe you left it at church," Mother suggested. "Call the office and ask if anyone turned it in." But the sweater wasn't there.

Several times that week, Phyllis searched in vain for her sweater. She wanted to wear it to a Sunday school party at Melissa's house on Friday evening, but now she'd have to choose something else. Arriving at the party, Phyllis stared in amazement at Marci, one of the girls in her class. Drawing Melissa close, she whispered, "Marci's wearing my sweater! She must have picked it up at Sunday school."

"Are you sure?" Melissa whispered back.

"Of course," Phyllis hissed. "She couldn't afford a sweater like that!"

As the girls were talking with Marci later, Melissa said, "That's a pretty sweater, Marci. Where did you get it?"

"My mother bought it at a garage sale," she told them.

"I'll bet," muttered Phyllis. She was angry and told several girls that Marci had stolen her sweater. The party wasn't much fun for her after that.

When Phyllis reached home, her grandmother met her at the door. Phyllis gave her a big hug as Mother said, "You'll be glad to see what Grandma brought you." Mother handed Phyllis her purple sweater.

"But where did you find this?" Phyllis stammered.

"You left it at my house last Sunday," Grandma told her.

Tears welled up in Phyllis's eyes. "I've made a terrible mistake," she sighed. "I'll tell you about it after I make some phone calls." *BJW*

HOW ABOUT YOU?

Have you ever falsely accused someone? Did you apologize? Next time you're tempted to accuse someone, wait! God says Christians should be slow to speak. He knows that hasty conclusions are often wrong.

MEMORIZE:

"Dear friends, be quick to listen, slow to speak, and slow to get angry."
James 1:19

DON'T ACCUSE FALSELY

BABY'S FIRST STEPS

(Read Romans 15:1-7)

"I give up!" exclaimed Ellen.

Mother looked up as she heard her daughter's words. "Give up on what?" she asked.

"Give up on Janet," explained Ellen as she tossed her school books on the kitchen table. "I was so glad when she became a Christian a month ago, but now she's getting tiresome! One day she acts like a Christian, and the next she lies or cheats or uses bad language. She'll never make a good Christian!"

"I hope you won't really give up on her," said Mother. "You need to pray for her and help her understand how to live for the Lord."

"Oh, I don't know," muttered Ellen with a sigh. "I think it's hopeless!"

After supper that evening, Ellen was playing with her baby brother. Suddenly she called out, "Mom! Look at Davy! He wants to walk!" Sure enough, when Ellen stood Davy on his feet, he took a tottering step toward her. "He took his first step by himself!" exclaimed Ellen. "I'm going to teach him to take more."

Ellen spent half an hour trying to teach her brother to walk. Mother smiled as she heard Ellen encourage and help the baby. "Come to Ellen, Davy," coaxed the girl. "Come on, honey. You can walk!" Over and over Ellen put the tottering baby back on his feet, for he was never able to take more than two steps before he tumbled to the floor.

"Better give up," advised Mother. "He'll never be able to walk. He just keeps falling down."

Ellen looked at her mother in surprise. "Give up? What do you mean?" she asked as she picked up the baby. "He just needs more help. Isn't that right, Davy?" Ellen put him down and patiently started to help him again.

Mother chuckled as she spoke. "You're exactly right, Ellen. Davy does need your help. And so does Janet. She's a 'baby' Christian. She's going to need lots of help in learning to walk spiritually—that is, to live as a Christian should live." *GW*

HOW ABOUT YOU?

Do you know a Christian whose spiritual walk is not as good as you think it should be? Perhaps he or she is a baby Christian who is learning the first steps of Christian living. This person needs your prayers, encouragement, and help, even as you need the help of older Christians.

NEW CHRISTIANS NEED HELP

MEMORIZE:

"We who are strong ought to bear with the failings of the weak."
Romans 5:1, NIV

FEBRUARY
28

I WISH I COULD

(Read Genesis 37:19-27)

Jody put her hands over her ears and intently read the bulletin on her lap. She didn't want to hear her friend Laura play the piano solo. After church everyone would talk about how Laura had mastered the piano, and Jody didn't want to hear that, either. She was envious, that was all there was to it! She wished *she* could play in church.

That week, the annual all-school track meet was held at Jody's school. All the classes were competing against one another in running events. Jody confidently waited on the sidelines. She had been chosen to run the cross-country race. She had always been the fastest runner in her class.

"You running the last event?" Jody turned to see Laura standing next to her.

"Probably."

"I wish I could run as fast as you do," said Laura.

Jody looked at Laura in surprise. After a moment, she laughed. "That's funny. I always wished I could play the piano as well as you do, and at the same time you were wishing you could run as fast as I can."

Laura grinned. "I guess we've both been pretty silly."

"I even tried not to listen last Sunday," confessed Jody, "but I heard you anyway. You did a great job."

"Thanks," said Laura, just as Jody's teacher came to get her for the next race. "Hope you win your race."

When Jody got home that afternoon, she told her mother about her conversation with Laura. Mother smiled. "Our job is to use the abilities God gave us the best way we know how. We should not waste our time wishing we could do something someone else is doing," said Mother. "I think you and Laura both learned an important lesson." *LMW*

HOW ABOUT YOU?

Have you ever wished you could write, play an instrument, or draw as well as someone else could? Have you ever disliked someone because of his or her abilities? Today's Scripture gives an example of terrible sin that resulted from envy. Remember, God made each person unique and gave each one different abilities. Don't be envious of someone else's talent. Instead, be happy with the talent you have.

MEMORIZE:

"Love is patient and kind. Love is not jealous or boastful or proud."
1 Corinthians 13:4

DON'T ENVY
ANOTHER'S TALENT

GOOD SERVANTS

(Matthew 25:14-29)

A smiling young lady carrying a tray of water glasses approached the Adams family. "My name is Joanna and I'll be your waitress tonight," she said. "Are you ready to order, or will you need a few minutes?"

"I think we know what we want," replied Dad. The waitress jotted down each order and then walked back to the kitchen. Before long, the family was enjoying a delicious meal.

"Why do they call those girls waitresses?" Penny asked as they finished dessert.

"Because you wait while they bring you the food," Peter answered.

Mom smiled. "That's not exactly the reason," she said. "One meaning for 'wait' is to 'serve meals.' That's what waitresses—or waiters—do. They serve the customers who come in to eat."

"Hey," said Penny, "I learned a Bible verse once that says, 'Wait on the Lord.'"

"Wait on *God?*" interrupted Peter. "We can't feed him meals."

Dad smiled. "No," he said, "and when the Bible tells us to 'wait on the Lord,' it generally means we are to be patient and trust him. But although we can't serve the Lord meals, we can serve him in other ways." Dad picked up the check. "Do you think Joanna has been a good waitress?" he asked as he took out his wallet. Both children nodded. "I agree," said Dad. "What makes a person a good waitress or waiter?"

"They need to bring you exactly what you ask for," Peter answered promptly.

"They need to be quick, too," Penny added. "When we asked for ketchup, Joanna brought it right away."

"And would those things help you be a good servant of God?" asked Dad. "If we obey his commands promptly, what will happen?"

"Maybe he'll give us a big tip—like Daddy is leaving for Joanna!" Peter exclaimed.

"God does bless us for obeying him and serving him," Dad said, "but the real rewards will come when we get to heaven. Imagine being greeted with the words, 'Well done, my good and faithful servant.' I can't imagine any tip better than that!" *RB*

HOW ABOUT YOU?

Are you serving the Lord? Do you promptly obey your parents and teachers? Are you kind to all the kids you meet—even those who don't treat you nicely? Do you "love your neighbor as yourself"? These are only a few of the things God tells you to do. Serve him by following his commandments.

SERVE GOD WELL

MEMORIZE:
"Well done, my good and faithful servant. . . . Let's celebrate together!" Matthew 25:21

MARCH
2

STAINS ON THE CARPET

(Read Colossians 3:8, 12-14)

"My friend is doing us a real favor in letting us stay in this neat place for a week," said Dad as he unlocked the door of a lovely condo. "And we're responsible for keeping it clean."

Almost immediately Jan and Lori were fighting over who would sleep in the top bunk of their room. More arguments followed over the closet space. The girls hurled unkind words and barbed comments back and forth. Their parents scolded and ordered them to stop fighting. Lori shrugged. "I guess we'll always fight," she said in a shrill, impatient voice. "The harder we try to quit, the worse it gets!" Jan nodded.

That evening, the girls were sitting in front of the fireplace tossing a ball back and forth. Jan, in a wild pitch, hit a glass of red punch in Lori's hand. It crashed to the floor, and in an instant, numerous bright red splatters appeared on the white rug.

"It's your fault!" Lori yelled at once. "You threw the ball!"

"It's not either my fault!" Jan insisted. "You picked up your punch at the wrong time. Why didn't you wait?"

Dad and Mom grabbed towels and they all worked to soak up the stains. But they wouldn't come out—even after Dad ran out to get some special detergent. "I know what we'll do," said Dad. "We'll rent a shampoo machine tomorrow and go over the entire rug. That should take care of it."

The next evening Lori looked at the spotless rug. "Wow!" she exclaimed. "When I saw all those red splotches, I thought we'd never get them out—especially when the detergent didn't do the job."

"Girls," Mother said, "that detergent reminds me of the weak efforts you've been making to stop your quarreling. You carelessly splatter ugly, angry words all over the place. Then you try to scrub away those splatters with flip apologies, insincere promises, and half-efforts. You'll never have a good relationship with each other until you ask the Lord to come with his powerful forgiveness and grace and do a thorough cleaning job on you!" *TVv*

HOW ABOUT YOU?

Do you quarrel with your family members or friends? Do you find it hard to stop? Good intentions or strong resolutions aren't enough. Ask Jesus to replace your angry words with positive ones.

MEMORIZE:

"Always keep yourselves united in the Holy Spirit, and bind yourselves together with peace." Ephesians 4:3

QUIT QUARRELING

KNOBBY KNEES AND FRECKLES

(Read Isaiah 45:9-10)

When Keli returned from school one day, she stomped in through the door, ran to her bedroom, and flopped down on her bed. She looked up when Mom came to the door. "Keli? What's wrong?" asked Mom.

Keli wiped tears from her eyes as she sat up on her bed. "It's Jeremy," she replied. Her voice trembled. "Remember that science project I did? I reported on the planets and made a model of them and everything. My teacher put it up on the bulletin board, and Jeremy keeps making fun of it. He and his friends say it looks dumb."

"I understand how that could make you feel bad," said Mother. "Jeremy shouldn't do that, but you know you did a good job, so try not to let it bother you, OK?"

The next morning Keli slipped on her favorite blue skirt as she got dressed for school. She walked over to the mirror, tossed her hair back over her shoulder, and sighed as she studied herself in the mirror. "Oh! I wish my knees weren't so knobby," she mumbled. "And why do I have to have freckles on my arms?"

Mom appeared in the doorway. "Keli, hurry or you'll be late for your bus," said Mom. She gave Keli a hug. "Did I hear you complaining?"

"Oh, Mom, my knees are too knobby, and I'm the only girl who looks like she has brown sugar sprinkled on her arms," grumbled Keli. "Why can't I be like Jenni?" She looked at her watch. "Oh, I've got to go, Mom . . . and I hope Jeremy minds his own business today."

"Me, too," said Mom. "It hurts to have someone criticize something you've made, doesn't it? Can you think of anyone else who might be feeling that way, too?"

"Well . . . not really. Who?" asked Keli.

"God," replied Mom. "The Bible tells us we are made by God. It states we were made for his good pleasure. Shouldn't you be thanking God for making you rather than complaining?"

"Oops! I never thought of that, Mom." Keli glanced at herself in the mirror. "I guess I'm OK after all." *CIR*

HOW ABOUT YOU?

Do you complain about your body? Do you compare yourself to other people and wish you looked like them? Thank God for making you. He made you just the way you are. You're perfect!

BE CONTENT WITH HOW GOD MADE YOU

MEMORIZE:
"Your workmanship is marvelous—
and how well I know
it." Psalm 139:14

ANSWER FOR THE DOUBTER

(Read Psalm 19:1-4; 111:2-4)

Emily sat on her porch step, staring out into space. She sighed. "What's wrong, honey?" asked her dad as he put down the garden hose.

"Daddy, this girl in my class—Jan—says there's no God," replied Emily. "I told her there is, but she said, 'Prove it.' I didn't know how. We can't see God. How could I show her proof?"

Dad nodded. "You may not be able to prove it to her satisfaction," he admitted, "but there are things she can see that may convince her of the truth. Come with me." Dad reached for her hand. Emily stood up and followed her father into the house. He pointed at the embroidered tablecloth on the dining room table. "Who made this?" he asked.

"Grandma did," Emily replied.

Dad then removed a drawing of a flower from the refrigerator door. "Who made this?"

Emily grinned. "I drew that in art class," she said.

"What about this cake?" asked Dad. "Who baked it?"

"Mom did," Emily answered.

Dad smiled. "See, no matter what I point to in this room, somebody made it," he said. Then he took Emily outside again. "What do you see?" he asked.

"I see the little birds in the trees," said Emily, "and a bee on a pink rose. And I see the sky and the sun shining and the grass and . . . and all kinds of things!"

"Who made them?" Dad asked.

"God did, of course," replied Emily.

"Yes, indeed he did," agreed Dad. "Everything made has a maker. Some things are made with human hands and others by God. One way we know God exists is that our eyes see the things that only God could make. Nature and our own bodies give us proof of God's existence and love for us."

Emily grinned. "That's true," she agreed. "I'll tell Jan about that." *SML*

HOW ABOUT YOU?

Do you know someone who doesn't believe in God? Even though we can't make people believe in God, we can help them by pointing out the wonderful things that only God could have made. The Bible teaches us that God is the creator of the universe. Let the wonders of his creation encourage you to speak about him to those who doubt his existence.

MEMORIZE:

"Who can forget the wonders he performs? How gracious and merciful is our Lord!" Psalm 111:4

**CREATION POINTS
TO GOD**

A DOG FOR RHONDA

(Read Matthew 7:9-11)

Rhonda sat down and began a letter to her dad, who was away on sea duty with the navy. Rhonda was eager to ask Dad if she could have a puppy from a neighbor's new litter. "I really hoped to have a dog just like Rex, Uncle Pete's dog," she wrote. "But this one is free, and it would be better than none." She could hardly wait for Dad's answer.

When Rhonda got home from school several days later, she was met by her smiling mother. "I just talked to Dad on the phone," Mother told her. "He'll be home next week and he can stay a whole month." Rhonda grinned broadly, but the grin disappeared when she heard that Dad had said no to the puppy. "I know this is hard for you to understand, but please trust your dad," urged Mother. "He loves you and wants what's best for you."

"Hard to believe," Rhonda muttered as she left the room. And for a while, her disappointment clouded the joy of looking forward to Dad's return.

But the days passed swiftly, and soon Rhonda was eagerly greeting her dad and making plans to do all sorts of things with him during the time he was home. "But I still don't see why I couldn't get that puppy, Dad," Rhonda said as she suddenly remembered her disappointment.

Just then a sound came from Dad's pile of luggage. "What is that noise?" asked Mother, looking startled.

But Rhonda recognized the sound. "A dog!" she exclaimed. "There's a dog in a box with your luggage!" She ran to see. "Dad!" she squealed, with a puppy in her arms. "He looks just like Rex!"

Dad nodded. "I did want you to have a dog," he explained. "The reason I said no to the other puppy was because I knew this was the kind of dog you really wanted." *AGL*

HOW ABOUT YOU?

Does your heavenly Father sometimes say no to the things you think you want and pray for? Remember, he loves you even more than earthly fathers love their children. When he says no, it's because he has something better for you. Trust God always, even when it looks to you like he's wrong!

GOD GIVES THE BEST

MEMORIZE:
"Whatever is good and perfect comes to us from God above." James 1:17

THE SCARE

(Read Hebrews 13:5-8)

Julie threw her books down on the kitchen counter. "I'm home, Mom!" she called. She ran into the living room and then called upstairs. "Mom?" A quick glance through the rooms showed that Mom and baby Ben weren't home. *That's funny,* Julie thought. *Mom is always here when I get home from school. I hope everything is OK!*

Julie walked slowly into the kitchen again. There on the table was half a cup of warm tea and a partially eaten cookie. Ben's bottle was under the high chair . . . and his "blanky" was on the floor! Ben never went anywhere without his blanky!

Julie shivered. *Where were they?*

"Julie?" There in the doorway stood Mom with little Ben in her arms. "Hi, honey," Mom said. "I'm so sorry we weren't here when you got home. Old Mrs. Henderson was locked out of her apartment and needed someone tall to reach the spare key. . . . Julie, are you OK?"

Julie threw herself into her mother's arms. "Oh, Mom!" she cried. "I thought something had happened to you and Ben. And I thought I might not ever see you again. And I began to think about how you told me once that if we are Christians, Jesus will never leave us. And since I'm not a Christian yet, I just felt so alone and scared."

Mom held Julie tightly. "Oh, Julie!" she said. "We are all safe. But it is a good thing to have Jesus in your life. For he never will leave you. Let's read from the Bible tonight and talk some more about what it means to be a Christian." *REB*

HOW ABOUT YOU?

Have you ever felt scared and alone? Remember, if you are a Christian, Jesus will never leave you. He is a forever friend.

MEMORIZE:

"Never will I leave you; never will I forsake you." Hebrews 13:5b, NIV

JESUS IS A FOREVER FRIEND

WHAT TO WEAR

(Read Ephesians 2:1-6)

Emma waved good-bye to Sherry's family as they drove off. Then she ran into the house. "Hi," Mom greeted her. "Did you enjoy going to church with Sherry?"

Emma shrugged. "It was OK, but I was too dressed up," she said. "Not many people dress up at Sherry's church. She says it makes strangers in the church feel uncomfortable if everybody's dressed up." Emma shook her head. "I don't get it," she added. "You and Dad want us to dress up to show respect for God's house, and that makes sense. But what Sherry said makes sense, too. Who's right?"

"That's not an easy question," replied Mom. "The Bible doesn't tell us exactly what to wear to church. But it does give us some guidelines. Do you know what they are?"

Emma thought for a moment. "It says to dress modestly," she said. "That means not too skimpy, right?"

"That's one thing," agreed Mother. "Perhaps it means not too 'showy' either. And we must treat people kindly no matter how they are dressed. The Bible also says we should try not to offend others."

"I think some people were offended when Daniel Dirks came to church in torn shorts," said Emma.

Mom frowned. "It wasn't just the way he dressed that caused the problem," she said. "His attitude showed that he wasn't being very modest or respectful."

"Well, maybe," admitted Emma, "but people complain about Tiffany Brooks, too, and she always looks great!"

"There again, they don't complain about her clothes so much. It's that she seems to spend a lot of time—even during the service—checking her hair and fixing her nails," replied Mom. "But do you know who Mr. Hales is? He always brings visitors from the homeless shelter, and he dresses in very casual clothes so they won't feel out of place. Nobody is offended by that."

Emma thought a moment then said, "So I guess what you're saying is as long as I follow the biblical standards of modesty, love, and respect, there is no right or wrong way." *HMT*

HOW ABOUT YOU?

How do you dress for church? It's easy to put on clothes to impress people, but God is looking at your heart. What you wear isn't as important as why you wear it.

MEMORIZE:

"The purpose of my instruction is that all the Christians there would be filled with love that comes from a pure heart, a clear conscience, and sincere faith." 1 Timothy 1:5

DRESS MODESTLY

A HELPING HAND

(Read Luke 10:25-37)

"Clumsy! Can't you even stand on your own two feet?" Kim heard jeering voices as she lay on the sidewalk, pain shooting through her skinned knees and hands. Her bulky corrective shoes made it difficult to go down steps, and she had tripped and fallen. Several girls glanced back as Kim lay sprawled on the ground. Then, except for one, they all sped off to the playground.

"Are you all right?" asked the girl who stayed. Kim nodded bravely but was too winded to answer. "Let me help you up," offered the girl. "Give me your hand. By the way, my name is Michelle. What's yours?"

Kim extended her hand. "K-K-Kim," she gasped, finally able to get her breath. "Thanks for helping me, Michelle. You're a Good Samaritan."

"What's that?" asked Michelle.

Kim smiled at her new friend. "We learned about him in church," she said. "Do you go to church?"

Michelle shook her head. "Tell me about your Good Samaritan," she said.

And so Kim told her the story. (See today's Scripture reading.) "You really are like the Good Samaritan," she said as she finished. "Two girls from my church were in that group that saw me fall, but like the religious leaders in the story, they didn't stop to help. You don't even go to church, but you stopped." She paused, then added shyly, "According to Jesus, you were a 'neighbor' to me. Hey, would you like to come to church with me?"

"Sure," agreed Michelle as the girls went out to play. "Sounds like you hear some good stories there." *CEY*

HOW ABOUT YOU?

When you see someone in trouble, do you stop to help? That isn't always the easy thing to do, especially when you're the only one who helps. Yet the Bible teaches that it's an important part of a Christian's life. If you love God, show his love to all those around you by being a good "neighbor" to them.

MEMORIZE:

"The man answered, 'You must love the Lord your God with all your heart, all your soul, all your strength, and all your mind.' And, 'Love your neighbor as yourself.'" Luke 10:27

LOVE YOUR "NEIGHBOR"

THE NEW BATTERY

(Read 1 John 1:5-9)

"I can stay at your house till four o'clock," Emily told Sara as she looked at the round, gold-colored watch on her wrist. "That gives us an hour to play."

The girls first played with Sara's new dollhouse. "Do we have time to roller skate?" asked Sara after a while.

"Sure. It's only twenty after three," replied Emily after checking her watch. "We have lots of time." So they got out Sara's roller skates and took turns skating up and down the driveway until Sara's dad came home.

"Your dad's home early today," Emily said. "It's only twenty after three." She looked at her watch again. "Twenty after three! That's what it was a long time ago. My watch must be broken!" She grabbed her schoolbooks and hurried home.

Mother was hanging up the phone when Emily ran into the kitchen. The clock on the wall said 4:45. "I'm sorry I'm late," said Emily quickly. "My beautiful watch that Grandma gave me—it's broken!" She burst into tears.

Mother put her arm around Emily. "I think I know what's wrong," she said after checking the watch. "After dinner we'll go get a new battery for it." They did, and when the new battery was in place, the watch ran as well as ever.

Mom explained, "The new battery gave it new power, and that did the trick. That reminds me of God. He made us to be his friends. But sometimes sin gets in the way, and our friendship with God is hurt. But when we confess our sin, he forgives us and gives us new power to do right."

Emily admired the watch on her arm. "It's like he gets us started running right again," she said with a smile. *BK*

HOW ABOUT YOU?

When you do wrong, do you think your friendship with God will be hurt forever? That is not so. If you're sorry and confess your sins to him, he'll forgive and make you clean again. Is there something for which you need to ask forgiveness? A lie? An unkind word? A nasty thought? Will you confess it to God right now? Ask him to forgive you and to give you new power to live for him.

MEMORIZE:

"But if we confess our sins to him, he is faithful and just to forgive us and to cleanse us from every wrong."

1 John 1:9

CONFESS ALL SIN

A PRETTY PACKAGE

(Read Matthew 23:27-28)

Lindsey skipped into the kitchen with a list of the children she wanted to invite to her birthday party. Mom glanced at the names on the list. "Aren't you inviting Melanie?" she asked.

Lindsey bit her lip. "Do I have to?"

"Melanie lives next door, so I'm sure she'll be hurt if she sees that you have a party and didn't invite her," said Mom. "Why wouldn't you want to invite her anyway?"

"Nobody invites her to their parties," replied Lindsey. "She talks with a lisp."

Mom frowned. "That's not a good reason," she said.

"OK, I'll invite her, but everybody will think I'm dumb," Lindsey grumbled.

On the day of her party, Lindsey took everyone to the dining room to see her chocolate cake with pink roses. "It's beautiful!" exclaimed Melanie.

Trish added, "My mother made a three-layer cake for my birthday."

When Lindsey opened her presents, Melanie exclaimed in delight over each one. But Trish informed everyone that *she'd* had more friends and better gifts at her party. When they played games, Melanie eagerly took part while Trish acted bored. "I wish we could play the games we had at *my* party," said Trish.

After all the kids had left, Mom brought in two last gifts. One was wrapped in beautiful paper and tied with a bow. The other was wrapped in a wrinkled brown paper bag that had been cut open. "These are from me and Dad," said Mom.

Lindsey eagerly tore open the beautifully wrapped gift, but she was disappointed to find only a cheap yo-yo inside. She opened the other package and found a lovely porcelain doll. "She's beautiful! I love her!" declared Lindsey. She grinned. "She sure looks better than her wrapping paper! Did you run out?"

"No, I just wanted to show you how misleading appearances can be," explained Mom. "One of these presents was pretty, yet it contained little inside. The other was plain, but when you opened it, you found a beautiful gift." Mom paused. "People can be like that, too." she added.

Like Melanie and Trish, thought Lindsey. *KEC*

HOW ABOUT YOU?

Are you more impressed by kind hearts or by pretty faces? Remember, God judges by what's in the heart. Use the same standard to choose your friends.

MEMORIZE:

"God blesses those whose hearts are pure, for they will see God."
Matthew 5:8

LOOK FOR KIND HEARTS

WHAT'S INSIDE

(Read Romans 14:10-13)

When the phone rang, Jody was quick to answer it. But when she heard who it was, she made a face. "Ah . . . no . . . I . . . ah . . . I have plans for Saturday," she stammered. "Maybe another time." As she hung up the phone, she noticed Mother looking at her. "Erica wanted me to come over on Saturday," explained Jody.

"Well, that's a surprise," said Mother. "I thought you always spent as much time with Erica as possible. I thought you were best friends."

"We were, but . . . well . . . there's a new girl at school—her name's Nora," said Jody. "I really want to be her friend, but she doesn't like Erica much. I don't want her to see me at Erica's house."

"And why doesn't she like Erica?" asked Mother.

"Well . . . Erica's family doesn't have much money, you know. They drive an old car and she doesn't dress very well." Jody felt ashamed as she answered.

Mom frowned. "I didn't think that bothered you."

"It does now." Hoping her mother would drop the subject, Jody quickly opened her favorite book and settled on the couch to read.

Mother looked at the book Jody held. "You're still reading that old thing?" asked Mother. "It's about worn out. The cover is a mess! Why don't you find something new?"

Jody frowned. "I don't care. It's still my favorite story," she said. "What it looks like on the outside isn't important."

Mother raised her brows. "Do you suppose that's true of people, too?" she asked. Jody felt her face flush. She knew Mother was thinking of Erica. Erica was a nice person, and that's really what counted. *KEC*

HOW ABOUT YOU?

Do you judge others by their appearance? If you choose your friends because they dress well, live in a nice house, or have new cars, you may be overlooking many good friends. What a person is like on the inside is what matters to God. Let that be what matters to you, too.

DON'T JUDGE BY APPEARANCE

MARCH
12

ARE YOU AN ADDICT?

(Read 1 Corinthians 16:13-18)

Kathy was busily working on her science report—writing about the effects of becoming physically addicted to things. "What are some things that people can become addicted to, Dad?" Kathy asked. "So far, all I can come up with is alcohol and cigarettes and drugs like cocaine and marijuana."

Dad looked up from his paper. "You might want to mention that lots of addictive drugs are found in medicines," suggested Dad. "They can cause us to be addicted, too. After I was hurt in an accident years ago, I had to take a lot of morphine as a pain killer. I became addicted and had withdrawal pains when they quit giving me the drug."

"Oh, that will be good to include in my report," Kathy said. "Can you think of anything else?"

"Well, sometimes people become addicted to caffeine in soda pop or coffee," said Dad. "It's a less serious problem, but it's something we should watch out for."

"Oh, yes, I want to cover that, too." Kathy nodded.

"Are you going to say anything about the good things a person can get addicted to?" asked Dad.

Kathy was surprised. "Good things? What do you mean?" she asked.

Dad grinned and said, "First Corinthians 16:15 tells us that the people in the house of Stephanas 'addicted themselves to the ministry of the saints' (KJV). Or, as another version says, they 'devoted themselves to the service of the saints' (NIV). In other words, they served the Lord and others as if they were addicted to it."

"That would be good," agreed Kathy. "If people can addict themselves to bad things by using them over and over, I guess they can addict themselves to good things by doing them over and over, too!" *REP*

HOW ABOUT YOU?

Wouldn't it be great if Christians served Jesus and others so regularly that they could hardly stop themselves from doing it? When the Bible says the people "addicted themselves," it indicates a deliberate act. Will you addict yourself to doing good?

MEMORIZE:

"You know that Stephanas and his household were the first to become Christians in Greece, and they are spending their lives in service to other Christians." 1 Corinthians 16:15

**ADDICT YOURSELF
TO DOING GOOD**

SHE LOVES ME, SHE LOVES ME NOT

(Read John 15:11-17)

"How was Mrs. Forsyth today?" asked Mother when Alyssa returned from her weekly visit with their elderly neighbor.

"Same as always," Alyssa answered. "As usual, she wanted to read her Bible."

"I'm so glad she can still read," said Mother. "She loves her Bible."

"But she reads it all the time," observed Alyssa.

"Well, Mrs. Forsyth loves God and wants to know all he has to say," explained Mother.

"She's read the Bible so often, she ought to know it by heart," Alyssa answered as her older sister, Kara, came in. "Hi, Kara," Alyssa greeted her. "I thought you'd be at Holly's house all morning."

"Holly went to apply for a job at Mandel's." Kara headed for the closet.

Alyssa followed her. "Did Holly talk about Jordan? Did she hear from him? Did they set a date for the wedding? When's he coming home?" she asked excitedly.

"No, she didn't talk about him. Yes, she got a letter from him. No, there's no wedding date that I know of. And he should be home some time next week," said Kara with a grin.

"What did the letter say?" Alyssa asked. "Jordan's through college now and will be starting his new job. I should think they'd have a date set soon. Didn't he say anything about it in his letter?"

"I wouldn't know. Holly never read it," answered Kara. "I thought that was odd."

"Doesn't she love him?" Alyssa was shocked. "Didn't she say *anything* about him?"

"She only mentioned that the letter her mother handed her was from Jordan," replied Kara, "and then she put it on her dresser. She hardly ever mentions him."

Alyssa frowned. "I can't believe she didn't read his letter," she said. "If I were her, I'd read it over and over!"

"Now this is interesting," said Mother as she put an arm around Alyssa. "You were wondering how Mrs. Forsyth could read her Bible over and over. It's because the Bible is God's love letter to her—and to everyone—and Mrs. Forsyth loves to hear from him. We should, too." *AGL*

HOW ABOUT YOU?

Do you read God's letter to you—the Bible? It tells you how much he loves you. It tells how he can help you anytime, anywhere. It will help you know how he wants you to live, and it will help you make right and wise choices.

THE BIBLE IS GOD'S LOVE LETTER TO YOU

MEMORIZE:

"I have hidden your word in my heart, that I might not sin against you."

Psalm 119:11

MARCH
14

WHO KNOWS BEST?

(Read Jeremiah 29:11-13)

Angela dropped her books on the kitchen table with an angry thud. "What's wrong?" asked Mom, looking up from brushing Sara's silky curls. "You look angry."

Angela's eyes filled with tears. "I prayed so hard to win a place in the art show, but I didn't get in," she complained.

"I'm sorry." Mom studied Angela as she picked up little Sara. "Maybe you need to get your mind off your disappointment. Why don't you come shopping with us?"

Angela sighed. "I might as well," she agreed.

At the store, Sara saw a toy that she wanted Mother to buy for her. Angela turned over the package and read, "Not for ages three and under." She put the box back on the shelf. "Sorry, Sara," she said. "This is for older kids."

Sara's eyes filled with tears. She stomped her little foot on the floor. "I want it now!" she insisted. "I can have it, can't I, Mommy?"

Mom looked at the package, then gave Sara a hug. "Not now, honey," she said. "You'll have to trust Mommy to know what's best for you."

That evening Angela's piano teacher called to let Angela know she had been chosen to play at a special recital to be held in a few weeks.

"Oh, wow!" squealed Angela. "Good thing I didn't get to be in the art show. The music recital is the same day, and I'd rather do that."

"So you're no longer angry that God didn't answer your prayer the way you thought he should?" asked Mom.

Angela stared at Mom. "I . . . I guess I was like Sara, getting angry because I couldn't have what I wanted," she admitted. "Now I'm glad the art show didn't work out."

Mom smiled. "God always knows best. And sometimes he says no even if it upsets us at first." *KEC*

HOW ABOUT YOU?

Do you trust God when things don't work out as you wish, or do you get angry? Like a wise parent, God allows only what is best. Trust him to bless you with just the right "presents."

MEMORIZE:

"'For I know the plans I have for you,'
says the Lord. 'They are plans for
good and not for disaster, to give you
a future and a hope.' "
Jeremiah 29:11

TRUST GOD

PARTY PROBLEMS

(Read Psalm 55:16-17, 22)

Megan brushed tears from her eyes as she sat next to her mother on the couch. *I've been looking forward to my birthday party for weeks,* she thought. *It's not fair that anything should ruin it!* Megan's mother could see that something was bothering her. "Did something happen at school today that upset you?" asked Mother.

Megan nodded. "Instead of coming to my birthday party next Saturday, Shari is planning her party for the same time," she said. "She's inviting the same kids, too . . . she even invited me! Why would she do that?" Megan wiped her eyes. "Since Shari's having a skating party and I'm only having pizza and games, everyone will choose her party instead of mine."

Mother hugged Megan close. "I think we can solve this problem," said Mother after a moment. "Since Shari's party is in the afternoon, we could change your party to Saturday evening. We could help pick up the kids from the skating rink and bring them over here for pizza and games. Shari could come then, too. Do you think they'd like two parties?"

Megan smiled. "That's a great idea! Thanks, Mom!" she exclaimed.

"I'm sorry you had a problem, but I'm glad you came to me," said Mother. She looked thoughtful as she added, "Do you remember when you asked last week why God let hurtful things happen to Christians?" Megan nodded. "I can't tell you exactly *why* God lets them happen," continued Mother, "but I do know that just as you came to me with your problem, God wants us to come to him. I think it brings us close when you come to me for help, and I think we feel closer to God when we turn to him for help, too. But if we never had any problems . . ." Mother paused.

"We probably wouldn't go to God as much," Megan finished, "or learn to trust him as much."

"That's right." Mother nodded. "I believe that one reason God allows Christians to have problems is to teach them to depend on him." *KEC*

HOW ABOUT YOU?

Do you see your problems as a way to grow in trust? Problems are not easy to go through, and God understands that, too. But when you lean completely upon him, he will be faithful to meet your needs.

MEMORIZE:

"Give your burdens to the Lord, and he will take care of you. He will not permit the godly to slip and fall."
Psalm 55:22

**TAKE PROBLEMS
TO GOD**

THE WINNING TEAM

(Read 1 John 2:15-17)

"Look at the score," moaned Kristi. "They'll never win." Kristi was spending the evening with her grandfather, and Grandpa had suggested that they watch a basketball game on TV. Kristi couldn't sit still. She jumped up, then collapsed on the sofa every time her team missed a shot at the basket. "They're doing awful," she mumbled. "We should be cheering for the other team." She got up to get a drink.

"Hold on!" Grandpa called her back. "Is that how you support your team?"

"It's not like they can hear me," mumbled Kristi as she trudged back.

A little later, Grandpa stopped the game in mid-play. "Let's get a snack to munch while we watch the rest of the game," he suggested.

"Hey!" Kristi exclaimed. "Is this game on tape?" Grandpa grinned and nodded. "So that's how you stay so calm," said Kristi. "You already know how it's going to end."

"I like it that way," confessed Grandpa. "There's less pressure. I hate surprise endings." He smiled and pointed to his Bible on the table. "That's why I'm so glad to have the Bible," he added. "It tells how the biggest match of all will end."

"There's a basketball game in the Bible?" Kristi asked in surprise.

"Not basketball," Grandpa said, "but a battle for the world! Satan wants the hearts and minds of everyone, and sometimes—" Grandpa shook his head sadly— "sometimes it seems like he might be winning. Then the pressure to give up and 'desert our team' can be pretty great, especially when others seem to be having a better time than we are." Kristi thought about her schoolmates. She didn't think many of them were Christians, but they did seem to be having a good time. "But when the battle is over and the Lord comes to claim his throne, the faithful will celebrate the victory with him," continued Grandpa. "That's one victory celebration you don't want to miss." *HMT*

HOW ABOUT YOU?

Do you ever feel like it isn't worth the effort to live for Jesus? Does it seem like Christians around you have a better or easier life? If you're a Christian, be confident that you are on the winning team. Someday you'll enjoy the rewards of victory with Jesus.

MEMORIZE:

"And this world is fading away, along with everything it craves. But if you do the will of God, you will live forever." 1 John 2:17

**JESUS WILL BE
THE FINAL VICTOR**

EVERYONE'S A WINNER

(Read 2 Timothy 3:14-17)

Linda was eager to start learning verses for the Sunday school contest. Anyone who learned fifty verses would receive a new Bible, and the person who learned the most verses would win a gift certificate at the Christian bookstore. Linda loved to read, and she was determined to win the grand prize! *But Sue Ellen says she's going to try to win it, too, and Sue Ellen is smart,* thought Linda. She tossed her head. *Oh, well, I'm smart, too, and I can do it.*

One evening, Linda recited some verses for her father—the first two verses of Psalm One, ending with, ". . . but his delight is in the law of the Lord, and on his law he meditates day and night (NIV)."

"That's a good verse for you," said Dad. "You've been meditating on God's Word a lot since the contest started."

"I know," said Linda, "and I've just got to win!"

"Well, there's no way you can lose," said Dad with a smile. "Even if you don't win a prize, you'll have learned all those valuable verses. They'll help you through life."

"I guess so," said Linda. "I really do want to win the grand prize, though."

The weeks passed quickly, and Linda continued to learn lots of verses. But . . . the last day of the contest arrived, and Sue Ellen won! "Does that make you mad?" asked Linda's brother.

"Well . . . it did at first," admitted Linda, "but then I remembered some verses I learned about loving others. I'm still disappointed, but I'm not mad. Sue Ellen won fairly."

"You see?" said Dad. "Those verses have helped you already. It's like I said— you're still a winner!" *BJW*

HOW ABOUT YOU?

Do you sometimes think you must be in first place in order to be a winner? Do you feel that you might as well not bother to learn verses for your Bible club, or for a contest, because somebody else will do better anyway? Whenever you learn God's Word, you're a winner. Do it for the help it will give you, rather than just to win a prize.

LEARN GOD'S WORD

MEMORIZE:
"Work hard and cheerfully at what-ever you do, as though you were working for the Lord rather than for people." Colossians 3:23

MARCH
18

THE YOUNGEST (PART 1)

(Read Luke 6:27-31)

"May I have more mashed potatoes?" asked Mia.

"Yes, but share them with Mike," replied Mother without even noticing there were only a few spoonfuls left.

Later, Mia watched an animal program she enjoyed, but soon she heard an all-too-familiar request. "Mia," Dad said, "Mike wants to watch 'Circus Hour.'"

Leaving the TV to Mike, Mia decided to try an experiment with her new beginner's science lab set. But soon there was a knock at the door. "I thought you wanted to see 'Circus Hour,' Mike," Mia said as Mike came in.

"I did, but now I want to do science," replied Mike.

"You can't," Mia told him. Mike ran out of the room. Soon Mother brought him back. Before Mia could explain that Mike was too young to understand the science experiment, she said, "Mia, can't you be kind and share your things with your younger brother?"

Later, Mother said, "It's bedtime," and both the children were sent to get ready for bed. When Mia went to kiss her parents good night, Dad noticed tears in her eyes. He gently questioned her about it, and Mia began to talk. "Oh, Dad," she sobbed, "I love Mike, but to me it just doesn't seem fair!"

"What do you mean?" asked Dad.

"Well, Mike gets his own way just because he's the youngest! Last Christmas he wouldn't even touch his own gifts, and everyone kept telling me to share my things with him. He played with my stuff more than I did! And it says right on my new science kit that it's for children eight years and older! But I have to let him do it with me, even though he messes things up. And I . . ." Mia couldn't go on because she was crying too hard.

Dad folded her into his arms and soothed her feelings. "You've put the Golden Rule into action many times," Dad said. "I'm proud of you, and I know God has been pleased, too. Go to sleep now, and we'll talk about it again tomorrow." *REP*

HOW ABOUT YOU?

Today's verse is called the Golden Rule. Do you practice it? Do you treat others the way you would like to be treated even if it doesn't seem fair to you? Jesus gave us this rule. Honor him by obeying it.

MEMORIZE:

"Do for others as you would like them to do for you." Luke 6:31

PRACTICE THE GOLDEN RULE

THE YOUNGEST (PART 2)

(Read Ephesians 4:32)

The next morning at breakfast, Dad told the kids he wanted to talk to them. "Mia and Mike, last night Mother and I realized that we haven't been treating you fairly, and we want to apologize," he said.

"What do you mean, Daddy?" asked Mia, while Mike just glanced at her and began to eat his cereal.

"Well," Dad answered, "after you and Mike were in bed, Mother and I talked about the things you told me. We realized we were always telling you to give in to your brother, to share your things with him, and to let him do everything you do because he is younger. We were always quoting Ephesians 4:32 to you."

"I know that verse," piped up little Mike. "Be kind to one another."

"That's right, Mike," nodded Dad, "and that verse applies just as much to you as it does to your older sister. From now on we want you to be as kind to her as she has always been to you. Sometimes being kind means allowing Mia to do her nine-year-old activities with no interference from a five-year-old."

As the kids left the table, Mother gave them each a hug as she said, "Oh, yes, one more thing. From now on Mia's bedtime is nine o'clock. Mike, when you are nine years old, your bedtime will change, too. OK?"

Both kids grinned. *REP*

HOW ABOUT YOU?

Do you ever feel that you're being treated unfairly by your parents? Perhaps if you would talk over the problems with them in a calm way—not angrily—something could be worked out. Apply the Bible verse to all family situations.

**TALK WITH
YOUR PARENTS**

MEMORIZE:
"Instead, be kind to each other, tenderhearted, forgiving one another, just as God through Christ has forgiven you." Ephesians 4:32

MARCH
20

ANYONE FOR GARBAGE?

(Read Philippians 4:4-9)

When Bethany came home from school, she was very hungry. She hadn't had an after-school snack because she'd stayed for basketball practice. She peered into the pot of spaghetti sauce simmering on the stove. "Oh, good! My favorite!" She smacked her lips. "When do we eat?"

"In about ten minutes," answered Mother. "I have some chores for you to do first."

By the time Bethany finished several chores, she was ravenous. Mother had one last chore for her—taking out the garbage. Before handing it to her Mom said, "Wait a minute." Then, taking a plate off the table, she carefully scooped some of the garbage from the bag onto the plate.

Bethany stared in disbelief at the peelings, coffee grounds, and leftovers heaped together in one soggy mess. "What in the world is that for?" she asked in surprise.

"This is your dinner, Bethany," said Mother.

"My dinner!" She stared at her mom in wonder. "I can't eat smelly garbage!"

"Why not?" asked Mother. "Garbage is what you're feeding your mind, so I figured we could feed garbage to your body, too." She took some CDs from the top of the refrigerator. "I found these under your blankets when I changed the sheets today. Do you think you should be listening to these?"

Bethany knew her mother was right. Those CDs with the foul language on them were garbage, and her mind shouldn't feed on them. Ever since she'd bought them, she'd felt guilty and unhappy. "I'll throw them out right now, Mother," she said, "and I won't buy any more." *MHN*

HOW ABOUT YOU?

Do you refuse to listen to music or look at pictures in magazines or on television that make your mind and heart "dirty"? If not, ask God to forgive you for feeding your mind on the world's garbage. Ask him to help you think on pure, good things instead.

MEMORIZE:

"I will refuse to look at anything vile and vulgar. I hate all crooked dealings; I will have nothing to do with them." Psalm 101:3

THINK ABOUT GOOD THINGS

LAVA LIPS

(Read James 3:3-10)

"Hi, Mom," called Tracie as she opened the front door. "We had the best class today! We learned about volcanoes."

"That sounds interesting," replied Mother. "Volcanoes are fascinating."

Tracie nodded. "My teacher, Mr. Hoover, had a small model of a volcano. He could even make it erupt. Do you know what erupts from a real volcano?"

"Lava, hot gasses, and rock fragments," answered Tracie's brother Jason, who had also come in from school.

Tracie frowned. "I asked Mom, not you," she growled. Then she went on telling about the volcano. "Pressure builds up and the red hot ash blasts through the surface. Do you know where it erupts from?" she asked, looking at her mother.

Jason answered again. "From the mouth. It's at the top of a cone-shaped mountain," he said.

"Wrong!" declared Tracie triumphantly. "That's what it looks like, but the actual opening is lower than the top, or mouth. It's called a vent." She made a face at her brother. "Shows how much you know. Next time mind your own business and don't answer unless I ask you."

"Tracie," Mother scolded, "a volcano isn't the only thing with a mouth. We have mouths, too. Our mouths can erupt with hot, vicious, unkind words that hurt other people. I'm afraid you've been allowing that to happen. We can't control volcanic eruptions, but we can learn to control our mouths." *NEK*

HOW ABOUT YOU?

Do unkind words sometimes slip out of your mouth? That happens to everyone. But remember that God made your mouth to praise and glorify him. Ask him to help you control your tongue when you feel a hot eruption building up.

MEMORIZE:

"And so blessing and cursing come pouring out of the same mouth. Surely, my brothers and sisters, this is not right!" James 3:10

CONTROL YOUR MOUTH

MARCH
22

FROM EARTH TO HEAVEN

(Read 2 Corinthians 5:1-8)

Becky was old enough to understand the reality of death. Her grandmother had died and gone to be with Jesus. But now it was different. Becky herself had a tumor that needed to be removed, and there was a possibility that it might be cancer. Her parents were honest with her when she asked about it, explaining that she could die.

It wasn't that Becky was afraid. She was a Christian, and she knew that when Christians die, they go to be with Jesus. Of course, she was sad when she thought about leaving her mother and father, but even that wasn't the thing that bothered her right now. She was just wondering what it would be like to die—how it would feel.

She decided to mention her feelings to her mother. "Honey," her mother answered after a time, "do you remember when you were a little girl, and you would crawl into bed with Daddy and me?" Becky nodded. Sometimes when she had been afraid in the night, she had climbed into bed with her parents and had felt safe again. "And where would you find yourself in the morning?" Mother asked.

Becky thought about it. "Why, back in my own bed," she said, remembering.

"That's right," Mother smiled. "After you had gone to sleep, Daddy would pick you up in his strong arms and move you to your own bed." Becky's mother suddenly was quiet. "I think that must be what death is like," she said at last. "We go to sleep here on earth and wake up in heaven."

As Becky thought about that explanation, she smiled. It was a beautiful thought. At the right time she would be taken to heaven to be with her Lord forever. When she thought of it that way, it definitely was not something to fear. It was something to look forward to. *RIJ*

HOW ABOUT YOU?

Are you afraid of death? If you're a Christian, you don't need to be afraid, for someday you, too, will be moved from earth to God's beautiful heaven. The most important thing is to be sure that you are a child of God. Then you can know that at just the right time God will take you to your new home in heaven. Won't that be wonderful?

MEMORIZE:

"Yes, we are fully confident, and we would rather be away from these bodies, for then we will be at home with the Lord." 2 Corinthians 5:8

CHRISTIANS NEED NOT FEAR DEATH

A WILLING HEART

(Read Matthew 6:1-4)

Janice smiled as she shook the coins out of her piggy bank. "Why, there must be at least ten dollars in here," she said happily. She planned to give two dollars for the special missionary offering at church, and that would leave a little more than eight dollars to spend on herself. She had worked hard for this money and was happy to have some for the offering.

When she arrived at church the next morning, she went straight to her Sunday school room, where several kids were already waiting for the teacher. "Hi, Janice!" Linda greeted her. "Did you remember your offering?"

"Sure did," Janice replied. "Did you?"

As Linda nodded, Katie piped up. "My mom gave me five dollars to put in the offering!"

"My aunt gave me money for my birthday, and I'm going to give five, too," said Jason proudly.

"How about you, Janice?" asked Linda.

Janice blushed. The two dollars she was going to give didn't sound like much anymore. "Uh—ten dollars," she mumbled. When the offering plate was passed, she dropped the money into it reluctantly.

Later Janice sat glumly as she rode home with her parents. Her mother was surprised at her mood. "You were so eager to get to church this morning," she said. "What happened?"

Janice shrugged and told what happened in her class. "I don't understand," she said. "I gave a lot more than I had planned to give, so I should be a lot more happy, right?"

"Not necessarily," Mother replied. "The two dollars you were going to give was of your own free will—a love gift to God. The extra dollars, however, were given just to impress your friends. When it comes to money, it would be better to not even discuss with your friends the amount you plan to give. You should decide what you believe the Lord wants you to give. Then give that amount joyfully and cheerfully." *SLK*

HOW ABOUT YOU?

Do you ever put money in your church offering simply because it's expected of you? Resist that impulse, for God is not pleased with gifts that are given just to impress others. Decide what God wants you to give, and do it with a cheerful, willing heart. Your attitude means more to God than your money does!

GIVE WILLINGLY

MEMORIZE:
"God loves a cheerful giver."
2 Corinthians 9:7, NIV

MARCH
24

A COMFORTER

(Read 2 Corinthians 1:3-7)

Jenny and Jamie. Bystanders thought they were twins, but their friends knew them as best buddies. They seemed inseparable. But one day that all changed.

"Jenny, aren't you going to stay for the pep assembly?" Jamie asked.

"No, I don't feel well," Jenny said. "I called my mom to come and get me."

"See you tomorrow then," said Jamie.

But Jenny didn't come to school the next day. Jamie stopped to see her at home, but she was resting. Jenny did come back to school the next week, but she seemed very tired. And before long, she was in the hospital.

Jamie went immediately to see Jenny. She brought their favorite flower, a pink rose. Jamie could tell Jenny liked the flower by the smile in her eyes, but Jenny couldn't say much. She was hooked to several tubes, and nurses kept checking her.

The longer Jenny stayed in the hospital, the less Jamie visited her. Finally Jamie stopped visiting.

"Jamie, who's your best friend now?" asked Mother one day.

Jamie looked puzzled. "Jenny, of course!"

"I thought best friends like to be together," answered Mom. "And you haven't seen Jenny in days."

Jamie burst into tears. "Mom, I can't go there. Jenny can barely talk. And she looks so different. What can I say?"

"You don't need to say anything," answered Mom. "Just be there. Jenny really needs a friend now. She misses you so much, Jamie."

"It's so hard," said Jamie, "but I want Jenny to know I care. So I'll go to see her as much as I can. After all, isn't that what friends are for?" *JLH*

HOW ABOUT YOU?

Do you know someone who is ill? Visit if possible. Send a card, a note, flowers, or a favorite item.

MEMORIZE:

"[God] comforts us in all our troubles, so that we can comfort those in any trouble with the comfort we ourselves have received from God."
2 Corinthians 1:4, NIV

SHOW YOUR FRIENDS YOU CARE

COMPANY'S COMING

(Read 1 Peter 4:7-11)

"Oh, no," cried Tanya, "not again! All we ever do is have missionaries stay at our house. If it's not missionaries, it's visiting preachers—or complete strangers, like when people got stranded in the snowstorm last winter!"

"I thought you enjoyed having company," Mother replied.

"Well, sure, once in a while," Tanya admitted.

"That's part of our ministry," Dad chimed in.

"Ministry?" Tanya questioned.

"That's right," her father answered. "Mother and I wanted to go to the mission field, but our health didn't permit that."

"So we decided we would open our home to missionaries whenever we could," finished Mother. "And we also want to use our home for a place that others can come to and learn about Jesus."

Tanya had never thought about entertaining people as a "ministry." All she could see was that it meant doing more dishes and often giving up her bedroom. "Does the Bible say you're supposed to have company?" Tanya asked her mother later that evening.

Mother smiled. "You won't find those exact words in the Bible," she said, "but 1 Timothy 3:2 does say we should 'enjoy having guests.' It also says in Hebrews 13:1-2 . . ." Mother picked up her Bible, opened it, and began to read aloud. "'Love each other with true Christian love. Don't forget to show hospitality to strangers, for some who have done this have entertained angels without realizing it!'"

"Is that like having missionaries come and stay?" Tanya asked.

Mother nodded. "That's part of it. It's sharing your house and your love with others."

Tanya took a deep breath. "Boy, I didn't know the Bible said anything about having company." She went to her room and picked up things that were scattered around. Suddenly she smiled and called to her mother, "Mom, what time are we going to 'give some hospitality' tonight?" *RIJ*

HOW ABOUT YOU?

When you have to help prepare a meal, wash extra dishes, or give up your room because your parents are entertaining, do you grumble about it, or do you think of it as sharing what you have with others? God wants you to share. Will you do it cheerfully?

MEMORIZE:

"Cheerfully share your home with those who need a meal or a place to stay." 1 Peter 4:9

ENTERTAIN CHEERFULLY

DANGER: MOSQUITOES!

(Read Hebrews 12:1-4)

Justina Phillips wanted to be a missionary when she grew up, so she was excited when Dr. Cook, a missionary on furlough from Africa, came to visit one evening. As they sat in the living room, Justina asked, "What is it really like in the jungle, Dr. Cook? I'll bet it's exciting!"

Justina's sister, Lisa, shuddered. "I think it would be scary, with all those lions and snakes and elephants."

"I'm not chicken!" Justina boasted. "If a big lion came at me, I'd just shoot him with my high-powered rifle. Bam! Bam! Bam!"

Dr. Cook laughed. "I'm glad you're so brave, Justina," he said. "I have seen some dangerous animals in Africa, but not the kind you're thinking of. Our biggest enemies in the jungle are not lions or elephants, but mosquitoes."

"Mosquitoes?" scoffed Justina in unbelief. "How can you even compare a little, dinky mosquito with a big, ferocious lion? Lions are mean and have big teeth and claws. They can kill people."

"It's true that occasionally someone is attacked by a lion in the jungle," responded the doctor, "but it doesn't happen very often. Actually, mosquitoes and other insects kill far more people than the big animals do, for they carry malaria, yellow fever, and other diseases. Many people have had to leave the mission field because of a mosquito."

At that point, Justina's father spoke up. "We ought to remember that principle when it comes to our Christian lives," he said. "Often it's not the big things that cause us to be discouraged. It's the little things like getting bored or not getting along with people."

"Hmmm. Well, I still want to be a missionary in Africa," said Justina, "but I promise to watch out for those really dangerous animals—the mosquitoes!" *SLK*

HOW ABOUT YOU?

You may think you'd be willing to fight great battles for Jesus, but how are you handling the little problems in your life—friends who tease you, tough homework assignments, a brother or sister you can't get along with, or a parent or teacher who just doesn't seem to understand? Don't let "mosquitoes" keep you from doing God's will.

MEMORIZE:

"For I can do everything with the help of Christ who gives me the strength I need." Philippians 4:13

OVERCOME "LITTLE" FAULTS

THE HOMECOMING

(Read 2 Corinthians 5:1, 6-8)

Linda was so sad. She and her family had just returned from her grandmother's funeral. Already Linda missed Grandma, and so did her brother, Jerry. An older sister, Josie, lived far away. She had a baby only three days old, so she wasn't able to come to the funeral. "Now Grannie will never get to see Josie's baby," Linda cried.

Her parents comforted her. "Try to understand that God knows how sad you are," they told her. "But he also knew that it was the right time for Grannie to go to heaven."

One night Linda went to a slumber party. The fun was just beginning when Linda's father telephoned to say she'd have to come home—he had a surprise for her. Linda protested and begged to stay, but Dad was firm and came to pick her up. She was very disappointed. Arriving at home, she opened the door to the house and heard a familiar voice call, "Surprise!" It was Josie and her husband, Bob, with baby Jane!

"Oooohhh!" breathed Linda. "Oh, let me see the baby! She looks just like me."

Jerry laughed. "Ha! You both have red noses, if that's what you mean."

What a happy time they had—visiting, admiring the baby, and just being together! "But I still wish Grannie could have seen Jane," said Linda.

"We all do," answered Dad. "But, Linda, aren't you glad I insisted that you come home from that party?" Linda nodded, and Dad continued. "Having Josie's family come home reminds me of the homecoming that is taking place in heaven because Grandma 'came home.' You know, it's been eight years since she has been with Granddad. And then there was her baby, who died when he was six years old, and her brother, who was killed in the war, and lots of other relatives and friends who went to heaven before she did."

Linda was thoughtful. "You mean God called her home to heaven just as you called me home tonight?" she asked.

"That's right," Dad said with a smile. *BJW*

HOW ABOUT YOU?
Has someone you love gone to heaven? It's OK to hurt. God understands. But it's also important to remember that you will see your loved one again some day in heaven.

HEAVEN IS THE CHRISTIAN'S "HOME"

MEMORIZE:
"For to me, living is for Christ, and dying is even better." Philippians 1:21

BLOOD IS IMPORTANT

(Read Hebrews 9:11-14, 22)

Karen needed surgery. "We've done this operation many times, and it's rather routine," her doctor assured her. "Some more good news is that your dad has the same rare blood type that you do. We'll have some of his blood on hand in case you need it." Karen's dad nodded and gave her hand a squeeze.

Before long, Karen had the surgery, and everything went well. Doctor Winter came to see her just before she went home from the hospital, and he was very pleased. "You're going to be as good as new," he told her. "You'll have to say an extra big 'thank you' to your dad. Without his blood, you could have been in serious trouble."

Karen nodded, thinking about it. Then she looked up at her doctor. "Did you know that Jesus gave his blood for the whole world?" she asked shyly.

"You going to start preaching?" asked the doctor with a grin.

Karen nodded again. "The Bible says without Jesus' blood, nobody could go to heaven."

The doctor seemed a little embarrassed. "Well, blood is important all right," he admitted.

Before he could say more, Karen asked him a question. "If blood is important," she began, "and if Jesus shed his blood for you, shouldn't you let his blood wash away your sins?"

The doctor stood there for a long time without saying anything. "I haven't thought about that for many years," he said finally. "Thank you for reminding me. I'm going to give this some thought." *RIJ*

HOW ABOUT YOU?

Maybe you know that Jesus shed his blood for the world, but do you realize that he did it for you, personally? If you have questions about how to accept him as your Savior, talk with a trusted friend or adult.

MEMORIZE:

"The blood of Jesus, his Son, cleanses us from every sin." 1 John 1:7

JESUS GAVE HIS BLOOD

LIVING PICTURES (PART 1)

(Read 1 Corinthians 11:23-26)

"Look, Mom!" Suzanne pointed to a wall of the bookstore they were visiting. On it were a number of religious paintings, including several of Jesus. "Mom, which of these pictures really look like Jesus?" Suzanne wanted to know.

"That's a good question," Mother replied. "You have to remember, Suzanne, that these are all imaginary pictures. Not one of the artists has actually seen Jesus in person."

"But don't we have any idea how Jesus looked?" asked Suzanne. "If we had a real picture of him, it would help us to remember him and think about him."

Mother smiled. "We do get a 'picture' of Jesus through the Bible," she said, "though it isn't a painting. I also think of the 'Lord's Supper' as a picture of Jesus—a living picture."

"Oh, you're talking about the communion service in church, when they pass the little crackers and the grape juice around, aren't you?" asked Suzanne. "How is that a picture?"

"Well, it's like a picture because it makes us think of Jesus," said Mother. "The crackers, or unleavened bread, picture the body of Jesus which was crucified for us. The juice pictures his blood, which was shed for our sins. Jesus taught his followers to remember him in this way."

"You said it was a living picture—how is it alive?" asked Suzanne.

"Most pictures are just to look at," explained Mother, "but the Lord's Supper is a picture that we take part in. Also, most pictures of people just show us what the person looked like, but the Lord's Supper makes us realize what Jesus did for us. What he did is much more important than how he looked."

"I guess so," agreed Suzanne, "but I'd still like to know what he looks like."

Mother smiled. "Soon he'll come back for us, and we'll all be able to see him," she said. "You'll just have to wait till then!" *SLK*

HOW ABOUT YOU?

Do you celebrate the Lord's Supper in the church you attend? It's an important way for believers to remember Jesus and his sacrifice for their sins. Jesus has given you this "living picture" to help you remember him until you see him in person.

**COMMUNION PICTURES
JESUS' DEATH**

MEMORIZE:
"For every time you eat this bread and drink this cup, you are announcing the Lord's death until he comes again." 1 Corinthians 11:26

LIVING PICTURES (PART 2)

(Read Romans 6:1-11)

The day after Suzanne and her mother visited the bookstore, Suzanne came running into the house after school. "Mom! Mom!" she called. "Cheryl's going to be baptized next Sunday night, and she asked if I could go to her church to see her. Can I, please?"

Mother smiled. "I guess that would be all right."

"Cheryl asked Jesus to save her one day after Bible club," Suzanne told her mother. "She says she wants to obey Jesus' command to be baptized. Mom, does the Bible say we have to be baptized?"

"Well, we don't have to be baptized, or do any other good work, in order to be saved," Mother answered. "Christ saves us when we call on him in faith and repentance. But when Christ told his disciples to spread the gospel, he said they should also baptize the new believers in his name. Do you remember that yesterday we talked about communion being a 'living picture'? Well, baptism is a picture, too."

"Another picture?" Suzanne grinned. "OK—tell me how it's a picture."

"When someone accepts Jesus as Savior, God sees that person as having been crucified, buried, and risen with Jesus," said Mother. "When a Christian is put under the water in the baptismal service, it's a picture of the old sinful nature dying and being buried with Jesus. When the person is lifted out of the water, it's a picture of being raised with Jesus to a new life—one no longer ruled by sin. Baptism is one of my favorite 'living pictures'—it pictures the death, burial, and resurrection of the believer with Jesus."

Suzanne listened thoughtfully. "I'd like to be baptized, too," she decided. "I'll go Sunday night and see Cheryl be baptized, and then maybe she can come one Sunday soon to see me. But I'm glad I don't have to wait till then to be saved. I'm glad I'm saved already!" *SLK*

HOW ABOUT YOU?

Baptism is a wonderful "living picture" of what happens when a person becomes a Christian. Have you been baptized yet?

MEMORIZE:

"I myself no longer live, but Christ lives in me. So I live my life in this earthly body by trusting in the Son of God, who loved me and gave himself for me." Galatians 2:20

BE DEAD TO SIN, ALIVE TO CHRIST

THE SACRIFICE

(Read Romans 5:6-10)

"Honey, what's the matter?" Mom asked, surprised to see her youngest child in tears in front of the television.

"A bear killed the girl's dog," Lori said with a sniffle.

Mom put her arm around Lori. "Honey, it was just a TV show," she said. "It didn't really happen."

"Yes, it did," said Lori, crying. "It was a true story about a girl named Myia who went to play in the woods with Kymie, her dog. As they played, an angry bear suddenly charged out at them. Myia tried to escape, but the bear was too fast. It was about to catch her when Kymie rushed up and attacked it. Then the bear went after Kymie and killed him." Lori started crying again. "The dog sacrificed its life for Myia," she said. "It loved her that much."

Mom hugged Lori. "What a sad story with a sad ending," she said. "No wonder you're crying." After a moment, she added thoughtfully, "Honey, did you know that once, a long time ago, Someone died for us like that? Only the story I'm thinking about has a happy ending."

Lori looked at her mother. "What do you mean?" she asked.

"Jesus gave his life to save us," explained Mom. "You see, sin, like a vicious bear, tries to destroy each of us. But Jesus took all our sins on himself and died for us, throwing away our sins forever. Then he arose from the dead, and now he reigns in heaven. Kymie saved Myia's life on this earth, but Jesus saves our lives for all eternity."

Lori was thoughtful. She had heard the story of Jesus many times, but until now she had never really understood what it meant. God had used a story about a girl and her dog to help Lori understand his wonderful love! *PCS*

HOW ABOUT YOU?

Do you understand the wonderful sacrifice Jesus made for you because he loves you? Do you understand that you can have eternal life through him? Talk with a trusted friend or adult about accepting the gift of salvation that God offers you.

JESUS DIED FOR YOU

MEMORIZE:

"But God showed his great love for us by sending Christ to die for us while we were still sinners." Romans 5:8

OFF DUTY

(Read 1 Timothy 1:15-17)

Elise walked beside her dad as they entered the big circus tent. Her little sister, Cindy, clutched Dad's hand. They saw their neighbor, Mr. Roberts, and waved to him. "Dad, since Mr. Roberts is a policeman, why isn't he wearing his uniform?" asked Elise.

Dad smiled down at Elise. "He's off duty," said Dad.

The action in the rings started. Elise and Cindy watched the trapeze artists swing on the bars. They held their breath as one of them swung through space to be caught by another. Cindy clapped her hands and laughed. "That man on the trapeze wasn't off duty, was he?" she said.

Elise laughed. "No, and it's a good thing, too!" she said. "If he had been, the one he was supposed to catch would have been in trouble!" Dad nodded and laughed, too.

At intermission time, Elise and Cindy went with Dad to buy hot dogs. As Elise followed Dad to get in line, a small boy stepped in front of her. Elise pushed rudely past him, nearly knocking him over.

When they got back to their seats, Cindy took a bite of her hot dog. "A boy stepped in front of Elise, but Elise just knocked him out of the way," she reported.

"Yeah," said Elise. "Can you believe it? I bet I taught him a good lesson!"

Dad frowned. "Maybe so, but I'm afraid you missed a chance to let your actions be a light for Jesus," he said.

Elise scowled. "He should have watched where he was going," she protested. "Besides, this isn't church."

Dad looked thoughtful. "So you think that as Christians we should go off duty when we leave church?" he asked. Elise didn't know what to say. But after a few minutes she said, "I never thought of it like that. I'll try to remember—no more being an off-duty Christian for me." *KEC*

HOW ABOUT YOU?

Do you leave your Christian behavior at church? If so, you may miss a chance to be a light for Jesus. Be alert for opportunities to respond as a Christian at all times and everywhere.

**STAY ON DUTY
FOR JESUS**

MEMORIZE:
"Take control of what I say, O Lord, and keep my lips sealed."
Psalm 141:3

APRIL
2

THE KITE AND THE BREEZE

(Read 2 Corinthians 3:4-6)

Dad had taken Tara and Jimmy to the park to try out their new kites. "I bet my kite will fly higher than yours," declared Jimmy, looking proudly at his bright yellow kite with its dark blue borders and perky red bows.

"We'll see about that!" said Tara, tweaking her little brother's ear and tossing her green and orange kite into the air.

For a few minutes both kites sailed merrily across the sky, flying higher and higher, making Jimmy jump up and down and squeal with delight.

But then, suddenly, Tara's kite plunged down toward the ground. "See, Tara's kite can't fly right; my kite's the KING of kites!" yelled Jimmy in glee. But the next moment his kite joined his sister's. "What's happening? Why isn't my kite flying anymore?" cried Jimmy, flapping his string in despair.

"Some king!" Tara teased him.

"Aha!" said Dad.

"What do you mean, 'aha'?" grumbled Jimmy.

"You were so proud of your kite that you forgot what makes it fly," said Dad. "It's very still now—there's almost no breeze at all—that's why neither of your kites will fly." He grinned at Jimmy. "You forgot about the breeze, didn't you?"

"Yeah, I guess I did," admitted Jimmy. "I guess I thought a supergood kite was all I needed."

"Lots of people think that way," said Dad.

"They do?" Tara was surprised. "I thought everybody knew you needed wind to fly a kite." She looked at her brother. "Except Jimmy, of course," she teased.

Dad smiled. "Jimmy forgot that the wind was needed, but people often forget that God is needed. They think they can do things all on their own and act like they don't need God in their lives; they forget that it's God who gives them power to do just about everything." *MTF*

HOW ABOUT YOU?

Are you intelligent? Smart? Talented? Do your abilities give you the feeling that you—all on your own—can accomplish just about anything you set your mind to? Like the breeze that sends a kite sailing across the sky, it is God, through the Holy Spirit, who gives the power for even the simple things that you do each day.

MEMORIZE:

"For apart from me you can do nothing." John 15:5

THE HOLY SPIRIT GIVES POWER

PIGS WILL BE PIGS

(Read Psalm 14)

"Isn't our new pig just darling, Mom?" squealed Mary as a big crate was unloaded from the truck.

"We're going to call her Annabelle," added Dave.

"I'd have preferred a lamb for your 4-H project," Mother said, "but I guess she'll do. Go put her in the pigpen."

"The pigpen!" exclaimed Mary as Mother returned to the house. "Annabelle would hate the dirty old pigpen."

"Yeah." Dave nodded. "People always expect pigs to be dirty, so they are. But not Annabelle. Let's give her a bath and fix her a nice bed of straw."

It wasn't easy, but the children managed to get the pig reasonably clean, and Mary tied a pretty pink bow around Annabelle's neck. Then they left the pig in the rose garden while they ran to get Mother.

When the children finally persuaded their mother to leave her work and come out to see Annabelle once again, disaster met their eyes. Plants were uprooted, the yard was a mess, and the pig was gone! "Oh no! Not my rose garden!" moaned Mother. "Well, I dare say I know where Annabelle is—in the pigpen where she belongs."

"No way!" exclaimed Dave. But that's where they found Annabelle, covered with mud!

"Annabelle!" cried Mary. "Why would you leave the rose garden and come here?"

"It's her nature to like mud," said Mother. "It's natural for birds to fly. It's natural for fish to swim. And it's natural for a pig to wallow in the mud. And I'll tell you something—people are like pigs in some ways."

"Mother! How can you say that?" protested Dave.

"It's natural for people to say things they shouldn't say and do things they shouldn't do. In fact, people often choose to wallow in the mire of sin," she explained.

"But we cleaned Annabelle all up, and I even gave her a pink bow," cried Mary.

"But that didn't change her nature," replied Mother. *HCT*

HOW ABOUT YOU?

Just as it's a pig's nature to wallow in mud, it's our nature to sin. A bath and a pretty bow can't change the pig's nature, and trying to clean up our life with good deeds doesn't change our nature. Only God can do that.

MEMORIZE:

"But no, all have turned away from God; all have become corrupt. No one does good, not even one!" Psalm 14:3

YOU HAVE SINNED

APRIL
4

THE HANDWOVEN DRESS

(Read Psalm 139:11-16)

Beth was excited. She and her mother were shopping for a new dress for her. "I hope we find the most beautiful dress in the world," said Beth.

They entered a store, and Beth looked through a colorful array of dresses. Her hand rested on a pale pink dress. She slipped it off its hanger and held it up against her. "Mom! I've found it!" she cried.

"It's certainly pretty," agreed Mom, fingering the soft material. She flipped it over and glanced at the price tag. "I'm sorry, honey, but this is way too expensive." Beth's face fell. She hung back, stroking the pink dress wistfully as Mom moved on to another group of dresses. "Look, honey! Another pink dress," called Mom. Beth reluctantly left the first dress and went to see what Mom had found. "And it's half the price," went on Mom triumphantly.

"That one's pretty, too," agreed Beth, cheering up. "How come it's so much cheaper, Mom?"

"The other one was handmade," explained Mom. "That means a lot more time and effort went into making it, and it's one-of-a-kind. There isn't another one like it in all the world."

"Wow! It would be neat to have a one-of-a-kind, handmade dress!" exclaimed Beth.

"Never mind, honey," said Mom. "Even though you won't have a handmade dress, you're handmade and one-of-a-kind!"

"Me?" asked Beth. "What do you mean?"

"Well, the Bible says that God knit you and wove you together—so you're his one-of-a-kind, handmade creation," explained Mom. She gave Beth a hug as she added, "That makes you very special." *MTF*

HOW ABOUT YOU?

Do you sometimes feel there's nothing special about you? Maybe you think you don't have any special talent. But there's something that makes you very special—you were skillfully handmade by God, and there's no one like you in all the world.

MEMORIZE:

"For we are God's masterpiece. He has created us anew in Christ Jesus, so that we can do the good things he planned for us long ago."
Ephesians 2:10

GOD MADE YOU SPECIAL

A HOME IN HEAVEN

(Read John 14:1-6)

"What are you doing, Mom?" Cami asked as she walked into the laundry room. Cami's mother was standing at the open back door and looking into the garage.

"Shhhh," said Mother. Then she crooked her finger and motioned for Cami to come.

Curious, Cami quickly went to stand beside her mother. A bird was flying into the garage with a piece of straw in its mouth. Together Cami and her mother watched as two birds put together a nest on one of the rafters in the garage.

Suddenly Cami sneezed, and the birds flew away. "Oh, I'm sorry, little birds. I didn't mean to scare you away," said Cami.

Cami's mother shut the door, and they both walked back into the kitchen. "What kind of birds are those, Mom?" Cami asked.

"Those birds are barn swallows," said Mom.

"Do they think our garage is a barn?" asked Cami.

Mother laughed. "I don't know," she said, "but they're building a mud nest in an excellent place for their coming family. It's fun watching them build their home, isn't it?"

"A mud nest!" exclaimed Cami. "That doesn't sound very exciting to me!"

Mom smiled. "I guess that's because you're not a barn swallow," she said. After a moment she added, "Did you know that Someone is making a special home for you?"

Cami's eyes opened wide. "Really? Who?"

"Jesus is," replied Mom. "Jesus is preparing a very special place for you in heaven."

"Just for me?" Cami asked with a grin.

"Jesus is preparing a special home for everyone who has trusted him as Savior. Isn't that a wonderful promise?" Mother asked. Cami nodded. *SKR*

HOW ABOUT YOU?

Is Jesus preparing a special place for you? He is if you've trusted him as your Savior. Have you done that? If not, won't you talk to a friend or trusted adult to find out more?

**JESUS IS PREPARING
A SPECIAL HOME**

MEMORIZE:
"There are many rooms in my Father's home, and I am going to prepare a place for you." John 14:2

APRIL
6

THE NURSERY

(Read Mark 1:40-45)

"Hey, Laura, wait up!" Laura turned at the door of her junior high Sunday school classroom to see Christy hurrying down the hall toward her. "You have nursery duty with me today, don't you?" asked Christy. "Let's go."

Laura dropped her gaze. "Well . . . ah . . . Jessie is going to take my place," she said.

Christy's forehead creased in a frown. "Why?" she demanded. "You and I always work in the nursery together. Why aren't you helping today?"

Laura squirmed uncomfortably. "I just don't feel like helping in the nursery anymore."

Christy eyed her suspiciously. "Laura McIntyre," she said firmly, "there is something funny about all this. I've never met anyone in my whole life who likes babies more than you do. What's up?"

Laura sighed. She knew it was no use trying to hide anything from her friend. Christy wouldn't be satisfied until she had found out the real reason she had decided to quit working in the nursery. "Well . . . kids have so many contagious diseases," she said, "and I just don't want to come down with them myself. There's always somebody with a cold or something. And . . . well, there's the Johnson's adopted baby who has AIDS."

"So that's it!" exclaimed Christy. She was silent for a moment before she spoke again. "Laura, the nursery staff uses special safety precautions with little Peter," she said. "And he needs our love and care just as much as any of the other babies. Maybe more." She paused, and added gently, "Remember the lesson we had in Sunday school last week? Whatever would have happened to the leper if Jesus hadn't been willing to help him?"

Laura stood silently, deep in thought. In her mind's eye, she could see that desperate man. Kneeling before Jesus. Pleading for his help. And then she saw the Savior with his outstretched hand. There was love in his face and in his touch. Thinking about it, Laura made a decision. She looked up and met Christy's gaze with a confident smile. "I'll tell Jessie she can go on into the worship service, after all," she said. "Meet you in the nursery in a few minutes!" *CAP*

HOW ABOUT YOU?

Is there someone God wants you to help, or something he wants you to do that you've been avoiding? Maybe you've been too busy to get involved. Maybe you've been too proud. Or perhaps, like Laura, you're just plain scared. Let God's love flow through you into the lives of others who need his touch today.

MEMORIZE:

"Such love has no fear because perfect love expels all fear."
1 John 4:18

BE A CHANNEL FOR GOD'S LOVE

AN UMBRELLA OF ANSWERS

(Read 2 Timothy 4:1-5)

Hannah excitedly told her Sunday school class about her trip to England. "The funniest thing," she said, "was that people carried umbrellas even on sunny days."

Mr. Hunt smiled, remembering his own visit to England. It had rained often. "And did you take your umbrella, too?" he asked. Hannah blushed and shook her head. "And?" prompted Mr. Hunt with a suspicious smile.

Hannah giggled. "One day I got really wet," she said. "It rains a lot in the area where we were—even when it looks like it won't."

"It pays to be prepared," Mr. Hunt said. He flipped open his Bible. "How many of you are prepared to go out into the streets today?" he asked.

"Prepared for rain?" asked Jose. "The weather report is for sunshine today, and it's not like it rains here all that often."

"I wasn't thinking of rain," replied Mr. Hunt. "I'm wondering how many of us are prepared for meeting people."

"What do you mean?" asked Hannah. "We meet people every day. How are we supposed to prepare for them?"

Mr. Hunt smiled. "You never know when one of them is going to 'shower' you with questions," he said. "Are you going to have an 'umbrella' of answers to give them?"

The class was quiet for a moment. Finally Hannah spoke. "How can we prepare an answer when we don't know what the questions will be?"

Mr. Hunt picked up his Bible. "The questions will be a surprise," he agreed, "but the answers are all right here. The trick is to keep them handy."

"You mean we have to carry our Bibles everywhere?" someone asked in disbelief.

"Well, that's not a bad idea," Mr. Hunt replied, "but it might be easier to just carry the words and meanings in your mind and heart."

"You mean memorize," Hannah said.

Mr. Hunt nodded. "Memorize and apply God's Word to your life," he said, "because you really can't tell when it's going to 'rain.'" *HMT*

HOW ABOUT YOU?

If a friend at school asks you about God, will you know what to say? If someone asks about right or wrong ways to live, will you have an answer? The Bible gives us answers, and it also gives us principles to live by.

BE PREPARED TO WITNESS

MEMORIZE:

"If you are asked about your Christian hope, always be ready to explain it."
1 Peter 3:15

THE BROKEN NEST

(Read Acts 2:22-24)

"It's not fair," grumbled Angie, pacing up and down the lawn. "Nothing good ever happens. First we leave our home and move to a new town, then I get sick and miss school and fail that stupid math test. . . ."

"Look, Angie! A bird's making a nest in our garden," interrupted Mom.

Angie stopped complaining and watched. "Little bird!" she cried suddenly. "That tree's no good; its leaves have all fallen off and it hasn't any fruit. Make your nest in the apple tree!" But, of course, the bird ignored her. Angie stood on tiptoe, picked up a few twigs from the nest the bird was making, and carried them over to the apple tree. "Here, bird, build your nest here," she said. The bird twittered angrily and carried the twigs back.

Mom laughed. "It's no use . . . it's made up its mind to nest there," she said. Angie got so interested in watching the bird finish its nest that she forgot to grumble anymore.

That night, there was a storm. The wind howled outside Angie's window and the rain fell down in great torrents. When Angie gazed out the window the next morning, she saw that the tree with the bird's nest lay flat on the ground and bits of straw and twigs were scattered nearby. "Mom, the bird's nest is broken," cried Angie. "Whatever will it do?"

"I suppose it will build another," replied Mom.

Angie watched the bird fly round and round the fallen tree, twittering and chirping. Then it began to collect the twigs and straw and, to Angie's surprise, flew across to the apple tree. "Well!" exclaimed Angie, "I guess it's a good thing that old tree fell down and the bird's nest got broken—now it will have a home with lots of leafy branches for protection and plenty of fruit, too."

Mom smiled. "God gave the bird wisdom and ability to make something good out of apparent disaster," she observed. "And he'll give us the ability to do that, too." She gave Angie a hug as she added, "Even disasters like moving into a strange place and falling sick and failing tests." *MTF*

HOW ABOUT YOU?

When bad things happen in your life—you lose a friend, you have to move to a strange place, you fail a test or you get sick—do you think things are hopeless? Or do you remember that God can work something good even out of what seems like disaster to you? You may not always see the good, but God will bring it.

MEMORIZE:

"And we know that God causes everything to work together for the good of those who love God." Romans 8:28

GOD CAN MAKE GOOD OUT OF BAD

STORMS AND SUNSHINE

(Read James 1:2-7)

Lightning pierced the darkness, and thunder boomed. Howling winds drove sheets of rain against the windows. Audra began to cry and, hearing the sobbing, Mother hurried into the room. "Don't be scared," said Mother. "It's a bad storm, but God will take care of us."

Audra wiped her eyes. "It's not just the storm," she said. "My whole life is falling to pieces. When I was sick, I missed so much school that I have to go to summer school now. Dad ran off and left us, and now Karen, my very best friend, is moving away."

"Things do look bad," agreed Mother, "and this miserable weather we've had all week is certainly depressing. But just as surely as the sun will shine again, our circumstances will get better, too. God promises that our trials will not be more than we can bear."

"But why doesn't God let only good things happen to us?" wailed Audra. "He can do anything he wants to."

"God doesn't keep us from hard times, honey, but he does promise to walk with us through them," answered Mom. "You know, the parts of the earth that get almost all sunshine are deserts. Just like the earth needs sunshine and rain so the plants will grow, we need good times and hard times to help us grow. Hard times draw us closer to the Lord, so we'll depend on him for help." Mother squeezed Audra's hand.

When the storm had passed, Audra finally went back to sleep. The next morning, bright sunshine streamed through her window. She jumped out of bed and looked outside. Seeing the oak tree standing tall and stout, she remembered what Mother had told her. "Thank you, Lord," she murmured. "I know the sun will shine again in my life, too. With your help, I want to become a stronger Christian with each of the storms I face." *MRP*

HOW ABOUT YOU?

Are you becoming stronger because of the troubles in your life? When someone you love is sick or moves away, when you have difficulties with school work, or when friends are unkind, ask God to use these things to help you grow. And remember, God understands that these hard times sometimes make us feel angry, hurt, and sad. Be sure to talk to him about your feelings, too.

MEMORIZE:

"For our present troubles are quite small and won't last very long. Yet they produce for us an immeasurably great glory that will last forever!"

2 Corinthians 4:17

GROW STRONG THROUGH TRIALS

APRIL
10

DOWN FROM THE MOUNTAIN

(Read Matthew 17:1-2, 5, 14-18)

Mandy sat slumped in Dad's armchair. A book lay open in her lap, but she just stared out the window. "What's wrong, Mandy?" asked Mom.

Mandy shrugged. "Oh . . . nothing, really."

Mom pulled up a chair beside her. "Then why are you looking so glum?"

"Well . . . last week after I sang my solo at church lots of people said I did so well and what a good voice I had and stuff like that," replied Mandy. "I know that's not so important, but some of them talked about how God was glorified through my singing, and I felt really good about all that. But since then, well . . . I feel kind of . . . of . . ."

"Let down?" suggested Mom. Mandy nodded. Mom thought a moment. "Mandy," she began slowly. "Remember the Bible story of the Transfiguration? Jesus was glorified up on that high mountain. His Father thundered forth from the heavens in praise of his Son. Don't you think that must have been a wonderful experience?"

"Sure," agreed Mandy.

"But what if Jesus had wanted to stay there, up on the mountain?" continued Mom. "Then he wouldn't have been able to get on with his next task—to heal a sick boy." Mandy looked thoughtful. "Mandy," said Mom gently, "you're trying to stay up on the mountain now—the mountain of success and praise. By doing that, you're missing opportunities to serve down below in the valley."

"But what can I do?" asked Mandy. "There are no more solos lined up."

"How about visiting Anita in the hospital?" suggested Mom. Mandy wrinkled her nose. "Yes, I know that doesn't sound very exciting," said Mom, "but that's coming down from the mountain and serving God the way he wants—and not just where people are going to praise you." *MTF*

HOW ABOUT YOU?

When you do something for Jesus—lead a Bible study, sing a solo, visit a sick person—you'll feel good inside, and that's fine. It's also nice if your pastor or parents or friends appreciate what you've done. But don't expect to go on feeling good or go on being praised for past achievements. That would be like Jesus wanting to stay on the mountaintop forever! Come down from the mountain and find out what God wants you to do next.

MEMORIZE:

"When you give a gift to someone in need, don't shout about it as the hypocrites do—blowing trumpets in the synagogues and streets to call attention to their acts of charity!" Matthew 6:2

**GLORIFY GOD,
NOT YOURSELF**

TOO YOUNG

(Read 1 Corinthians 6:18-20)

Note to parents: The following story may not be appropriate for very young children.

"Karen," said Mother, "I drove past school this afternoon and saw you holding hands with a boy."

Karen blushed. "Oh, that was just Kevin."

"Well," said Mother, "you're too young to center your attention on one boy. You're not allowed to date, and holding hands with Kevin is out, too. You need to wait until you're older."

"We weren't doing anything wrong," Karen argued. "Lots of kids in sixth grade hold hands."

"It doesn't matter what others are doing. Hand-holding usually leads to other kinds of physical contact. You are too young," Mother repeated.

"That's right," agreed Dad. "Far too many boys and girls your age are getting involved in sexual things too soon."

"Oh, Dad," said Karen, "hand-holding isn't sex. We just like each other."

"But often boys or girls soon want to go beyond hand-holding," added Dad.

Several days passed before the subject came up again. "Do you remember when we talked about holding hands?" Karen asked her mother one day when she came home from school. "Well, what you and Dad said is true. It can lead to other things. Kevin doesn't want to just hold hands now. He wants to do kissing and stuff. I said, 'No, I don't want to.' He just laughed and said he'd find someone who would."

Karen started to cry, and Mother put her arms around her. "You did the right thing, Karen," said Mother. "God commands us to keep ourselves pure. Our bodies belong to him. When a very young person shows affection in ways God has reserved for grown-ups, he or she often feels guilty and unhappy. Your body is very privately yours and God's." *DK*

HOW ABOUT YOU?

Do some of your young friends hold hands, put their arms around each other, or kiss? The Bible tells you to glorify God in your body. When this way of showing affection is permitted at a young age, it often leads to more and more physical contact. You need to learn to say no now. Touching privately is never a way for boys and girls to show they like each other. Say NO!

**YOUR BODY
BELONGS TO GOD**

MEMORIZE:
"God bought you with a high price. So you must honor God with your body." 1 Corinthians 6:20

STAY OUT OF THE MUD

(Read Joel 2:11-13)

Mary winced as the small child in her arms beat little fists against her shoulders. "Let me go!" Tabitha whined. She wanted to go for a walk even though it had just rained. Mary had picked her up, intending to carry her to the sidewalk so her feet wouldn't get muddy. Now Tabitha gave Mary one last punch and squirmed down. Mud oozed around her shoes as she sloshed stubbornly along. Her legs and clothes were soon splattered with mud. Mary sighed. She usually liked to baby-sit, but this child was so stubborn!

The next day, Mary was at her friend Kristin's home. "Wait till you see this movie," said Kristin, picking up a video tape.

Mary looked at the title and recognized it as one her parents had refused to let her see. "I'm not allowed to watch that," she said. "But," she added as she saw Kristin frown, "my parents are too strict anyway. Besides, who's going to know?" So she stayed and watched the movie. She winced when she heard God's name taken in vain in the movie.

"Did you have a good time?" asked Mother when Mary arrived home. How guilty Mary felt as she nodded and hurried to her room!

As Mary sat down on her bed, she noticed her Bible. Again she felt a stab of guilt. She had skipped Bible reading and prayer for several weeks. Now she had disobeyed her parents and dishonored God. Trying to forget all that, Mary began to leaf through her picture album. Turning a page, she saw a picture of Tabitha, the little girl she often cared for. In her mind, she saw Tabitha beating her fists and insisting on walking in the mud. *I guess what I've been doing is kinda like that,* she admitted to herself, *only I've been beating my stubborn fists against God, refusing to listen to him, and insisting on getting myself dirty with worldly things.*

Mary bowed her head, telling God she was sorry. *Maybe I should tell Mom what I did, too,* she decided. *Maybe she'll punish me, but I don't care. It will be worth it to know things are right again! CEY*

HOW ABOUT YOU?

Have you ignored and neglected God? Do you find yourself doing things you know are wrong? God wants you to come back to him and feel close again. He's waiting for you to return. If your friendship with him has been broken, ask him to forgive you now.

MEMORIZE:

"Yes, turn to our God, for he will abundantly pardon." Isaiah 55:7

RETURN TO GOD

MAKING RAINBOWS

(Read Philippians 1:21-26)

"Dad, isn't that just beautiful!" exclaimed Tiffany, gazing out the window.

Dad came and stood behind her. "Oh, a rainbow," he said. "Yes, that is beautiful."

"I wish I could see a rainbow every day," said Tiffany dreamily.

Dad smiled. "Would you like to make a rainbow to keep in your room?" he asked.

Tiffany's eyes grew big and round. "Really?"

Dad nodded. "Come on, I'll show you how."

Tiffany hopped along beside Dad and watched as he rummaged in his "odds-and-ends" cupboard. He picked up a ball of heavy string, a pair of scissors, and a small, triangular-shaped glass with a small hook on one end.

"What's that?" asked Tiffany.

"This is called a prism," said Dad as he tied one end of the string to the hook on the glass. He held it out toward Tiffany. "Cut here," he said. Tiffany took the scissors and cut the string. "OK," said Dad, "let's take this to your room."

"What are you going to do with it?" asked Tiffany.

He took the glass triangle and tied the string to the curtain rod. "Look!"

Dancing lightly on her desk and even spilling over onto the floor, Tiffany saw . . . a rainbow! "Cool!" exclaimed Tiffany. "Now I have my very own baby rainbow."

"You'll have it only when the sun is shining," Dad warned her. "The prism can't make a rainbow unless the sun shines through it." He smiled at Tiffany. "How would you like to make something beautiful like a prism does?" he asked.

"Sorry, Dad, but I'm afraid the sun won't shine through me," she replied.

Dad smiled. "I'm not thinking about the sun in the sky," he said. "I'm thinking about God's Son—and about God's love. If you let his love shine through you, you can make something even more beautiful than that rainbow. You can bring God's joy and peace and love to other people." *MTF*

HOW ABOUT YOU?

What can you do to make "rainbows"—to make something beautiful—in your world today? How about a word of encouragement to someone who is discouraged? A helping hand to someone who needs help? A listening ear to someone in trouble? If you are willing to give of your time and talents and possessions, God can use you to make a "rainbow of happiness" in someone else's life.

MEMORIZE:

"Then when I return to you, you will have even more reason to boast about what Christ Jesus has done for me."

Philippians 1:26

BE A PRISM FOR GOD

AFTER THE BATH

(Read Colossians 3:1-11)

"Mom! Where are you?" called Linda.

"Helping Dana with her bath," answered Mom. Linda ran upstairs. "Actually, we're finished. Dana just needs to get dried off and dressed."

Four-year-old Dana peeped out from behind the shower curtain. "Mommy, I want my red pants and flowered shirt," she said.

"But honey, you were wearing that before your bath and it's dirty," said Mom. "You can wear this nice clean yellow outfit."

"But the red one's my favorite!" protested Dana, pouting.

"Yeah, but you're clean now," Linda told her little sister, "so you have to wear clean clothes."

"Exactly!" said Mom.

"Hey, that's kinda like what Mrs. Richards was talking about in Bible Club today," said Linda. "She talked about accepting Jesus and putting off our old self and putting on a new one. Like Dana needs to change her dirty old clothes for clean ones."

Mom nodded. "Before we received Christ into our heart, we were like Dana before her bath—and you know what that's like!" she said.

Linda giggled as she pictured her chubby sister, clothes spattered with mud, face sticky and sweaty, arms and legs covered with dust and dirt. "I sure do," she said. "And when we ask Jesus to come into our life, it's like taking a bath, right?"

Mom nodded. "Yes, and after that, we must put aside our 'dirty clothes'—our sinful practices like lying and gossiping and disobedience. Sometimes we don't want to. We cling to them, like Dana clings to her favorite red outfit. But our old clothes—our old selves—are no longer fit to be worn." She helped Dana slip into the yellow outfit. "We need to put on fresh, new 'clothes'—kindness, humility, patience, love—that are appropriate for our new life in Christ." *MTF*

HOW ABOUT YOU?

Have you asked Jesus to forgive your sins and make you clean? Then you must put aside your sinful ways. Put aside the lying, the deceit, the selfishness, the greed that was part of your old way of life. Put on a "new self" by developing and showing such qualities as kindness, humility, gentleness, patience, and love.

MEMORIZE:

"What this means is that those who become Christians become new persons. They are not the same anymore, for the old life is gone. A new life has begun!"
2 Corinthians 5:17

LIVE A NEW LIFE

THE ESCAPE PLAN

(Read 1 Corinthians 10:12-14)

Mara sat on her bed. Her face was red and splotchy from crying. She had been caught cheating at school, and her teacher had called and talked to her mother about it. Mara knew she'd be punished.

There was a quiet knock on her door. Mother entered with a very serious look on her face. "We need to talk about this problem," she said softly. "Mrs. Davis says she's seen you looking at other students' papers before."

Mara burst into tears once more. "I can't help it, Mother," she whined. "Our tests are always so hard! I try to stop cheating, but I just can't!"

Mara's mother was silent a moment, then she asked, "Mara, what would you do if we had a fire in our house?"

Mara looked at her mother, puzzled by the question. She answered slowly. "Well, I'd follow our fire escape plan. I'd crawl on my hands and knees down the hallway to the front door, and then I'd open it and go outside—unless the fire was in that area. Then I'd use the back door."

"That's right! We've told you over and over again how to escape in case of a fire, and you've remembered it." Mother nodded. "God also has an escape plan for us to follow. He tells us in the Bible that he has made a way to escape temptation."

Mara sniffled. "He does? But how?"

"By obeying his Word," replied Mother. "In Corinthians it says that we don't have to let temptation overtake us; we can escape. And when the apostle Paul wrote to Timothy, a young man, he told him to 'flee youthful lusts' and follow righteousness. We need to do that, too, and with God's help, we can." *LSR*

HOW ABOUT YOU?

Are you tempted to tell a lie instead of the truth? To disobey when you think you can get away with it? To help yourself to something you really want? Do you feel that you can't resist temptation? You can. God will show you the way to escape the temptation. Ask him to help you find it.

MEMORIZE:

"But remember that the temptations that come into your life are no different from what others experience. And God is faithful. He will keep the temptation from becoming so strong that you can't stand up against it. When you are tempted, he will show you a way out so that you will not give in to it." 1 Corinthians 10:13

YOU CAN ESCAPE TEMPTATION

THE BEST KIND OF GIFT

(Read Romans 12:1-3)

Rachel was worried. It was her mother's birthday, and she was sure everybody else's gift for Mom was nicer than hers. Dad had bought her a new dress; Doug had gotten a CD; Mandy had bought Mom a bottle of her favorite perfume. *But I haven't got anything . . . well, not much of anything,* thought Rachel. *Just the recipe book I made in my class at school and the flowers I picked by the side of the road.*

Mom "ohhhed" and "ahhhed" over each gift, including Rachel's. But Doug looked at the flowers and snorted. "Those are weeds," he said.

Mandy looked at the recipe book and pointed out that the front cover looked pretty messy. "Can't you color any better than that?" she asked.

Ignoring her mother's protests, Rachel ran from the room, crying.

Soon Mom came to Rachel's room, looking pretty in her new dress and smelling like her new perfume. Rachel cried harder as her mother gathered her into her lap. "My gift for you wasn't nearly as nice as the others," sobbed Rachel.

Mom kissed Rachel's forehead. "I love your gift," she said. "I can see that you spent a lot of time coloring the recipe book, and picking flowers for me was a sweet idea."

Rachel sniffed. "I know how much you like flowers," she said, "but I didn't have any money, so I rode my bike to the edge of town. I found the flowers beside the road. I thought they were pretty."

"They are pretty," Mom answered, "and it was thoughtful of you to find them for me. Your gift came from your heart, and a gift from the heart is the nicest kind of all."

"Really?" asked Rachel.

"Really," said Mom. She hugged Rachel close. "Your gift is a wonderful example of the kind of gift we can give to God," she added. "He gave the greatest gift of all when he gave Jesus to die on the cross for our sins. In return, we should give him ourselves in both love and service. That's the best gift we can give." *JW*

HOW ABOUT YOU?

Have you accepted the gift God offers you? Have you given him yourself in return? If not, talk to a friend or trusted adult about how you can ask Jesus to be in your life, too.

MEMORIZE:

"Their first action was to dedicate themselves to the Lord and to us for whatever directions God might give them." 2 Corinthians 8:5

GIVE YOURSELF TO GOD

CALLUSES

(Read Ephesians 5:1-2, 6-11)

Katie crossed her arms defiantly and scowled angrily at her mother. "How could you?" she demanded. "I have never been more humiliated in my life! Do you know how embarrassing it is to have your mother come and drag you home?"

"Katie, that's enough!" said Mother quietly, but firmly. "What has come over you? You've deliberately broken guidelines we have set for you—not just one of them, but two! You not only were out past your curfew, but you did not have permission to be at the mall!" Mom sighed deeply and sat on the edge of Katie's bed. "What has been going on the last couple of months? I don't think you just suddenly decided to rebel."

Katie began to cry. "I . . . I don't know. A lot of the girls don't have such strict rules as I do, and they always want me to join them. After a while, the things that seemed so wrong before didn't seem so bad anymore," she admitted. "I don't know how it happened."

"Katie," said Mom, "do you remember when you first started playing the cello?" Katie nodded. "Do you remember how, if you played very long, it hurt your fingers terribly?" asked Mom. "Why was that?"

Katie looked at her hand. "My fingers hurt because they weren't used to it," she said. "But now I have calluses, so they don't hurt anymore."

"Did your calluses just appear magically one day, or did they build up over a period of time?" asked Mom.

"They built up gradually," said Katie. "Why?"

"Your fingers gradually got used to the pressure of the strings, and the pain grew less and less until it disappeared completely," said Mom. "That's a picture of what happens when you practice doing something wrong. At first, doing things that are wrong pricks your conscience and you feel guilty, but after a while, you get used to it and your conscience doesn't bother you anymore. That's not a good situation to be in!" *BRE*

HOW ABOUT YOU?

Are you getting "callused" toward sin? Are wrong things starting to seem not so wrong anymore? Ask the Lord to help you recognize when that is happening. When the Holy Spirit gives you an uncomfortable feeling about some activity, don't take part in it.

MEMORIZE:

"And do not bring sorrow to God's Holy Spirit by the way you live. Remember, he is the one who has identified you as his own, guaranteeing that you will be saved on the day of redemption."

Ephesians 4:30

DON'T GET "CALLUSED" TOWARD SIN

ME WORK?

(Read 2 Thessalonians 3:7-13)

Saturdays were boring for Marjorie. "Oh, Mother," she complained as she returned from making a tour of the neighborhood, "there's no one to play with. Mary has to clean her room, Jeff has to rake the yard, and Karen has to take care of her little brother."

"Well, why don't you go help your friends with their chores?" suggested her mother. "That is, if you've finished cleaning your own room."

"Yuk! Who wants to just work all day!" complained Marjorie. "That's no fun."

"You can find pleasure even in work, when you do it as unto the Lord," encouraged Mother. "With a little imagination, you can make it fun, too. When I was a little girl and had to clean my own room, I used to pretend I was a princess and that everything in my room was made of shiny gold."

Marjorie made a face. "My room's done. I'll just go over and keep Mary company while she cleans her room," she decided.

It was late Saturday afternoon before Marjorie returned home. She came bursting into the house, just popping with stories about her day! "Mom, I had a ball!" she said. "You should see how great Mary's room looks. We pretended we were getting ready to open a toy shop and everything had to look just right for our customers. Later we went over to Jeff's. We all got a rake and pretended we were the gardeners at the White House. Jeff's yard looks terrific now! Then we went to Karen's. We got so silly over there! We were turning somersaults and imitating Karen's baby brother—'Goo-goo. Ga-ga!' What a cute baby! We kept him laughing all afternoon." She grinned at her mother. "Next time I think I'll play princess while I clean my room." *PR*

HOW ABOUT YOU?

Do you tackle work and make the best of it? Or do you hate it and try to avoid it? The Bible teaches us to do everything—including work—as unto God. When you do, it's a good testimony for him, and you'll probably be surprised at how much you enjoy yourself, too.

MEMORIZE:

"Work brings profit, but mere talk leads to poverty!" Proverbs 14:23

WORK JOYFULLY

A LESSON IN MUD

(Read 2 Corinthians 6:14-18)

"You just don't understand," whined Julie when her parents wouldn't allow her to join her friends in an activity she really knew was wrong. "Everybody's doing it! Besides, I'm just trying to be a witness to my friends. If you never let me do anything with them, how can I ever tell them about Jesus?"

"I'm glad you want to win them," replied Dad, "but believe me, honey, that's not the way to do it."

As they were talking, there was a knock on the door. A friend of Julie's dad had gotten his car stuck in the muddy, country road in front of their house.

Julie and Dad jumped in the truck and were "off to the rescue." Then, to Julie's astonishment, her dad did a very foolish thing. He backed the truck right down into the mud hole where the car was stuck. "Dad!" exclaimed Julie. "We'll get stuck, too!"

"This truck has a lot of power," Dad replied. "I think we'll be all right." But just as Julie had predicted, they got stuck. As Julie sputtered about it, Dad turned to her. "You were right," he admitted quietly. "This mud is deeper than I thought." Dad paused, then added, "You know, Julie, this reminds me of what we were discussing earlier. Being like your non-Christian friends won't help them any more than my getting stuck in the mud with my friend helps him. You can't help others who have fallen into sin by going down with them and joining in."

Julie knew it was true. "I never thought of it that way," she admitted slowly. "I guess the way to really help my friends is to be the kind of Christian I should be." *SLK*

HOW ABOUT YOU?

Do you want to win your friends to Christ? Be sure you do it in the right way, and not by going along with the wrong things they do. Instead of you helping them, they will probably draw you away from Jesus. Live the way you know God wants you to live, and you can be a real testimony and help to your friends.

**DON'T GO ALONG
WITH THE CROWD**

APRIL
20

THE DONOR
(Read Romans 5:6-11)

Sam was nervous as she sat in the hospital waiting room. Her baby brother, Mark, had been in an accident and needed a blood transfusion. But he had a very rare blood type, and Sam was the only one they knew of with the same type of blood as Mark. When Dr. Griffin explained to her that Mark needed some of her blood in order that he might live, Sam hesitated a few moments. Then she said in a shaky voice, "O-OK. I love Mark lots, so if my blood will make him live, I . . . I want to give it to him."

Soon everything was ready, and the doctor prepared to take some of Sam's blood. She was very tense and held tightly to her mother's hand. After a few minutes, she asked, "How soon will I die?"

"Die?" asked Dr. Griffin in surprise. "Did you think giving blood would make you die, Sam?" Fearfully, Sam nodded. "Oh, honey," said Dr. Griffin, "you're not going to die. You'll be giving only a little of your blood—it might make you feel a little weak, but you'll be up and running around again in no time."

Her mother hugged her tightly. "I'm so sorry you thought that, honey," she said. "We should have explained more carefully what would happen."

The transfusion helped Mark, and he recovered rapidly. On the day he was ready to come home from the hospital, everyone was excited. Dad gave Sam an extra big hug. "This whole experience reminds me of what the Lord Jesus did," he said. "You were willing to give your blood for Mark. Because of that, he can live longer here on earth. Jesus, God's Son, gave his blood—he gave his life—for every man, woman, boy, and girl. Because of what he did, we can have our sins forgiven and live forever with God." He patted Sam's curls. "I am very proud of you," he said. "You did a brave thing." *HCT*

HOW ABOUT YOU?
Have you asked Jesus to be your Savior? If not, talk to a friend or trusted adult to find out more.

MEMORIZE:
"But God showed his great love for us by sending Christ to die for us while we were still sinners." Romans 5:8

JESUS DIED SO
YOU CAN LIVE

I DO . . . LOVE YOU

(Read John 14:21-23)

Josie was so excited! She had been invited to her cousin Nancy's wedding. "Oh, Mother, I just can't wait," she said. "It seems like Nancy's wedding will never come."

"Oh, it will come fast enough," Mother assured her. "Since we're having special services at church all next week, we'll be busy, and time will go fast." Josie moaned and asked if they would have to go to every meeting. "No, we don't have to," answered Mother, "but we want to try to go to all of them—at least Dad and I do."

Josie did go to the services with her parents, but she didn't listen much. She spent the time daydreaming about her own wedding.

The day of Nancy's wedding came, and after the reception she was off on her honeymoon with her new husband. "Nancy's little sister didn't want Nancy to go with Jerry," said Josie with a smile. "She cried when they left."

"She didn't understand that Nancy's place is with Jerry now," said Mother.

Dad nodded. "Weddings always remind me of Christ and the church—the people who are Christians," he said. "In the Bible, Christ's love for the church is compared to a husband's love for his wife."

"Right," said Mother. "And it would have been very hard for Nancy to convince Jerry that she loved him if she hadn't wanted to go with him today, wouldn't it? When you love a person, you like to be with him, and talk to him and about him."

"You know," said Dad, "I wonder if Jesus believes us when we say we love him, but we don't want to go to church or talk about him or to him."

"You mean . . . like if we say we love Jesus but don't like to go to church, or pray, or witness, then we must not really love him very much?" asked Josie.

Dad nodded. "It seems that way to me," he said. "After all, real love is more than words." *BJW*

HOW ABOUT YOU?

Do you really love Jesus, or do you just say you do? Do your actions show that you love him? Do you love his people and his Word? Do you like to talk to Jesus? If you love him, show it!

SHOW LOVE FOR JESUS

MEMORIZE:
"If you love me, obey my
commandments." John 14:15

STRONG FENCES

(Read 1 Corinthians 1:4-9)

Courtney hurried to tie her sneakers. It was a Saturday morning, and she was going to go with Mom on her morning walk.

Mom smiled as Courtney skipped along beside her. "I enjoy having you along when I go for a walk," said Mom. "Why don't you come with me more often?"

"I think I will," agreed Courtney. "Maybe not every Saturday." She grinned. "I have to sleep in once in a while, you know. But I do like to come with you, too. I like to look at all the flowers blooming in the yards and . . ." Courtney broke off her sentence as two large dogs ran barking toward her across their fenced backyard. She shrank against Mom.

Mom smiled down at her. "Don't worry. That's a strong fence," said Mom. "I walk this way every morning, and I've never seen those dogs get out."

Courtney shuddered as she hurried past the dogs. "I don't like big dogs."

"I know," said Mom, "but you can trust the fence to hold them."

That evening, Courtney's friend Sara called. After hanging up the phone, Courtney talked with Mom. "Sara wanted me to go with her to a movie that I knew I shouldn't see, but I said no," she reported.

"Good," said Mom, giving her a hug. "As you get older, honey, you'll face many temptations. You will need to build strong fences to keep from giving in to things you shouldn't do."

Courtney looked puzzled, and Mom explained. "There are several things we can do to build fences that hold back temptation," she said. "Listening in church, reading the Bible and obeying it, talking to God in prayer, and spending time with Christian friends are all ways to help strengthen our fences of resistance. Then, even though temptation can come at us like those dogs you saw today, all it can do is bark at the fence. If you build a strong fence, it will be sure to hold." *KEC*

HOW ABOUT YOU?

There are many temptations that are hard to resist. Are you building "fences" against them? You need to do that now so that you don't give in, even to the strongest temptation.

MEMORIZE:

"For he will conceal me there when troubles come; he will hide me in his sanctuary. He will place me out of reach on a high rock." Psalm 27:5

BUILD A FENCE AGAINST SIN

MINING FOR WISDOM

(Read Job 28:12-23)

Tanya hurried ahead of her family to reach the train that would take them down into the old mine shaft. She could hardly wait for the trip to begin as she settled into a seat beside Dad. "It must have been a lot of fun to dig for treasures like diamonds and gold," said Tanya. "I wish I could have been a miner."

Dad laughed. "I don't think you'd really like it so much," he said as the train began to move. "These mine shafts were cramped and uncomfortable—often dangerous, too."

Tanya listened eagerly as the guide explained various aspects of mining. "That was cool!" she exclaimed when they came up into the sunshine again. "Mining would be hard work, but I still think finding gold would be worth the effort." And all day she talked about how much she wished she could find treasure.

That evening Dad reached for the family Bible. "Time to do a little mining," he said.

Tanya looked at Dad in surprise. "Mining?" she repeated.

Dad smiled. "Studying the Bible is a little like digging for treasure," he said. "It takes work to mine for the truth and wisdom God wishes to teach us. It's dangerous, too . . . dangerous to old habits, ideas, and maybe even friendships that are not right. It can be uncomfortable to give them up. But if we discipline ourselves to mine for God's truths, we discover gems."

Tanya grinned. "Guess I can be a miner after all . . . even though I won't find diamonds or gold," she said.

"Diamonds and gold are only human treasure," said Dad. "Since the Bible shows the way to salvation and spiritual growth, the riches we get from it are far better than finding diamonds and gold." *KEC*

HOW ABOUT YOU?

Do you understand that no earthly treasure can compare with the gifts of wisdom and understanding that God wishes to give? Choose to "mine" for Bible treasure.

"MINE" GOD'S GOLD—THE BIBLE

MEMORIZE:

"My gifts are better than the purest gold, my wages better than sterling silver!" Proverbs 8:19

APRIL
24

GOD'S HANDIWORK

(Read Psalm 139:13-16)

Kelley tossed her pencil and sketchbook aside and scowled into the mirror. "How's your self-portrait assignment going?" asked Mom, peeking into Kelley's room.

Kelley scowled. "I'm too ugly for a portrait," she complained.

"You're not being very fair to God when you say that," Mom told her softly. "God says that you are wonderfully complex. He thinks you're beautiful."

"Well, then he's the only one who thinks so." Kelley sighed.

"I think so, too," said Mom.

"You're my mother," said Kelley. "You have to say that."

Mom flipped through one of Kelley's art books and stopped at a famous portrait. "Now see," she said, pointing to it, "you are much prettier than that person."

"Oh, Mom," groaned Kelley, peeking over her mother's shoulder. "That's the *Mona Lisa!* She's beautiful!"

"Well, I don't think so," said Mom.

Kelley shook her head and laughed. "The Mona Lisa is a work of art, made by one of the best artists in history!" she said.

"So are you," said Mom, closing the book. "In fact, I'd say you were created by the very best artist in history—God!"

Kelley had never thought of God as an artist. She peered into the mirror again. "Why do you suppose he gave me green eyes?" she asked, still skeptical.

"I don't know that, but I like them. And I do know it wasn't an accident," said Mom. "God planned just how he wanted you to look before you were even born. And God doesn't make mistakes. In his eyes, you are a work of art."

As Kelley smiled thoughtfully, she caught a glance of her reflection in the mirror. She hardly looked like the same girl who was scowling a few moments ago. *Hmmm,* she thought as she picked up her pencil again. *That smile would be perfect for my portrait. HMT*

HOW ABOUT YOU?

Do you ever wish you had a nose just like your friend's, or a different color eyes and hair? Do you complain about the way that God made you? Try to look at yourself the way God does. He thinks you're perfect because he made you that way.

MEMORIZE:

"Thank you for making me so wonderfully complex! Your workmanship is marvelous—and how well I know it." Psalm 139:14

GOD MADE YOU SPECIAL

TREASURES IN HEAVEN

(Read Matthew 6:19-21)

"Look at these pretty stones!" called Lily. She and her parents were enjoying a visit to a park, and she had run ahead down the path. She held out the rocks for her parents to see and then slipped them into her pocket. "I'm going to put these in my aquarium," she said.

"Hold on," Mom said. "I'm afraid you can't do that."

"Why not?" asked Lily.

"We're in a national park, and we walked past several signs warning tourists that it's illegal to remove anything from this property," explained Mom. She pointed. "In fact, there's another one now."

"But I need these for my art class," whined Lily. "I found some other neat stuff, too." She pulled several rocks, leaves, pieces of wood, and other things from her pocket. "Can't I take at least a few of these home?" she begged. "I want to make drawings of some of them." Mom shook her head, and Lily sat down on a log and crossed her arms angrily across her chest.

"Sorry," said Mom, "but I'm afraid that's the way it has to be."

After pizza that evening, Mom read from the book of Matthew. "These verses make me think of all those things you picked up this morning, Lily," she said. "You spent a lot of time collecting them. Would you have done that if you had thought about the signs?"

"Of course not," Lily answered. "I would have taken my art pad and made sketches of them right there. I sure wasted a lot of time, didn't I?"

Mom nodded. "Yes, and I'm afraid you're no different than many Christians. We're ignoring God's signs when we are too busy collecting things. For example, we see signs that Jesus is coming soon, yet it's easy to spend a lot of time collecting money and lots of possessions."

"None of that stuff is really important, right?" asked Lily.

Mom nodded. *HMT*

HOW ABOUT YOU?

Do you dream about the things you want to own? A new bike? Video games? Designer shoes or clothes? God doesn't want you to become attached to these things, because he has something so much better. Think of something you can do today that will be of value when you get to heaven.

**USE YOUR TIME
FOR GOD**

MEMORIZE:
"After all, we didn't bring anything with us when we came into the world, and we certainly cannot carry anything with us when we die."
1 Timothy 6:7

THE FLOOD

(Read Genesis 6:14; 7:10; 8:13-14)

Ellen and Andy were visiting their Grandpa Wilson, who lived in a cottage on the Paranak River. One day a wild storm caused the river to rise rapidly, and Grandpa was concerned. "I'm afraid this whole area might be flooded if the Paranak Dam breaks, but the roads are not passable," he said. "I think the best thing for us to do is to get into my boat and head downriver." So they hastily gathered a few things and set off.

As they moved downstream, they stopped at each cottage they passed, inviting the families to come along. At some places, the people were polite, thanking them for stopping. At others, they were told in no uncertain terms that they were a nuisance and should go away. "The dam has never broken, and I'm sure it won't now," they were told over and over. "We'll be fine."

At one place, a party was in progress. Again Grandpa warned the people that a flood might occur. "Oh, ho-ho! If it isn't just like Noah and his ark!" came the taunting reply. "Where are all your animals, Noah?" Unable to persuade anyone to join them, Grandpa and the children went on.

Soon after they reached a safe place, the dam did break. Tons of water rushed over the river banks, resulting in much loss of life and property. "I feel awful about the people who could have come with us but wouldn't," said Ellen sadly.

"Remember the one who called Grandpa 'Noah'?" asked Andy. "Well, Grandpa's first name is Noah," he said. "And we were a little like Noah in the Bible, warning people about a flood. No one believed him, either."

"That's true," mused Grandpa. "It's sad when lives are lost because folks don't believe warnings of coming trouble. It's even more sad when souls are lost because they don't believe warnings about the trouble they will have after they die. Noah and his family were safe because they believed God. That's a picture of those who trust Christ." *HCT*

HOW ABOUT YOU?

Have you trusted Christ as your Savior? Or are you—like the people at the party—having too much fun? Do you feel there is no danger? Come into God's ark of safety before it's too late. Don't put it off. Trust the Lord Jesus as your Savior while the door of salvation is still open.

MEMORIZE:

"What makes us think that we can escape if we are indifferent to this great salvation that was announced by the Lord Jesus himself?" Hebrews 2:3

THERE'S SAFETY IN JESUS

UNCOMMON SENSE

(Read Psalm 19:1-4)

Kyle and Janae helped their grandmother clear the lunch table. "I should have brought you some turtles from the pond," said Kyle. "Frogs, too. You could have fixed turtle soup and frog legs for lunch." Janae shuddered, but Grandma just grinned.

"I wish I could have gone along on your walk," said Grandma. "I love to see the things in nature that God created."

"How do we know for sure he created them?" asked Kyle. "My science teacher says everything began with a big explosion. He also says there's not any God."

"Do you think that makes sense?" asked Grandma.

"We-e-ell, probably not," replied Kyle. "I don't know."

"Let's see," said Grandma. "Let's try an experiment. She took out some small cards. "Write a letter of the alphabet on each of these," she said, "starting with *A* and going all the way through *Z*." When Kyle and Janae were finished, Grandma took the cards. "OK, Kyle," she said, "I want you to climb up on this chair."

So Kyle got up on the chair and Grandma handed him the cards. "Toss these up and let them fall," she said. Kyle did as he was told. "Now look at them—they're all in order from *A* to *Z*, right?" asked Grandma.

"Are you kidding?" said Janae. "Of course they're not."

"Oh, well, then let's try it again," said Grandma. "Janae, you toss the cards this time. If we try often enough, they'll eventually move into the right spots, don't you think?"

"No, I don't," grumbled Kyle. "This is silly, Grandma. You know they'll never fall in order no matter how often we do this."

"You're right," agreed Grandma. "It takes an intelligent person to put the letters in order. It's silly to think it could just happen. And it's just as silly—in fact, it's more silly—to believe that the magnificent world in which we live just 'happened' to come into being by itself." *HWM*

HOW ABOUT YOU?

Do you wonder about God? Would you like to learn more about him? Look at the wonders of nature and space. Read a little about the marvelous way your body is made. Common sense will tell you that only an all-powerful God could have put everything together—but the best place to learn about him is your Bible.

GOD IS THE CREATOR

NO STEPMOTHER CARD

(Read Psalm 133)

Paula Johnson was not happy about her father's new wife, and she allowed those feelings to show. "I wish you would try to accept your stepmother for who she is," suggested Dad. "I think you would find her kind and loving."

"I've never said that she wasn't nice," Paula protested. "It's just that she isn't my mother, so I don't know why I have to treat her as if she is."

Paula's father looked at her with sadness. "No, she's not your mother," he admitted. "But your mother is gone, and there is nothing we can do about that. We just have to accept her death as a fact, whether we like it or not."

"But why did you have to bring Marian here?" Paula asked, choking back tears. "And just before Mother's Day!"

Dad nodded understandingly. "Tomorrow is going to be a difficult day for all of us," he admitted. "But just remember, it's going to be a difficult day for Marian, too."

"Marian!" Paula snapped. "Why should this be a hard day for her? You and Kenny both act like you've forgotten all about Mom. Kenny even bought a Mother's Day card!"

"Don't you plan to do that, too?" Dad asked seriously.

Paula shook her head. "They don't make stepmother cards," she said with sarcasm.

A light tap on the door interrupted their conversation. It was Marian. "Look what was just delivered!" She beamed, bringing in a small plant. "It's lovely. Thank you!" The card that came with it was signed in Kenny's handwriting, and it read, "Your new family."

Paula bit her lower lip to keep herself under control. Quickly she slipped out the door. She felt anger building up inside of her, and she didn't know what to do with it. She felt guilty. Somehow, she knew, she would eventually have to accept Marian for who she was—not her real mother, but someone who was willing to step in and take on a new family. *RIJ*

HOW ABOUT YOU?

Is there someone you are not accepting? God has brought that person into your life for a purpose. Ask him to help you to show love, kindness, and thoughtfulness to that person. Look for the good in the situation.

MEMORIZE:

"How wonderful it is, how pleasant, when brothers live together in harmony!" Psalm 133:1

ACCEPT WHAT GOD ALLOWS

A BAD START

(Read Philippians 4:4-9)

"Mayla, get up! Time to get ready for school," called Mother. Mayla pulled the covers over her head and burrowed deeper into the warm cocoon of blankets. She didn't even open her eyes. She was too busy dreaming about being the pilot of a 747. It would be exciting to travel around the world. "Mayla," Mother called again. "I told you to get up, and I want you to get up now! Do you hear me?"

"Yes." Mayla's voice was muffled by the pillow over her head.

"Mayla, I said now!"

Oh, bother! Why do my good dreams always have to be interrupted? Mayla thought as she finally stumbled out of bed and into the shower.

"It's raining," she moaned as she entered the kitchen a little later. "Why can't the sun ever shine?" She eyed the breakfast table. "Oh, yuck!" she said with a frown. "Oatmeal! I can't stand oatmeal!"

Just then her sister, Nancy, came to the table. She was chattering excitedly about the field trip her class would be taking that day. "We never go on field trips. I hate school," complained Mayla.

"Mayla," asked Mother, "would you please give thanks before we eat?"

"Dear heavenly Father," prayed Mayla, "thank you for the beautiful day you have given us, and thank you for the good food. In Jesus' name, Amen."

"Mayla, I think something is very wrong," said Mother as she passed the oatmeal.

Mayla looked up in surprise. "What do you mean?"

"You thanked the Lord for the beautiful day, but all you've done so far is grumble," she told her.

Mayla thought about that. Yes, she had been grumbling. In fact, she had been out of bed for only half an hour, and she had grumbled the entire time!

"I'm sorry, Lord," she whispered. "Help me to get a new start on this day!"

LMW

HOW ABOUT YOU?

Do you grumble when Mom calls you in the morning? Do you complain about the food and then thank the Lord for it? Sometimes boys and girls get in the habit of grumbling about everything. The Bible tells you to rejoice. Be a joyful Christian, not a grumbling Christian.

MEMORIZE:

"This is the day the Lord has made. We will rejoice and be glad in it."
Psalm 118:24

DON'T BE A GRUMBLER!

CRACKING THE SHELL

(Read Hebrews 12:5-11)

Katie was impatient to get home and ask Mother an important question.

"Have Martha's chicks been born yet, Mom?"

"Not yet," replied her mother.

"Can we go and see right after lunch?" asked Katie eagerly.

Mother nodded. So right after lunch, they went down to the henhouse. "No chicks yet," said Katie, turning away, disappointment clouding her big brown eyes.

"Wait a minute," said Mother. Katie turned around, surprised to hear a note of excitement in her mother's voice. "Look at that egg, Katie, the one near Martha's leg."

Katie looked. The egg was cracked. As she watched, the crack widened. "What's happening? Why is the egg breaking?" asked Katie, alarmed.

"The little chick is trying to come out," said Mother.

After a short time, Katie went down to the hen house again. A moment later, she was yelling at the top of her voice, "Mom, the chick is trapped. He's struggling so hard, but he can't get out of the shell!" Mother came to look. Katie's eyes filled with tears. "Look, Mom. The poor little chick! Can't we break the shell for him so that he can come out?"

Mother put her arm around Katie. "I know you don't like to watch the chick struggle, but we can't interfere," she said. "The struggle to break the shell makes the chick strong. If we break the shell for him, then he won't go through that struggle, and he might come out weak."

"But, Mom, it's so hard for him," protested Katie.

"God knows that sometimes hard things are good for us, Katie," said Mom. "If we accept hard things and face up to the challenges they bring, God helps us become stronger people." *MTF*

HOW ABOUT YOU?

Do you grumble and complain when you face difficulties and hardships? Or do you talk to God about your anger and sadness and ask for his help to overcome and grow through them? If you face up to struggles in your life—moving to a new place, failing an exam, illness, losing a friend—and trust God to help you through them, you will become a stronger person.

MEMORIZE:

"We can rejoice, too, when we run into problems and trials, for we know that they are good for us—they help us learn to endure." Romans 5:3

LEARN FROM DIFFICULTIES

DELAYED, NOT DENIED!

(Read Psalm 40:1-5, 16-17)

In spite of their earnest prayers, things seemed to go from bad to worse, and Janet and Jared were beginning to wonder if God really answered prayer at all. First, Dad was laid off from his job, and he couldn't seem to find another one. Next, Mother became ill and had to be taken to the hospital. And a few days later, a big storm knocked down part of the old barn on their property.

After a simple dinner one evening, Dad picked up the Bible for family devotions. "I waited patiently for the Lord to help me, and he turned to me and heard my cry," Dad read slowly. "That's a good verse for us," he said. "We must be patient and wait for the Lord to help us."

Jared frowned. "But why doesn't God answer our prayers?" he asked. "We've prayed and prayed, but you're still out of work, and Mom's still in the hospital."

"Well," said Dad, "God always answers prayers, but he doesn't always say yes. Sometimes he says no, and sometimes he says to wait awhile. Jared, do you remember when Janet got her first two-wheel bike?"

"I remember!" exclaimed Janet. She grinned. "Jared begged for one, too, but that was silly. He was too little to ride one anyway."

Dad nodded. "Later on, when you were old enough, we were happy to get you a bike, Jared," he said. "It's like that with God—he knows what's right for us. And if something is good for us, he'll give it to us at just the right time."

A few days later, Dad went to talk to Mr. Johnson at the bank about getting a loan. When he returned home, he was smiling. "God answered our prayers through our old barn," he said. "Mr. Johnson's brother is in the construction business and buys old barn wood. I talked with him on the phone. Not only will he pay us for the wood, but he offered me a job!"

"Wow! God did work everything out!" exclaimed Jared. "I guess I should have known he would." *JLH*

HOW ABOUT YOU?

Do you sometimes think your prayers aren't being answered? Recognize that God's answers, though not always what you would choose, are best for you. Then keep praying and waiting for God's answer. And remember, he knows how difficult waiting can be. So, if you get angry, frustrated, or impatient, talk to him about those feelings, too.

GOD ANSWERS PRAYER

MEMORIZE:
"I waited patiently for the Lord to help me, and he turned to me and heard my cry." Psalm 40:1

NEW SKIN AND NEW HABITS

(Read Colossians 3:8-14)

"Grandma! Grandpa!" Casey and Tyler ran outside to greet their grandparents.

"My! How you've grown!" Grandma exclaimed. "Did you have a good time on your trip?"

"We sure did—and come see what we brought home," said Tyler. He led his grandparents into the house. After greeting the rest of the family, Grandma and Grandpa followed the children into the family room. "Look," said Casey as she pointed to a covered glass bowl filled with living green plants.

"Nice plants," Grandpa said. "Very nice."

"Look again, Grandpa," suggested Casey. "Look right there." She pointed to a small branch resting on the bottom of the bowl.

Grandpa looked where Casey pointed. He grinned. "I see it," he said. "It's a chameleon. God colored chameleons so they could blend in with their surroundings. He gave them camouflage uniforms!"

"It looks almost like a little leaf," Grandma said in amazement.

"Chameleons are interesting creatures. Their skin doesn't grow," Grandpa said. "When they get too big for their skin, they begin shedding it."

"Yeah—we learned about that in school," said Tyler.

"Kind of like what we should do, isn't it?" observed Grandma.

Casey and Tyler looked at her. "We should get rid of our skin?" they asked.

"No." Grandma laughed. "I guess I was thinking out loud," she said. "The chameleon sheds his skin, and we are to shed sinful things. The Bible gives a whole list of things we need to get rid of. The chameleon puts on new skin, and we are to put on new, Jesus-like characteristics."

Casey nodded. "The Bible says in Ephesians 4 that we're to throw off our old way of life and show new attitudes. We learned about that in school, too," she said. "In Sunday school." *LJR*

HOW ABOUT YOU?

Are you getting rid of sinful habits? Are you becoming more like Jesus every day?

MEMORIZE:

"What this means is that those who become Christians become new persons. They are not the same anymore, for the old life is gone. A new life has begun!" 2 Corinthians 5:17

SHED OLD, BAD HABITS

SHOW YOUR COLORS

(Read James 4:4b-10)

Grandpa Wells was sitting on his porch one day when Sherry, a neighbor girl, approached. She looked as if she had been crying. When he greeted her, she stopped to talk to him. "My friends are all mad at me," she told him with trembling lips.

"That's too bad," sympathized Grandpa Wells. "Want to tell me about it?"

"I . . . I'm just so miserable," Sherry replied, and the story spilled out. "Some of my school friends told some of the kids at church that I smoke."

"And do you?" asked Grandpa Wells.

"I . . . I . . . well, I've tried it," admitted Sherry, "but only a couple of times—when I was with some school kids." She paused to wipe her eyes. "But I am a Christian, and I haven't smoked very often," she defended herself. "It's just that I hate to be odd. But now the kids all say I'm two-faced, and no one likes me anymore."

Grandpa Wells sighed. "Sherry," he said, "you remind me of a chameleon—a kind of lizard that changes colors. When it's against the bark of a tree, it turns brown. When it's against a leaf, it turns green. Now, God intended chameleons to be that way—it's for protection from their enemies. But God did not intend for Christians to be like that. God intended us to show true Christian colors all the time. We are to act like Christians no matter who we're with."

Sherry sniffed. "Oh, Grandpa, I'm s-s-so sorry. I'm never going to smoke another cigarette," she declared. "From now on I'm going to take care of my body like a Christian should."

Grandpa Wells nodded. "I'm glad to hear you say that," he said. "I think it would be easier for you if you ran around with Christian kids at school, too. But even if you're with unsaved kids, there's no excuse for not acting like a Christian." *BJW*

HOW ABOUT YOU?

Are you trying to be like a chameleon, blending in with your surroundings? There's no way you can please the Lord and non-Christians all the time. Ask God to help you be courageous as you determine to be true to him.

MEMORIZE:

"Don't you realize that friendship with this world makes you an enemy of God? I say it again, that if your aim is to enjoy this world, you can't be a friend of God." James 4:4

BE TRUE TO GOD

THE THREE-LEGGED RACE

(Read Genesis 2:21-24)

"Mom, why did you tell Karen she shouldn't date Steve?" asked Lisa as they waited for the three-legged race to start. It was Field Day at the elementary school, and Lisa's little brother Joel and his friend Ben were hoping to win the kindergarten lap of the race. "I think Steve's a really nice guy," added Lisa.

"I know he is, honey," replied Mom, "but he's not a Christian, you know."

"But why does that . . . oh, look! They're starting!" cried Lisa. "I hope Ben and Joel win!" She watched her little brother eagerly.

After watching a few moments, Mom began to laugh. "What is Ben doing?" she asked.

Lisa watched in horror. "Mom! He's pulling Joel backwards. What's he doing that for?" She impatiently bounced up and down in her seat.

"I think he's heading for that ice-cream stand," said Mom. The window at the ice-cream stand had just opened.

"Oh, poor Joel!" cried Lisa as she watched her brother trying desperately to pull his friend forward. "Now they're just standing still—neither of them is moving an inch!"

Others in the crowd were smiling as they watched the antics of the two little kindergartners. At last Joel gave up and let himself be dragged away by Ben toward the ice-cream stand. "They're out of the race now," said Lisa, shaking her head sadly. "Joel should have chosen another partner—someone who wouldn't have dragged him away from the finish line."

"Honey, that's why I told Karen she shouldn't date Steve," Mom said.

"What?" asked Lisa in surprise. "What do you mean?"

"Christian marriage is something like that three-legged race," explained Mom. "If both people aren't believers, then they're like Ben and Joel—pulling in two different directions and not getting anywhere."

"Or ending up in the wrong place!" added Lisa. She nodded. "I think we should tell Karen about the three-legged race. Then maybe she'll understand about Steve, too." *MTF*

HOW ABOUT YOU?

Are you thinking of getting married soon? No, of course you're not! You're much too young. But you're not too young to know that when you do marry someday, it is wise to marry another Christian.

MEMORIZE:

"Don't team up with those who are unbelievers. How can goodness be a partner with wickedness? How can light live with darkness?" 2 Corinthians 6:14

CHRISTIAN MARRIAGE REQUIRES TWO CHRISTIANS

SEEDS, FLOWERS, AND HEAVEN

(Read 1 Corinthians 15:35-44)

Cathy and her mother were busily digging and burying tiny brown seeds in the rich, dark earth. "I wonder whether there'll be flowers in heaven," said Cathy.

Grandma, who had sent the seeds, had recently died. Cathy knew she was now in heaven.

Mom laughed. "I hope so!" she said.

"It's hard to understand what will happen to us in heaven, isn't it, Mom?" asked Cathy. "I know Grandma is there now, but I don't really understand it."

"I know," said Mom. "I guess that's one reason why we say heaven is a mystery."

"But, Mom, we'll still have bodies, right?" asked Cathy. "Pastor Holmes said that Grandma left her body and went to be with Jesus, but that her body would be raised up again someday."

"That's right," agreed Mom. "The Bible says they'll be glorious, heavenly bodies."

"But how can that be?" asked Cathy. "I think of how crippled and sick Grandma was, and I wouldn't think she'd even want that body back. It just doesn't seem possible that it could ever become something so wonderful."

Mom thought a moment, then smiled. "Cathy, maybe those seeds you're planting won't grow into flowers after all," she said casually.

Cathy looked at her mother in astonishment. "Why not?"

"How can they, Cathy?" asked Mom. "Look . . . they're ugly little seeds, so they can't turn into something as beautiful and as different as flowers."

"Mom! You're kidding! Of course they can!" exclaimed Cathy.

Mom smiled again. "Yes, Cathy, I am kidding. But that's to show you that, just like seeds are changed into the flowers that are so different from them, we can be transformed by God into something very different from what we are now." *MTF*

HOW ABOUT YOU?

Do you wonder—even worry—about what heaven will be like? Do you find it hard to believe that God will give you a perfect, heavenly body? Think of how God makes flowers of all shapes, sizes, and colors to grow out of small, uninteresting-looking seeds. Surely he will work even greater miracles with his children whom he loves.

MEMORIZE:

"So will it be with the resurrection of the dead. The body that is sown is perishable, it is raised imperishable; it is sown in dishonor, it is raised in glory; it is sown in weakness, it is raised in power; it is sown a natural body, it is raised a spiritual body. If there is a natural body, there is also a spiritual body." 1 Corinthians 15:42-44, NIV

GOD WILL GIVE US IMPERISHABLE BODIES

THE LEAKING PITCHER

(Read 2 Timothy 2:20-21)

Jalanna watched as her mother took a piece of clay from her potter's wheel and tossed it in the scrap heap in her hobby room. Jalanna picked it up. "Mom, why did you throw this away?" she asked as her mother began working on a new piece. "This is a pitcher, isn't it?"

Mother nodded. "It was going to be. I want to make a pitcher like one I saw in the store the other day," she said, "but I can't get it right. So I decided to give up that project for now and try again later." She frowned as she looked at Jalanna. "By the way, did you tell your friend Amy that your brother wets his bed?" asked Mother.

Jalanna blushed. "He was teasing us!" she said, trying to excuse herself. "Besides, I told him I was sorry!"

"I'm glad you did," said Mother, "but an apology can't take away Shawn's embarrassment." She looked at the pitcher Jalanna still held. "God is the Potter for our lives," she added. "He wants good vessels he can use, not vessels that crack under temptation's pressure and hurt others by leaking secrets."

Jalanna put the pitcher back on the scrap heap. "Does . . . does that mean God will throw me away like you did this pitcher, Mom?" she asked.

Mother smiled. "No, of course not, honey," she said. "Actually, I'm not throwing away those defective items in the trash bin, either. I'll break up the clay, screen out any hard lumps, and make good vessels from them. God does that, too." *NIM*

HOW ABOUT YOU?

Are you a vessel God can use to pour out his love to others? Or are you a cracked vessel, leaking out secrets that hurt or embarrass others? If you are guilty of being a tattletale, ask God to help you become a good vessel. Ask him to fill you so full of his love that there will be no room inside you for mean thoughts.

MEMORIZE:

"But we have this treasure in jars of clay to show that this all-surpassing power is from God and not from us." 2 Corinthians 4:7, NIV

DON'T LEAK HATE, POUR OUT LOVE

THE BLUE MOUSE

(Read Ecclesiastes 4:9-12)

Sandi sat cross-legged on the bedroom floor, surrounded by snapshots. "Look, Mom!" she exclaimed. "Here's another picture of me and Mousie. I really loved that old stuffed animal."

Sandi's mother peeked over her daughter's shoulder at the child in the photographs—Sandi swinging in the backyard, Sandi in a red Christmas dress, Sandi riding her first bike. There were a number of pictures of her blowing out candles on a succession of birthday cakes. In many of the pictures, the little girl clutched a blue stuffed toy. "Why did you love that grubby old bear so much?" asked Mother. She added with a smile, "It really was a bear, you know, not a mouse."

Sandi laughed. "I know it, but I thought he looked more like a mouse. I guess I loved him because he was a good guy to talk to. He just sat and listened." Sandi could remember long-ago times when she had sobbed her hurts into the fur of her faded, blue friend. "I told Mousie all my secrets, and he seemed to understand, even though he never could tell me so or hug me back," she said thoughtfully as she gathered the snapshots and put them into a shoebox.

Mother nodded. "We need a friend like that, don't we?" she said. Then she added, "Mrs. March and her daughter Jody invited us to go with them to church tomorrow, Sandi. Mrs. March said the pastor of their church is giving a message called 'God, Our Best Friend,' and I think I'd like to hear it. Shall we go?"

Sandi snapped a rubber band over the lid of the shoebox. "OK," she agreed. "I've been a little lonesome since we moved here. Maybe if we go to church with them, Jody will be my friend. I'd like that."

"And I'd like to know more about God as my friend," Mother said.

"Me, too," agreed Sandi. *PIK*

HOW ABOUT YOU?

Do you need a friend—someone with whom you can share all your thoughts? The Bible speaks of the value of friendships. And it tells about the best friend of all—Jesus. He wants to be your friend throughout your whole life.

JESUS WILL BE YOUR BEST FRIEND

MEMORIZE:
"There are 'friends' who destroy each other, but a real friend sticks closer than a brother." Proverbs 18:24

MIRROR ON THE WALL

(Read 1 Peter 3:1-6)

"Mom! I'm home," called Janice. "Guess what, Mom! I was voted to represent my classroom in the 'Princess Contest'!"

"Great!" said Mother.

"I'm going to win—I know I am!" said Janice. "The school kids will be voting on three of us, and one of the girls has freckles and red hair. The other one is shy, and hardly anyone knows her." Mother frowned slightly but didn't comment.

During the next days, Janice spent a lot of time in front of the mirror. She expected the rest of the family to make way for her at any time. "Be careful," cautioned Dad, as he noticed her interest in herself and the trouble it was causing others.

One afternoon, Dad took Janice and her brother, Pete, to the animal shelter to choose a dog. "Oh, look at this puppy!" exclaimed Janice. "Isn't he beautiful?" But when they tried to make friends with the puppy, he growled angrily. They learned from the attendant that he seemed to have a nasty temper. "But he's so beautiful," said Janice.

"Beauty isn't everything," Dad reminded her, and they finally chose a somewhat homely, but friendly, little dog that Pete discovered.

Soon the day arrived for the students at Janice's school to vote for their "princess" . . . and Janice came home in tears. "I didn't w-w-win!" she wailed. "I c-can't understand it. Betsy, with her r-r-ed hair and f-f-freckles and s-sloppy clothes won!"

"Janice," said Dad gently, "remember the beautiful white puppy at the animal shelter? Why didn't we bring him home instead of our shaggy little Buffy?"

Janice wiped her eyes as she looked at Dad in surprise. "Because he was so mean and Buffy was so friendly and . . ."

"And you've been acting more like the white dog," interrupted Pete, "and Betsy acts more like Buffy."

Janice gasped, but Dad nodded. "I'm afraid that's true," he said. "Always remember that true beauty comes from within." *BJW*

HOW ABOUT YOU?

Are you too concerned about your appearance? Boys as well as girls need to develop inner beauty. How can you do this? By treating others like Jesus would.

MEMORIZE:

"Charm is deceptive, and beauty does not last; but a woman who fears the Lord will be greatly praised."
Proverbs 31:30

BEAUTY IS AS BEAUTY DOES

SARA'S DISAPPOINTMENT

(Read 1 Samuel 23:14-18)

Sara's bed shook as she sobbed into her pillow. *It isn't fair! It isn't fair!* she kept repeating to herself. All winter long she had helped shovel the walks and driveway for Grandma Atkins. As a reward, Grandma had promised to take Sara on a special weekend trip for her birthday. And now, just a week before the promised outing, Grandma was sick. Mother was staying with her at night, and Sara had to help take care of her after school each day. It just wasn't fair.

"Sara, are you OK?" Dad's concerned voice came from the doorway. "I thought I heard you moving around. Why aren't you sleeping? You'll be too tired to help Grandma tomorrow." Sara squirmed with anger. Didn't anyone care about *her?* "What's troubling you, honey?" asked Dad when he saw she was crying.

"How . . . how would you feel if you worked all winter and didn't get what you were promised and . . . and nobody even c-c-cared?" Sara's voice rose to a loud wail.

"So that's it," Dad answered softly. "Sara, we do care. When I talked to your mother on the phone this evening, she told me Grandma is terribly upset because she can't keep her promise to you."

Sara wiped her eyes. "I-I guess I never thought of how she might feel."

Dad nodded. "When we get hurt, we often forget about others," he told her. "That's why I like the Bible story of David and Jonathan so much. Jonathan, as King Saul's son, was expected to be the next king of Israel, but God chose David to rule instead. I'm sure Jonathan was disappointed, but he loved David and risked his life to help and encourage him. Sara, your mother and I know you're disappointed, and we're going to try to make it up to you. So is Grandma. But for right now, will you think of Grandma and help her all you can?"

Sara grinned sheepishly. "I love Grandma, and I'll do everything I can to make her get well quick. I promise!" *AGL*

HOW ABOUT YOU?

When things go wrong, do you think only of how badly you're feeling? Or do you think of how others might be hurting? Remembering that others also suffer will make you a kinder person and help you to forget your own hurts.

MEMORIZE:
"The greatest love is shown when people lay down their lives for their friends." John 15:13

THINK OF OTHERS

TOO BUSY

(Read Psalm 143:8-10)

When band practice was canceled on Saturday morning, Julie thought she would head to the pool to practice for the swim meet. Instead, Mom insisted that she help Grandpa with the new vegetable garden he had planted.

Julie wiped her hand across her brow as she followed Grandpa out to the garden. It was a warm day, and she could smell the scent of roses and honeysuckle. She remembered how she used to pick bouquets and give them to Grandpa. But she'd been so busy lately, she hardly had time to see Grandpa anymore. She felt bad about that.

Julie looked up to see her grandfather watching her. "Is something wrong?" he asked.

"I just have so many things to do," said Julie with a sigh. "There's school and band and Bible club and swimming and choir at church. And now my friends want me to join a drama club. Mom says I'm not spending enough time helping with chores around the house or seeing the people I care about. And she's right!"

Grandpa picked up the hoe. "Do you think you should cut down on your activities?" he asked. "Maybe give up a few of them?"

Julie shrugged. "But they're all such good things!" she protested. "I like them all." She watched as Grandpa began to weed out the plants that were crowded together. "Why are you throwing out those healthy plants?" asked Julie.

"They are healthy. But they're growing too close together," explained Grandpa. "If I let them stay, none of the plants will grow well. Plants don't do well when they're crowded for space, and people don't do well when they're crowded for time," he said gently.

Julie bit her lip. "You mean . . . like my activities. There's nothing wrong with any of them. It's just that my life is so crowded I can't do any of them as well as I should?"

Grandpa nodded. "God says we are to do everything to his glory," he reminded her. "I'm afraid he doesn't get much glory from the things we don't do well."

Julie sighed. "I think I better 'weed out' some of my activities so I'll have time for the things that matter most, like schoolwork and spending time with my family and friends," she remarked. *KEC*

HOW ABOUT YOU?

Is your life so crowded with activities that you don't have time for the things that really matter? Even good activities can take too much time. Check to see if you should do some "weeding" to make room for family, friends, schoolwork, or responsibilities at home.

MEMORIZE:

"Whatever you do, you must do all for the glory of God." 1 Corinthians 10:31

DO ALL FOR GOD'S GLORY

DANGER! TURN AROUND!

(Read Proverbs 4:18-27)

Rain splashed hard against the windshield. Gina sat back in her seat and watched the windshield wipers slapping the raindrops away. Soon the car slowed to a stop. Mom eased her window down just enough to talk with a man standing in the road, waving a flashlight. "The bridge ahead is washed out," shouted the man above the roar of the rain. "You'll need to take a different route." He showed her where she could turn around.

Mom thanked the man and closed the window. "Well," she said with a sigh, "we won't be home quite as soon as we hoped, but it shouldn't take too much longer." She carefully turned the car around, and they headed in the other direction.

"Mom," Gina said the next morning at breakfast, "I just heard on the news that some people were hurt last night during the storm. They didn't know the bridge was washed out and drove right off a big drop-off into the river."

Mom placed a box of cereal on the table. "I heard the news, too," she said. "I'm sure glad that man was there to warn us of danger ahead." She smiled. "You know," she added, *God often warns us when danger is ahead, too, and tells us to turn around.*"

"What do you mean?" Gina asked curiously.

"Well, we often face choices in life—who to be close friends with, whether or not to cheat on a test in school, whether or not to tell a lie—things like that. When we're tempted to make the wrong choice, God always warns us to turn around. Sometimes he shows us something in the Bible to warn us of danger. Sometimes he uses parents or other Christians. If we obey him, we'll be kept safe. If we ignore his warning, we'll end up hurt or in trouble."

Gina sat at the table and looked out the kitchen window. Finally she said, "So instead of getting mad that we can't do something the way we want to, we should be glad when we're warned about it, right?"

"Right!" agreed Mom. *RSM*

HOW ABOUT YOU?

Do you pay attention when parents warn you against doing something wrong? Do you listen to warnings given by your pastor, teachers, or other Christian friends? Sometimes they may tell you things you don't want to hear, but God has given them to you to help and protect you. He also uses his Word, the Bible, to instruct you and show you what things please him. Read and obey what he says.

MEMORIZE:

"Obey your leaders and submit to their authority. They keep watch over you as men who must give an account." Hebrews 13:17, NIV

HEED GOD'S WARNINGS

LESSON FROM A RUBBER BAND

(Read Romans 12:6-11)

Leah sighed as she dropped her backpack on the floor. "What's the matter, Leah?" asked her mother.

"Aw, I wanted to get on the softball team this year, but I can never quite make it." Leah flopped on the sofa. "I wish I were better at sports."

"I know you've always wanted to make the team," said Mother as she filled a shoebox with items to be taken to the attic. "But perhaps there are some other talents you should be developing." Leah grunted and headed toward the kitchen. "Look in the drawer by the stove and find a rubber band to fit around this box so it can be stored in the attic," Mother called after her.

Leah reluctantly found the rubber bands and came back with several sizes. She tried a narrow band, but it snapped before she got it around the box. She tried another. It looked big enough, but it was too stiff. Mother watched her efforts. Leah finally found a sturdy band that reached comfortably around the shoebox.

"Leah, it occurs to me that the manufacturer of the rubber bands created each one to do a certain job, and that reminds me of you," said Mother. "A small band is not made to handle large jobs. Nor is a large band to be used for small jobs. Right?"

Leah looked at her. "Sure," she said, "but what does that have to do with me?"

"Well, you were created for certain jobs, too," said Mother. "God gave you talents to use . . . maybe not in the area of sports, but maybe in art or music. Or maybe God wants you to develop your talent for writing."

"Are you saying I should give up sports then?" asked Leah.

Mother shook her head. "No. I think it's fine for you to develop whatever ability you have in that area," she encouraged her. "But don't fret if the sports area doesn't 'fit you' perfectly. Try to determine just which 'rubber band'—just which talent—does perfectly suit you. Then use that talent for the Lord." *LAW*

HOW ABOUT YOU?

Do you know which talents God has given you? It's fine to try out many different things, but don't be discouraged when some of them don't seem to work out. Look for the areas in which God has given you special ability. Maybe it's in art or music. Maybe it's in the area of class leadership. Or maybe you have a special talent for seeing ways to help others.

MEMORIZE:

"God has given gifts to each of you from his great variety of spiritual gifts. Manage them well so that God's generosity can flow through you." 1 Peter 4:10

DEVELOP YOUR TALENTS

PROMISES, PROMISES

(Read Proverbs 20:5-11)

"Mom," called fourteen-year-old Carmen as she ran into the house, "I might have a job this summer. The Webers and the Kings are both looking for summer baby-sitters." She frowned as she continued. "But there are four of us who applied for the two jobs," she added. "We should know in a couple of days which ones they pick. I really hope I get to work for the Kings. They pay more and have a computer and a swimming pool."

A couple of days later, Mrs. Weber called. "Would you like the job?" she asked Carmen.

"I sure would!" exclaimed Carmen. Though it wasn't the job she preferred, she was thrilled to have been chosen.

When Carmen got home from school a few days later, she found a note from her brother. It read: *Mrs. King called and wants you to baby-sit for her this summer.* "Oh, Mom," wailed Carmen, "what should I do? The Kings have such a gorgeous house, a neat computer, and the pool would be great on a hot day. I really want to work there."

"I can understand that," said Mom, "but how do you think Mrs. Weber will feel if you back out on her now? You made a promise when you accepted the baby-sitting job from her, and you really don't have a good reason to change your mind."

"But I didn't know I'd hear from the Kings," moaned Carmen.

Mother picked up her Bible. "I was reading in Nehemiah this morning," she said. "Read this verse—Nehemiah 7:2." She handed the Bible to Carmen.

Carmen read, "I gave the responsibility of governing Jerusalem to my brother Hanani, along with Hananiah, the commander of the fortress, for he was a faithful man who feared God more than most." She looked up at her mother. "I don't get it," she said.

"Let's put that verse in our own words, using your name," Mother suggested. "How about, 'I gave Carmen the job as baby-sitter for the Webers, because she is faithful and can be counted on to do a good job, and she fears God.' "

Carmen frowned. "You're saying if that verse is really true about me, I'll keep my word to Mrs. Weber, aren't you?" she asked. She sighed. "I know that's really the right thing to do." *MAM*

HOW ABOUT YOU?

Is it hard to do what you've agreed to do, when something you'd rather do opens up? Be careful about what you promise. If you've made a commitment, keep it. Occasionally, a compromise may be agreeable to both parties involved, but as a rule you need to follow through on what you have said.

DO WHAT YOU PROMISE

MEMORIZE:
"People with integrity have firm footing, but those who follow crooked paths will slip and fall." Proverbs 10:9

FEELING ITCHY-SCRATCHY

(Read 1 Corinthians 13:4-7)

"I need that red marker!" hissed Ellie, snatching it from her big brother, Tad. She dropped it on top of the card she was coloring and bent to scratch the big mosquito bite on her leg. "Oooh, this will never go away!" she moaned. The big, swollen bump stung and throbbed and itched again. Ellie straightened up, intending to color, but Tad had grabbed the marker back. "Give it here!" ordered Ellie, her voice rising. "Making a card for Mom was my idea. You're always copying me!"

"Well, I draw better than you," retorted Tad. "And I want the red."

"Give me that marker right now!" Ellie was almost shouting, and all the time her sharp fingernails scratched, scratched, and scratched the bite.

Hannah, their older sister, staggered into the room with a big laundry basket. "Quiet down, you two!" she said. "Remember, Mom needs lots of rest!" She sat down with a sigh and gave them a smile. "What's the problem this time?"

Ellie thought of her mother, trying to grow strong again after her operation. But the mosquito bite was burning and itching—just like her anger at Tad. "Tad took my marker," grumbled Ellie. "And besides . . . I just feel so 'itchy-scratchy' from this mosquito bite!"

Hannah nodded sympathetically. "You know, scratching an insect bite just makes it worse, Ellie. You need to soothe the itch away," she said. She ran a cloth under the cold water faucet and handed it to Ellie. "Try this," she suggested. Ellie smiled in relief as she held the cold, wet cloth against the bite. "It's soothing, isn't it?" asked Hannah. "Try to remember that God's love is soothing, too—it's patient and kind. If your heart is filled with his love, you won't be so 'itchy-scratchy' with other people. If someone makes you 'itch,' remember that scratching back only makes the argument worse. Show God's love instead."

"OK," agreed Ellie, grinning over at Tad. He grinned, too, and together they finished their cards. *MGH*

HOW ABOUT YOU?

What irritates you? A bossy big sister, or a whining little brother? When you feel annoyed with someone, ask God to help you show patience. It will be like a cool cloth, soothing away the "itchy-scratchy" feelings.

MEMORIZE:

"Love is patient and kind. Love is not jealous or boastful or proud."
1 Corinthians 13:4

SHOW PATIENT LOVE

THE BROKEN THREAD

(Read Matthew 7:7-11)

Linda was making a new shirt. It was the first time she was doing a sewing project all by herself, and she began to carefully sew the first seam. After only a few stitches, however, the thread broke and pulled loose from the needle. Linda threaded the needle again. After a few more stitches, the thread pulled loose again. Linda sighed and tried again. But the thread kept breaking. "What's wrong with you?" she demanded angrily.

She found Mother putting away groceries in the kitchen. "Mom, something's wrong with the sewing machine," complained Linda. "I can't finish my shirt." So Mother went to check. Linda followed her to the sewing room. "I prayed so hard that this shirt would turn out well," said Linda with a sigh. "When the thread started breaking, I even prayed that God would make the machine work so I could sew this seam! But he didn't."

Mother checked the machine. "Oh, it's threaded wrong!" she exclaimed. She showed Linda where she had made a mistake in threading the machine, and then she looked at the seams Linda had started. "You know, honey, I think maybe God answered your prayer after all," she said. "You're sewing the wrong pieces together."

"I am?" asked Linda in surprise.

Mother nodded. "If you had finished that seam, you would have had to take it all apart again," she said. "What you saw as an irritation saved you lots of work."

Mother showed Linda how to correct her mistake. Then she said thoughtfully, "This reminds me of how we often pray for God to help us, then become irritated when things don't go the way we plan. Sometimes when God says no to our prayers, it keeps us from making a mistake."

Linda grinned. "I guess so," she agreed. "I'm glad I didn't get what I asked for this time. If I had, I'd be picking stitches all afternoon."

Mother smiled. "Trusting God means being patient when we run into a problem," she said. "It may be God's way of getting us back on course." *KEC*

HOW ABOUT YOU?

When you ask God to help you, are you patient? Or do you get angry when something seems to go wrong? Remember that what you may think is a problem may be God's guidance, keeping you from making a painful mistake.

SEEK UNDERSTANDING

MEMORIZE:
"He leads the humble in what is right, teaching them his way." Psalm 25:9

"GOODY-GOODY"

(Read 1 Peter 3:12-17)

Joni put her baseball glove on the table and went to get a glass of milk from the refrigerator. "Wow, what a day!" she said to her mom.

"What happened?" asked Mother.

"During recess a bunch of girls were playing kickball, and Chandra King asked if she could play. A lot of girls make fun of Chandra because of the way she acts, but it's a rule that you have to let anyone play that wants to, so the girls said she could. Well, Chandra kicked the ball and took off running toward first base, except she tripped and fell flat on her face! You should've heard the girls tease her! I noticed she was actually hurt, so I went over, helped her to her feet, and went to the nurse's office with her. When I came out again, the girls started calling me a 'goody-goody.' "

"Then what?" Mother was giving Joni her full attention.

"Well, they stopped when the bell rang," explained Joni, "but two of the girls followed me home, kidding me and calling me 'Ms. Goody-Goody' all the way home."

"It's hard to be called names as a result of kindness, isn't it?" asked Mother sympathetically.

Joni nodded. "Yes," she admitted, "it sure is."

"You have to remember, Joni, that there's nothing wrong with being good," Mother told her. "As a Christian, you have the responsibility of being kind to others, but we can't expect everyone to understand. The apostle Paul wrote that the gospel is foolishness to those who don't believe in Christ. Because unbelievers choose to think the Bible is foolishness, they are also going to think we are foolish at times."

Joni nodded. "Those kids didn't understand how I could be friendly to Chandra, but I'm glad I was. Chandra needs friends!" *LMW*

HOW ABOUT YOU?

Is it hard for your non-Christian friends to understand why you won't join them in cheating, swearing, or treating someone unkindly? Do you get teased for doing what is right? God says it's better to suffer for doing good than for doing evil. Continue to follow his way, even when your friends don't understand.

MEMORIZE:

"I know very well how foolish the message of the cross sounds to those who are on the road to destruction. But we who are being saved recognize this message as the very power of God." 1 Corinthians 1:18

GOD'S WAY IS BEST

PEACE

(Read Colossians 3:15, Philippians 4:6-9)

The fire alarm was ringing! As the children got up from their seats, some were saying, "Oh, why do they always have fire drills when it's raining?" But wait! The alarm was not staying on! It was just ringing for a short period of time, stopping, and then starting again. Mrs. Elders said, "Now, children, you know what this means! It's a tornado drill! You all know what to do. Quiet now!"

Chad closed the curtains so any flying glass would not hit the children. The other children filed silently into the hall. They lined up against the inside wall, crouched down with their heads against the wall, and put their arms over their heads to protect themselves.

Kelly began to wonder how long they were going to have to stay in this uncomfortable position, when suddenly she realized that there were many sirens screaming outside. She began to tremble uncontrollably when she heard the principal's voice over the intercom saying, "This is not a drill! I repeat, this is not a drill! A tornado has been spotted. Please remain calm and stay in your positions!"

Some children began to cry, and Kelly heard several kids say, "I don't want to die!" However, the boy right next to Kelly seemed perfectly calm. "How can you be so calm, Michael?" Kelly asked, her voice shaking. "Listen to the wind and the alarm! Why aren't you afraid like the rest of us?"

"I did feel scared at first," Michael answered, "but I asked Jesus to help me not to be afraid."

Before long they realized that the tornado had missed the school. The students were allowed to return to their classrooms. Michael would probably never realize what a big effect his calm, peaceful attitude had on the other children. *REP*

HOW ABOUT YOU?

Do storms frighten you? Are you scared in the dark? Whatever fear you have, talk to Jesus about it. Then choose to let God's peace "rule in your heart." It will help others who are fearful themselves.

JESUS CAN CALM FEAR

MEMORIZE:
"But when the Holy Spirit controls our lives, he will produce this kind of fruit in us: love, joy, peace." Galatians 5:22

GOD'S MOUTHPIECE

(Read Exodus 4:10-12)

It was youth night at Centerville Church, and the young people were in charge of the entire evening service. They used their talents to serve the Lord as they sang, played instruments, worked in the nursery, put on a skit, ushered, took up the offering, and even preached.

After the special program, Mr. Jenkins approached Connie. "You did a fine job with your wooden puppet," he complimented. "The skit was cute, and it had a good message, too. I'm in charge of a special program that we're planning where I work. Would you do a skit there?"

Connie was so pleased with Mr. Jenkins's comments that she readily agreed. But when she thought about it later, she became apprehensive about what she had done. "I forgot that Mr. Jenkins works at that center for children who have been in trouble with the law," she told her mother. "I can't give a talk there!"

"Why not, dear?" asked Mother. "Those children need to hear about Jesus, too."

"But they're so tough," explained Connie. "They aren't church kids. They'll laugh at me. I can't do it—I just can't!"

To Connie's surprise, Mother agreed with her. "You're right, Connie," she said. "They're too tough! Just send your puppet with Mr. Jenkins. Let the puppet handle those kids."

Connie glanced at her mother in surprise. "Mom," she protested, "you know he can't talk without me! I put the words in his mouth."

Mother smiled and nodded. "That's how God works, too," she reminded Connie. "He'll give you his power and the words to say if you ask him." *JLH*

HOW ABOUT YOU?

Do you speak up for Jesus whenever you get a chance? Are you using your talents to serve him?

MEMORIZE:

"For I will give you the right words and such wisdom that none of your opponents will be able to reply!" Luke 21:15

SPEAK UP FOR GOD

THIS ISN'T SUGAR!

(Read Isaiah 5:18-21)

"Mom, can I bake a cake?" asked Cindy.

Mother smiled. "Sure, Cindy, but I'm going to be busy, so I won't be able to help. Follow the directions exactly."

"Oh, I will, Mom," promised Cindy eagerly.

Cindy did follow the directions. She carefully measured the correct amount of each ingredient she needed. But when the finished product looked and tasted awful, she was almost in tears.

"What's up?" asked Dad, walking into the kitchen. Cindy explained about the ruined cake. "Oh no!" Dad exclaimed. "I know what happened. I stopped at the grocery store on the way home last night, remember? Well, the bag ripped and a few things fell out. Nothing broke, but the box of salt was leaking. When I saw that the sugar canister was empty, I poured the salt into it and threw the box away. I meant to mention it, but then the phone rang and I forgot."

"So what I thought was sugar was really salt?" Cindy asked. "I can't believe I wouldn't have noticed that!"

"I'm surprised, too, but it's my fault, and I'm sorry, Cindy."

"What a perfect illustration for the pastor's message last Sunday," commented Mother. "He talked about the verse in Isaiah where people called evil good, remember? And they said light was darkness and the bitter was sweet. Of course, salt isn't bitter, but the idea is still the same."

"Right," Dad nodded. "That jar said sugar, but it was really salt, and so the cake was ruined. That's not so bad because you can make another cake. But if people say a thing is good when God says it's bad—and if they say things are bad when God says they're good—that can ruin an entire life. That's not so easy to fix!" *LMW*

HOW ABOUT YOU?

Do you know what things God says are good? Do you know what things God says are bad? In today's world many people change it around so that the good seems to be bad and the bad seems to be good. It's sad that so many people think that things like dishonesty, immorality, and cheating are sometimes OK. That isn't true. Know what God says in the Bible, and follow his guidelines.

**DON'T CALL BAD
THINGS GOOD**

MEMORIZE:
"Destruction is certain for those who say that evil is good and good is evil."
Isaiah 5:20

THE WRONG FINGER

(Read John 3:1-7)

"Well, I'm a Christian, that's for sure," Mia told her friend Karen. "My mom and dad go to church all the time. Dad's on the church board, and Mom teaches Sunday school." She paused, then added, "And last week they both talked about when they became Christians."

"So what?" retorted Karen. "That doesn't make you a Christian."

"Does too," insisted Mia.

Overhearing the conversation, Mia's mother decided to have a talk with her daughter. Soon the door opened, and Mia came in. "Mom," she said, holding up a finger, "can I have a Band-Aid?"

Mother looked at the cut on Mia's finger and nodded. "Sure," she said. "I'll get one." After getting the Band-Aid, she tore it open and carefully put it on her own finger. "There," she said. "That should take care of the problem."

Mia stared at her mother. "Mom! It's my finger that's hurt!" she exclaimed.

Mother looked at her. "You mean the bandage on my finger doesn't help yours?"

"Of course not!" Mia couldn't understand her mother's behavior at all.

"Well, I don't know," Mother said. "A little while ago I heard you claim that because Dad and I are Christians, you are, too. We took the cure for sin—we accepted Jesus as Savior. If that makes you a Christian, too, then I think this Band-Aid on my finger should also take care of your cut."

Mia stared thoughtfully at her mother. "I guess you're right," she admitted. "I need to accept Jesus myself, don't I? Can we talk about what it means to accept Jesus?" *HWM*

HOW ABOUT YOU?

Are your parents Christians? If you answered yes, that's wonderful. But here's the real question—have you accepted Jesus as your Savior? If you want to know more, talk to a trusted friend or adult.

MEMORIZE:

"For you have been born again. Your new life did not come from your earthly parents because the life they gave you will end in death. But this new life will last forever because it comes from the eternal, living word of God." 1 Peter 1:23

YOU MUST BE BORN AGAIN

GROWING UP (PART 1)

(Read Psalm 139:13-16)

Judy and Bob were so happy to have a new baby brother. Judy especially liked to help Mother take care of little Jason. But one day when the children came home from school, they found Dad in deep thought and Mother wiping her eyes. "Mother! What's wrong?" Judy exclaimed. "You took Jason to the doctor today, didn't you? Is there something wrong with him?"

"Yes, Judy, there is," answered Mother. "Jason isn't growing normally. He's not doing the things he should be doing at his age. The doctor calls it being developmentally disabled or handicapped. Many people would say he's retarded."

Bob and Judy were stunned! Their baby brother was retarded? How could God allow such a thing to happen? "But why, Mother?" they asked. "Why?"

Dad answered. "We don't know why. Some day, perhaps in heaven, we'll know why. But for now we'll just go on loving him and caring for him."

Judy burst into tears. "Not normal!" she exclaimed. "Jason's not normal!"

Dad spoke again. "This is hard to accept," he said, "but God will help us to help Jason. Jason needs us more, so we'll love him more. In giving him love and happiness, we'll gain love and happiness, too." *AGL*

HOW ABOUT YOU?

Do you know any disabled persons? For reasons known only to him, God made some people special, with either physical or mental handicaps. Make an effort to smile at them and talk to them. Never stare at them, make fun of them, or say unkind things about them. There are many wonderful, lovable human beings with special problems, and they have much to offer. Remember, God made them. He loves them, and you can love them, too.

MEMORIZE:
"'Who makes mouths?' the Lord asked him. 'Who makes people so they can speak or not speak, hear or not hear, see or not see? Is it not I, the Lord?'" Exodus 4:11

LOVE THE DISABLED

GROWING UP (PART 2)

(Read 1 Peter 2:1-5)

After Judy and Bob learned that their baby brother would never be able to do some of the things most children do, their attitudes toward him seemed to change. Bob played with him more than before and encouraged him to learn new things. But Judy gave him less and less attention. She helped take care of him when she had to, but whenever possible, she busied herself with some other task.

"Judy," said Mother one day, "you used to love to take Jason for a ride in the park. Why is it you never want to do that anymore?"

Judy blushed. "It . . . it just isn't the same as before," she stammered.

"What isn't the same, honey?" asked Mother.

"Jason!" Judy cried. "Jason's not the same! He's not like other babies. Taking care of him isn't fun anymore."

"But Jason is the same," Mother told her. "He's still the same sweet baby he always was. *You* have changed! You're not the same sweet, happy girl that you were."

"But Mother," objected Judy, "you can't blame me for being disappointed!"

"We are all disappointed," Mother replied, "but we didn't all grow bitter. Judy, you became a Christian several years ago. If you were growing spiritually, as you should be, you would be concerned about Jason instead of yourself. You wouldn't be ashamed. Judy, you are disabled, too! You see, dear, I have two disabled children—one mentally disabled, and one spiritually disabled."

"Oh, Mother," Judy said, her eyes glistening with tears. "I never thought of myself that way! Please forgive me. Here—give Jason to me! I'll take care of him. And I'll hug and love him, too. Oh Jason, you *are* sweet."

Mother smiled. "And so are you, dear—now! You are growing again." *AGL*

HOW ABOUT YOU?

Are you growing spiritually? Are you learning to be more cheerful and to be more kind to your brothers and sisters? Are you being more and more helpful around the house? Growing physically and mentally is important, but we often forget that growing spiritually is even more important.

MEMORIZE:

"But grow in the special favor and knowledge of our Lord and Savior Jesus Christ." 2 Peter 3:18

GROW SPIRITUALLY

DON'T BE A CHICKEN

(Read 2 Peter 1:4-9)

Randy followed Grandpa into the chicken coop, and Grandpa closed the door as the chickens crowded noisily around them. Randy scattered a handful of grain over the floor. The chickens scrambled madly for it. But one chicken was having trouble. Every time it tried to eat, the others pecked it. Randy saw a small, red spot on the chicken's neck.

"Look, Grandpa!" he exclaimed. "That chicken is hurt!"

Just then a big rooster jabbed the sore on the neck of the chicken, making it even larger. Grandpa picked up the chicken and carried the squawking bird out of the pen. "Come on, old girl. We'll put you in a separate place until your neck heals."

Randy watched as Grandpa rubbed medicine into the sore. "Why do the other chickens peck this one?" he asked.

"Well, Randy, I can't tell you exactly why," answered Grandpa, "but this is typical chicken behavior. They always pick on those who are hurt or different from the rest. And they always peck right at the spot that is already sore or hurt."

"That seems stupid," said Randy.

"Right you are, Randy," said Grandpa. "But do you know that people often do the same thing?"

"They do?" asked Randy, surprised. "How?"

"When others have skin that is a different color, or perhaps their eyes, nose, or ears look a little different, some people make fun of them," explained Grandpa. Randy immediately thought of a boy named Darrin. Some of the other boys teased Darrin about his bright, red-orange hair. Randy was glad now that he had not joined in the teasing—but he hadn't made any effort to be friendly, either. "It's too bad when people act like chickens," continued Grandpa.

Randy nodded. When he got home, he was going to invite Darrin to play with him. *CEY*

HOW ABOUT YOU?

Do you accept those who do not look or talk the way you do? Perhaps there is a "different" person in your school or neighborhood who needs your friendship. God loves that person. Will you show him or her God's love?

ACCEPT OTHERS' DIFFERENCES

MEMORIZE:

"So now I am giving you a new commandment: Love each other. Just as I have loved you, you should love each other." John 13:34

FREE AS THE AIR

(Read Romans 4:4-8)

"I can't understand Sherri," complained Rachel as she looked down at the candy in her hand. "A couple of days ago she gave me a cute little eraser to pay me back for helping her with her math. Now she gave me this Tootsie Roll to pay me back for a cookie I gave her yesterday. It's not that I don't want the candy, but it's getting so I'm not sure I should ever do anything for her because she always thinks she has to give me something back."

Mother nodded. "Some people are like that. It takes the fun out of doing things for them, doesn't it? But I don't think you should stop helping her."

"I guess so," said Rachel. "But you know, Mom, she even thinks she has to pay God for everything he gives. When we were talking after Bible club the other day, she told me she didn't see how anybody could accept the idea that they could go to heaven just by believing. She said she intends to earn her way by being baptized and joining the church and by living a good, honest life."

"Oh, that is serious!" exclaimed Mother. "Let's pray that she'll see how foolish that is."

A couple days later, Rachel and Sherri conducted an experiment in their science class. By combining several chemicals, they made a gas that smelled just like rotten eggs! "Oh, air! Air! Give me air!" gasped Sherri as she rushed to a window. Rachel, too, eagerly gulped cold air. Suddenly Rachel got an idea. "Hold your breath," she commanded, "until you pay for the air!"

"What! Are you crazy?" asked Sherri.

"But you said you wouldn't take something for nothing, remember?" reminded Rachel. "Yet every day, all day, you breathe the air God gave us and don't pay for it. If you can accept God's gift of air, why is it so hard to accept his gift of salvation?"

"You might be right," Sherri said slowly. "Maybe I better think that over again." *HWM*

HOW ABOUT YOU?

The air that God gives us is a wonderful gift, isn't it? It would be foolish to think we could ever pay for it. Salvation is an even more wonderful gift. You can never earn it.

MEMORIZE:

"For the wages of sin is death, but the free gift of God is eternal life through Christ Jesus our Lord." Romans 6:23

SALVATION CANNOT BE EARNED

AN IMPORTANT SEAL

(Read 2 Timothy 2:19-22)

Callie watched as her father made a stamp on several letters with an embosser. "What are you doing, Dad?" she asked.

"This is our company's seal, Callie. It displays our trademark and our motto," explained Dad. "The raised marks make it impossible for anyone to erase it."

"What's your company motto?" asked Callie.

"'Old-fashioned service with new-fashioned materials,'" said Dad with a smile.

"Do all companies have seals?" Callie wondered.

"Some do," answered Dad. "So do the fifty states. Our Wisconsin seal says, 'Forward.' Our country has a seal, too. It's a Latin phrase that means, 'Out of many, one.'"

Callie grinned. "Hey, that's neat," she said.

"There's another important seal, too, Callie," said Dad. "Take your Bible and look up 2 Timothy 2:19."

Callie got her Bible and quickly turned to the New Testament. She found the verse and read, "Nevertheless, the foundation of God standeth sure, having this seal, The Lord knoweth them that are his (KJV)."

"You see, Callie, when we became Christians we were sealed with the Holy Spirit," said Dad, "and I guess we could say that the motto of our seal is 'The Lord knoweth them that are his.'"

Callie thought about that. "It's kinda like your company's seal, Dad," she decided. "It's something that can't be erased. And when people see that special mark on a letter, they know it's from your business. When we're sealed with the Holy Spirit, people should be able to see that we belong to the Lord!" *LMW*

HOW ABOUT YOU?

Have you ever seen a seal with a motto or a picture representing a country or a business? If you're a Christian, you were sealed with the Holy Spirit when you accepted Christ. You belong to the Lord, and nothing can change that. But, remember, others should be able to see by your life that you have his seal upon you.

**THE HOLY SPIRIT
IS OUR SEAL**

MEMORIZE:
"Having believed, you were marked in him with a seal, the promised Holy Spirit." Ephesians 1:13, NIV

STAR OR SUN?

(Read Mark 9:33-35)

Revival meetings were being held at Sharon's church, and many people had become Christians. Many others had rededicated their lives to God. This all bothered Sharon! You see, her dad was pastor of the church, but for some time nobody had become a Christian. Then the special evangelist came, and lots of the people to whom her dad had preached every week accepted Jesus under this new man's ministry.

Sharon's father wondered what was bothering her. "You seem awfully quiet lately, honey. Don't you like Reverend Henderson?" he asked after the meeting one evening.

"Yes, but you're every bit as good as he is, Dad!" Sharon responded. "Now all these people are becoming Christians under his preaching, and he's getting all the credit."

Dad was quiet for a moment, then asked her to come with him outdoors. "Now, which star is the brightest in the sky?" he asked.

Sharon gazed upward. "That one up there is," she decided. "Or . . . no, maybe that one way over there. Or is it . . . I don't know! Why do you ask, Dad?"

He smiled. "It's hard to decide, isn't it? Now think in the morning when the sun comes up, which star will be the brightest?"

"Well, I don't know," she began. Then she thought of something. "It won't make any difference because the sun is the brightest of all!"

"Exactly," said Dad, "and it's that way in the ministry, too. We sometimes try to decide which preacher is the best, but it doesn't make any difference. When Jesus, God's Son, is preached, he is the best and brightest of all." *REP*

HOW ABOUT YOU?

Do you think one pastor is better than another because he seems to lead some people to the Lord? Or maybe you have witnessed to somebody yourself and then thought it was unfair because another person led him or her to Jesus. Be careful. Remember that we should not worry who will be greatest in God's kingdom. Jesus will be the greatest of all!

MEMORIZE:

"The ones who do the planting or watering aren't important, but God is important because he is the one who makes the seed grow."
1 Corinthians 3:7

**PRAISE CHRIST,
NOT MEN**

FEEDING THE FIRE

(Read Proverbs 6:12-19)

Tami was on the phone when Mother came into the room. ". . . and that's what she said, Staci. She said that you're stupid! But don't tell Marsha that I told you, OK? See you tomorrow."

When Tami hung up the phone, Mother asked, "Why did you tell Staci that Marsha said she was stupid?"

"Because she did," Tami replied quickly. "Staci and Marsha fuss all the time." Mother raised her eyebrows. "Could it be because you add fuel to the fire?"

"What do you mean?" asked Tami.

"Come into the family room." Mother led the way to the fireplace. She pointed at the smoldering fire. "What would happen if I added a log to the fire, Tami?"

"It would get bigger," Tami replied.

"What if I didn't add any wood to it?" Mother asked.

"It would die out," Tami answered.

"Right! And it's like that when there's a quarrel between two people. It usually dies out if there isn't anyone to stir it up and keep it going. God hates gossiping, Tami. And usually it's the gossip spreader who gets hurt." The ring of the telephone interrupted her.

"I'll get it. It's probably Marsha. She was going to call me." Tami was glad to end the conversation.

Later when Mother called the family to dinner, Tami came to the table with red, puffy eyes. "What's the matter, Tami?"

"Marsha and Staci are going to the riding stables tomorrow." Tami choked back a sob. "Marsha can't invite both of us, 'cuz her mother says we fuss too much when we're all together. So she asked Staci because she's mad at me for telling Staci what she said about her."

"I'm not surprised," Mother said. "Didn't I warn you that it's usually the gossip spreader who gets hurt?" *BJW*

HOW ABOUT YOU?

Are you tempted to "carry tales" or gossip? It's dangerous. Not only will it hurt others, but you'll be hurt yourself. God suggests a better way—he says, "Blessed are the peacemakers." If you know two people who don't get along well, do what you can to keep peace between them.

MEMORIZE:

"Disregarding another person's faults preserves love; telling about them separates close friends."
Proverbs 17:9

DON'T CARRY TALES

THE HIDDEN GARDEN

(Read Galatians 5:19-25)

As Ken and Becky explored behind the barn at their new home in the country, Becky pointed to some plants. "Look over there, Ken—under those tall weeds! Are those tomato plants?" she asked. Sure enough, they were! The children found other vegetables as well. Evidently someone had planted a garden but had not been able to take care of it, and the weeds had grown more than waist high.

"Let's show Mom and Dad!" exclaimed Ken.

"How about that!" said Mother when the children took their parents to see the hidden garden. "I didn't know these plants were here. I could only see the weeds."

"You know something?" Dad spoke up. "Our heart is a little like a garden. When we trust Jesus as Savior, he plants seeds of such things as happiness, joy, patience, and self-control in the 'garden' of our heart. It's up to us, with God's help, to keep the weeds of sin from coming back." *CVM*

HOW ABOUT YOU?

Are you careful to keep the "weeds of sin" from growing in the garden of your heart? When you tell a lie, cheat, or disobey, be sure to confess that sin immediately. Don't allow it to grow and cover up the fruit of the Spirit.

MEMORIZE:

"Their life will be like a watered garden." Jeremiah 31:12

DON'T ALLOW SIN TO GROW

INSTANT EVERYTHING

(Read Galatians 6:1-5)

Since Mom and Dad would be gone, Chris would have to get supper for herself and her brother, Doug. "There is pizza," Mother was saying. "Just follow the directions on the box. There's also instant pudding. You know how to do that."

"And there's a salad in the refrigerator," said Chris.

Mother put on her coat. "Yes, and if you need Dad or me, the phone number is on the table in the dining room."

Chris had no trouble with the meal. Doug even admitted that it was pretty good!

The next day when Chris got home from school, she was very upset with one of her friends. "You know what Sandy did today, Mom?" she exclaimed. "Our teacher didn't collect our homework assignments. Instead, she just asked everyone if they had it done. Sandy told me this morning that she hadn't finished it, but when Miss Derks asked her, Sandy said she had it done! She lied! And she calls herself a Christian!"

"You have to remember that Sandy has only been a Christian for a little while," responded Mom.

"But, Mom," shrieked Chris, "she lied! You make it sound like it doesn't even matter!"

"I'm not excusing what Sandy did," answered Mom. "I'm just suggesting that you shouldn't be too hard on her. You do wrong things too, you know."

"I know, but that's different. She—"

"Hold on a minute," said Mom. "I'm afraid that in this day and age we get the idea that everything should be 'instant'—like the pizza you made last night. It was easy and quick to make. But spiritual maturity doesn't come that way. It's more like the salad I made. It takes a lot of time to become mature."

"I get it!" said Chris thoughtfully. "I was expecting too much from Sandy too soon." *DSM*

HOW ABOUT YOU?

Do you have any friends who are new Christians? Remember, when you ask Jesus into your heart, you instantly become a Christian, but you aren't instantly grown-up. Be patient with your friends.

GROWTH TAKES TIME

MEMORIZE:
"We should please others. If we do what helps them, we will build them up in the Lord." Romans 15:2

TRASH OR TREASURE?

(Read James 2:5-9)

Pam was glad she and her parents had come to spend a weekend in the country with Aunt Clara and Uncle Bill. With her uncle's permission, she decided to go digging in the old trash pile behind the barn. To her delight, she found an old fruit jar with "1898" stamped on the bottom. Pam took it into the house to show her aunt and mother. "I saw one like it in the antique store, priced at twenty dollars," she told them.

Aunt Clara smiled. "Well, good," she said. "You found it, and you may keep it." Pam squealed with pleasure. Then Aunt Clara asked, "Do you remember Rebecca, who lives across the road? She's coming over this afternoon."

"Oh, no!" groaned Pam. "I don't like her. She isn't a Christian, and I don't think she ever will be. She doesn't seem like the kind, if you know what I mean."

"Pamela!" scolded her mother. "You aren't acting like a Christian, either. And no, I don't know what you mean."

Aunt Clara looked thoughtful. "Pam," she said, "go clean that old fruit jar and then bring it back to me." Pam was surprised, but she did as she was told.

"It's quite pretty, now that it's cleaned up," said Aunt Clara later, taking the jar. "Strange, isn't it, that for years it was in the rubbish pile. Until today. No one realized its value and saved it. In a way, Rebecca is like this jar."

"What does it have to do with her?" asked Pam.

"A lot," Aunt Clara told her, "and with me, and with you, too. We were both dirty from our sin, but God recognized our value. He picked us up, washed us, and gave us a new shine. Rebecca may not have been "cleaned up" yet, but she is very valuable! So valuable that Jesus died for her."

Pam answered, "I hadn't thought about it like that." *BJW*

HOW ABOUT YOU?

Is there someone that you think is too unpopular to play with? What does it really matter if a person's clothes are wrinkled or torn or if the person doesn't always use correct English? God looks beyond all that and sees a precious treasure.

MEMORIZE:

"Stop judging by mere appearances, and make a right judgment."
John 7:24, NIV

EVERYONE IS VALUABLE

WHOSE FAULT?

(Read Ezekiel 34:11-16)

Christy's whole body shook with sobs. "Oh, honey," said Aunt Mary, comforting her, "see if you can stop crying so you can tell me what's wrong."

With great effort, Christy did her best to control her crying. Her breath caught in her throat as she said, "Dad and Mom just told me they're getting a divorce. I think it's all my fault." Fresh tears rolled down her cheeks.

Aunt Mary put her arms around Christy. "I can understand how hurt you are, but you must not blame yourself, Christy. Your behavior had nothing to do with your parents' divorce."

"But if I had been a better daughter, maybe Dad and Mom would have gotten along," Christy answered. "I haven't kept my room clean and haven't always obeyed like I should. If I hadn't caused them trouble or made them worry, they might have had a better marriage."

"Many children feel that way," said Aunt Mary, "but believe me, it's not your fault. You certainly should obey and be as helpful and cheerful as you can, but failing to do so is not the cause of the divorce."

"Are you sure?" asked Christy tearfully.

"Absolutely!" replied Aunt Mary. "I know you're hurting because of this, but blaming yourself won't help." She picked up her Bible from the coffee table and turned the pages. "God has some comforting words for those whose hearts hurt deeply. Here in Ezekiel, chapter 34, it says, 'I will bind up the injured.' You're 'injured' now, Christy. But God has promised that he'll bind up your hurts."

Christy wiped her eyes. "How will he do that?" she asked.

"God will put people into your life who will help you through this hard time," said Aunt Mary. "Read your Bible and pray every day, so he can help you by reminding you of his promises. Little by little, you'll begin to feel better. Would you like for us to pray together?"

Christy nodded. Although she still felt very sad, she prayed quietly while Aunt Mary prayed aloud. *CEY*

HOW ABOUT YOU?

Are you hurting because your parents have been divorced? If you are blaming yourself for that, realize that it is something between only them. Divorce is not fun for anyone, but God will help you through the hurting time if you'll trust him.

**GOD CAN HEAL
BROKEN HEARTS**

MEMORIZE:
"I will bind up the injured and strengthen the weak." Ezekiel 34:16

MOVING BLUES

(Read Ephesians 4:13-15)

It was an unhappy day for Scott and Sandy. They were leaving their familiar neighborhood and school and moving to a town several miles away. Mother tried to cheer them up. "You'll soon have new friends there," she comforted, "and you'll love our new house and yard." Sandy just shook her head as she carried a bowl with fish to the car.

One day not long after they moved into their new house, Dad came home from work with a large aquarium. "Dad," Sandy exclaimed, "is that for our little goldfish?"

"Yep," replied Dad. "Your little fish need a larger living space as much as we did." He watched as Scott and Sandy transferred the fish to their new home.

A few months later, Scott called his sister over to the aquarium. "Hey, Sandy, look at these fish!" he exclaimed. "They've grown."

Dad looked up from his newspaper. "Goldfish need space in order to grow," he told them, "so the change to a bigger aquarium was good for them. Change is often good for people, too. It gives them new opportunities. For example, since we moved here, you've met new friends who have interests that are new to you. That's growth."

"Yeah," said Sandy. "I like it here now."

"Me, too," agreed Scott, "but I hope we don't have to move soon again."

Dad smiled. "Moving is sometimes God's plan for bringing us new opportunities, but not always," he assured them. "But even when we don't move, things around us are always changing. We need to be open to the lessons God wants to teach us through the changes he brings into our lives." *PR*

HOW ABOUT YOU?

Are you afraid of change? Many people are, but change brings growth. Ask God to show you how the changes in your life can help you to win someone to him, to develop the talents he's given you, or to teach you more about him.

MEMORIZE:

"Instead, we will hold to the truth in love, becoming more and more in every way like Christ, who is the head of his body, the church."
Ephesians 4:15

GROW IN CHRIST

JUNE
2

A TRIP BACK IN TIME (PART 1)

(Read Matthew 5:14-16)

The Bell family had read about a resort that "takes you back in time to the year 1800." They thought it would be great fun! So, for one week they left electricity, running water, and all modern conveniences to live in a log cabin. They were eager to see what it would have been like to live "way back then." Soon they found out!

At first Brandon and Mary had worried about how they would spend their evenings. They hadn't brought any games, and of course there was no TV. But they soon discovered that the simple games pioneer children played were lots of fun. On the other hand, some things that had sounded like so much fun (splitting wood and bringing water from a well, for instance) very quickly proved to be a lot of work! Living pioneer style left them very tired, and they were ready to go to bed in the loft quite early.

"What's wrong with the oil lamp?" asked Brandon one night. "It isn't throwing as much light as usual."

"That's because you turned the wick up way too high when you lit it," Mary told him. "That made the glass chimney smoky!"

Brandon was ready to argue, but Mother interrupted. "It used to be the girl's chore to clean and polish the lamps," she said. "So how about you taking care of that tomorrow, Mary?"

The next day, Mary made a trip to the well, heated the water on the cookstove, shaved some lye soap into the hot water, and began to clean all the lamp chimneys. "You know what?" she said after working awhile. "My Bible verse last week was about letting our lights shine before men. I know that means we should be a good witness for Jesus, but I was thinking about these oil lamps. Smoke on the chimney messes up the light, and sin in my life will mess up my witness and keep the light from shining brightly."

Mother smiled and nodded. "Good thinking!" she said. *REP*

HOW ABOUT YOU?

Is the light of your witness shining bright and clear, or is the "glass chimney" of your life all smoky with sin? If you need to rid your life of sin, confess it and be clean.

MEMORIZE:

"But if we confess our sins to him, he is faithful and just to forgive us and to cleanse us from every wrong."
1 John 1:9

KEEP YOUR LIGHT CLEAN

A TRIP BACK IN TIME (PART 2)

(Read Mark 12:28-31)

By the end of the week, Brandon and Mary were beginning to think it wouldn't have been much fun to be a pioneer. Modern life began to look better and better. As they went together to get water from the well one evening, they made a game of saying what they were going to do when they reached "civilization" again.

"I'm going to blow-dry my hair!" began Mary.

"I'm going to call Frank on the telephone and tell him to come over and see these muscles in my arms. This vacation sure has toughened me up!" boasted Brandon.

Mary giggled. "I'm going to drink some soda pop!"

"I'm going to watch a baseball game on TV. I don't even know which team is in first place anymore." Brandon shook his head sadly.

"I'm going to bake some cookies in our good old oven," said Mary, and on and on they went until they brought the water into the cabin.

After supper, the family had devotions as usual. Then they talked about their vacation. All agreed that it had been a great experience to go back in time. They agreed that pioneer life was lots harder than they had expected it to be. "Brandon, you look awfully thoughtful," observed Mother.

"Well, I don't exactly know how to say it, but I . . . um . . . I've liked having our devotions as a family out here more than I do at home," Brandon stammered.

Mary agreed. "Out here we aren't in such a hurry to be done so we can watch TV or go out to play or something," she said. "I've felt closer to God out here than I do at home. I've read my Bible more this week than I have in a long time."

The family was quiet for a while until Dad interrupted their thoughts. "I think you both have discovered what I've felt for a long time," he said. "I think our family has allowed TV and other things to crowd God out of the center of our life. Before we go back to the city, let's all determine to put God first—at home as well as here in this cabin." *REP*

HOW ABOUT YOU?

Do you allow things to crowd God out of your life? Is playing ball more important to you than God is? How about watching TV? Or how about that video game? Anything in your life that comes ahead of God is an idol.

PUT GOD BEFORE THINGS

MEMORIZE:
"Dear children, keep away from anything that might take God's place in your hearts." 1 John 5:21

JUNE
4

WHY DO I HAVE TO?

(Read Ephesians 4:30-32; Philippians 2:14)

"Why do *I* always have to take out the trash?" grumbled Chad. He glared at his sister. "Why can't you help, Angela?"

"*Me?* Look at all these dishes I have to do!" complained Angela. "I don't think Mom did any today while we were in school. And she can't help now, because she just found out the Watsons are coming for supper, so she had to go to the store. When she gets back, she'll have to start supper."

Their brother, Jon, had some complaints, too. "Have you seen the garage?" he asked. "I have to clean it. I'd gladly trade jobs with either of you!" He headed for the door.

Finally, the three children finished their chores—though they didn't do them happily.

Suppertime came, and so did Mr. and Mrs. Watson. After everyone enjoyed the delicious meal, Mother looked at the children. "Chad and Jon, would you two clear the table, please?" she said. "And, Angela, you can load the dishwasher."

Immediately the children set to work. Mr. Watson watched for a few minutes. "What helpful kids you have!" he exclaimed. "And you had to ask them only once."

"This time—that is. Angela here doesn't always jump so fast," teased Chad.

"Yeah—you should have heard her complain this afternoon about a few dishes she had to take care of," added Jon.

Angela blushed. "OK, I admit I'm not always so quick to help, but look who's talking," she said. "Earlier today I didn't see you guys hurrying to do your chores either. And I didn't see any big smiles on your faces while you did them."

"Oops! I'm sorry I mentioned it!" Chad grinned. "It's true," he admitted. "Dad and Mom have taught us to be obedient, but I'm afraid we don't always have the right attitude or move as quickly as we should. I guess it's easier to be obedient when others are around watching us."

Mr. Watson nodded. "Yes, that's true," he agreed. "Next time you're tempted to grumble, remind yourself that Someone is watching. That 'Someone' is God. Maybe that will help you to want to do things more quickly and cheerfully." *BR*

HOW ABOUT YOU?

Do you respond quickly and cheerfully when your parents ask you to do something? Or do you often grumble and complain? Don't forget that God is always watching and listening. He wants you to be a cheerful "doer."

MEMORIZE:

"In everything you do, stay away from complaining and arguing."
Philippians 2:14

DO THINGS CHEERFULLY

HOLD YOUR NOSE

(Read 2 Corinthians 2:14-17)

"Rod," Mother called. "Take out the trash, please."

Rod scowled. "I don't see why lazy Becky can't take it out for once," he answered sarcastically.

Becky looked angry. "Tell my ugly brother . . ."

"Why must you children constantly bicker and fight?" interrupted Mother sadly. "Why can't you show more love to each other?"

The trash didn't get emptied after all, for the trash can was missing from the alley. Days passed, and they still had not purchased a new one. "Phee-yew!" exclaimed Rod one day. He held his nose. "Something stinks!"

"It's the trash!" exclaimed Mother, opening the door of the closet where it was piled. "Here. Let's put these smelly bags in the carport until we can get a trash can."

"Make Becky help, too," grumbled Rod.

"Shut up, Dum-Dum," retorted Becky.

"That will do!" Mother said sternly. "You'll both help." When they were finished, Mother made them both sit on chairs in the kitchen. "I'm wondering how long it's been since you cleaned the trash out of your lives." The children looked at the floor as she continued. "Things like bad attitudes, selfishness, and jealousy need to be cleaned out regularly."

Becky and Rod looked at each other. They both nodded. "I'm sorry," they said together. Then they laughed.

"Good," said Mother. "I hope you'll tell God you're sorry, too. And remember—sorry is more than just words." *BJW*

HOW ABOUT YOU?

Have you noticed any things that need to be cleaned out of your life lately? Ask God to show you what needs to be cleaned out so that your actions and attitude suggest a sweet aroma to all who know you.

MEMORIZE:
"Create in me a clean heart, O God.
Renew a right spirit within me."
Psalm 51:10

KEEP YOUR LIFE CLEAN

BY ANY OTHER NAME

(Read Romans 3:10-12, 20-23)

"Come on, Tyler. Eat your beans." Roxanne was trying to get the baby to finish his supper. But Tyler turned his head away, mouth firmly closed.

"He thinks he doesn't like beans—call them something else," suggested Matthew. He put a bean on a spoon and held it out to Tyler. "Here—have some ice cream, Tyler," he coaxed. But his little brother just looked at the bean on the spoon and turned away.

Roxanne laughed. "What a dumb idea," she scoffed. Then she quoted, "A rose by any other name would smell as sweet." She laughed again. "And a bean by any other name would taste the same. Even Tyler knows that."

Dad smiled at the dialogue between the children. Then he added a thought of his own. "And going to church doesn't make a person a Christian," he said. Roxanne and Matthew looked at him in surprise. "I was thinking of a conversation I had with a couple of the men at work today," explained Dad. "They're both nice, decent guys—in fact, they're so 'good' that it's hard to get them to see that they need Christ."

"What do you mean, they're so good?" asked Matthew. "My Bible verse last week said nobody is good."

Dad nodded. "I mean they're good in their own eyes," he said. "Pete is a young, good-looking fellow, a hard worker, and a faithful church member. Jeff, who also goes to church, is a little older. He manages a Little League team, heads the fund-raising committee for the city youth center, and is active in the fight against pornography. Each thinks he's going to get to heaven because of all the good things he does."

"So what do you tell them?" asked Roxanne.

"Well, basically, what I said before," replied Dad. "Going to church doesn't make a person a Christian. I try to show them that, although their work is commendable, they still need Christ." *HWM*

HOW ABOUT YOU?

Are you a "good kid"? One your parents and teachers can be proud of? That's great, but not great enough to get you to heaven. God says everyone has sinned, and that means you, too. Only by accepting Jesus as Savior can your sin be washed away and can you have the promise of heaven.

MEMORIZE:

"No one does good, not even one."
Romans 3:12

NO ONE IS GOOD

DARLA DELAYS (PART 1)

(Read Ephesians 6:1-3)

Darla yawned as she came down the stairs. "Good morning, sleepyhead," Mother greeted her. "I'm leaving now for the mall, but I'll be home by noon. I want you to weed the flowers today. I asked you to do it last week, but you didn't get it done."

"Oh, Mother, I hate bugs and spiders and weeding," wailed Darla. "And I did clean the garage instead."

"But I asked you to do the weeding," Mother reminded. "Be sure it gets done today. Bye, now."

Darla sighed as she prepared to go out to the garden. Suddenly she remembered something—Mother's birthday! Today was Mother's birthday! *Wouldn't it be nice if Mother could have a birthday cake?* she thought. I know how to make one. So Darla bustled about the kitchen, and the cake was ready just in time—only minutes before Mother arrived home.

How pleased and surprised Mother was when she saw the lovely cake! And when she had a piece for dessert, she declared it was the best she had ever eaten! "But how did you have time to weed the flowers and bake a cake, too?" she wondered. Then seeing Darla's expression, she added, "You did weed the flowers, didn't you?"

When Darla admitted that she had not, Mother sighed. "I appreciate the work you did in the garage last Saturday," Mother told her. "And I appreciate this lovely cake. But the fact remains that the weeds are still in the garden."

"But I thought you would want a cake," protested Darla.

"A cake is nice, honey, but I wanted even more for you to obey me," answered Mother. "For that would be the best birthday present indeed." *BJW*

HOW ABOUT YOU?

Do you think that as long as you do something helpful—perhaps even something sacrificial—it doesn't matter if you don't do exactly as you're told? Today's verse points out how important obedience is.

**OBEDIENCE IS
IMPORTANT**

MEMORIZE:
"Obedience is far better than sacrifice." 1 Samuel 15:22

JUNE
8

DARLA DELAYS (PART 2)

(Read Psalm 19:12-14)

Darla struggled to pull weeds from the flower bed while Grandpa Wilson, who lived next door, watched. As they talked, he learned that she was missing a shopping trip because she had failed to weed the garden when she was told. "That's too bad," said Grandpa, "but why did you put it off so long? I always enjoyed working in the garden and watching the miracle of growing things. If it weren't for this crippled leg, I'd love to help you."

"But, Grandpa, I hate bugs," moaned Darla.

Grandpa smiled. "I guess some people do," he said, "but all the sweet, good things of life have a few unpleasant things mixed with them. Flower beds have spiders and weeds. Life has problems and responsibilities."

"Ugh!" Darla puffed as she pulled a particularly large weed. "These things sure are big and stubborn."

Grandpa nodded. "They would have been much easier to pull last week," he pointed out. "The sooner they're pulled, the better." After a moment he added, "It's the same way with bad habits in our life—the longer they grow, the harder it is to get rid of them. Your life is like a flower garden, Darla, full of sweet, beautiful things . . . but if you don't keep the bad habits and sins pulled out, your life will lose its beauty." *BJW*

HOW ABOUT YOU?

What "weeds" need to be pulled out of your life? Disobedience? Gossiping? Unkindness? Whatever they are, pull them out. Ask the Lord to help you. The sooner you do it, the better it will be.

MEMORIZE:

"Cleanse me from these hidden faults." Psalm 19:12

WEED OUT BAD HABITS

BIRDS AND FLIES

(Read Matthew 7:21-27)

"Look, there's a ladybird!" cried Kristie.

Annie dropped her doll on the grass and ran across the lawn. "Where?" she demanded, looking up at the sky. She frowned. "I don't see any birds or any lady, either," she protested. "Besides Mom, that is," she added, smiling at her mother.

Kristie squealed with laughter. "Annie, you're such a baby! A ladybird isn't a bird—or a lady." She pointed to a small red and black creature crawling its way up the stem of Mom's tomato plant. "That's a ladybird."

Annie stared. "Well!" she exclaimed, placing her hands on her hips. "How was I to know that? Why is it called a ladybird when it's not a bird at all? It's a bug." She tossed her head and picked up her doll again.

"Some people refer to it as a 'ladybug,'" said Mom. "That name really does fit it better, doesn't it?" She smiled. "I can think of another creature with a name that doesn't really fit. What did Dad show you last night?"

"Fireflies!" squealed Annie.

"Oh, yeah," said Kristie. "Dad said they aren't flies at all. They're beetles."

"That's right," said Mom. After a moment she added, "Sometimes people use names that don't match what they really are, either. For example, we can call ourselves 'Christian,' but that doesn't make us Christians."

"That's right!" said Kristie. "Only those people who know Jesus are true Christians!" *MTF*

HOW ABOUT YOU?

Are you a Christian? If you answered 'Yes,' try these questions: Are you a Christian only by name? Or have you really committed your life to Jesus? Do you really try to live as he has asked you to live? Jesus doesn't want you to just be called a Christian. He wants you to be a Christian—a follower of him.

BECOME A CHRISTIAN

MEMORIZE:
"But to all who believed him and accepted him, he gave the right to become children of God." John 1:12

POPCORN PEOPLE

(Read Hebrews 3:8-15)

"Mmmmm . . . this popcorn is so good!" exclaimed Marissa as she stuffed more kernels into her mouth. "I could eat a whole pan of it."

"Me, too," agreed Sally. Several other girls nodded as they eagerly crunched the popcorn. They were having a sleepover at the home of their Sunday school teacher, Miss Eckler.

"Ow!" exclaimed Kim. "I bit into a hard, burnt kernel!"

Miss Eckler gave her a napkin and then asked thoughtfully, "How are people's hearts like this popcorn we've been eating?"

"Well, some people's hearts are hard like Kim's burnt kernel," offered Shari quickly.

Miss Eckler smiled. "Right."

"And the people with hard hearts are those who hear about Jesus over and over again, but they don't believe in him," added Marissa.

Miss Eckler nodded. "Right again," she said. "But Christians can also have hard hearts. How can that be?"

Shari responded, "By not doing what we know is right."

"Correct, Shari," answered Miss Eckler. "But how can Christians keep their hearts soft and teachable?"

"By trying to do right and by confessing when you don't," said Kim.

"And by going to church, reading your Bible, and praying," finished Marissa.

"Exactly right, girls," answered Miss Eckler. "And my prayer for all of us is that our heart will remain soft and teachable and not become hard like Kim's burnt kernel." *JLH*

HOW ABOUT YOU?

How is your heart today? Is it soft and teachable or hard? Ask God to help you have a heart that will yield to him when he wants to teach you something new or show you something in your life that needs to change.

MEMORIZE:

"Today you must listen to his voice. Don't harden your hearts against him." Hebrews 3:15

YIELD TO FAITH IN JESUS

INVITATION NEEDED

(Read Matthew 7:21-23; Titus 3:5)

Wendy eagerly answered the door as her friends began to arrive for the sleepover. "I'm so glad you could come," she greeted the girls. "Help yourselves to snacks."

Soon the family room was filled with sleeping bags and girls in pajamas. Wendy glanced around. "I wonder why Julie isn't here," she said. "I'm sure she was planning to come. I'm going to call and see if she's sick." Wendy went to the phone and dialed Julie's number. She was surprised when Julie herself answered the phone. "Hi, Julie," said Wendy. "You didn't forget about my party, did you? I thought you'd be here long ago! Aren't you coming?"

"Well . . . uh . . . I'm not sure," stammered Julie. "I mean . . . I didn't get an invitation or anything, so I wasn't sure if I was supposed to come."

"Of course I want you to come! I've talked to you about this party so much that I thought you knew automatically that you were invited. Please come!"

"OK!" Julie exclaimed eagerly. "Dad will bring me right over!"

Later that evening, Wendy's mom was giving devotions. "I think we can all learn something from the little mix-up that took place here this evening," she began. "Julie knew about the party, and she knew Wendy liked her, but she had not actually been invited. She didn't come until she received that invitation—and we're so glad she's here now." She smiled at Julie, then continued her lesson. "Just as Julie didn't come to the party uninvited, so Jesus doesn't come into our life uninvited," she said. Mother talked a few more minutes—telling the girls how Jesus died so they could have eternal life in heaven. As she ended her talk, she said, "If any of you would like to know more about Jesus, come and talk to me after we pray." *DLR*

HOW ABOUT YOU?

Have you asked Jesus to come into your life? The Bible tells us to turn away from sin and trust in Jesus to be saved. You invite him in by believing in him and accepting what he has done for you. Until you do that, he'll still be waiting. Once you do invite him in, he promises to stay forever!

MEMORIZE:

"Look! Here I stand at the door and knock. If you hear me calling and open the door, I will come in, and we will share a meal as friends."
Revelation 3:20

INVITE JESUS INTO YOUR LIFE

THE BRIDE (PART 1)

(Read Matthew 19:3-6)

"Oh, Lisa," gasped Tina as she entered the room she shared with her older sister, "your dress is beautiful! You look like a princess!"

Lisa laughed. "I hope I look like a bride," she said.

Tina giggled. "Try on the veil, too. I want to see it. Please, Lisa?" As Lisa placed the veil on her dark hair, Tina sighed wistfully. "I'd love to wear a dress like that and march down the church aisle," she said.

Lisa laughed. "Whoa, Tina!" she said. "You're only thirteen. It'll be a long time before you're old enough to get married."

"With these braces and glasses, I'll probably never get married," Tina pouted. "No guy in his right mind would even look at me twice!"

"By the time you're old enough to get married, you won't have braces. And glasses can look really smart—or you could get contact lenses some day," Lisa encouraged. "Besides, if a guy really loves you, he won't care if you have glasses, or braces, or warts on your nose!"

Tina laughed. "Well, at least I don't have warts. Lisa, how do you know that you really love Doug?"

Lisa thought awhile. "Well, love isn't just a good feeling. It includes respect, commitment, and friendship. When there's real love between a man and a woman, they want to commit themselves to one another for a lifetime. Never get married unless you're sure you've found someone you want to live with the rest of your life," she advised.

"Wow!" Tina whistled. "Maybe I never will get married! It must be hard to love someone that much."

Lisa smiled. "God will give you love for the right guy as you seek to do his will," she said. "But the important thing to remember, Tina, is to be willing to do what God wants." *BD*

HOW ABOUT YOU?

Do you wonder who you'll marry or whether you ever will get married? Don't fret. You have lots of time. Remember, God says that marriage is to last as long as you both live, so it's a very serious decision. Pray for God's wisdom.

MEMORIZE:

"Since they are no longer two but one, let no one separate them, for God has joined them together."
Matthew 19:6

MARRIAGE IS FOR LIFE

THE BRIDE (PART 2)

(Read Ephesians 5:25-33)

Tina was nearly as excited about her sister's wedding plans as Lisa was. One night not long before the marriage was to take place, Lisa looked up from her desk with a smile. "I thought I'd read my Sunday school lesson and forget all about weddings for a few minutes," she said, "but guess what the lesson is about?"

"What?" asked Tina, who was sprawled on her bed.

"It's about how believers are God's church," Lisa answered. "They're called the bride of Christ. He's the Bridegroom, and he'll come back for his bride." She paused, a thoughtful look on her face. "I've worked so hard to make sure everything is just right for my wedding! I wonder if I've been as careful in preparing to meet Jesus."

"What things are we supposed to be doing to be ready to meet him?" asked Tina.

"Trusting in Christ to forgive our sins is the beginning, of course," Lisa answered. "And then, according to 1 John, chapter 3, we should be purifying ourselves."

"What does that mean?" Tina asked.

"Well, think about it," said Lisa. "I know that when Doug is coming over, I want to be always looking my best. And I want to do the things that please him just like he wants to do the things that please me." She grinned. "I'm even glad to go fishing with him!"

Tina laughed with her sister, remembering how Lisa had always disliked squiggly worms. "I think I get it," said Tina. "If we really believe Jesus is coming, we should want to live pure, clean lives for him and do the things that please him."

Lisa nodded as she climbed into bed. "That's right," she agreed. "Let's both remember to work on that as well as on wedding plans." *BD*

HOW ABOUT YOU?

If Jesus came today, would you be ready? Are you keeping your life pure? Do your thoughts and actions please him? Remember, Jesus is coming! Live as though you believe that.

MEMORIZE:

"But we know that when he appears, we shall be like him, for we shall see him as he is. Everyone who has this hope in him purifies himself, just as he is pure." 1 John 3:2-3, NIV

LIVE A PURE LIFE

JUNE
14

SUNSHINE OR RAIN

(Read Matthew 5:43-48)

Jenny was gardening with her mother. "I don't like weeds," she said, pulling one of the many tiny green weeds that had sprung up in the flower bed. "And it takes a lot of work getting them out." She scowled. "Why do weeds grow anyway?" she asked.

"Well, if the soil is good enough for the flowers, I guess it's good enough for the weeds!" said her mother. "As long as they get sunshine and rain just like the flowers do, they grow, too. In fact, it seems like they grow even better than the flowers!"

"Well, I wish God would make only the flowers grow," declared Jenny.

Mother laughed. "That would be nice, wouldn't it?" she agreed. "But when it comes to sunshine and rain, God doesn't make distinctions between flowers and weeds. He makes the sun shine on everything. And when he sends rain, he doesn't pick and choose. His rain waters weeds as well as flowers."

"Mmmm." Jenny was quiet for a few minutes, digging busily, uprooting weeds and tossing them onto the rubbish heap. Then she sat down on the grass and looked up at her mother. "That's kind of like us, isn't it, Mom? God loves and cares for all of us, no matter what we look like or what we do."

"That's a very good point, Jenny," said Mother. "We're often attracted to people who look nice, and especially to those who are nice to us. But God loves everyone, even those we consider our enemies. He wants us to show love to them, too. It may be that he wants to use us to tell them about him." *MTF*

HOW ABOUT YOU?

Do you make distinctions between people? Do you show concern only for people who are friendly and lovable and easy to get along with? Do you make friends only with the kids who are good-looking or rich or popular? How about those who seem like "weeds" and don't look attractive or act nice—those no one likes? Remember, God loves everyone. Demonstrate his love to them.

MEMORIZE:

"For he gives his sunlight to both the evil and the good, and he sends rain on the just and on the unjust, too."
Matthew 5:45

GOD LOVES EVERYONE

OUTDONE BY ANTS

(Read Proverbs 6:6-11)

Jill and Cathy were sprawled on the living room floor, reading comic books. "Girls," called Mother, "how about going out and watering the flowers?"

"It's too hot to work," Jill complained with a scowl.

"Yeah!" agreed Cathy. "Besides, this is summer vacation. Who wants to work in the summertime?"

"I know some who do," said Mother mysteriously. "They're already out on the driveway now. Maybe you could learn something from them."

Surprised, Jill and Cathy jumped up and ran to the window. "There's nobody out there," said Cathy with a frown.

"Go outside and look closely," Mother replied.

So the girls went out and looked around curiously. "I don't see anybody," Jill said. "Maybe Mother was . . ." Then she stopped. "Hey, look! See the anthill in this crack in the pavement? I bet that's what she meant!"

The girls sat down on the warm cement to watch the little creatures. "Look at them scurrying around," said Jill. "The heat doesn't seem to bother them, does it?"

"They sure work hard," agreed Cathy. "Some carry grains of sand; some carry food. Look at that one! He's dragging a twig that's ten times bigger than he is!"

Jill nodded. "Yeah, ants are strong. We studied about them in school. We learned that some anthills can stretch out for miles underground, and that ants are our friends. They get rid of dead animals and plants."

Cathy laughed. "Maybe so, but Mom sure doesn't act very friendly toward them if she finds them around her cabinets," she said. "They sure do rush around. They're as busy as bees."

Jill giggled. "No—as busy as ants," she corrected. "They're so hard-working that . . ." She stopped and looked at her sister. "I bet that's the lesson Mom wanted us to learn!"

"Yeah!" replied Cathy. "All right . . . let's go water the flowers like she asked us to. After all, we can't let ourselves be outdone by a bunch of ants!" *SLK*

HOW ABOUT YOU?

Do you work hard? Or do you put off work because it's too hard, it's too hot, or maybe you just don't feel like doing it? Go and watch some ants for a while. Then find something useful to do.

DON'T BE LAZY

MEMORIZE:
"Take a lesson from the ants, you lazybones. Learn from their ways and be wise!" Proverbs 6:6

JUNE
16

"GOD'S GOODNESS" BOOK

(Read Psalm 77:10-15)

"I wonder what's in here," said Stacy as she tore away the wrappings from a large birthday present. "Oh, boy! A scrapbook! I can put all my favorite drawings and awards and stuff in it. Thank you! This will be really neat."

Soon Stacy was eagerly at work, sorting through her old school papers and pictures. "These math facts look so easy now," she said as she tossed aside an addition test.

"Didn't you study hard and then pray about each test last year?" Mother asked. Stacy was thoughtful for a moment, then nodded. "Why don't you save a few to help remember how God answered prayer?" suggested Mother.

As Stacy set a few of the old tests aside, her dog came in and began sniffing the pages. Stacy laughed. "Bootsie wants us to put something in the scrapbook so we can remember her," she said.

"Not a bad idea," Mother said thoughtfully. "It's good to remember all of God's blessings—including a pet."

"That's right," agreed Stacy, "and Bootsie has sure been a good one. I'll put a picture of her in my scrapbook."

"Arf! Arf!" Bootsie barked her agreement.

Stacy soon had Bootsie's picture, several test papers, and many other items pasted in her scrapbook.

"Instead of calling it a scrapbook, you could call it a 'God's Goodness' book," Mother suggested. "God knows how important it is for his children to be reminded of his goodness. That's why he gave us his Word. As we read and learn how God answered prayer for the people of the Bible, and as we look back on our own life and see how God helped us, it's not hard to trust him for the future."

Stacy smiled. "That's a good idea," she said. *JAG*

HOW ABOUT YOU?

Do you worry about your next math test, science project, making new friends, or keeping old ones? Take a moment to look back, and see how God helped you last year in school or with a family problem. He has not changed, so you can trust him for your concerns today and for the future.

MEMORIZE:

"I recall all you have done, O Lord;
I remember your wonderful deeds of
long ago." Psalm 77:11

REMEMBER GOD'S GOODNESS

TRUE LOVE

(Read John 10:11-18)

Erica loved to take her dog, Butch, and go exploring along the creek on their ranch. One day after they headed across the pasture, Erica could see the cattle a safe distance away. But when they stopped to examine some tracks, Erica heard an angry bellow and the sound of something crashing through the brush. Her feet froze as a black Angus cow charged toward her.

Just then, Butch, who had been taught to leave the cows alone, lunged at the cow, snarling furiously. The cow shook her head, turned her attention to Butch, and a moment later, rammed the dog against the ground.

Erica pulled herself into a tree, thinking Butch could take care of himself. But when she looked back down, she knew she was wrong. "Please, God, take care of Butch," she pleaded as the angry cow charged Butch again.

Erica watched until the cow finally returned to the brush. She could see her newborn calf, half hidden by bushes. Erica climbed from the tree and hurried to Butch's still form. A lump rose in her throat as she picked up her dog and struggled toward the house. "Dad! Mom!" she called frantically. "Help me!" They came running, and tears streamed down Erica's cheeks as she told about the cow.

Dad put his ear to Butch's chest. "His heart is still beating," he said. "Let's get him to the vet."

While Erica sat in the waiting room, Dr. Colby spent a very long time examining and caring for Butch. "Your dog is going to be OK," said Dr. Colby when he finally returned, "but he has several broken ribs, a punctured lung, and a concussion. I'll keep him here until he's stronger."

"Butch went after that cow so it wouldn't hurt me," said Erica.

Dad nodded. "Butch willingly faced death so you could live," he said, "and do you know what that reminds me of? It reminds me of Jesus' sacrifice. He loved us so much that he suffered to save us from our sins." *KLB*

HOW ABOUT YOU?

Have you accepted Jesus' sacrifice of love? Like everyone, you have sinned, and God requires that sin must be punished. Jesus took the punishment you deserve by willingly giving his life. If you would like to find out more, talk to a trusted friend or adult.

**JESUS GAVE HIS
LIFE FOR YOU**

MEMORIZE:
"We know what real love is because Christ gave up his life for us. And so we also ought to give up our lives for our Christian friends." 1 John 3:16

THE GOLDEN RULER

(Read Matthew 5:38-48)

Joy came down the hall, pulling her little brother with her. "If Josh doesn't stay out of my room . . ."

Mother looked up. "Now what?"

"He's been in my stationery again!" Joy reported.

Mother sighed. "There's a verse in the Bible you two should learn. It would stop all this fussing if you'd do what it says to do."

Joy interrupted. "I'll stop if he'll . . ."

Mother held up her hand. "If you'd both practice the Golden Rule, there would be no more quarrels between the two of you. Why don't you give it a try?"

"What's the Golden Ruler, Mommy?" little Josh asked.

"Not 'ruler,'" his big sister corrected. "It's 'rule.' "

"Yes, and it's a rule that Jesus gave. It tells us to treat others like we want them to treat us," explained Mother. "Josh, would you want Joy to go into your room and help herself to your felt markers?"

"No!" Josh exploded. "And she'd better not! She won't let me have any of her dumb old . . ."

"Enough!" Mother said sternly. "If you don't want Joy to use your things without asking, you shouldn't use hers without asking, either."

Mother turned to Joy. "I saw you and Carrie in Josh's room yesterday," said Mother. "You were looking at his Beanie Babies. Had you asked permission?" Joy felt a little embarrassed. "If only you'd treat each other like you want to be treated, how much happier we'd all be," Mother added with a sigh.

"OK!" Josh nodded his head. He grabbed his sister's hand. "We won't fuss anymore. We promise, don't we, Joy?"

Joy grinned sheepishly. "Well, we'll try not to," she agreed.

"I'm going to 'member what the Golden Ruler says every day of my life!" declared Josh. *BJW*

HOW ABOUT YOU?

Do you practice the Golden Rule? Ask yourself, "Would I want someone to treat me this way?" If not, don't treat others that way, either. If you follow this biblical principle, you'll be much happier, and so will everyone around you.

MEMORIZE:

"So in everything, do to others what you would have them do to you." Matthew 7:12, NIV

OBEY THE GOLDEN RULE

DOES IT DO ANY GOOD?

(Read Isaiah 55:10-12)

Darlene's Sunday school class was going to spend Saturday morning at the mall, passing out gospel tracts. They did this once a month. "Why don't you come with us this time?" urged Darlene's friend Anna.

Darlene shook her head. "Do you think it does any good?" she asked. "I mean . . . do you think anybody really reads those things?"

"I think so," said Anna. "Mrs. Hyde says God promises that if we give out his Word, it will do good. She says that even though we may never see anyone become a Christian because of our tracts, God always blesses his Word—spoken or written."

"Well, I bet a lot of people won't even take them," said Darlene.

The next evening, Darlene went to the mall with her mother. In one of the large department stores, a lady was passing out literature describing various gift boxes of soaps and perfumes. *Oh, what a good idea,* thought Darlene. *Mom's birthday is coming up. I bet she'd like some of this.*

When she went to school the next day, she took the literature along. "Help me decide which of these gift boxes to get for Mom's birthday," she said to Anna as she spread out the papers on a desk. "I have enough money saved for any one of these," she added, pointing out three of the boxes. "Which do you think she'd like best?"

Anna studied the attractive literature. "I know which one I like," she said, "but I don't know what your mother would like best." Then she frowned. "What are you doing with this literature anyway?" she asked. "Why did you take it? And why are you reading it? I thought you said nobody reads these kinds of things."

Darlene stared at her friend. "I get the point," she said slowly. "I guess passing out tracts is worthwhile after all." *REP*

HOW ABOUT YOU?

Have you given out tracts or literature that might help someone get to know Jesus? It's a good thing to do. Why not enclose a gospel tract with cards or letters you send? Keep a few tracts handy in your desk or pocket.

MEMORIZE:

"It is the same with my word. I send it out, and it always produces fruit. It will accomplish all I want it to, and it will prosper everywhere I send it."

Isaiah 55:11

GIVE OUT GOD'S WORD

JUNE
20

SUSAN'S POTTERY

(Read Jeremiah 18:1-6; Romans 9:20-21)

Susan had never had a better birthday! Grandma and Grandpa had given her a real potter's wheel, and Susan was thrilled. The next day, however, she found that using the wheel was much harder than it looked. The wheel spun very rapidly, and bits of wet clay flew everywhere! But Susan was patient and persistent. "If at first you don't succeed, try, try again!" she mumbled to herself as she worked. Things were going well, but just as she was shaping the clay into a vase, it slipped off the center of the wheel. Her vase instantly became lopsided.

Susan sighed and started over. Her persistence paid off, and this time she successfully formed a small vase. She set it in the sun to dry.

The next day, Susan walked to her grandparents' home to show them the vase. As she darted up the porch steps, she heard Grandma singing, "Have thine own way, Lord; have thine own way. Thou art the Potter, I am the clay."

Grandpa and Grandma both praised Susan's vase. Then she told them of the problems she had while making it. "It was just like the clay had a mind of its own and didn't want to be molded into a vase," she said, "but I finally got it done."

Grandpa smiled. "People are like clay," he observed. "God wants to mold us into something beautiful for his use, but sometimes we fight against his will and don't want to be molded. That's why I like the song Grandma was singing earlier. In that song, we ask God to mold us and make us according to his will."

"It sure would be easier if my clay would want to be molded," Susan said with a grin.

"Yes," Grandma agreed. "Our life is much easier, too, if we willingly let God mold us into whatever he wants." She smiled at Susan. "That's something you can remember every time you use your potter's wheel!" *REP*

HOW ABOUT YOU?

Do you willingly accept God's leading in your life? He uses parents, teachers, and friends to help mold you. Sometimes he uses difficult experiences, and sometimes happy ones. Remember, he is the Potter. Let him make you into a beautiful vessel that he can use.

MEMORIZE:

"And yet, Lord, you are our Father. We are the clay, and you are the potter. We are all formed by your hand." Isaiah 64:8

LET GOD MOLD YOU

BLOCK OR BRIDGE?

(Read Genesis 37:23-28; 45:4-5)

Johnny and Ann were visiting their grandparents. They had gone to the barn only to find that their favorite kitten was missing. "Grandpa, have you seen Tabby?" asked Ann.

"Not today, but yesterday she was playing on the other side of the creek," answered Grandpa. "The creek was nearly dry then, but after all that rain last night, it's almost full. Come on, kids. I'll help you find Tabby."

As they walked along the edge of the creek, Ann tripped on a log. "Ouch! Oh-h-h! My toe!" she groaned.

"Here, kitty, kitty," called Johnny.

"Look, kids!" Grandpa pointed. "Over there on the other side of the creek."

"It's Tabby!" shouted Ann.

"How can we get her, Grandpa?" asked Johnny. "The water's too deep to walk across, and it's too wide to jump."

"Let's think." Grandpa paused. "Let's get that log Ann tripped over. Maybe we could use it as a bridge."

So they dragged the log to the edge of the river. After much tugging and heaving, they had it in place, and Johnny crawled across and rescued Tabby.

On the way back to the barn Grandpa suddenly stopped and said, "I just thought of something."

"What?" asked Johnny.

"Well, I was just thinking that Ann could have reacted to tripping over that log in either of two ways," said Grandpa. "She could have complained because she stumbled over it, or she could have thanked God for it because he put it there so we could have a bridge over the creek. Which do you think she should have done?"

"Thanked him," said Ann quickly, hugging Tabby.

"You see," said Grandpa, "when God brings tough situations into our lives, like that log, we can look on them as helpful. They help our character to grow." *BJW*

HOW ABOUT YOU?

Have you been complaining about situations and people in your life? Try to view them as something helpful. Ask God to show you how they can be bridges instead of stumbling blocks in your life!

MEMORIZE:

"And we know that God causes everything to work together for the good of those who love God and are called according to his purpose for them." Romans 8:28

EVERYTHING HAS A PURPOSE

JUNE
22

CAMP COUNSELOR

(Read Deuteronomy 6:6-9)

Bethany fought the urge to bite her nails as Miss Lewis told the older girls what would be expected of them as church-camp counselors. "You'll be teaching Bible stories to the younger children, and it's important that your behavior is a good example to them," said Miss Lewis. Bethany was excited about the opportunity, but she also felt like a huge block of responsibility rested on her shoulders. *Some of the kids who are going to be counselors act like we're just going for a good time. What if they tempt me to goof off?* she worried. *I don't want to disappoint Miss Lewis—or God!*

When Bethany got home, Mother was getting ready to leave for a meeting at church. "While I'm gone, I'd like you to fix a meatloaf for dinner," said Mother. "The directions are in the cookbook."

Bethany sighed as Mother hurried away. *I hope I can do this right,* she thought.

When Mother returned, dinner was all ready. Everyone complimented Bethany on doing a good job. Even her little brother, Pete, had two helpings of meatloaf.

As they washed the dishes, Bethany told Mother about her concerns regarding camp. "Hmmm," murmured Mother. "Tell me . . . did you have any trouble making the meatloaf?"

"No," replied Bethany. "It was easy. I just followed the cookbook."

Mother smiled. "I knew you could," she said. "There are also directions for us to follow when we're worried, afraid, or need encouragement to remain strong. Do you know where to find them?"

Bethany nodded. "I bet you mean the Bible," she said.

"That's right," said Mother. "Think of the verses you've memorized and use them as recipes while you're at camp. They'll help you find faith and courage to do what you know is right." Mother dried the last plate. "Follow those directions, and you can't help but do a good job." *KEC*

HOW ABOUT YOU?

Do you know where to turn for directions when you're worried, afraid, or tempted? The Bible has verses to help you know what to do no matter what problem or worry you might face. Memorize verses that are especially helpful to you.

MEMORIZE:

"Your word is a lamp for my feet and a light for my path." Psalm 119:105

LEAN ON GOD'S WORD

GRAVEL AND SIN

(Read Numbers 5:5-7)

Cindy tried to slow her bike when one of the neighborhood kids turned right in front of her, but her front wheel skidded and she toppled onto the hard gravel. After a moment of stunned fright, she stood up and inspected the damage. Her bike was OK, but her right knee was a mess. Small pieces of gravel were imbedded in the cut. Slowly, she wheeled her bike home and parked it in the garage.

She found her mother in the kitchen. "Look at my knee, Mom," said Cindy. "It hurts! That Jason makes me so mad! He cut right in front of me, and I fell."

"I'm sure he didn't mean to make you fall," said Mom as she examined Cindy's knee. "I'm afraid we'll have to do more than wash this. We'll have to get all the bits of gravel out of the cut. Otherwise it may fester, and the sore spot might get infected."

Mom sterilized some tweezers and carefully dislodged each tiny piece of gravel. Cindy winced and felt her eyes fill with tears, but she clenched her teeth and didn't complain. She was glad when Mom finished and the cut was bandaged.

"Your knee may be sore for a few days," said Mom, "but it should heal just fine."

Cindy studied her bandaged knee. "Well, I'm never going to play with Jason again," she declared. "It's all his fault."

"Whoa!" cautioned Mom. "Be careful! Don't let anger or bitterness fester in your heart. They're like gravel."

"Like gravel? What do you mean?" asked Cindy.

"Sins such as bitterness and anger—actually, any sin . . . even so-called little sins—are like the gravel in your cut," Mom told her. "If we don't do anything about our sin, it can lead to more sin . . . like germs lead to an infection. So when you sin, what should you do about it?"

"Ask Jesus for forgiveness," said Cindy promptly. "And we should also ask forgiveness of anyone who's been hurt by our sin."

"That's right," answered Mother. *KEC*

HOW ABOUT YOU?

Have you checked for sin in your life that needs attention? It may be painful to examine your sin and ask for forgiveness, but if you ignore it, it will be even more painful later. Get rid of sin quickly.

MEMORIZE:

"Guide my steps by your word, so I will not be overcome by any evil."
Psalm 119:133

DON'T IGNORE SIN

JUNE
24

A HAPPY REUNION

(Read 1 Thessalonians 4:13-18)

Cassandra and Crystal were so excited! A year ago Dad's job had required them to leave their hometown while he received some special training, but tomorrow they were moving back home. "It seems like ages since we left Fenberg," said Cassandra. "Won't it be exciting to get back and see all of our friends?"

"Yeah," Crystal replied. "Until this year, Judy and I were in the same room every year since kindergarten. I hope I get to be in her room again."

"I wonder what our teachers will be like," said Cassandra. "I hope mine is nice. Oh, I can hardly wait to see Mrs. Hind again. I liked her so much! I do hate to leave Kathy and Susan from my school here, though. They're good friends, too—but not as good as Ruth and Ellen back home."

"I'm not going to sleep a wink tonight," declared Crystal. "I'm so excited!"

"We're just gonna have one o' them old-fashioned reunions with all our old friends that we haven't seen for months," drawled Cassandra, imitating a TV character.

Mother laughed at the girls' excited chatter as she thought about her own friends and how good it would be to see them once again. Then she thought of something else. "A few weeks ago, Pastor Burns talked about a reunion," she said. "Do you girls remember that?"

Cassandra and Crystal looked at Mother. "Pastor Burns?" said Cassandra. "Oh . . . I guess you mean when he talked about Jesus coming again and about how all Christians will be together in heaven, don't you?"

Mother nodded. "That will be a celebration and reunion much greater than what we'll enjoy going back to Fenberg," she said. "Christian friends we haven't seen in a long time will be there. But best of all, we'll get to see our Savior—Jesus." *BMc*

HOW ABOUT YOU?

Have you been excited when you were going to see old friends? Maybe when school was soon to begin in the fall, or when a favorite friend or relative from far away was coming to visit? Meeting loved ones in heaven will be far more wonderful than meeting them here on earth. And meeting Jesus face-to-face will be best of all.

MEMORIZE:

"Then, together with them, we who are still alive and remain on the earth will be caught up in the clouds to meet the Lord in the air and remain with him forever."
1 Thessalonians 4:17

HEAVEN IS A REUNION

A NEW BEGINNING

(Read Lamentations 3:18-26)

Natalie hadn't been very happy lately. Her father's work had moved the family from the Midwest to the South, and Natalie missed her friends and the happy times they had together. She was sure she never could be happy here.

One day, the family took a trip to the beach. They all went swimming, but Natalie refused to admit it was fun. Later, the family hunted for shells on the beach. Natalie found a starfish, but two of its arms were broken off. She was about to throw it away when Dad spoke up. "Let me see it," said Dad, holding out his hand. Natalie handed the starfish to him, and Dad turned it over. "See the little moving feet?"

"You mean it's alive?" Natalie asked in surprise. Dad nodded. "But it's gonna die," continued Natalie. "It only has three arms instead of five."

Dad nodded. "Yes, but it will survive. Starfish can regenerate."

"What does that mean?"

"In time, the starfish will grow new arms to replace the old ones," Dad explained.

"And I thought it was useless," Natalie said thoughtfully.

"Natalie, right now you're something like that starfish. You've been cut off from your old friends and associations, and you're hurting. It's scary to begin again, but with God's help, you can make new friends and develop new interests," encouraged Dad.

Natalie looked at the starfish and smiled. "If he can begin again, I guess I can, too." *JLH*

HOW ABOUT YOU?

How do you face new situations? Do you accept them as a challenge to learn and grow? Or do you look at them with discouragement and refuse to try again? Perhaps a loved one has died, a friend has moved away, or you've gained a new stepparent, and things seem so uncertain for you. Ask God for strength to accept your new situation.

MEMORIZE:

"The unfailing love of the Lord never ends! By his mercies we have been kept from complete destruction. Great is his faithfulness; his mercies begin afresh each day."
Lamentations 3:22-23

**ACCEPT NEW
SITUATIONS**

JUNE
26

THE ROOSTER LAYS AN EGG

(Read 2 Timothy 3:13-17)

"Why don't roosters lay eggs?" asked Martin as he watched his aunt and his cousin, Lynne, stuff a big Rhode Island Red rooster.

Lynne laughed. "Oh, but they do," she said. "Marty, will you please get out the meat thermometer from that cupboard behind you?" she asked. Martin found the thermometer, and when he turned back again, Lynne withdrew her hand from inside the bird. "I found an egg!" she exclaimed. "Look!" Martin could hardly believe his eyes.

Aunt Marcia hid a smile. "Martin," she said, "I think Lynne is playing a joke on you. Go take a look at the book on the coffee table—it tells a lot about birds."

Martin went to see. As he paged through the book, he read, "The male fowl does not lay eggs." He ran to show his aunt and cousin.

"While you were getting the meat thermometer, I put an egg in the old rooster just for fun," Lynne chuckled. "I guess I didn't really expect you to believe me."

"Your joke reminded me of something serious," said Aunt Marcia. "It reminded me that we need to watch out for others who would try to fool us. Satan is like that—he wants to trick us, and he's not doing it just for fun like Lynne did with the egg. Can you think of some ways he tries to trick us?"

"He wants us to think that we have no need of a Savior," suggested Lynne.

"Yeah," agreed Martin, "and he wants us to think we don't need to go to church."

Aunt Marcia nodded. "And just like Martin checked a book to learn the truth about chickens, you must keep checking God's Book, the Bible, so you will not be fooled." *PR*

HOW ABOUT YOU?

Have you ever felt foolish over being deceived? It's not so serious when someone fools you just to tease, but don't let Satan deceive you. He may try to convince you that it's OK to tell a "little" lie. He may say it's all right to cheat sometimes. He may encourage you to disobey your parents. He tries many ways to deceive you, so keep checking the Book!

MEMORIZE:

"He must have a strong and steadfast belief in the trustworthy message he was taught; then he will be able to encourage others with right teaching and show those who oppose it where they are wrong." Titus 1:9

CHECK THE BOOK (THE BIBLE)

GRANDMA AND THE BUTTERFLY

(Read 1 Corinthians 15:51-57)

"Do you really think this thing is ever going to turn into something beautiful, Grandma?" asked Nisha, bringing a jar to the sofa where her grandmother was resting. She had caught a caterpillar, and it had spun itself into a cocoon. Nisha liked to share things with Grandma. She was always interested even though she was sick.

Grandma smiled as she looked at the dried-up, greenish thing in the jar Nisha held. "Oh, yes. Just wait," she answered. "Sit down a minute, Nisha, and let's talk." She patted the seat beside her. "Nisha, someday soon I'm going to be like the pupa inside that cocoon," Grandma continued. "The doctor says I won't be here much longer—I will die soon." A big lump came into Nisha's throat, and tears sprang into her eyes.

Grandma patted her hand. "I don't want you to feel too bad when that happens, Nisha, because I'll be going to heaven. My old body will be buried in the ground, but the real me will be with Jesus, because I have received him as my Savior. And someday I'll get a wonderful new body that won't get sick anymore. You keep watching the cocoon, and when you see the beautiful creature that comes out of it, think about the beautiful new body your Grandma is going to get."

One night while Nisha was asleep, Grandma died. When Nisha saw her lying so still in her casket, she knew it was only her body. Grandma was with Jesus. Thinking about that helped, but she still felt sad.

The morning after Grandma's funeral, Nisha noticed something that made her very excited. "Mom! Dad!" she called. "Look at my butterfly!" Sure enough, a beautiful butterfly had emerged from the cocoon.

As they admired the lovely creature together, Nisha decided to let it go free. "Just like Grandma," she said as she watched the butterfly stretch its wings and fly away. "Someday she'll have a new body, too." *MHN*

HOW ABOUT YOU?

Do you realize that you don't need to fear death when you have trusted Jesus to be your Savior? Just as the caterpillar turned into a beautiful butterfly, so you will receive a new body that will live forever. Thank God for this wonderful hope.

MEMORIZE:

"In a flash, in the twinkling of an eye, at the last trumpet. For the trumpet will sound, the dead will be raised imperishable, and we will be changed."

1 Corinthians 15:52, NIV

**WE WILL HAVE
NEW BODIES**

JUNE
28

PEACEMAKERS

(Read Psalm 34:11-15)

Joy liked Tina, who lived in a big house and had a "doctor dad." She also liked Carol, who was smart and pretty, had no dad, and lived in an average house. But Tina and Carol didn't like each other, and often Joy felt caught in the middle, with both girls getting mad at her as well as at each other.

One day Joy discussed the problem with her father. "Hmmm," he murmured. "What do you do, Joy, when you hear one of the girls say something unkind about the other? Do you keep it to yourself? Or do you repeat it?"

Joy flushed. "Well, I don't repeat it too often," she stammered.

"Any repeating of such words is too often, Joy," Dad told her. "The Bible says, 'Quarrels disappear when gossip stops.' As a Christian, you don't want to be stirring up quarrels between the girls. Now if Tina says good things about Carol, or if Carol says good things about Tina, it might be a good idea to repeat that. If they hear that the other has said something good about them, perhaps they'll decide to like one another."

This was a new idea to Joy. "You mean I should start listening for compliments instead of criticism?" she asked.

Her dad smiled. "Could be. Pray about it and keep your eyes and ears open. And determine never to repeat any of the things that would cause anger." *BJW*

HOW ABOUT YOU?

Are you a talebearer? Do you stir up trouble by telling your friends and classmates the unkind things someone has said about them? Refuse to be a talebearer.

MEMORIZE:

"Fire goes out for lack of fuel, and quarrels disappear when gossip stops."
Proverbs 26:20

DON'T BE A TALEBEARER

THE BEST ARTIST

(Read Psalm 107:21-24, 31)

Every summer, Katie and Scott spent a whole day at the zoo with their Uncle Bill. It was so much fun to watch all the different kinds of animals. There were big ones, tiny ones, scary ones, and some very funny ones. They had fun when they got back home, too. Uncle Bill would sit on the couch, and Katie and Scott would sit close beside him to watch him draw. He was an artist, and he would draw pictures of the animals they had seen at the zoo. Katie and Scott would try to guess what animal it was.

"I know! That's a bear!" said Scott, smiling. "The ones we saw had great big mouths like that!"

"Right," said Uncle Bill. "How about this?" Quickly, he made another drawing.

"A giraffe!" shouted Katie. "I can tell by the long neck. You're such a good artist that it's easy to tell what you're drawing."

"Yeah," chimed in Scott, "all of your pictures are so neat! I think you're the best artist in the world!"

"Thanks for the compliments, kids." Uncle Bill smiled. "I appreciate them. But you know, if it weren't for the greatest artist of all, I wouldn't have anything to draw."

"What do you mean?" the kids wanted to know.

Uncle Bill motioned toward the window. "Look out of the picture window," he directed. "What do you see?"

"Lots of things!" exclaimed Katie. "There's the apple tree, the flower garden, and even a robin in the birdbath."

"And that's not all," added Scott. "There goes David's dog running across the lawn."

"And who's the artist of our big picture?" asked Uncle Bill.

"God!" said Scott. "He's the artist you were talking about."

"That's right." Uncle Bill nodded. "I love to look at God's pictures. He created so many things, and each thing is just the right color, just the right shape, and just the right size! His pictures really are the very best!" *DLR*

HOW ABOUT YOU?

Have you thought of God as an artist? Have you noticed how creative he is? He created the cold white snow and the warm summer sunshine. He made the water wet and the desert dry. Kittens are soft, and the porcupine is all prickly! Look around at God's pictures today, and thank him for them.

**GOD'S CREATION
IS BEAUTIFUL**

MEMORIZE:

"The heavens tell of the glory of God. The skies display his marvelous craftsmanship." Psalm 19:1

JUNE 30

WINNING FIRST PLACE

(Read Matthew 6:25-34)

Kylea gulped down her dinner, asked to be excused, then jumped up from the dinner table. "Where are you going in such a hurry?" Dad asked.

"To get Misty ready for the Fourth of July parade," Kylea replied. "It's coming up fast, and I registered her in the riding contest. Remember?"

"But you have choir practice tonight!" Mother reminded her.

"I know, but I can't go, Mom," mumbled Kylea. "I still have lots to do to get Misty ready if I want to win first place."

"I'm sure you do," said Dad, "but isn't Mr. Robinson counting on you to sing the solo part on Sunday? You need to practice. You still have time to get Misty ready."

Kylea frowned. "I know, but I promised my friend Chelsea I'd help her, too," she said. "We're riding to the parade together, and it's her first time to be in one."

"Kylea, have you forgotten your best friend?" asked Mother.

"Chelsea is my best friend," said Kylea. But she frowned as she thought about it. It seemed that Chelsea sometimes forgot that they were friends at all—like the time she had ignored Kylea for days after a new girl came to school. Kylea had talked to her horse about her unhappiness with Chelsea, and Misty had cheered her by nuzzling her ears. *Maybe it's Misty who is really my best friend,* thought Kylea uncertainly.

"What about Jesus?" Mother said softly.

Kylea gulped. How could she forget Jesus? "Oh, yeah," she said. She remembered that she had also told Jesus how she felt when Chelsea ignored her. "Jesus is always there for me," she said thoughtfully. Kylea hurried toward the stairs.

"Where are you going?" Mother called after her.

"To get ready for choir practice," Kylea said. "I do want to win first place in the riding contest, but I'll work with Misty later. Jesus is my best friend, and I want to do what honors him."

Dad smiled. "Looks like Jesus just won first place," he said. *NIM*

HOW ABOUT YOU?

Do you give Jesus the time he deserves? He wants you to have fun and friends, but he doesn't want you to put them first and ignore him. Talk to Jesus every day, read the Bible—his letters to you—and do special things for him . . . using your talents for him.

MEMORIZE:

"Don't let the excitement of youth cause you to forget your Creator. Honor him in your youth before you grow old and no longer enjoy living." Ecclesiastes 12:1

NEVER FORGET JESUS

THE VACATION

(Read 2 Kings 22:8-13)

"Vacation time is the best time of the year," Traci declared as they neared the Rocky Mountains.

"Not as good as Christmas," argued Trent.

"Do you two have to quarrel about everything?" asked Dad with a sigh. "Where's the map? See how far it is to Garden City. We're about out of gas!"

Mother reached under the seat. She looked puzzled. "Is the map in the backseat, Trent?" she asked.

Trent glanced around him. "I don't think so. Could be, though, and we'd never find it. Traci brought every game and paper doll she had."

"Help Trent look for the map, Traci," said Mother. She also searched, looking through the books, snacks, and souvenirs.

Dad pulled to the side of the road and stopped. "We have to find that map," he said. "There's an intersection ahead, and I don't know which way to go."

"Here it is," announced Mother. She handed it to her husband, who silently studied it for several minutes.

Dad folded the map and started the car. "About 20 miles to Garden City," he said. "We should make it."

Mother picked up her Bible. "Losing our map reminds me of a Bible story." She flipped the pages. "Here it is; I'll read it to you. It's found in 2 Kings 22:8-13."

When Mother finished reading, Dad nodded. "Because the nation of Judah lost the Word of the Lord, the people lost their way," he said. "They didn't know how to serve God or worship him. The Bible is God's map for our life, too."

"That's why we need to read it every day. If we don't check God's map, we'll lose our way," Traci said thoughtfully.

Trent chuckled. "You're a poet and don't know it."

Mother laughed. "It's a good poem to remember. Let's say it together." She smiled as they all repeated, "We must read the Bible every day. If we don't check God's map, we'll lose our way." *BJW*

HOW ABOUT YOU?

Do you follow the "map" God has given? Do you read it every day? It's very important. Don't take a chance on losing your way.

**READ THE BIBLE
EVERY DAY**

MEMORIZE:
"Teach me how to live, O Lord. Lead me along the path of honesty."
Psalm 27:11

JULY
2

TWO TREES

(Read Jeremiah 17:5-10)

After camping for a week, the Pearson family began the drive home. Twins Tammy and Kirk looked out the car windows to get a final glimpse of all the mountain scenery. "Look at that river," exclaimed Tammy. "It's way down there!"

"Look at how far down it is compared to how tall the rocks are!" shouted Kirk.

"And see that tree growing right out of the rocks!" exclaimed Tammy. "I thought trees needed soil to grow."

"It's so tiny," observed Kirk. "Look at the trees down by the river, though. They're big and so tall!"

Dad and Mom were listening to the children's conversation. Finally Dad brought the car to a stop beside the river. They all got out to stretch as they looked at the scenery and compared the trees.

"Look at that lonely, scrawny tree down there," Dad said, pointing to the left. "Then notice the big, strong tree right here in front of us."

"What makes the difference?" asked Tammy.

"The big tree is close to the river and gets lots of water and food. Its roots are well anchored in the soil by the riverbank. The little tree is too far away from the water, and its roots can't anchor very well in the rock," replied Dad. After a moment he added, "The Bible talks about trees like these—it compares them to people. Kirk, can you get the Bible from the car and look up some verses for me?"

When Kirk returned, Dad asked him to read some verses from Jeremiah 17. (See today's Scripture reading.) "The trees in the rock are like people who trust in man," Dad explained. "They have no real roots. Christians—those who trust in God—are like the trees by the river. They are well rooted and have a source of spiritual food and water as they study God's Word." *BR*

HOW ABOUT YOU?

Which kind of "tree" are you? Are you trusting in your own good works to get you to heaven? Read Jeremiah 17:5 again to see what God says about that. Won't you trust in God? Accept the salvation he offers you through Jesus. Then verse seven will apply to you.

MEMORIZE:

"But blessed are those who trust in the Lord and have made the Lord their hope and confidence."
Jeremiah 17:7

TRUST IN GOD

ASK THE ONE WHO KNOWS

(Read Deuteronomy 18:10-13)

It was Katy who rushed home and told her parents the news. "He died," she gasped. "Jerry died!"

"Oh, how sad!" comforted Mother. "I'm so glad he came to vacation Bible school last summer and accepted Jesus as Savior. For even though we will miss him, we know he is with Jesus and we will see him again some day."

Weeks passed. Then one day, Jerry's sister Rita had some exciting news for Katy and her brother, Dan. "We're going to hear from Jerry," she told them. "Did you know the dead can talk to you?"

Dan scowled. "I don't believe it," he said.

"Well, it's true," insisted Rita. "Tomorrow we're going to a meeting, called a seance, where there's a medium—someone who contacts the dead spirits. We asked the Ouija board, and it said Jerry will come and talk to us." Rita showed them the Ouija board. "Put your hands on the pointers with me, and ask it a question," she said. "The pointer shows the answer. Come on—try it."

"No way," declared Dan. "I don't want anything to do with it!"

Back home the children asked their parents about it. "To put faith in a Ouija board or seances is wrong," Mother told them.

Dad nodded. "The Bible tells us to have nothing to do with such things," he said. "There are often evil spirits involved in seances. The medium you spoke of is the person who yields himself, or herself, to spirits—evil spirits who imitate and pretend to be the dead person talking." He picked up his Bible. "Listen to what God says. This is Leviticus 20:27. 'Men and women among you who act as mediums or psychics must be put to death by stoning. They are guilty of a capital offense.'"

"Wow!" exclaimed Dan. "That makes it plain enough!"

"There are two powers on earth—God's and Satan's," continued Dad. "But God is stronger than Satan. He's the only one who knows all about the future."
AGL

HOW ABOUT YOU?

Do you wish you could see into the future? Have you seen a Ouija board? In today's Scripture reading, God says that such things are an "abomination" (something hateful) to him. It's foolish and dangerous to play with such things. Instead, look to God and his Word to learn all you need to know.

MEMORIZE:

"The Spirit who lives in you is greater than the spirit who lives in the world."
1 John 4:4

GOD HAS THE ANSWER

FAMILY REUNION

(Read 1 Thessalonians 4:13-18)

The Johnsons were on their way home from a family reunion. "Oh-h-h," groaned Heather as she sank back in the seat, "I think I ate too much of Aunt Margie's chocolate cake. It sure was good, though!"

"And I think I played too much ball." Dad laughed.

"You know what I liked?" Kayla asked. "I liked seeing Mom's Uncle Harold and some of the other old people. They have such interesting stories to tell."

"Yeah," said Heather. "I've heard Mom talk about some of those things, but it's even more interesting to hear stories from the people they actually happened to."

Mother smiled. "That's exactly what family reunions are for, girls," she said. "They give you an opportunity to learn about your heritage."

"Our family is sure getting big," observed Kayla. "There must have been a hundred people there today."

"I think so," agreed Dad. A little later he added, "But I know an even bigger reunion we'll be attending."

Heather gave her dad a puzzled look, but then she smiled. "I know what you're talking about!" she exclaimed. "You're talking about the reunion we'll have with our Christian family in heaven, right?"

"Right." Dad grinned and nodded. "There we can meet members of our spiritual family—people like the apostle Paul . . . or Moses."

"We should hear some really good stories then—maybe we can ask Noah what it was like living on an ark with all those animals," suggested Kayla.

"Yeah!" exclaimed Heather. "And I'd like to ask Jonah how it felt to be inside a fish!"

Mother grinned at the two girls. "Now that will be a special reunion!" she agreed. *LMW*

HOW ABOUT YOU?

Do you ask your grandparents what it was like when they were young? It's interesting to hear about life long ago, isn't it? Just think about the Christian's spiritual family reunion in heaven! Perhaps you're having such a good time here on earth that you're not very eager for heaven. That's natural, but think about it—people you've read about in the Bible and all Christians throughout history will be there. Best of all, you'll meet your Savior! It will be a wonderful time!

MEMORIZE:

"Then, together with them, we who are still alive and remain on the earth will be caught up in the clouds to meet the Lord in the air and remain with him forever." 1 Thessalonians 4:17

HEAVEN WILL BE A WONDERFUL REUNION

THE WRECKERS

(Read Genesis 3:1-6)

The Hamiltons, who were on vacation by the sea, visited an old lighthouse in the area. "What does a lighthouse do, Daddy?" asked little Joanne.

"It shines its light far and wide, so ships out at sea are guided to a safe place to land," Dad told her. "Can you see those rocks way over there?" he asked. "Well, sometimes evil men, called wreckers, would light their lamps and swing them over there near those rocks. The ships' captains would think that was a safe place to land, and then they'd end up on the rocks."

"That's horrible!" gasped Mary Ann. "Why would anyone do that?"

"Well, after the ship crashed into the rocks, the wreckers would steal the cargo," replied Mom. "Ships often carried gold in those days."

"I'm glad there are no wreckers now," said Joanne fervently.

Mary Ann nodded. She shuddered as she studied the sharp, cruel looking rocks.

"You know, kids, there are still some wreckers around," said Dad, "though I don't mean the shipwrecking kind." He frowned. "Satan is a wrecker—a master wrecker," Dad continued. "He makes evil things look so attractive and appealing that we're tempted to do them."

"Like what?" asked Joanne curiously.

"Well, how about some of the popular music that has a catchy tune but bad words and ideas?" suggested Dad. "Satan would like us to listen to it."

Mary Ann nodded. "Or how about taking drugs? Some of the kids at school try it in order to get in with the popular kids."

"Right," said Dad. "Sometimes Satan manages to persuade us that it's all right to do those kinds of things."

"And like the ships that got wrecked upon the rocks, our lives can get wrecked by sin when we're misled by Satan's false light," added Mom. *MTF*

HOW ABOUT YOU?

Is Satan making something appear good to you—something that you really know is wrong? Remember that he's a wrecker of lives. He will sometimes make evil things appear good and attractive to you—like he made the forbidden fruit seem good and attractive to Eve. He wants you to believe that it's OK to do things God forbids. Don't let him fool you into doing them.

DON'T LISTEN TO SATAN

MEMORIZE:
"But I am not surprised! Even Satan can disguise himself as an angel of light." 2 Corinthians 11:14

JULY
6

HEAVENLY HOMECOMING

(Read John 14:1-4)

Jennifer sighed as she put down the last of the envelopes she was addressing. "That's 215 envelopes, Mom," she said. "I'm all done, but my hand hurts."

"Thank you so much, dear," replied Mom. "I don't know what I would have done without your help. When I accepted the job of sending out invitations for Old Home Day, I had no idea so many emergencies would come up."

Several months later Mom and Jennifer and the rest of the family joined the crowds at the local high school where the Old Home Day festivities were being held. "I see Mr. and Mrs. Wood!" exclaimed Jennifer. "I sent them an invitation and they came!" She and her parents hurried over to greet the Woods, who were former neighbors.

"There's Mr. Burns," said Dad a little later. "He used to be principal here at the school." Dad made his way over to talk to Mr. Burns.

Mom headed for Mrs. Smith, who had been a member of the Young Mothers' Club many years before. She and her old friend had much news to share.

That night, tired but happy from seeing so many former residents of the town, Jennifer and her parents sat down at the kitchen table to talk. "I was hoping the York family would come," said Jennifer. "I wanted to see the twins again. The Hills weren't there either." She shook her head. "A lot of the people we sent invitations to came, but there were a whole lot who didn't come, too. I wonder why not."

"Well, there are many reasons why people can't take a trip at a certain time," said Mom. "I was just glad to see the ones that did come."

"Yeah," agreed Jennifer, "but I still would like to know the reasons why the others didn't come."

Dad smiled. "You know," he said, "we wonder why some people ignored this invitation, but I'm thinking of an invitation that's much more important than those we sent out for today's homecoming. I'm thinking of our heavenly homecoming. Jesus said he was going to prepare a place for us, so we could be with him in heaven. He also said, 'Whosoever will may come,' but many people pay no attention to his invitation." *LAS*

HOW ABOUT YOU?

Have you heard about the invitation Jesus has given? If you accept him as your Savior, you will also be with him one day in heaven.

MEMORIZE:

"For God so loved the world that he gave his only Son, so that everyone who believes in him will not perish but have eternal life." John 3:16

JESUS INVITES YOU
TO COME TO HIM

IN YOUR HEAD

(Read Joshua 1:7-9)

"I think you've got a bite!" Lori pointed excitedly.

"Oh, you're right!" exclaimed Dad. He quickly raised the line and brought up a fish. The boat bobbed gently in the breeze as he took the fish off the hook and put it into the bucket.

"You almost lost him, Dad," Lori said. "I guess you were daydreaming, huh?"

Dad smiled. "Well, I wasn't exactly daydreaming. I was just thinking about a Bible verse I memorized this morning," he explained. "I don't want to forget it."

"I thought only us kids had to memorize verses," said Lori in surprise.

Dad shook his head. "It's important to memorize verses all your life, Lori. Knowing God's Word by heart lets you think about it when your hands are busy—like right now, while we're out here in the boat."

Lori grinned. "I guess it would be kind of hard to hold a fishing pole and read the Bible at the same time."

Dad laughed. "That's right. Another thing I like about memorizing Scripture is that it will come to your mind over and over. For instance, when I was pulling up that fish, I suddenly thought of a verse in Matthew—'Follow me, and I will make you fishers of men.' And when your mind is full of Scripture, there isn't much room for unkind thoughts and ungodly ideas."

Lori was thoughtful. "There's lots more to memorizing Scripture than just winning contests, isn't there?"

"Yes, there is," agreed Dad. "Take every opportunity to learn verses in Sunday school, camp, Bible club—and keep on reviewing. You can never learn too much Scripture." *CR*

HOW ABOUT YOU?

Have you ever wondered what you would do if you had no Bible to read? Or have you needed to know Scripture when you didn't have a Bible with you? What do you understand best—something you have read once or twice, or something you know by heart? If you have God's Word in your head, it will also go deeper and deeper into your heart and life, and will be there when you need it.

MEMORIZE:

"Study this Book of the Law continually. Meditate on it day and night so you may be sure to obey all that is written in it. Only then will you succeed." Joshua 1:8

MEMORIZE GOD'S WORD

JULY
8

TREASURES THAT MATTER

(Read 1 Timothy 6:6-11, 17-19)

"How did school go today?" Mother asked as Christy came into the kitchen.

"OK, I guess," Christy muttered.

"What's the matter?" Mother asked, looking up at Christy. "Your sad face tells me something is not right."

Christy's words came in a rush. "I can't stand Abbie anymore, Mom. She's always bragging about how much money she has, her gold jewelry, and all the places she gets to go. She even goes a lot of times to get her hair and nails done. I'm so tired of hearing about it."

Mother looked thoughtful. "You're not jealous, are you, honey?" she asked. Christy blushed a little. "Christy," said Mother, "I'm going to give you two gifts. Here's the first one." Reaching out, she pulled Christy to her and gave her a big hug. "I love you, love you, love you," Mother told her, using a favorite family phrase. Then Mother went and got her purse. She handed Christy some money. "Here's your second gift."

"Oh, goody!" squealed Christy. "May I run to the store and get an ice cream bar?" Mother nodded, and Christy hurried out.

When Mother tucked Christy into bed that night, she asked, "What do you have left of the two gifts I gave you?"

"Well, the ice cream is long gone—unless it made me a little fatter," said Christy with a laugh. She hugged her mother. "But I still have your love. And I'll give you some of mine."

Mother smiled. "Good—I'll take it," she said. "Christy, I wanted you to see that you have treasure far more valuable than the things your friend Abbie tells you about. All her 'things' are like the money. They don't last. Love does. And in addition to the love of your family, you know God's love. You've accepted his gift of eternal life which lasts forever, so you're really a very 'rich' young lady." *SMc*

HOW ABOUT YOU?

Do you place more value on clothes, games, and activities than you do on salvation and living for God? Don't get your values mixed up. Earthly treasures are not nearly as important as the love of family and friends—and especially the love of God.

MEMORIZE:

"Beware! Don't be greedy for what you don't have. Real life is not measured by how much we own."
Luke 12:15

SEEK HEAVENLY TREASURES

THORNS AND BERRIES

(Read 2 Corinthians 4:8, 15-18)

"That was your father," said Kate's mom as she hung up the phone. "There was a fire at Grandma Reed's house this morning. She wasn't at home and she's all right, but she did lose most of her things."

"Oh, no," groaned Kate. "Why Grandma? She's a Christian, Mom! Why would God let something like this happen to a Christian?"

"I don't know," replied Mom, "but let's just thank the Lord that Grandma is OK."

"But to lose everything!" moaned Kate. "It's too much!"

Later that morning, Kate took her little sister, Grace, outdoors to play. But before long, Kate flung open the kitchen door. Little Grace stood beside her, holding out her hands and sobbing. "Mama! Hurt!" she cried.

"We were picking blackberries," explained Kate. "Grace was having fun until she got her hands scratched on a bush."

"Bush!" screamed Grace. "Bad bush!"

"It's not a bad bush," Kate told her as Mom cleaned the little girl's hands. "It has yummy berries on it. You just have to be more careful."

Mom gave Grace a hug. "Kate is right," Mom told her. "The berries were good, weren't they?" Grace nodded her head. "You know, Kate," continued Mom, "I'm afraid we're often like Grace."

Kate looked up. "What do you mean?" she asked.

"Because she was hurt by that blackberry bush, little Grace couldn't see any good in it," replied Mom. "She quickly forgot how good the berries were. In much the same way, when things that happen hurt us, we often can't see that there's anything good about them. For example, we don't see why Grandma Reed had to lose her home, since she's a Christian. Yet God says everything that happens to a Christian will eventually work out for the good. We can't always see it, but God can."

"I guess you're right, Mom," said Kate slowly. After a moment she asked, "Do you think Grandma would like a blackberry cobbler?" Mom smiled and nodded. *AM*

HOW ABOUT YOU?

Do you become angry at God when something bad happens to you or to someone you love? You may not always understand how a bad situation could work out for good, but God does. Trust him with your circumstances!

**TRUST GOD IN
THE BAD TIMES**

MEMORIZE:
"And we know that God causes everything to work together for the good of those who love God and are called according to his purpose for them." Romans 8:28

JULY 10

BETTER THAN REWARDS

(Read Psalm 119:9-16)

"Oh, here's a letter for me!" exclaimed Whitney as she came in from roller-blading. Putting her skates by the door, she picked up the envelope from the table. "Who's it from?"

Mother laughed. "Open it and find out," she said.

Whitney did, and she found that the letter was from her cousin, Jill. It told all about the wonderful week Jill was having at camp—swimming, boating, playing games, and taking part in skits. "And it didn't cost me anything," wrote Jill. "I learned some Bible verses for Sunday school and got to go for free."

"I wish our Sunday school had a plan like that," murmured Whitney. "I'd learn verses, too, if I could go to camp."

"It's fine to memorize verses to win a week at camp," Mother replied, "but it's also good to learn them to experience the way God can use those verses to speak to you."

Whitney was skeptical. "How can verses speak to me?"

"Tell you what—I'll give you a list of verses to work on. Start learning them, and see what happens," Mother challenged. So Whitney did just that, and she was surprised to see how quickly she could learn them when she really tried.

One morning as she walked to her friend Laura's house, a big black dog started following her. She caught her breath—she was afraid of dogs! Suddenly a Bible verse came to her mind. "I will trust and not be afraid." She kept saying the verse over and over, and soon her fears were quieted.

As the girls played a bit later, Laura said some unkind things about another girl. Whitney was ready to add her own unkind comments when Psalm 19:14 came to her mind. "May the words of my mouth and the thoughts of my heart be pleasing to you, O Lord, my rock and my redeemer." Whitney held the words back and quietly told Laura she would really rather talk about something else.

"Mom, you were right," Whitney called excitedly when she arrived back home. "There are more good reasons for learning verses than just to go to camp."
CVM

HOW ABOUT YOU?

Do you learn Bible verses even if nobody promises a reward for doing so? It's nice to receive rewards from people, but it's even more important to receive the help that knowing Scriptures can bring.

MEMORIZE:

"I have hidden your word in my heart,
that I might not sin against you."
Psalm 119:11

LEARN GOD'S WORD

THE FIRST TOMATOES

(Read 1 Chronicles 29:10-17)

"I don't see why I always gotta put some of the money I earn in the church collection," grumbled Julie. She fumbled in her pocket and reluctantly took out some coins, which she set aside. "I've only a couple of dollars left," she complained.

"Julie," began Mom, but before she could continue, the kitchen door jerked open and Melissa ran into the room, flushed and panting.

"Mom! Julie!" gasped Melissa, leaning against the fridge to catch her breath.

"Melissa! What's wrong?" Mom asked.

Melissa shook her head so hard that her long, brown curls streamed down over her face, muffling her voice. "Nothing," she said, flashing her mother a triumphant grin. "Look!" She held out her hands. In each small sunburnt hand lay a big, red tomato! "My very first tomatoes are ripe already!"

"Wonderful!" exclaimed Mom. "Would you like to have them for dinner?"

"Mm-m-m! Yeah," said Melissa, smacking her lips.

Julie frowned at her sister. "I think you should give these two to Grandma and Grandpa," she said. "After all, Grandma gave you the plants, and Grandpa helped you plant them and taught you how to take care of them."

"Hey, that's a neat idea," agreed Melissa. "I'll wait for the next ones to get ripe. Grandma and Grandpa get these!"

Mom smiled a secret smile. "That was a good idea, Julie," she said gently. "Now here's something else to think about. God has given you everything you own, right?"

"Yes," replied Julie easily.

"Then," said Mom, "why do you have such a hard time giving your offering?"

"Oh," mumbled Julie. She touched a tomato gently with one finger. "I guess I didn't think of it like that." *MTF*

HOW ABOUT YOU?

Do you give a portion of your allowance or earnings to the Lord's work? Do you give it willingly and cheerfully or grumpily? Remember that everything you have is God's good and generous gift to you, and when you "give" to him—to his needy people, or to his work here on earth—you are only "giving back" what you received from him in the first place.

MEMORIZE:

"But who am I, and who are my people, that we could give anything to you? Everything we have has come from you, and we give you only what you have already given us."
1 Chronicles 29:14

**GIVE CHEERFULLY
TO GOD**

THE PRINCESS AND THE PEA

(Read Isaiah 57:19-21)

"Grandma, will you read me the story of 'The Princess and the Pea' before I go to bed?" begged Alonya.

"I'll read it," agreed Grandma with a smile, and she did. When Grandma tucked Alonya into bed a little later, she began feeling under Alonya's mattress.

"What are you doing, Grandma?" Alonya asked.

"I'm looking for peas, Princess!" Grandma replied.

Alonya giggled. "There aren't any there, Grandma," she said.

"Good," said Grandma. "I hope there aren't any in your life, either."

"My life?" asked Alonya.

Grandma nodded. "The pea in the story reminds me of a time when I did something wrong," she said. "I told a little, bitty lie. I thought it wasn't important, and it didn't hurt anyone. But what does God say about lying?"

"He says we should never tell lies," replied Alonya.

"That's right," agreed Grandma. "My lie was like the pea in the story. It was hidden, but it really bothered me. Sometimes I would lie awake at night, tossing and turning, thinking about it."

"Just like in 'The Princess and the Pea'!" Alonya cried. "But you're not a princess."

"In a way I am," said Grandma. "God our heavenly Father is the King of kings and we're his children, so doesn't that make us both princesses?"

"Wow! I never thought about that before," said Alonya, her eyes wide open in awe.

"Finally, I couldn't stand trying to hide my lie any longer. I had to ask Jesus and my mother to forgive me," said Grandma.

"And did you live happily ever after?" Alonya asked, grinning.

"I must admit I still sin sometimes," said Grandma, "but it's been a good reminder to always confess my sin. I don't want any more 'peas under my mattress.' " *LJR*

HOW ABOUT YOU?

Do you have any "peas under your mattress"? Are there things you have done that you feel guilty about? Sometimes we say it's our conscience that bothers us. If you're a Christian, it's the Holy Spirit who makes you feel guilty when you sin. Confess your sin and get right with God. It's the only way to have peace.

MEMORIZE:

"Because of this, I always try to maintain a clear conscience before God and everyone else." Acts 24:16

IT'S BEST TO CONFESS

TANGLED OR ATTRACTIVE?

(Read Romans 12:1-2, 21)

"Oh, no!" exclaimed Joyce as she and her parents walked into the house. They could hardly believe their eyes. Pink yarn went around table and chair legs and over and under the chair rungs in the kitchen. Then the yarn went from the kitchen to the dining room where it went over and around more chair legs and rungs. Then back to the kitchen!

It didn't take long to know where to pin the guilt—Patches, Joyce's kitten, had to be the culprit. "But how could one little kitten accomplish such a mess?" groaned Joyce.

"I'm sorry, Joyce," said Mother, "but it looks like you'll lose most of it. We might as well get a scissors and start cutting."

"Wait," said Dad. "That's a lot of yarn to waste. Let me try to untangle it." And with that he started to work. Joyce and Mother helped, too. It was no easy task, but finally the yarn was rolled into a ball.

"Well," said Joyce. "I'm glad we could save this. But it doesn't look like it did when it was new. Look . . . some of the threads are pulled apart."

Mother nodded. "I guess Patches' claws did that. It looks a little dingy, too," she said.

Joyce sighed. "It won't ever be quite the same again, but I'll still use it," she decided.

"This reminds me of people," said Dad thoughtfully. "God made them and wants to use them in his own wonderful way. But sometimes people, especially young people—even Christian young people—mess up their lives. They rebel against parents and become entangled with the world. Perhaps they join a gang; or maybe they begin to harm their bodies by using cigarettes or alcohol or drugs. Even if they come back to God, their lives will never be quite the same. There will be scars left." *VMH*

HOW ABOUT YOU?

Do you say no to the temptations that come your way? As you keep untangled from the world, Jesus will make your life something beautiful and special. Let him do that for you. Ask him daily to help you live for him.

MEMORIZE:

"Pure and lasting religion in the sight of God our Father means that we must care for orphans and widows in their troubles, and refuse to let the world corrupt us." James 1:27

KEEP UNTANGLED FROM THE WORLD

LEARNING AND DOING

(Read James 1:22-25)

Shannon had been memorizing verses for a contest her Sunday school class was having with the boys' class. Memorizing was easy for her.

When she came home from school one day, her little brother, Jeff, ran up to her, wanting to play. She pushed him away. "Leave me alone," she scolded. "I have to memorize verses." When Mother asked her to set the table, she grumbled, saying she had to study her verses so the girls would win the contest. When it was time for her to do the dishes, she pouted. Before Jeff went to bed, he again wanted her to play with him, and once more she told him to leave her alone and go away.

"Shannon," said Dad at last, "you've been learning lots of verses for your class. I believe you learned Ephesians 4:32. Can you recite it for me?"

Shannon beamed. She liked to have Dad quiz her on her verses. "Be kind to each other," she quoted.

"Good," said Dad. "Now, how about James 1:22?"

"And remember, it is a message to obey, not just to listen to," replied Shannon promptly.

"That's right." Dad nodded. "Now let's think about what happened here this evening. Were you obeying the message of God's Word? Were you kind to Jeff? Or to Mother?"

Shannon's smile was gone. She knew exactly what Dad meant. "You see, Shannon," Dad went on, "memorizing all those verses isn't worth much unless you also do what they say."

Shannon nodded slowly. "I'm going to start doing," she promised. Then she grinned. "Hey," she added, "wouldn't it be great if we could have a contest with the boys to see which group has the best 'obeyers' instead of the best 'memorizers'?" *BR*

HOW ABOUT YOU?

Are you a "memorizer"? Wonderful! More important—are you a "doer"? Memorizing verses isn't worth much unless you allow them to change your life as well. What's the last verse you learned? Find an opportunity today to put it into practice—to be a doer of the Word.

MEMORIZE:

"And remember, it is a message to obey, not just to listen to. If you don't obey, you are only fooling yourself." James 1:22

BE A "DOER" OF THE WORD

DESERVING TO DIE

(Read Psalm 103:8-14, 17-18)

"Mo-m-m-m!" wailed Felicia as she ran into the house, followed by her brother. "Juan has a dirty old fly, and he's chasing me with it! Make him kill it, Mother!"

Juan was carrying a glass jar. Inside was a large horse fly. "Now this little old fly is plumb unhappy in this jar," he declared, laughing. "There isn't a horse for miles around for him to pester, so I'm going to set him free in your room. You'll do just as well." He started toward Felicia's room.

At Felicia's angry squeal of protest, Mother spoke up. "Stop teasing your sister," she scolded mildly, "and take that thing outside and get rid of it."

"Kill it!" ordered Felicia.

"Awww, have a little mercy," Juan answered. "I'd just let it go, but it's been pestering me while I work on my bike. I tried to chase it away, but it won't leave me alone. I know! I'll take it to Bryson's Woods and let it go there."

Felicia watched Juan pedal down the street on his bike. "Now why would he go to all that trouble?" she wanted to know.

Mother smiled. "I don't really know," she said, "but Juan has always hated to see anything hurt."

"Well," Felicia added, "saving the life of something like a dirty old fly that's been pestering you and deserves to die anyway is going a bit too far, if you ask me."

"Hmmmm," murmured Mother, "you may be right. But on the other hand, I'm glad God doesn't feel that way." Mother laughed at Felicia's surprised look. "In some ways we're like that fly," she explained. "We're dirty from our sins. But just as Juan showed mercy to the fly, God shows mercy to us. He gives us the opportunity to have a new life. I'm glad God is merciful." *HWM*

HOW ABOUT YOU?

Have you experienced God's mercy? God loves you so much that he sent his Son, Jesus, to die on the cross and take that punishment for you. Be truly sorry for your sin and accept what Jesus did for you. If you have more questions, ask a trusted friend or adult.

MEMORIZE:

"For the Lord your God is gracious and merciful. If you return to him, he will not continue to turn his face from you." 2 Chronicles 30:9

GOD SHOWS MERCY

JULY
16

A HOLY RESIDENCE

(Read 1 Corinthians 6:19-20)

"Let's stop for some ice cream," suggested Kayla as she and her friend Jenny walked home from school.

Jenny shook her head as she looked at her chubby friend. "I thought you said your doctor wanted you to cut out sweet stuff," she said.

"Well, I'm hungry," said Kayla as she waved Jenny on and turned to go into the ice-cream store. But she felt a bit guilty as she ordered a banana split. The doctor had said she should lose weight, and she knew she didn't eat properly. As she ate, she told herself the fruit was good for her.

When Kayla arrived home, her mother had good news. "I've decided to quit smoking, Kayla," she said. "I went to a Bible study at church this morning, and the group discussed how our body is the temple of the Holy Spirit. I guess he must be tired of living in a smoke-filled residence!"

Kayla was delighted. Her mother had been a Christian only a short time, and Kayla had been praying that she would give up smoking before it harmed her permanently. "Great, Mom," cheered Kayla. "I'll help you all I can."

"Good." Mother smiled. "Will you go for a walk with me every day?" Inwardly, Kayla groaned. It sounded like such a lot of effort! "One of my excuses for smoking has always been that it kept me from gaining weight," Mother continued, "so I'm going to eat a well-balanced diet and get lots of exercise." She paused a moment before adding, "After all, having a proper temple not only involves ridding it of smoke but also of excess weight, I should think."

Kayla sighed. "All right. I can take a hint. I'll walk with you and try to improve my diet, too. But don't expect any miracles," she warned.

"We'll do our best," said Mother, "and we'll let Jesus handle the miracles." *JN*

HOW ABOUT YOU?

Do you take good care of your body? Do you eat properly? Get enough rest? Exercise? Maintaining a proper temple for the Holy Spirit means doing the right things as well as staying away from things that harm you (such as cigarettes, alcohol, drugs, and too much food). Ask the Lord to help you take proper care of his temple.

MEMORIZE:

"Don't you realize that all of you together are the temple of God and that the Spirit of God lives in you?" 1 Corinthians 3:16

TAKE CARE OF YOUR BODY

MOTHER'S HELPERS

(Read Hebrews 6:9-12)

Mother rubbed her hot forehead. "Jeremy, fill the ice trays, please," she said. "We'll need ice for the cooler tomorrow." The family would be leaving on their vacation trip, and Mother had already spent hours cleaning, cooking, and packing.

"It's Susan's turn," Jeremy hollered. "Make her do it."

"Susan's not here. You do it this time," said Mother.

"Susan left on purpose," Jeremy protested angrily as he filled the trays. Mother sighed. It would have been less tiring to do it herself.

The baby began crying just as Susan got home. "Susan, could you rock Tommy for a while? I still need to pack some things for tomorrow."

"But, Mom," replied Susan, "Kim's coming over in a few minutes. Let Jeremy rock him." Mother started to speak, then picked up Tommy and rocked him herself. Feeling as she did, Susan would probably not be much help to the baby.

Mother was still rocking Tommy when the children came in for a snack. Jeremy peeked in the cookie jar. "I thought you were going to bake cookies, Mom."

"I haven't had time yet," Mother said. "Maybe you could make some, Susan."

Susan groaned. "They wouldn't taste as good as yours. We'll eat crackers for now."

When Dad came home very late that evening, Mother was still working. Noticing her hot, tired face, he sent her right to bed.

Early the next day, the children found Dad cooking breakfast. "Where's Mom?" Susan asked. "Today's our trip. We gotta get moving."

"She's in bed," Dad replied. "And we'll have to postpone our trip for a day."

"Postpone it!" exclaimed Jeremy. "That means one less day at the beach! And one less day for sightseeing!"

"I'm sorry," said Dad, "but your mom is exhausted." He looked at them sternly. "If Mom had been given some help yesterday, she wouldn't be so tired today." *JLH*

HOW ABOUT YOU?

Do you grumble when you're asked to help? Do you stand around when you should take action? Make yourself available to those who need your help. Offer to help your mom, even if you have done all your chores.

DON'T BE LAZY

MEMORIZE:
"We do not want you to become lazy." Hebrews 6:12, NIV

JULY
18

NO DEPOSIT, NO RETURN

(Read Ephesians 4:30-32)

Scott wiped the back of his hand across his damp forehead. "It's time to quit," he called to his sister. Her flushed cheeks reminded him that he was not alone in his discomfort. "This is incredible, Carrie! We collected lots of cans and bottles today! We'll make good money for a few hours of work!" Scott and Carrie lived in a resort town on the east coast and collected pop bottles and cans that had been discarded by tourists. They received money for each one they turned in at the local supermarket.

At the store, the children waited patiently in line to redeem their bottles. Their favorite cashier winked at them as she finished with another customer. Scott grinned back as he and Carrie began to unload the cart.

"Whoops, this one is no good," said the cashier, setting one can aside. "It doesn't have a deposit stamp on it." Scott quickly apologized. He and Carrie were usually careful to check each bottle and can for the mark. When the cashier was finished, she paid them, and they headed home.

"Guess what, Dad," said Carrie that evening. "Scott and I made almost fifteen dollars collecting pop cans today." She grinned at her brother. "Scott tried to sneak one in without the deposit stamp on it, though," she teased.

"Did not!" protested Scott. "You're probably the one who put that can in our bag."

"Well," admitted Carrie, "we could make worse mistakes."

Dad nodded. "Actually, a lot of people do," he said. "They make the mistake of thinking they don't need God's stamp—his Spirit—to get into heaven. They think that going to church and acting like Christians will be good enough to get them there. But unless a person has received God's seal by trusting in Jesus for salvation, that person will not get to heaven. Having the Holy Spirit in our life is kind of like a deposit to guarantee our salvation. That's one deposit stamp you don't want to be missing." *GDB*

HOW ABOUT YOU?

Examine your heart and life carefully. Do you trust Jesus as Savior? Is the Holy Spirit living within you? If you are unsure of your salvation, talk to Christian parents, your Sunday school teacher, a friend, or your pastor about it.

MEMORIZE:

"It is God who gives us, along with you, the ability to stand firm for Christ. He has commissioned us, and he has identified us as his own by placing the Holy Spirit in our hearts as the first installment of everything he will give us." 2 Corinthians 1:21-22

MAKE SURE YOU HAVE GOD'S HOLY SPIRIT

IT STILL STANDS

(Read Psalm 33:11-20)

Drums beat, flags waved, and trumpets blew! Bethany's and Brad's eyes darted here and there trying to capture all the excitement. Suddenly, a shot split the air! The parade had begun!

The school band proudly marched down the street in new uniforms. When they began playing "The Star Spangled Banner," the crowd sang along. "I know who wrote the words to our national anthem," said Brad later as the family drove home.

"You do?" asked Mother. "Tell us about it."

"They were written by Francis Scott Key," Brad told them. "While British ships were firing at Fort McHenry all through the night, Mr. Key watched from a ship just offshore. If Fort McHenry fell, Baltimore and other key cities would probably tumble, too. At dawn, the guns stopped, and what do you think Mr. Key finally saw?"

"What?" asked Bethany.

"The American flag," Brad replied. "My teacher read a story about him, and it said that he shouted, 'The flag still stands!' Right after that, he wrote the song."

Bethany was impressed. "Will it always stand, Dad?"

"We pray it will," answered Dad.

Brad was more confident. "Sure, it will! We're the strongest nation in the world. If anybody dares . . ."

"Whoa!" cautioned Mother. "God's Word teaches that nations do not rise or fall because of their great strength. Proverbs 29:25 says that 'to trust the Lord means safety,' so our safety doesn't come from preparation for battle."

Dad nodded. "God has been very good to our country. We have many privileges and blessings, and we should be thankful," he said. "But we should also pray for our leaders and our people. Our nation needs to turn back to God." *JLH*

HOW ABOUT YOU?

Did you thank God today for your country? Did you pray today for its leaders? Will you pray for them? Pray, too, for all the people—your neighbors, your town, your state, yourself. Pray that you and your nation will put away the things that displease God.

PRAY FOR YOUR GOVERNMENT

MEMORIZE:
"What joy for the nation whose God is the Lord." Psalm 33:12

THE BUG LIGHT

(Read 1 Corinthians 3:16-21)

"Let's sit on the back porch, Rob, and watch the sun go down," Dad suggested one evening. He walked toward the door, and Rob followed silently. They sat several minutes without talking, then Dad spoke. "Rob, you're usually so cheerful, but you've been very quiet lately."

"Everything's fine—really! We don't need to talk about anything," Rob answered quickly, not looking at his dad.

Soon the sun was down, and the only sound they heard was the *zzztt!* of the bug light on the post. It cast an eerie blue shadow on the backyard.

Dad decided to try again. "Rob, I hope everything is fine," he said, "but if it isn't, would you talk to me about it? I'm available any time."

"Sure," said Rob as he stared at the bug light.

The next day it was Rob who suggested that they sit on the porch. "Dad, you were right," he said. "Everything isn't fine." Then Rob told how a friend had offered him a cigarette. After saying no a few times, he had smoked one. Since then he had smoked several times, and now he was starting to want a cigarette more often.

Dad put an arm around Rob. "Thanks, Rob, for telling me," he said.

"Last night I watched the bugs fly into that bug light," continued Rob. "They were attracted to the light, not knowing it was drawing them to their death. They got closer and closer and didn't realize they would be harmed. Then I realized that it was the same with smoking. I took the first cigarette because lots of my friends smoked. Then I smoked because I thought it made me feel good. But I'm getting closer and closer to being harmed, too. I could get addicted if I don't stop now."

"Smart thinking, Rob," Dad said. "Sin often looks very pleasant to us. It's easy to get involved in it, but it can destroy us."

"This afternoon I told God I'm not going to smoke again," said Rob quietly. *DK*

HOW ABOUT YOU?

Has anyone ever asked you to smoke a cigarette? God's Word says Christians are not to defile (do anything to hurt) their bodies. A person who encourages you to smoke or take drugs is not a true friend. Don't try those things—not even once. Keep your body pure for the Lord Jesus.

MEMORIZE:

"Or don't you know that your body is the temple of the Holy Spirit, who lives in you and was given to you by God? You do not belong to yourself." 1 Corinthians 6:19

STAY AWAY FROM SIN

REALLY EMPTY

(Read Ephesians 2:1-10)

"Mom," said Janice, "can I make some lemonade?"

"I doubt it," teased her brother, Russ. "It takes far more talent than you possess."

"Oh, hush," scolded Janice. "*May* I make some, Mother?"

Mother laughed. "You can, and you may," she said. "I bought several packages of fruit drinks yesterday. Just add the sugar and water."

"I will," agreed Janice. She went to the cupboard and took out the box containing the mixes.

"Stick with lemonade," advised Russ. "It's my favorite."

Janice took out an envelope showing a bright yellow lemon. After carefully measuring sugar into a pitcher, she picked up the lemonade packet. She was going to tear it open but held it up and inspected it closely instead. She ran her fingers up and down both sides. Then she took a different packet from the box and compared the two, shaking them and feeling them with her hands.

"I was right," declared Russ. "She can't make lemonade. See, she's all confused."

Janice ignored him. "Mother," she said, "I don't think this packet has a thing in it. It feels empty."

Mother took the packet and checked it. "You're right, Janice. It is empty, but don't tear it open. I want to use it as an object lesson for my Sunday school class."

"An object lesson?" asked Janice. "Of what?"

"It reminds me of some people—people who pretend to be Christians," replied Mother. "Like this packet, they look fine on the outside—they're faithful in church, they're generous and kind. Others are often fooled by them."

"Just like you were fooled by this packet when you bought it," said Russ.

Mother nodded. "But God isn't fooled by anyone." *HWM*

HOW ABOUT YOU?

Are you putting on a good front and fooling people? Remember, you're not fooling God. All the fine, nice-looking things you do cannot save you. You need to accept Jesus as your personal Savior, and then you will be a Christian. God wants to make you the "real thing."

MEMORIZE:

"For by grace you have been saved through faith, and that not of yourselves; it is the gift of God, not of works, lest anyone should boast." Ephesians 2:8-9, NKJV

WORKS DON'T SAVE

I DON'T WANT TO GO!

(Read Ruth 1:8-18)

"England!" Amanda was stunned. "We're really moving to England?"

"That's right, honey," said Dad. "The company wants to start a branch overseas, and they've chosen me to get it started. We'll be living in England for at least five years."

Amanda walked over to the living room window and looked out at the familiar street. She had lived in this same house ever since she was a baby. What would it be like not only to live in a different house but in a different country? Amanda couldn't imagine. She'd have to leave her friends, her school, and her church. "I don't think I want to move," Amanda whispered in a trembly voice. "I want to stay here."

Amanda's dad put his arm around her. "I know it'll be hard to leave your friends and everything that is familiar. But you can choose to look at the move as a special experience that very few of your friends will ever have. Remember, too, that no matter where we move, God will be with us, and he promises to take care of us."

As Amanda sat in her room later, she remembered what her dad had said about choosing to see the move as a good thing. She knew they were going to England whether she liked it or not, so she might as well choose to like it. Amanda called her best friend, Julie, that very night. "Guess what! We're moving to England!" she said.

Julie almost sounded jealous after Amanda explained. "How neat!" she squealed. "You can send me lots of letters, and I can put the stamps in my stamp collection!"

Amanda smiled. Moving to England might be a good adventure. *LMW*

HOW ABOUT YOU?

Does your family move a lot? Have you had to change schools? Did you find it hard to make friends at your new school or church? It isn't easy to move away from everything familiar. Remember, though, the Lord promises to be with you anytime and anywhere. You can always talk with him. So try to see the advantages of living in several different places. Learn to enjoy the unique experiences and the wide array of friends. Be content wherever God places you.

MEMORIZE:

"Not that I was ever in need, for I have learned how to get along happily whether I have much or little."
Philippians 4:11

ACCEPT NECESSARY CHANGES

CALM IN THE STORM

(Read Isaiah 43:1-3)

As rain pattered against Dana's bedroom window, two big tears dampened her pillow. The storm inside her heart seemed far greater than the one outside. Her dad had left the family a year ago, and Dana had been praying he'd come back and rejoin them. But today the awful news had come. Dad was getting married again. Now there was no chance of restoring the family to the way it was.

A few minutes later Dana heard her door opening softly, and Mother came in. "Is the storm bothering you, honey?" asked Mother.

Dana sniffed. "No, I hardly noticed it," she said.

Mother smiled. "That's good. When you were small, you were terribly afraid of lightning."

"I was?" asked Dana. "I don't remember that. I wonder how I got over it."

Mother sat in the rocker next to the bed and stroked Dana's hair fondly. "When there was a bad storm, I used to come and sit in this chair sometimes. For some reason, just having me here seemed to make your fear go away."

Dana looked up at her mother and grinned. After a moment she added, "You really don't need to stay in here tonight, Mom. I'll be OK."

"I know you will," replied Mother as she stood up. "You see, I know how upset you've been lately, and I've been praying that God's presence will help you through this tough time. I know I'd never make it without him, and I hope you'll always remember that he's here to help you."

After Mother had left, Dana looked at the empty rocking chair. She tried to imagine the Lord sitting there, watching over her during this crisis in her life. Suddenly she knew that even though the problems in her life were still there, things were different now because she was trusting God to take care of her. Dana rolled over and was soon sound asleep. *SLK*

HOW ABOUT YOU?

Are there some difficult problems in your life right now? God is able to change your situation, but he may let you go through hard times so that you'll learn to trust in him completely. Learning to trust God, no matter what happens, is the secret to real happiness. Remember, he's always there!

TRUSTING GOD BRINGS PEACE

MEMORIZE:

"You will keep in perfect peace all who trust in you, whose thoughts are fixed on you!" Isaiah 26:3

KATHY'S CREATION

(Read Genesis 1:1, 31; Hebrews 11:3)

The hum of the sewing machine sounded throughout the house. "My creation is almost ready for you to see," said twelve-year-old Kathy. She had been measuring and cutting and stitching ever since she arrived home from school, only taking time out for supper.

Mother smiled. "I'm eager to see it—whatever it is," she said. "You've certainly spent a lot of time on it."

"Oh, you'll like it," said Kathy as she stood up and shook out the material she was using. "Ta-da! Here it is—my own special creation! It's an apron for Dad to use when he barbecues hamburgers or steak."

"Just what he needs," said Mother, "especially one that has flowered pockets and a polka-dot bib."

Kathy laughed. "Some creation, isn't it?"

"You keep saying 'creation,' Kathy, and I know what you mean," said Mother. "But the dictionary says the main meaning of 'create' is 'to cause to exist'—or in other words to make something out of nothing. I like to remember this because it reminds me of God's power. He's the only One who can really create anything in that sense."

Kathy nodded. "I hadn't thought of that," she said as she looked at the apron she was holding. "OK, Mom. I'm a fashion designer, not a creator." *GW*

HOW ABOUT YOU?

Do you realize what a great thing God did when he created the world and everything in it? When you draw a picture, sew something unusual, or cook some concoction no one ever heard of, remind yourself that you are not creating in the same way God did. Only he can create like that.

MEMORIZE:
"In the beginning God created the heavens and the earth." Genesis 1:1

GOD CREATED THE WORLD

NOT A TAURUS

(Read Isaiah 47:1-14)

"Mother, Linda told me I'm a Taurus!" exclaimed Jenny as she burst through the front door. "Her mother says the stars can tell us all about ourselves and advise us about what we should do according to what day we were born. She says we can read the horoscope in the paper every day to find out what the stars say."

Jenny's mother looked up. "And does it make sense to you to believe that the stars have power over a person's life?" she asked. "Does it make sense for people to have to wait until the newspaper arrives to find out what the stars advise them to do that day?"

Jenny thought about that. She remembered a girl at summer camp who'd always worn a rabbit's foot on her belt, even to go swimming. She had believed it would bring her luck, until another little girl had asked, "How much luck can a foot bring? Look what happened to the rabbit, and he had four of them!" Believing in the power of the stars to direct her life, Jenny decided, made about as much sense as believing in a rabbit's foot.

Jenny glanced at the family Bible lying on a nearby shelf. "Linda may say I was born under the sign of Taurus," she said, "but I've been born again." She smiled at her mother. "I'm a Christian, not a Taurus. I have Jesus in my life. He's more powerful than any star—he made them! And I don't have to wait for the newspaper. I have God's Word to tell me how to live!" *LBM*

HOW ABOUT YOU?

Do you ever find yourself avoiding the cracks in the sidewalk? Crossing the street to dodge a black cat? Reading the horoscope section of the paper? Astrology and superstition have no place in a Christian's life.

**DON'T TRUST
SUPERSTITIONS**

MEMORIZE:
"Let all the world look to me for salvation! For I am God; there is no other." Isaiah 45:22

WHO GETS THE CREDIT?

(Read 1 Corinthians 3:1-11)

"Laura Graham was at our Sunday school party today," announced Lindsey. "What a bummer!"

"Why, I thought you wanted her to go," said Mother. "Didn't you invite her?"

"That's just the point," said Lindsey. "I've invited her for three years in a row, and she always said no. Then today she shows up with Bonnie."

"Well, I'm sure Mr. Patterson had a good Bible message, just as he always does," observed Mother. "I should think you'd be happy Laura came." The doorbell interrupted her. "That must be Grandma with those marigold plants."

After Grandma had left, Lindsey and her mom decided to plant the marigolds.

"You know something, honey?" Mother handed Lindsey a trowel. "These plants remind me of you and Laura."

"Of me and Laura?" exclaimed Lindsey. "How?"

Mother dug in the dirt as she explained. "Well, Grandma started these plants and nursed them along until they developed healthy roots," she said. "Now we must back up Grandma's efforts and care for these plants. And, in a way, you 'started' Laura—you first invited her. Then Bonnie backed up your efforts by inviting her, too. Right?"

"I guess so," said Lindsey. "But why couldn't Laura have come when I invited her?"

Mother shook her head. "I don't know," she said, "but sharing Christ is not a competition. When we tell someone about Jesus, we don't always see the final result. God is using both you and Bonnie to help Laura spiritually, just as Grandma, you, and I are helping these plants." *LMW*

HOW ABOUT YOU?

Have you ever been upset because someone else received credit for bringing your friend to church? Did that seem more important to you than the fact that your friend would hear about Jesus? You need to work together with other Christians in winning others to Jesus. Paul understood this. He knew the Lord was using him and Apollos to further the gospel. Witnessing is not a competition where one person wins and another loses.

MEMORIZE:

"My job was to plant the seed in your hearts, and Apollos watered it, but it was God, not we, who made it grow."
1 Corinthians 3:6

**WORK TOGETHER
FOR CHRIST**

GUILTY CONSCIENCE

(Read Hebrews 9:11-14)

Misha whistled as she sauntered out of Brown's grocery store. Then, with a flying leap, she jumped on her bicycle and raced down the street. Every few seconds she glanced over her shoulder. Only when she was a safe nine blocks from the store did she stop and pull a package of chocolate-covered nuts from her pocket. But the candy didn't taste very good after the first few bites. Misha got rid of the rest of the evidence and went home.

"Misha, I'm glad you're home," Mother smiled. "Will you run to Brown's store and get me some sugar, please?"

"B-B-Brown's? B-b-but I don't feel good," stammered Misha. "Can't Michelle go?" Concerned, Mother agreed.

When Mother answered the phone a bit later, Misha heard her say, "Yes, Mr. Brown." After that she could hear only snatches of the conversation. Soon Mother hung up, and with a sigh she hurried out to the garage to talk to Dad. Misha could tell Mother was upset. She felt sick!

When Dad came in, Misha's feelings poured out. "I didn't think Mr. Brown saw me in the store, but he told Mother, didn't he? Oh, Dad, I don't know what made me do it."

Dad looked puzzled. "Mr. Brown?" he asked. "Mr. Brown told Mother there was a check he had to return to her. It was one a lady had given her at the garage sale. Mr. Brown had cashed it for her, but the bank said it wasn't any good. Now what are you talking about?"

"I stole some c-c-candy today," stammered Misha. "I've been scared ever since."

Dad shook his head. "You were unhappy and scared because you were trying to run from a guilty conscience. This reminds me of a Bible verse that says, 'The wicked run away when no one is chasing them.' That's what you were doing."

"So I didn't have to tell you about the candy at all," said Misha, "but I'm glad I did! I'd hate to spend the rest of my life with a guilty conscience, running from nobody."

"Good," said Dad, "because now you're going to go and pay Mr. Brown for that candy." *BJW*

HOW ABOUT YOU?

God has given each one of us a conscience. If you have accepted Jesus, the Holy Spirit will work through your conscience. Listen to him. Obey him.

LISTEN TO THE HOLY SPIRIT

MEMORIZE:
"The wicked run away when no one is chasing them." Proverbs 28:1

BUILDING BLOCKS

(Read 1 Thessalonians 5:11-15)

Lisa and her friend Shawna sat at the table talking. Little Joel sat on the floor nearby, playing with his new building blocks. "Did you see Rachel today?" asked Lisa. "She got her hair all chopped off, and it looks just awful!"

"If she were smart, she'd dye it," said Shawna with a laugh.

"Did you know that Mona dyes her hair?" asked Lisa.

"No!" Shawna gasped. "No wonder it's so blonde. Well, she's so fat, she may as well do something to try to improve herself." She nibbled on a cookie.

Mother, who was listening, began to speak, but just then a horn sounded outside. "There's my mom," said Shawna, getting up quickly. "Bye, everybody." As she headed for the door, her long coat brushed against the tall block building Joel had just finished, knocking it over. "Mommy," he moaned, "Shawna tore my building down."

"I know, honey," sympathized Mother, "but it was an accident. Why don't you build it back up again?" As Joel got busy, Mother looked at Lisa and added, "I'm afraid Shawna's not the only one who knocked down in a moment what it took a long time to build. I'm afraid you've done the same thing."

"Me?" asked Lisa. "I didn't touch Joel's blocks."

"No," said Mother, "but you girls tore apart half your friends. I think that's even more serious than knocking down a few blocks, don't you?"

Lisa stared down at the table. "I guess so."

"People are a little like Joel's building," said Mother. "They need to be built up by compliments and kind words, not torn down by criticism. If you have knocked them down, you'll feel a lot better about yourself when you build them back up again."

Lisa nodded. "But how do I do that?" she asked.

"From now on, when you hear a criticism of another person, try to replace it with a compliment," suggested Mother. "Why not begin by calling Shawna and telling her something nice about each person you knocked down?" *VLR*

HOW ABOUT YOU?

Do you compliment or criticize? The Bible says to speak evil of no one. Don't tear down—build up instead.

MEMORIZE:

"Get rid of all bitterness, rage, anger, harsh words, and slander, as well as all types of malicious behavior."
Ephesians 4:31

DON'T CRITICIZE

FINALLY THIRTEEN

(Read 2 Peter 3:11-14, 18)

Reaching her 13th birthday had seemed like the most important thing in Rozanne's life. "How come you want to be 13?" asked Julie, her little sister.

"Because now, people will think of me as grown-up," Rozanne replied.

Julie still didn't understand. "You mean that last night, when you were 12, you were just a kid, and now, today, you're a grown-up?"

Before Rozanne could answer, Mother came into the room. "Rozanne, your father just called from Boston. He's not going to get home in time for your birthday party, and that means we won't have a car to pick up the cake we ordered at the bakery."

Something inside of Rozanne flashed, and before she knew what she was doing, she shouted at her mother about people not caring how important this day was to her and spoiling it for her. Without giving her mother a chance to make any suggestions for getting the cake, she blurted out angry things she did not mean to say.

Julie looked at her. "Are you being 13 or 12?" she asked innocently.

The words struck Rozanne's heart. She sighed. "I'm 13 in numbers but only 12 in my actions, I guess. I'm sorry," she apologized, turning toward her mother. "I've still got a lot to learn about being grown-up."

Mother smiled at her. "Why don't you take your bike and get the cake," she suggested. "I think your bike basket is big enough."

"But I'm too old to run errands on my bike," Rozanne began. Suddenly she stopped and whispered a prayer for help. "Dear Lord," she said sincerely, "I think you're going to have to help me be 13." *RIJ*

HOW ABOUT YOU?

Are you eager to be older? Do you think being "grown-up" happens automatically at a certain age? It doesn't. It's a gradual process, just as growing physically is a process. Growing in the Lord takes time, too. We need to pray for help to become more mature every day.

MEMORIZE:

"But grow in the special favor and knowledge of our Lord and Savior Jesus Christ." 2 Peter 3:18

GROW INTO MATURITY

THE EMPTY COCOON

(Read 1 Corinthians 15:35-44)

"EEEEK!" Lina ran up on the porch screaming.

Kyle followed, laughing. "It's just a caterpillar," he said.

Lina shuddered. "I don't like caterpillars." As she slammed the door behind her, she saw Mother wiping tears from her eyes. "What's the matter?" asked Lina anxiously.

"I just got a phone call. Grannie Carter died."

"I don't want her to die," Lina said as she started to cry also. Grannie Carter had been their next-door neighbor.

Mother smiled faintly. "Well, at least Grannie Carter is happy. She wanted to be with Jesus and her husband again."

Lina and Kyle dreaded the funeral. It would be their first one. But when the time came, they found that, except for the casket and the flowers, it was like a regular church service. At the end, everyone walked out past the casket where Grannie lay. "She looks like she's asleep," Lina whispered.

Later at home, Lina asked, "How can Grannie be in the ground and in heaven, too?"

"Well," said Mom, "it's sort of like Kyle's caterpillar. The caterpillar makes a chrysalis (like a cocoon). And at the right time, the caterpillar comes out of the chrysalis as a beautiful butterfly."

"I get it," said Kyle. "Grannie's body is like the chrysalis or cocoon. She has left it behind. But her spirit is like the butterfly. It has gone to heaven."

"That's right," said Mom.

"Wow!" said Lina. "I'll never look at a caterpillar the same way again." *BJW*

HOW ABOUT YOU?

Has someone you love died and gone to heaven? Don't worry about the old body that was buried in a grave. Remember that the real person has left the old body and gone to be with the Lord. God will give that person a wonderful new body someday.

MEMORIZE:

"Our bodies now disappoint us, but when they are raised, they will be full of glory. They are weak now, but when they are raised, they will be full of power." 1 Corinthians 15:43

CHRISTIANS WILL HAVE NEW BODIES

A DIFFICULT MOVE

(Read Joshua 1:1-5)

At the close of the church service, Carrie listened in disbelief as Pastor Allen said, "After much prayer, we feel the Lord is calling our family to serve him at an Indian reservation. We will be leaving in a month." Carrie was saddened by the news. Her best friend was Becky, the pastor's daughter. That meant Becky would move, too.

When the service ended, Carrie dashed out to the car. She was too upset to even speak to Becky. "How could Pastor Allen do this?" Carrie sobbed on the way home.

"He must obey the Lord's leading," Dad said gently.

"But I don't want him to leave," Carrie wailed. "Becky's my best friend."

Carrie was upset all day. At bedtime Mother gave her a hug. "Honey," she said, "your old crib is set up in the guest room. Why don't you sleep in it tonight?" Carrie stared at her mother. "I remember how you fought against the idea of moving out of it when you got your first bed," Mother continued, "so I thought maybe it would make you feel better to sleep in it again tonight."

Carrie laughed. "You can't be serious, Mother! I don't want to sleep in a crib anymore. Besides, I wouldn't fit."

Mother smiled. "That's true," she agreed. "Part of growing up means leaving behind old things and adjusting to new ways. People may change or move away, but God is still with us, planning things for our good. And keeping the Allens here apparently doesn't fit into God's plan."

"Right," said Dad. "Let's thank God for the good years we've had with them and make their last days at our church extra special."

"I guess you're right," Carrie said slowly. "It won't be easy for Becky, either, but I'll help her all I can." *JLH*

HOW ABOUT YOU?

Are you faced with a move, a new family member, or a new church or school? Are you angry about changes or new circumstances in your life? It isn't easy to let the familiar go, but God understands your feelings, and he will be with you in your new situation.

MEMORIZE:

"No one will be able to stand their ground against you as long as you live. For I will be with you as I was with Moses. I will not fail you or abandon you." Joshua 1:5

ACCEPT GOD'S LEADING

BUTTERFLY WISDOM

(Read Proverbs 31:29-31)

"Look!" exclaimed Mother. Melissa's eyes followed her mother's pointing finger. Her blue eyes sparkled as she spotted a striking orange and black butterfly flitting daintily from flower to flower.

"He's so pretty!" Melissa exclaimed in delight. "Let's see where he goes." So they walked on, following the butterfly's progress through Grandma's garden. "Look at those red flowers," said Melissa a moment later. "They're the prettiest flowers in the garden. I'll bet that butterfly will like them." She looked around, but the butterfly had disappeared.

Mom pointed toward a tiny cluster of weeds just below the red flowers. "He's there," she said.

"But why is he wasting time on weeds?" asked Melissa.

"That's one wise little butterfly," said Mom. "He knows that the prettiest flowers aren't always the ones with the sweetest nectar."

With wonder in her voice Melissa asked, "You mean those tiny purple flowers taste sweeter to the butterfly than the red ones?"

Her mother nodded. "I expect they do," she said. "Perhaps we should be as wise as that butterfly. Sometimes we get carried away by how people look, the color of their skin, how tall they are or how slim they are, how they dress, how they talk . . . and we forget that real sweetness and beauty come from their character, from the kind of people they are."

"Yeah." Melissa nodded. "Some of the least popular kids at school are the nicest ones I know," she said.

"Another thing we tend to do is worry and fret and spend time and money trying to make ourself beautiful on the outside, without giving any thought to our character," added Mom. "We need to remember that what we are on the inside is what's important." *MTF*

HOW ABOUT YOU?

While it is natural that you would want to look attractive and wear nice clothes, remember that real beauty in God's eyes is on the inside—in the kind of person you are. What kind of person are you?

MEMORIZE:

"Don't be concerned about the outward beauty that depends on fancy hairstyles, expensive jewelry, or beautiful clothes. You should be known for the beauty that comes from within, the unfading beauty of a gentle and quiet spirit." 1 Peter 3:3-4

BE BEAUTIFUL INSIDE

LAZY SUSAN

(Read Ephesians 6:18-19; Philippians 1:20)

Susan sat on the porch, waiting impatiently for her father. *I wish Dad would hurry home,* she thought. *I need money to get a birthday present for Janice before the party this afternoon. I suppose Mom's right when she says I could have earned it by mowing the lawn for Dad or baby-sitting for Mrs. Greene, but it's been just too hot for all that.* Mother looked out. "Susan, why don't you walk over and see if Jill Ryan would like to go along to church tomorrow?" she suggested.

Susan made a face. "Oh, Mom," she whined. "It's too hot. Jill would never go in this weather anyway." Susan stretched lazily.

By the time Dad came home, it was too late to get a present. "Oh, well," said Susan, "I'll get a gift for Janice later."

When the gifts were opened at the party, Susan explained that she hadn't had time to get one. "I'm going to bring one next week," she said. Janice was very nice about it, but the other kids whispered together. Susan just knew they were calling her by her nickname—"Lazy Susan." She complained about it when she got home. "I was so embarrassed," she said.

"I imagine you were," said Mother. "After all, when Janice invited you to her party, you accepted her invitation. Yet you didn't bother to get a gift for her." After a moment she added, "This reminds me of the invitation that Jesus gave you to his home in heaven. You believed him and accepted that invitation, too— but do you have a gift ready for him? Once you get to heaven, you can't promise to bring something later."

Susan looked thoughtful. "But what gift can I bring Jesus?" she wondered out loud. Suddenly she jumped up and started for the door. "Oh, I know! He wants us to bring other people to him. Do I have time before dinner to go invite Jill to church? I don't want to be known as 'Lazy Susan' anymore—especially not in heaven." *AGL*

HOW ABOUT YOU?

Have you accepted Jesus' invitation to heaven? That's great, but do you have a gift for him? Is there someone to whom you could witness or to whom you should show kindness? Someone whom you should invite to church?

MEMORIZE:

"He who wins souls is wise."
Proverbs 11:30, NIV

WIN SOULS FOR JESUS

TO GRANDMOTHER'S HOUSE (PART 1)

(Read John 14:16-18, 26)

Jamie's grandparents had called and offered to buy her a plane ticket so she could spend a couple of weeks with them. She was excited at the thought of flying, but she was scared, too. "Do you really think I should go?" she asked. "I won't know what to do. I might get lost by myself."

Mother gave her a hug. "You won't be alone," she said. "The flight attendant on the plane will look after you. And when you get off the plane, she'll stay right with you until you meet Grandma and Grandpa. It will be fun."

At dinner that night, Jamie eagerly told Dad all about the plan. "You're sure the flight attendant will take care of me?" she asked, still a bit uncertain.

Dad smiled. "I'm sure she will," he assured her as he reached for the family Bible. "Time for devotions," he added, and he read several verses about the Holy Spirit. "Your trip to your grandparents will be a little like Christians on their way to heaven to see Jesus," said Dad. "Sometimes we don't know just what to do. We feel uncertain and kind of alone. But we're never alone. The flight attendant will help you on your trip, and the Holy Spirit helps us each day. He lives within us. He will keep us and guide us until we get safely to heaven." Dad looked at Jamie. "He'll be there with you on that plane, too." *JLH*

HOW ABOUT YOU?

Do you sometimes feel alone and uncertain about what you should do? Do you feel like you don't know how to pray or witness? If you're a Christian, God has given you the Holy Spirit to teach you. He will speak to you through God's Word. He will help you pray, witness, perform an act of kindness, or do any number of other things pleasing to God. When you feel him prompting you to do those things, don't hold back.

MEMORIZE:

"But when the Father sends the Counselor as my representative— and by the Counselor I mean the Holy Spirit—he will teach you everything and will remind you of everything I myself have told you." John 14:26

THE HOLY SPIRIT GUIDES

AUGUST
4 **TO GRANDMOTHER'S HOUSE (PART 2)**

(Read 1 Thessalonians 4:13-18)

Jamie fastened her seat belt. She was glad she was sitting near the window. This was her first plane trip, and she didn't want to miss a thing!

Soon the plane was roaring down the runway. *Oh! This is fun!* thought Jamie. When they were airborne, she looked down. The rivers and highways wound through the countryside like yards of ribbon. *Everything looks so tiny from up here!* she thought. The fluffy, white clouds looked so soft and warm, and they flew right through some of them! Jamie wondered what it would be like to sit on a cloud and softly float along.

Jamie enjoyed every minute of her trip. She was almost sorry when it ended, but she was glad to see her grandparents, who were waiting for her. Soon she was hugging them tightly. After thanking the flight attendant for her kindness, they were on their way home. "How was the trip?" Grandpa asked.

Jamie's eyes sparkled. "It was super, Grandpa! Everything looked so tiny and pretty. I wish I could have reached out and touched a cloud. They looked so fluffy."

"Someday you just might do that," Grandpa said.

Jamie was puzzled. "How, Grandpa?" she asked.

"Someday Jesus is coming back to earth to take the Christians with him to heaven," Grandpa explained. "The Bible tells us that Christians who have died will rise from the graves first. Then Christians who are alive will be caught up with them 'in the clouds' where we'll meet the Lord in the air. Maybe you can check out the clouds then."

Grandma joined in. "I think we'll have more important things to think about then."

Jamie laughed out loud. "Yeah," she agreed. "That will be even more exciting than this trip. Mom and Dad couldn't afford to come along with me this time, but they'll be there when Jesus takes us all to heaven."

"That's right," Grandma replied. "We'll all be together forever! We'll never have to say good-bye again!" *JLH*

HOW ABOUT YOU?

Are you on your way to heaven? You can't buy a ticket to get there. Neither money nor good works will get you to heaven. There's only one way to go. Jesus died on the cross to pay for your sins. You must confess your need to him and accept Jesus as your personal Savior to receive the gift of salvation. If you do that, you can look forward to the day when Jesus will take you to heaven to live with him forever.

MEMORIZE:

"Then, together with them, we who are still alive and remain on the earth will be caught up in the clouds to meet the Lord in the air and remain with him forever." 1 Thessalonians 4:17

BE READY FOR HEAVEN

TO GRANDMOTHER'S HOUSE (PART 3)

(Read Isaiah 45:9-13)

Jamie was excited to be with her grandparents again. One morning they packed a lunch and set off for a trip through the Black Hills of South Dakota. Jamie was enjoying the beautiful scenery when Grandpa slowed the car and said, "Look ahead, Jamie. What do you see?"

Jamie blinked her eyes. Carved into the sides of the mountain were four human faces. "Mount Rushmore!" she exclaimed. "We learned about that in school. One of the men is George Washington and another is Abraham Lincoln. Who are the other two?"

"Thomas Jefferson and Theodore Roosevelt," answered Grandpa. "They were all United States presidents. The man who started dynamiting the rock to form the faces died before it was finished, and then his son took over the job. It wasn't an easy task. But look how beautiful it is today!"

"I like it here," Jamie said after they had parked the car and gotten out for a closer look. "I wish we lived nearer to you. Then Mom and Dad could see this, too, and we could see you more often."

Grandma hugged Jamie. "We'd like that, too," she said, "but we must remember that God knows our needs. He carves into our life the experiences that make us grow to be more like Jesus."

"It's like this rock formation," added Grandpa. "If you got up really close, you would see just parts of the rocks. You need to be at a distance to see all the men's faces—the whole group together. And right now, we're too close to the events of our life to see how they fit. But God sees the entire picture of our life from the distance of eternity, and he fashions a work of lasting beauty as we yield to his touch."

Jamie nodded. "I need a picture of this," she said, lifting up her camera.

"It can be a reminder to you," suggested Grandpa. "It can help you remember that God sees your whole life and is carving it out just right." *JLH*

HOW ABOUT YOU?

Are you upset about a difficult circumstance in your life? Does it seem that what is happening to you is just all wrong? Be patient and trust God to work things out for your future good. He won't fail you.

MEMORIZE:

"And yet, Lord, you are our Father. We are the clay, and you are the potter. We are all formed by your hand." Isaiah 64:8

GOD WORKS FOR YOUR GOOD

AUGUST
6

THE FORTRESS
(Read Psalm 18:1-3)

"Early American settlers built fortresses to protect them in case of an attack," read Tina from the brochure she held. She and her parents were on vacation and were visiting an old fort. The brochure explained that forts were often built on a hill so it would be difficult for the enemy to sneak up on them. Tina looked around. "Look at the towers at each corner," she said. "Let's climb up and look out."

"You surely can see a long way in every direction," commented Mother after they had climbed the steep steps to one of the towers.

"That was the purpose of the towers," Dad replied. "Lookouts were posted in them. When an enemy was sighted, the lookout could warn the people in time for them to close the gate and prepare for battle."

Tina and her parents went down the ladder and walked all around the fortress with its thick, sturdy walls. Her father pointed to bullet holes in the outside walls. The bullets had gone in only a short distance. "The people must have felt safe when they were inside," Tina said.

"Perhaps they did," Dad agreed, "but sometimes the enemy was very strong and was able to get inside the fortress. When that happened, many people were killed."

"The Bible says God is our rock and our fortress," said Mother, "but he offers much better protection than any fortress made by people. He not only provided salvation through his Son, Jesus Christ, but he watches over us throughout our life."

"Yes, and the Bible also says God is our high tower," Dad replied. "He sees what's in the future for us. We can be sure he'll take care of us no matter what comes into our life."

For devotions that evening, Dad asked Tina to read from Psalm 18. Somehow she felt especially secure as she climbed into bed that night. *Thank you, Lord,* she prayed silently, *that I know I'm safe in your care. TB*

HOW ABOUT YOU?

Are you afraid of something or someone? Do you worry about what may happen next week, next month, or even next year? God doesn't promise that you won't have any problems in your life, but he does promise that he will guide you through them.

MEMORIZE:

"You are my rock and my fortress. For the honor of your name, lead me out of this peril." Psalm 31:3

GOD WILL TAKE CARE OF YOU

TOO LITTLE

(Read 2 Kings 5:1-4, 9-14)

For the weekend family retreat, the children and teens had their own special meetings each morning while Mom and Dad were at a Bible study. One day, just as Andrea was going to tell Mom what fun she'd had playing the Bible memory games, her older brother, Mark, spoke up. "The speaker for the teens is great!" he said. "He challenged us to give money for the Lord's work. When we get back home, one-tenth of all the money I make is going to the Lord." Andrea could see that her parents were pleased.

Once again Andrea opened her mouth to speak, but this time Julie, her college-age sister, spoke first. "When I get back to school, I may change my major," said Julie. "I think the Lord wants me in some kind of full-time service for him."

Andrea's parents were so thrilled with this announcement that they both hugged Julie. Amid all the hubbub, Andrea left the room and went to the lake. Her own announcement didn't seem very important now. She sat on a stump and skipped stones on the water. "Hey! Why so glum?" The voice belonged to Uncle Max, the children's evangelist.

Uncle Max listened sympathetically as Andrea told him about her brother and sister. "I wish I could do something for Jesus, too," she said, "but I'm too little."

"Are you sure?" asked Uncle Max. "I can think of some children in the Bible who served God."

Andrea thought about that. Then she smiled. "Like Naaman's servant girl?" she asked. "I remember that story. And like Miriam? She watched over baby Moses."

Uncle Max nodded. "I can tell you're busy learning God's Word," he said. "I think that's exactly what God wants you to be doing at this time. And I dare say you can find ways to serve him, too—maybe by inviting your friends to church or by helping your mom at home or perhaps by being a Christian example at school." *REP*

HOW ABOUT YOU?

Do you sometimes think you're too little to do anything worthwhile for Jesus? Regardless of your age, Jesus can use you. Learn all you can from his Word. Then ask him to help you be bold enough to speak out for him at every opportunity.

MEMORIZE:

"Then Jesus called for the children and said to the disciples, 'Let the children come to me. Don't stop them! For the Kingdom of God belongs to such as these.'" Luke 18:16

YOU CAN SERVE JESUS

AUGUST *- Thank U Lord*
8

GOD'S NEVER-EMPTY NEST

(Read Psalm 23:1-6)

Shelly examined the bird's nest her dad brought home from work. It was empty now, but it had once held four chirping baby robins. "It's neat!" Shelly exclaimed.

Mother stopped to examine the nest more closely. She looked thoughtful. "What are you thinking about?" Dad asked, laughing. "Do you want a robin's nest, too?"

"No." Mother smiled. "I was just thinking about you and Shelly and the lovely nest God has provided for us."

"Nest?" Shelly asked with surprise.

"Our home could be compared to a nest," explained Mother. "Like the baby robins, you too will leave your nest, Shelly. You'll go to college, or get married, or find a job."

"Not right away, I hope," said Dad, giving Shelly a hug.

"No." Mother laughed. "But growing up and leaving home is all part of God's plan for children. It will happen some day, and we'll miss her."

Shelly looked at the nest again. "I'll miss you, too," she said. "It sounds kind of exciting all right, but I'm glad I'm not leaving for a while. Who would take care of me?"

"Always remember that you won't ever have to leave God's 'nest,' or his care," advised Dad. "Genesis 28:15 is a good verse to remember. If you put your name in place of the word 'you,' it will have a special meaning to you." He smiled. "It would read, 'What's more, I will be with Shelly, and I will protect Shelly wherever Shelly goes.' "

"That's a good verse for all of us to remember," said Mother. "God will keep you while you're here in our 'nest' and also when the time comes for you to leave." *JAG*

HOW ABOUT YOU?

Do you wonder how you'll ever be able to get along without your parents? Most people look forward to being on their own, but it's a scary idea, too, isn't it? As you read Genesis 28:15, you, too, can put your name in the place of "you." God promises to be with you and keep you if you have put your trust in him. Remember, you never have to leave God's "nest," or his care.

MEMORIZE:

"What's more, I will be with you, and I will protect you wherever you go."
Genesis 28:15

GOD'S CARE NEVER ENDS

THE GOSPEL ACCORDING TO YOU

(Read Titus 2:7-10)

"Mom, it's just no use," said Sarah. "I've tried and tried to get Marcia to come to church, but she won't."

Jenny flipped through a small booklet. "And I tried giving her some of these booklets Dad bought for us, but she won't even look at them."

"I started telling her a story about Jesus, Mommy," said little Alicia, cradling her doll. "But she said, 'Not interested!' She wouldn't even listen to me."

"So how's she ever going to hear the gospel?" asked Sarah.

Mom smiled at her daughters. "Why, she's got all of you, hasn't she?"

"But, Mom," protested Jenny, "we just told you—she won't listen to us."

"Well, she may not hear the gospel the way we do—by hearing it read in church or by reading the Bible," said Mom, "but I hope she will see it and hear it as she gets to know you better." The girls looked at each other and frowned. Then they looked at Mom, waiting for an explanation. "You know that some of the New Testament books are actually letters to churches, don't you?" asked Mom. "And that all these letters—which we also call God's Word—are inspired by God himself?" They nodded solemnly. "Well, did you know the Bible also says that each of you is a letter from Christ?"

The girls shook their heads. "What does that mean, Mommy?" asked Jenny.

"That means that giving out the gospel doesn't mean only telling it," answered Mom. "When you live in a way that is pleasing to God, you touch people's hearts and often open the door for you or someone else to communicate his good news to them." *MTF*

HOW ABOUT YOU?

Do you think the only way you can be a witness for Christ is by taking someone to church? Or by telling people that Jesus died for them? Of course God wants you to speak out his Good News to others, but he also wants you to be a witness by the way you live. Next time a friend refuses to listen when you talk about Jesus, don't be discouraged. Be kind; be friendly; live as you know Jesus wants you to live.

YOU ARE CHRIST'S LETTER

MEMORIZE:

"Clearly, you are a letter from Christ prepared by us. It is written not with pen and ink, but with the Spirit of the living God. It is carved not on stone, but on human hearts."

2 Corinthians 3:3

AUGUST
10

SPACE TRAVELERS

(Read 1 Thessalonians 4:16-17; Isaiah 61:10)

After spending a day visiting the launch sites at the Kennedy Space Center and marveling at the space capsule and other exhibits, Corey talked of nothing but the space program for days. "Corey," said Dad, "did you know that space travel has been around since Jesus' time?"

"Awww, Dad, you heard the guide," objected Corey. "The first manned space flight was made in 1961."

"Read this." Dad handed Corey a Bible opened to the book of Acts. "Read verses ten and eleven of the first chapter," said Dad.

Corey silently read the verses. "So?" she asked, when she was finished.

"Jesus went up into heaven—space travel!" said Dad with a grin. "And some day all those who have accepted Jesus as Savior will be taken up to heaven to be with him. We'll be space travelers, too."

"Hey, cool!" exclaimed Corey. "The guide at the space center said the government spends thousands of dollars getting astronauts ready for their space missions, but our space travel will be free, won't it?"

"Free to us," agreed Dad, "but it cost Jesus a great deal. He gave his life and took the punishment we deserve."

"The astronauts need special clothes, too," observed Corey, "but we won't need space suits and helmets, either, will we?"

"Not exactly," said Dad, "although God does call our salvation a garment and a robe of righteousness. So in a sense, only those who have on their special 'space suit of salvation' will be taken to heaven."

"I have mine on!" Corey said happily.

Dad grinned and nodded. "I'm glad," he said, "and I have mine on, too." *LJR*

HOW ABOUT YOU?

Are you ready for your "space trip"? You can be ready by believing that Jesus died to take the punishment for your sin. Ask him to forgive you and to be your Savior.

MEMORIZE:

"After that, we who are still alive and are left will be caught up together with them in the clouds to meet the Lord in the air. And so we will be with the Lord forever." 1 Thessalonians 4:17, NIV

BE READY FOR JESUS' RETURN

PULLING ON THE LEASH

(Read Psalm 25:4-9)

Amanda panted as she pulled her Labrador puppy into the house. Prince was only six months old, but he was strong and already weighed half as much as Amanda. Mom looked up from setting the table and smiled. "I'm not sure who took whom for a walk," she said.

Amanda frowned. "Prince makes me so mad," she complained. "He tugs and pulls on the leash the whole way. He acts like he knows where he's going! If I let him go wherever he wants to, he'll just get us lost, but he's not smart enough to know that."

"He's still just a puppy," said Mom.

"I know," grumbled Amanda, "but he should know that I'm his owner and listen to me. He should let me lead him."

"Maybe we'll have to take him to dog obedience school," said Mom, "or at least start some dog obedience lessons on our own." Mom studied Amanda a moment, then said softly, "Sometimes people behave a lot like Prince. Sometimes they pull and tug on their 'leashes,' too . . . not listening to God or to parents who really know best. Like last week when I wouldn't let you go to Jessica's party. I'm not sure you've quite forgiven me for that yet!"

Amanda felt embarrassed. "I guess I have been acting pretty bad, haven't I? But I've gotta admit you were right about that. Jessica's parents weren't home, and I found out today that some of the kids got so loud, the neighbors called the police. I'm really glad I wasn't there."

"I'm glad you weren't, too!" responded Mom.

Amanda sighed. "Just like Prince, I wanted my own way even though you knew better," she said. "I'm sorry."

Mom gave her a hug. "It's hard for all of us to remember that we are not wise enough to choose our own way," she said. "That's why God gave children parents. And that's why we all need to rely on God."

Amanda nodded. "From now on, I'll try to do less tugging and more listening," she promised. *KEC*

HOW ABOUT YOU?

How do you respond when your parents, grandparents, or other adults guide you? Do you realize that they may know the best path for your life? God provided them for you because he knows they may help you avoid some of life's pitfalls.

MEMORIZE:

"I will teach you wisdom's ways and lead you in straight paths."
Proverbs 4:11

OBEY YOUR PARENTS

AUGUST
12

BOUGHT BACK

(Read Ephesians 1:3-8)

"You won't believe what I saw at Kelsey's!" Sharlene was almost in tears. "She's selling *my* doll at her garage sale!"

"Your doll?" asked Mom.

"Yes! My doll!" answered Sharlene. "I know it's mine . . . it has a scribble mark on one arm, the same dress, and the eye that sticks shut. It's the one Grandma gave me."

"How did Kelsey get it?" asked Mom.

Sharlene shrugged. "I don't know. Maybe I left it over there or something. When I said it was mine, Kelsey grabbed it. She said it was hers and she was going to sell it."

"I'll check it out," offered Carla, Sharlene's older sister. She headed down the street. When she returned a few minutes later, Carla nodded. "That's Sharlene's doll all right," she said. "I would have talked to Kelsey's mom, but she wasn't home."

Sharlene burst into tears. "But it's mine!" she protested. "And it's from Grandma."

Mom sighed. "Well," she said, "if Kelsey feels that way, you may have to buy your doll back."

"She shouldn't have to pay for something she owns," muttered Carla. But Sharlene was already up in her bedroom shaking coins out of her bank. She put the money into her pocket and dashed down the street. A few minutes later she came skipping back, the doll hugged tightly in her arms.

Mom smiled. "You redeemed her," she said.

"I what?" asked Sharlene.

"You did for your doll what Jesus did for us," explained Mom. "He made us for himself, but when Adam and Eve sinned, it made all the people who came after them prone to sin. But Jesus paid the price so that we could become God's children."

"He did that when he died on the cross, didn't he?" said Carla.

Mom nodded. "That's right," she said. "He bought us back with his own blood. When we trust in him, we no longer have to be afraid of death." *VEN*

HOW ABOUT YOU?
Did you realize that Jesus paid the price to redeem you—to buy you back from sin? He offers you the gift of salvation. If you haven't received Jesus as your Savior, won't you do so today?

MEMORIZE:
"For he has rescued us from the one who rules in the kingdom of darkness, and he has brought us into the Kingdom of his dear Son. God has purchased our freedom with his blood and has forgiven all our sins." Colossians 1:13-14

JESUS' BLOOD REDEEMED YOU

SARAH'S SOUR MILK

(Read Luke 18:9-14)

The milk tasted terrible! As Sarah thought about it, she remembered that as Mother left for the grocery store, she had mentioned that the milk was turning sour. *Well, now what?* thought Sarah. Then she had an idea. *If I add some choco-late, it will cover the sour taste,* she thought. She got out a can of powdered chocolate drink and spooned some of the sweet mixture into the milk. She licked her finger where a little of it had stuck. *Mmmm, good!* she thought. But after taking a big gulp of the chocolate milk, she groaned. It still tasted awful!

Later that morning, Sarah skipped off to vacation Bible school. She listened carefully as Mrs. Wilson shared a story Jesus had told his disciples. "Two men went into the temple to pray," began Mrs. Wilson. "One was a Pharisee—a man who did many good works and went to the temple often. The other man was a dishonest tax collector. The Pharisee prayed first, telling God that he was glad he was good and not bad like the other man. He reminded God of all the good things he did."

Mrs. Wilson paused and looked around at the boys and girls. "Now let me tell you about the other man—the tax collector," she continued. "He didn't even lift up his head. He just cried out to God, pleading for forgiveness from his sins. And do you know what Jesus told his disciples? Jesus said that the tax collector—not the Pharisee—went home 'justified,' or forgiven. You see, the tax collector knew that only God could take away his sins, but the Pharisee was trying to cover up his sins with good works. He was not really a good man at all. He was proud and haughty—a sinner just like the tax collector. His good works didn't change his sinful heart."

As Sarah listened, she smiled and nodded. She remembered the sour milk, and she understood that good things don't necessarily cover up the bad. Good chocolate hadn't covered the bad taste of the sour milk, and good works wouldn't cover up sin. *Only Jesus can forgive sin,* she thought. *I'm going to remember that. RH*

HOW ABOUT YOU?

Do you obey your parents? Behave politely? Help with the chores? Go to church? Are you a "good" person? None of the good things you do can cover up the "sour taste" of sin. Only Jesus can do that. If you have questions about this, talk to a friend or trusted adult.

**GOOD WORKS
CAN'T SAVE**

MEMORIZE:
"O God, be merciful to me, for
I am a sinner." Luke 18:13

AUGUST
14

FORGOTTEN INVITATION
(Read Acts 1:6-8)

One day Lisa's grandmother told her a story. "Once upon a time, there was a poor little girl, named Helena, who had to go about in a ragged dress and without any shoes," began Grandma. "Each day she was given one piece of bread for lunch and one piece for supper. Oh, how miserable she felt.

"One day as Helena walked through the park, she saw some children having a picnic. *Maybe they'll leave some scraps behind,* she thought, *and I'll have something to eat.* Quietly she crept up and crouched behind a bush. As she waited, she overheard the children talking about all the nice things the king of that land had been giving them—food, clothes, homes, and servants. Helena crept a little closer. 'How do they get the king to give them all those things?' she asked herself, not realizing that she had spoken aloud. The startled children began to run away, so Helena boldly stepped out and repeated her question.

"'What a silly question!' exclaimed one child when she saw who it was. 'Everybody knows the answer to that.'

"'I don't,' said Helena. 'Nobody has ever told me.'

"'Oh, that reminds me,' said another child, pulling an old, wrinkled paper from his pocket. 'I was supposed to give you this long ago. It's an invitation from the king to come to the palace. Whenever people accept his invitation, he gladly gives them whatever they need. In return, he asks that they pass out invitations to other people. I'm supposed to give out invitations to all the poor children I can find.'

"Happily, Helena skipped off toward the king's palace to accept his invitation, wondering why the other children had forgotten to give it to her. She was sure she would never forget to give out invitations. In fact, she made up her mind to spend her whole life doing so."

After Lisa heard the story, she became thoughtful. Then she got up and headed for the telephone. There were a few "invitations" she needed to give out. *JVA*

HOW ABOUT YOU?
Have you accepted the invitation from the King of all creation? Have you invited others to come to Jesus so that they may become Christians, too?

MEMORIZE:
"The Spirit of the Sovereign Lord is upon me, because the Lord has appointed me to bring good news to the poor." Isaiah 61:1

**INVITE OTHERS
TO JESUS**

DISCONTENTED BESSIE

(Read 1 Timothy 6:6-8)

"I've never seen so many cows before in my life," observed Amy as she strolled across the pasture with her Uncle Steve. "I'm glad I could come and visit you here at the ranch." Just then Amy noticed something unusual ahead. "Uncle Steve, it looks like that cow is caught in the fence!" she exclaimed.

"She sure is!" agreed Uncle Steve. "How about giving me a hand at getting her loose?" Amy nodded, and they hurried toward the struggling cow. "Bessie, you sure got yourself in a mess," Uncle Steve said, as they untangled the strands of wire that pinned the cow's foot and head.

When they had loosened the last wire, Bessie loped back to join the rest of the cows. "How did she get caught in the fence?" Amy asked.

"Well," replied Uncle Steve, "Bessie has a bad habit of trying to reach through the fence to the grass on the other side, and you saw what can happen." He chuckled. "You know that 'the grass is always greener on the other side of the fence,' don't you?" he asked.

Amy grinned. "I've heard that old saying," she said. "I guess Bessie doesn't know it isn't true."

"Unfortunately not," said Uncle Steve, "so she gets into trouble. But what's even worse is that sometimes we don't seem to know it, either, and then we act like Bessie."

"How?" asked Amy. "What do you mean?"

"Bessie thinks something else is better than the good grass I've provided for her, and we sometimes think something else would be better than what God has provided for us," explained Uncle Steve. "When we aren't content with what God has given us, we're apt to get ourselves into a mess, just like Bessie did." *SK*

HOW ABOUT YOU?

Have you learned to be content with what God has given you? No matter what the circumstances, God will never leave you or forsake you. That's reason enough to be content. Next time you feel like complaining, take a moment to thank the Lord for what he has given you. You can begin by thanking him for always being with you.

MEMORIZE:

"Stay away from the love of money; be satisfied with what you have. For God has said, "I will never fail you. I will never forsake you." Hebrews 13:5

BE CONTENT

AUGUST
16

A GOOD DECISION

(Read 1 Corinthians 6:18-20)

Note to parents: The following story may not be appropriate for very young children.

"Mom," said Jill hesitantly, "I hate it when Uncle Roy comes over. He . . . he always wants to hug and kiss me. He makes me feel strange, and . . . and sort of dirty. And he touches me too much."

Mother sighed. "Jill," she said slowly, "are you sure about what you're saying? Could his hugs and kisses be merely affectionate?"

"I . . . I guess so," mumbled Jill, "but it's not like when you and Daddy hug me, Mom. It's different somehow."

Mother looked sad as she thought about what Jill was saying. "You did the right thing in coming to me, Jill. I'm very, very proud of you," she said finally. "We'll certainly check into this right away."

Jill began to feel better when Mother said that. "What's wrong with Uncle Roy, Mom?" she asked. "Why does he act that way?"

"I don't know if I can answer that," said Mother. "But Uncle Roy needs help, and he needs our prayers. Dad and I will talk with him and urge him to get the help he needs. And we'll do anything we have to do to make sure he never bothers you again." Mother gave Jill a hug. "Honey, you know that love and affection are very precious things. I don't want you to get the idea that all hugging and kissing is wrong."

Jill nodded. "I know, Mom," she replied. "But what should I have done to stop Uncle Roy?"

Mother patted Jill's shoulder reassuringly. "What happened was Uncle Roy's fault, not yours, so don't feel guilty. And don't ever be afraid to speak up if you think someone is behaving in a wrong way toward you."

"Thanks, Mom." Jill smiled. "I'm glad I decided to talk to you." And she gave her mother a big hug. *SLK*

HOW ABOUT YOU?

If you belong to Jesus, your body is the temple of the Holy Spirit and should be treated with respect—by you and by others. If someone is forcing his affections on you, tell that person to stop. If it continues, by all means tell another adult. It's never right to allow someone to get away with something you know is wrong. Ask God to give you the courage to stand up for what's right.

MEMORIZE:

"For God bought you with a high price. So you must honor God with your body." 1 Corinthians 6:20

YOUR BODY
DESERVES RESPECT

THE IMITATOR

(Read 1 John 2:1-6)

Abby tied a ribbon in her hair. Turning away from the mirror, she bumped into her little sister Clara, who had been glued to her side all afternoon. "Mom!" yelled Abby, grabbing Clara by the hand and pulling her to the head of the stairs. "Can't you keep Clara with you? She's driving me crazy! She follows me and copies everything I do!"

Mom came to the foot of the stairs. She smiled when she saw Clara. The little girl was mimicking her adored older sister, standing with one hand on her hip and the other thumping away in midair. Her eyes never left Abby's face.

Mom motioned for Abby to bring the toddler downstairs. "You know, honey, you should consider it an honor that Clara wants to be like you," said Mother. "It means she loves you."

Abby sighed. "I know, Mom. I love her, too," she said, "but I'd like to be able to have *some* time to myself."

Mom nodded. "Come on, sweetie, let's give your sister some privacy," she said, "Come and help me in the kitchen." Abby sighed and returned to her room.

That evening during family devotions, Dad read from the fifth chapter of Ephesians. The very first verse said, "Be imitators of God."

"How can anybody do that?" asked Abby. "What does it mean?"

Mother smiled. "Remember how Clara stuck close to you this afternoon?" she asked. Abby nodded as she looked at Clara sitting on her mother's lap. "Clara watched you and tried to do everything you did," continued Mother. "If we are to be like Christ we need to stick close to him."

Dad nodded. "We do that by spending time with him and studying his Word so that we get to know him better and to know what pleases him. Then we need to copy the example he left us."

Abby smiled. "So we need to be copycats," she said. *MMB*

HOW ABOUT YOU?

Do you want to be more like Jesus? Then study the Bible and become familiar with how Jesus responded to every situation. Consider what he would do in your situation.

MEMORIZE:

"Follow God's example in everything you do, because you are his dear children. Live a life filled with love for others, following the example of Christ, who loved you and gave himself as a sacrifice to take away your sins." Ephesians 5:1-2

IMITATE CHRIST

AUGUST
18

BROKEN SHELLS

(Read Psalm 139:14-16; Exodus 4:10-11)

The Martin children were having a wonderful vacation at the seashore. They spent hours on the beach . . . swimming, building sand castles, finding shells, and making new friends. "Want to come with Scott and me to find shells?" asked Mark one day.

"Scott!" echoed Laura. "You're not going to play with him, are you? He talks funny—he sounds like a baby. And he doesn't walk very well!"

"Just because he's different doesn't mean we can't play with him," replied Mark. "Besides, he's really nice. I like him."

"Well, if you're not careful, no one will want to play with you, either," declared Laura. "I'll find my own shells." She turned and went in the opposite direction.

When Laura returned home that afternoon, she found that Mark had gotten there first. And he *did* have some fine shells. "Ooohhh! These are nice," murmured Laura as she picked one up. "But look . . . there's a broken edge! I kept only perfect ones." She picked up another. "This one has a little crack, too," she said. She inspected it more closely, then put it down. "Even with their cracks," she said, "I like your shells a lot better than mine—I wish I had gone with you."

"Even though Scott went, too?" asked Mark. Laura blushed and glanced at Mother.

"That's a fair question," said Mother. "Mark told me how you feel about Scott. It seems to me you're treating people the same way you treated shells. Scott doesn't look perfect, so you 'threw him away'—you ignored him. God made Scott, just as he made all of us," she reminded Laura. "We look at the outward appearance of a person, but God looks on his heart. He sees what a person is like inside. That's what's important." *PR*

HOW ABOUT YOU?

Do you know people who look "different" or can't do everything you can do? God allowed them to be the way they are for reasons we may never understand. But God expects us to accept those people as they are. Talk with them. Play with them. Show Jesus' love.

MEMORIZE:

"'Who makes mouths?' the Lord asked him. 'Who makes people so they can speak or not speak, hear or not hear, see or not see? Is it not I, the Lord?' " Exodus 4:11

GOD MADE EVERYONE

A CRAZY AFTERNOON

(Read Titus 2:1-8)

Carrie wondered if the afternoon would ever end. She was baby-sitting the three Norris children while their mother ran some errands, and things weren't going well. So far Tina had unrolled an entire package of paper towels, Tracy had spilled a box of cereal, and Tommy kept crying for his mother.

"Can't you make us some popcorn?" Tracy whined.

Carrie shook her head. "No, Tracy. Your mother said you could have some cereal and that was all."

"Please," Tracy begged. "I'm hungry."

"No, but I could read you a story," suggested Carrie.

Surprisingly, Carrie's suggestion worked, and Tommy even stopped crying to listen. By the time Carrie finished reading, Tommy was asleep on the couch. "Girls, let's see how quietly we can walk to the playroom," whispered Carrie, "and I'll help you with that big puzzle."

"Really?" Tracy whispered back. "The big, big one with the three hundred pieces?"

"That's the one," Carrie promised.

They were busily working the puzzle when Mrs. Norris arrived home. "Looks as if everything is under control." She smiled. "Thanks a lot, Carrie."

Later Carrie told her mother about the afternoon. "Once we got busy doing something together, I even enjoyed it," she said.

"Great," approved Mother, "and did you know you got some good training?"

"Good training for what?" asked Carrie.

"In Titus 2, the Lord gives a list of things young men and women are to learn from older men and women," explained Mother. "One of the things is to learn to love children."

"Wow," Carrie said, "I didn't realize I was taking a course in loving children this afternoon." *LMW*

HOW ABOUT YOU?

Do you ever take care of younger children? Perhaps you're still too young to baby-sit, but there are probably times when you have the opportunity to entertain a young child for an hour or so. Learning to love and care for children is a good thing to do.

MEMORIZE:

"These older women must train the younger women to love their husbands and their children."

Titus 2:4

LOVE CHILDREN

AUGUST
20

ITS PROPER PLACE (PART 1)

(Read Psalm 78:1-6)

Lynn was excited! She was almost certain she was going to be named captain of the cheerleading squad!

"That's really important to you, isn't it?" her mother asked as they talked about it.

"Important!" Lynn cried out. "Mom, this is the most important thing in my whole life! If I'm elected, all the kids will treat me special!"

"And after you've accomplished this goal, and you get all the kids in school to think of you as something special, then what will you strive for?"

"Mother!" Lynn exclaimed, raising her voice noticeably. "After that I won't need to strive for anything. I'll have it made!"

Lynn's mother took a deep breath and let it out slowly. "That's what worries me, honey. I think it's great to have this opportunity if you don't allow it to go to your head or to replace more important things."

"You just don't want me to make it, do you?" Lynn retorted, a touch of bitterness in her voice.

"That's not what I'm saying at all, but I do want you to think about it carefully."

"What is there to think about?" Lynn countered, trying to keep her voice steady.

"Priorities," her mother said simply. "Matthew 6:33 says we are to seek God's kingdom first." Then Mother went back to the kitchen.

Lynn stood there for a long time. Her mother always did that—always quoted Scripture to her. It made her so mad! Why couldn't Mother just leave her alone? As Lynn sat down on the couch, she noticed her mother's Bible. Suddenly she felt ashamed of herself. She really knew why Mother cautioned her about things and quoted Scripture so often. Just last week in church they had talked about the responsibility of parents to teach their children the things that God had taught them. And children have a responsibility to listen. Maybe she should think about what Mother had said. *RIJ*

HOW ABOUT YOU?

Do you sometimes feel as though your parents are always "preaching" at you? Next time it happens, remember that they are doing their best. Don't be angry with them. Instead, honor them by listening and by thinking about what they say.

MEMORIZE:

"Honor your father and mother, as the Lord your God commanded you."
Deuteronomy 5:16

HONOR YOUR PARENTS

ITS PROPER PLACE (PART 2)

(Read Colossians 3:1-4)

Lynn was still thinking about her chances of being the cheerleading captain as she and her mother left for a missionary conference at church. But by the time the meeting was over, Lynn was no longer thinking about the school group. She had heard about great needs in various places and actually found herself thinking about her responsibility to let people know about Jesus. She remembered once telling her mother she wanted to be a missionary someday, but that was probably just a childish whim. Lynn's thoughts were still on missions as they left the church and even after they reached home.

"Those missionary pictures certainly do something to your heart, don't they?" Mother commented.

"My heart?" Lynn replied.

Mother laughed. "Oh, I mean any person's heart—mine, really."

"They did make me wonder, too," Lynn said at last.

Her mother looked up at her. "About what, honey?"

"Maybe *wonder* isn't the word," Lynn began slowly. "But I've been thinking of what you said this afternoon about needing to keep things in their proper place. Now after seeing those pictures and hearing about all those needy people, being the cheerleading captain just doesn't seem so important anymore."

Just then the telephone interrupted their conversation, and Lynn went to answer it. "Congratulations," a voice said enthusiastically. "You've just been elected captain of the cheerleaders."

Though Lynn was thrilled to get the news, the last few hours had made her realize there were many things in life that were more important than being the captain of the cheerleaders. She would do her best at the job, but some other things would receive equal or more attention. She wondered if perhaps God would call her to the mission field someday. *RIJ*

HOW ABOUT YOU?

What is most important to you? Is it good grades? Popularity? Athletics? Pretty clothes? The list goes on and on. It may be OK for these things to be important in your life, but they should never be the most important. Put God and his will first, and other things will fall into their rightful places.

PUT FIRST THINGS FIRST

MEMORIZE:
"Let heaven fill your thoughts. Do not think only about things down here on earth." Colossians 3:2

AUGUST
22

UNDER THE SURFACE

(Read Mark 12:28-33)

"I hate having to be nice to Sue," said Kathy. "She's never nice to me."

"Well, it's a church picnic, so you have to do it," replied Amy. "Just pretend."

Mother frowned as she looked at her daughters in the rearview mirror. "Who said you should pretend to like someone just because you're at a church function?"

"Isn't that the Christian thing to do?" asked Amy.

"Hmmm," said Mother as she tapped her finger against the steering wheel. "Do you remember last summer when you wanted to paint that old desk?"

"Sure," said Amy.

"Yeah. You wanted to just paint over the old paint," said Kathy, "but Dad made you sand it first."

"Right," said Mother, "and why was that?"

"He said if I didn't, the new paint would eventually chip off and the old paint would show through," replied Amy.

"Pretending to like someone is like painting over old, chipped paint," said Mother. "All the old feelings are still under the surface, and sooner or later they'll show through."

"So should we just not bother to be nice to Sue at all then?" asked Amy.

Mother shook her head. "You didn't 'just not paint' the old desk," she said. "You sanded and got rid of the rough spots. You need to get rid of the old feelings, too."

"But how?" asked Kathy.

"It isn't easy," admitted Mother, "but a good place to start is with prayer. It's hard to dislike someone you're praying for." She handed Kathy a picnic basket. "Before we head out, shall we ask the Lord to help you love Sue as he does?" The girls nodded, and they bowed their heads.

As they got out of the car, they saw that Sue was just arriving, too. "Shall we go and talk to Sue?" asked Amy.

"Yes," said Kathy. "Let's go." *GLJ*

HOW ABOUT YOU?

Do you ever just pretend to like someone? Why not ask God to teach you to love somebody you find it difficult to like. He loves that person. Ask him to fill your heart with his love.

MEMORIZE:

"I command you to love each other in the same way that I love you."
John 15:12

LEARN TO LOVE OTHERS

T-SHIRT DAY

(Read Matthew 26:69-75)

Jenny and her family were spending vacation at Mountain View Bible Camp, and Jenny was having a wonderful time. "Can I please buy a camp T-shirt?" she begged one day. "Everyone else has one."

Mother agreed, and Jenny promptly put the shirt on. On the front was a picture of the chapel with the words "Proclaiming his Word to the World." On the back it said "Mountain View Bible Camp." Jenny wore the shirt regularly, proud to be a part of the group.

Back home, Jenny stuffed the shirt in a drawer and forgot about it. Mother didn't forget, though. From time to time she suggested that Jenny wear it, but Jenny always refused. "I like it," she insisted, "but it just wouldn't look right here."

One Friday was declared T-Shirt Day at school. Again Jenny begged for a new shirt. "Not this time," Mother replied. "Wear your camp shirt. It's almost new."

"I can't wear that," protested Jenny. "It wouldn't look right. Everyone else will wear shirts with cute sayings on them, or they'll be from exciting places."

"Wasn't camp exciting?" asked Mother. "You loved your shirt before."

Jenny bit her lip. "It was different at camp," she said.

"Yes, it was," Mother admitted. "It was comfortable to be identified as a Christian then, because others shared your faith."

Jenny bristled. "Are you saying I'm ashamed now to let others see I'm a Christian?"

"Are you?" asked Mother softly.

Jenny thought about it. "I guess maybe I have been," she confessed. "I'll wear my camp shirt to school after all. Maybe I can interest my friends in attending Bible camp in the summer."

"Good," Mother said. "Then you'll be proclaiming God's Word, just like your shirt says!" *JLH*

HOW ABOUT YOU?

Do your friends and teachers know you're a Christian? Do you pray before you eat, witness when you can, and speak up for your faith in the classroom? Don't be ashamed of Jesus. Others need to know him, too.

MEMORIZE:

"So you must never be ashamed to tell others about our Lord. And don't be ashamed of me, either, even though I'm in prison for Christ."
2 Timothy 1:8

DON'T BE ASHAMED OF JESUS

THE "WHITE" PILLOWCASE

(Read 1 Peter 2:21-25)

Julie quickly ran to the telephone. It was her friend Shawna. "I'm sorry, Shawna, but I can't come over now," said Julie. "My mother needs my help with the laundry." Julie hung up the phone and began helping Mom fold clothes.

"Why, Julie," Mother said with surprise, "I never mentioned needing help with the laundry. Why did you tell Shawna I needed you?"

"Don't you want me to help you?" Julie asked.

"That would be nice," agreed Mother. "However, what you told Shawna wasn't true."

"In a way it was, even though you hadn't asked for my help," argued Julie. "If you needed me to help, I would. Besides, a lot of people say things that aren't completely true, so is that so bad?"

"Julie," said Mother, "hand me that pillowcase from the top of the laundry basket, please. What color do you think it is?"

"It's white, Mom," replied Julie.

"Now dig to the bottom of the basket and get me another one," Mother directed. Julie looked puzzled but did as she was told. "What color is that one?" asked Mother.

Julie looked at it. "It's white, too," she said, "but next to this one, the first one looks yellowish."

"That's right, Julie." Mother nodded. "Until you had a really white pillowcase, you couldn't tell the first one was actually old and yellowed. It's the same with our life. If we compare it with the lives of people around us, it seems that we are doing all right. But when we compare ourselves with Jesus, we see how sinful we are. People may think it's all right to tell what they call 'little white lies,' but God says Jesus, the Son of God, never lied or sinned in any way. He left a perfect example for us to follow. Be careful to use Jesus as your example instead of watching how others play with sin." *BB*

HOW ABOUT YOU?

Do you try to live like Jesus? Don't compare your life with anyone else. He is the only perfect pattern after which to shape our life.

MEMORIZE:

"This suffering is all part of what God has called you to. Christ, who suffered for you, is your example. Follow in his steps." 1 Peter 2:21

FOLLOW JESUS' EXAMPLE

NOT HOPELESS

(Read Philippians 1:3-11)

Carla stirred Jell-O into boiling water, added some ice cubes, and put the bowl with the watery mixture in the refrigerator to set. "What can I do now?" she asked her mother after a while. "I wish I had a real good Christian friend to play with."

"Isn't Dana a Christian?" asked Mother.

Carla nodded. "Yeah, but I'm beginning to think she's hopeless. She always wants her own way, and she says mean things about other kids."

"That's too bad," said Mother. "Well, maybe it's time to check your Jell-O."

Carla went to the refrigerator. "It's getting there," she said. "It's ready for the fruit." She added apples and bananas while she continued to complain about Dana.

"Tell me something," said Mother. "Has she changed at all since she became a Christian?"

"Oh, sure," Carla nodded, "but not enough. She used to be just awful. Nobody liked her. Now she's not so bad, but she still has a long way to go."

"Like the Jell-O," said Mother.

"The Jell-O," repeated Carla. "What do you mean?"

"The Jell-O has improved since you started it, but it has a long way to go, too," explained Mother. "In time it will be set and ready to eat. It reminds me of Christians. They don't usually 'set' all at once. It takes time. As they grow in the Lord, they improve in outward behavior. We need to be patient with them."

"Maybe we can add some 'fruit' to help them." Carla was enjoying the comparison. "We can pray for them, and we can be friendly."

"Good," approved Mother, "and let's remember that you and I aren't finished yet, either." *HWM*

HOW ABOUT YOU?

Do you know Christians who need a lot of improvement? Are you praying for them? Are you helping them by being friendly and encouraging them to attend church and study God's Word? Do you set a good example for them? God finishes what he starts. He'll finish what he has begun in them—and in you.

GOD FINISHES WHAT HE STARTED

MEMORIZE:

"And I am sure that God, who began the good work within you, will continue his work until it is finally finished on that day when Christ Jesus comes back again." Philippians 1:6

AUGUST
26

NO MORE DOUBTS
(Read John 20:24-31)

I wish this feeling would never end, Julie thought as she sat near the campfire with her youth group friends. At this moment, as she and her Christian friends sang God's praises, she felt closer to him than ever before. But the feeling would end. She'd been to retreats before, and she knew that on Monday morning she wouldn't feel nearly as close to God. *If I don't feel close to God on Monday, maybe this feeling of God's presence is just in my head. Maybe he isn't real at all.* Julie tried to forget these ideas, but she couldn't.

When Julie arrived home the next day, Mom was busy with dinner preparations. "My cousin Pauline is coming for dinner," Mom explained as she scurried about.

"I didn't know you had a cousin named Pauline," said Julie as she began to help.

Julie found Pauline delightful. She entertained them all during dinner with funny stories about Mom's childhood. "I'm glad I got to know you," Julie told her. "And just think, a few hours ago I didn't know you existed."

"Shame on your mom for not mentioning me," Pauline said with a wink. "But I've been here all along."

The words stuck with Julie. Cousin Pauline's existence wasn't dependent on Julie knowing about her or "feeling her presence." It was the same with God. *I've been a doubting Thomas,* Julie told herself. Thomas doubted Jesus was really alive until he saw him. Julie had doubted God was real because she didn't always feel his presence.

"Tell us about the retreat," suggested Mom.

"It was great," Julie said. "Really great." *KRA*

HOW ABOUT YOU?
Have you ever felt God to be especially close, only to be doubtful of his presence when you no longer felt that way? It's nice to feel God's presence, but it's important to know he is there whether you have the "feeling" or not. Don't rely on feelings. Rely on God's Word.

MEMORIZE:
"Blessed are those who haven't seen me and believe anyway." John 20:29

TRUST GOD'S WORD, NOT FEELINGS

REFLECTIONS

(Read Exodus 34:29-35)

"Well?" Lisa looked at her sister, Beth. "Do I look like Tara?" Lisa held a picture in a magazine under her chin as she gazed into the mirror. She had worked a long time to get her hair arranged like that of the famous movie star.

Beth shrugged. "A little, maybe. Come on, we've got to go." They were on their way to the lake before Lisa mentioned the movie star again.

"Tara's so beautiful." Lisa sighed as she stared at the picture in the magazine.

"Why do you want to be like her?" asked Beth.

"Hasn't she been married several times?" asked Mom.

"Yes," said Beth, "and she's been arrested for drugs."

"This magazine says she has the most exciting life in the world," Lisa said.

When they reached the lake, everyone piled out of the car, and soon they were enjoying a picnic lunch. "The lake's lovely today. Look how blue it is," Mom observed.

"The water isn't really blue, though," said Dad. "The lake is reflecting the sky."

After the picnic, they were busy with hiking, fishing, and other activities. "It looks like rain," said Dad when he noticed the gathering clouds. "We'd better go."

Soon they were on their way. "Look at the lake now." Mom pointed toward the water.

"It's not blue anymore—it's gray. It's reflecting the clouds," said Beth.

"And it isn't beautiful anymore," added Lisa.

"The lake doesn't have a choice about what it reflects," said Mom thoughtfully, "but in our life, we can choose."

Lisa knew Mom was thinking about Tara Tarton. *Tara's life is gray compared to the beautiful life of Jesus,* Lisa admitted to herself. *I should be reflecting him.* KRA

HOW ABOUT YOU?

Is your life reflecting the beauty of Jesus? Compared to him, the life of any singer or ball player, or of any friend or relative, is gray. Reflect Jesus and his way of life, not that of someone else.

MEMORIZE:

"And all of us have had that veil removed so that we can be mirrors that brightly reflect the glory of the Lord. And as the Spirit of the Lord works within us, we become more and more like him and reflect his glory even more." 2 Corinthians 3:18

REFLECT JESUS

LOVE RETURNED

(Read 1 John 4:16-21)

Sandy was so happy! When she opened her birthday present, she found a beautiful doll! Every day after that, Sandy played with her doll. She pretended it was a real baby, and she treated it like one, pretending to feed it and put it to bed.

One day as Sandy was playing with her doll, she felt as though she needed to be with her mother for a while. Mother was always so busy with the new baby, and it had been a long time since Sandy and her mother had played a game together. "Please, Mother," begged Sandy, "will you play this game with me?"

"Not now, dear," answered Mother. "I'm giving the baby her bath. Just play with your doll until I get finished. Then I'll play with you."

So Sandy sat and pretended to rock her doll to sleep. But she felt lonely. She still loved her doll, but she wanted someone to talk with her. Though she often talked to her doll, it couldn't answer her.

It seemed like a long time before Mother finished taking care of the baby. Finally Mother said, "Ready, Sandy?" Together they sat down on the floor and began the game. Sandy was happy now. It felt so good to be able to talk and laugh with Mother. She gave a contented sigh.

Mother put her arms around Sandy and said, "You were feeling lonely, weren't you, honey?"

"Yes, I was. But I'm not now," answered Sandy.

"But don't you love your doll anymore?" asked Mother.

"Oh yes," said Sandy. "I still love her as much as I ever did. But I needed someone to love me back."

"Oh, Sandy," said Mother, giving her a kiss, "I love you very much. You know, I think God must feel the same way you do. He could have made us just like dolls, to do whatever he makes us do. But he made us real people so we'd be able to love him back. Let's tell God right now that we're glad he loves us, and that we love him, too." *CEY*

HOW ABOUT YOU?

God shows you every day how much he loves you. Do you show him that you love him back? One way to do this is by obeying his commands. Another is by telling him in prayer that you love him. If you do love God, tell him right now.

MEMORIZE:

"God is love, and all who live in love live in God, and God lives in them."
1 John 4:16

TELL GOD YOU LOVE HIM

THE VIEWPOINT

(Read Colossians 3:12-17)

"Look behind you, Mom," said Rhonda as she and her mother picked raspberries. "Down low there are some berries you missed."

"Oh, and they're nice ones." Mother bent to pick them.

"There are more in the bush behind them," said Rhonda.

Mother looked as Rhonda pointed, but she shook her head. "No, those aren't ripe yet. But I see some in the bush you just finished."

"I guess we should pick each other's bushes," laughed Rhonda. "This is fun. Remember when Carla and her mom used to come with us?"

"Yes, I miss them." Mother sighed. "How is Carla doing since her mother left home?"

"Oh, she whines all the time about how she would rather live with her mother than with her dad. We girls get sick of hearing about it," said Rhonda. "After all, this way she's still in the same house and the same school. But she doesn't see that she's better off with her dad."

"I guess it all depends on your viewpoint," suggested Mother. "You see Carla's problems from a distance, so you see things she doesn't see. But don't forget that she also can see things you can't see. It's like these berries—we miss some good ones and mistake others for good, depending on how we view them."

Rhonda nodded slowly. "I see what you mean."

"As Christians, we need to be more understanding and less critical of others," added Mother. "Tell me, what bothers Carla most now that her mother's gone?"

Rhonda thought for a minute. "Well, for one thing, her father is dating. I can see how that would be hard to take. And she says she misses her mom. They were so close. She could tell her mom anything."

"God can use you to help make this change easier for her," said Mother. "Show her good things about her situation and help her with the hard ones. She needs understanding." *AGL*

HOW ABOUT YOU?

Are you annoyed when your friends talk about their troubles? Does it bug you because it spoils your fun when you hear about the sad things happening to them? Remember, the Bible says "a friend loves at all times."

MEMORIZE:

"Give me an understanding mind so that I can govern your people well and know the difference between right and wrong." 1 Kings 3:9, NIV

BE UNDERSTANDING

DEE AND THE DANDELIONS

(Read Psalm 19:12-14)

"There goes Melinda—that new girl," said Dee to her friends at recess. "She wears funny clothes. And you should see her father! He looks like a criminal."

"Do you think he's really a criminal?" asked Lois. "What do you suppose he did?"

Dee shrugged. "Who knows? Robbed a bank maybe."

As Dee slid into her seat, she heard Lois whisper to Pam, "Beware of Melinda—her dad's a bank robber."

The rumor flew and grew until everyone in the class was whispering about Melinda and avoiding her. A little voice in Dee's heart said, *Dee, what have you done?* But she tried not to listen.

Sprawling on the lawn after school to enjoy the sunshine, Dee picked a dandelion that had gone to seed. She blew on it, and the seeds floated off into the air like dozens of tiny parachutes.

"Oh dear!" said Mother, who had come out with a glass of lemonade for Dee. "Those little seeds are going to take root and become more pesky dandelions!"

"Oops!" said Dee. "Sorry, Mom."

Mother sat down in a lawn chair. "Well, if you hadn't blown them, the wind would have," she said. Then she added thoughtfully, "Those little seeds remind me of words. Those seeds are gone forever. There's no way you could gather them back. Words are like that. Once we've said them, they're gone. The good ones bring happiness and help to people, and the unkind ones bring sorrow." Dee squirmed uncomfortably as she remembered her words about Melinda and her father. "Before we speak about anyone," continued Mother, "we should ask ourselves, 'Is what I'm about to say true? Is it kind? Would God be pleased to hear me say it?' "

Dee's conscience seemed to be shouting now. Her words about Melinda's father had certainly not been kind. Probably they were not even true! "Mother," she said as she started for the house, "I've got some phone calls to make. I'll tell you all about it later." *MHN*

HOW ABOUT YOU?

What kind of words do you speak? Are they true? Kind? Pleasing to God? Do they build, or do they destroy? Ask God to help you watch your words.

MEMORIZE:

"Take control of what I say, O Lord, and keep my lips sealed." Psalm 141:3

SPEAK KIND WORDS

FLOWERPOT SHOES

(Read Philippians 4:6-9)

"Nancy," called Mom, "the guests are arriving for our good-bye party. Are you coming down?"

"Soon," Nancy mumbled from up in the tree fort, but it was the last thing she wanted to do.

Mom climbed the ladder and crawled into the fort. "You're going to miss this place, aren't you?" she asked. "You had a lot of good times here."

Tears welled up in Nancy's eyes. "I still don't understand why we have to be missionaries," she said.

Mom put her arm around Nancy. "I know it's hard to say good-bye." Mom looked fondly around until her eyes rested on a flower growing in the corner. "Is that one of my old shoes you're using for a flowerpot?"

Through her tears, Nancy smiled proudly. "It looks good, doesn't it?"

"Yes," Mom said, "but I gave those shoes to you to wear for dress-up parties."

"I know," said Nancy, "but I really needed a flowerpot."

"Nancy," Mom said thoughtfully, "when someone gives a gift, who owns it and gets to decide how to use it—the one who gives the gift or the one who gets it?"

Nancy answered quickly. "The one who gets the gift. So I can use the shoe for a flowerpot if I want to, right?"

"Yes," Mom said, "it's your shoe now—I mean flowerpot. You can use it however you think is best. And that reminds me of another gift we once gave. Do you remember when we all gave our lives to Jesus?" Nancy nodded. "After we did that, God let us continue to live our lives pretty much the way we did before— same school, same house, same job—for a long time. But now God has another use for us. He wants us to go to the mission field. If our lives really belong to him, do we have any right to argue?"

"N-no," admitted Nancy, "but it's so scary."

"Maybe a little," Mom agreed, "but God is never careless with his belongings. Just like you care for all your treasures up here in your tree fort, he'll take care of us wherever we are." *HMT*

HOW ABOUT YOU?

Are you moving, changing schools, or going through other changes in your family? Your life is God's special treasure. He knows what is best for you, and he will take care of you, no matter what happens.

YOU BELONG TO GOD

MEMORIZE:
"You are not your own; you were bought at a price."
1 Corinthians 6:19-20, NIV

KNOCK KNOCK

(Read Luke 11:9-13)

Kendall had forgotten his key. All the way home from school he worried about how he would get into the house. *Maybe Mom will be home early today,* he thought, *and then she'll let me in.* But when he reached home, Mom's car wasn't in the driveway. So Kendall went to the side of the house and checked the basement windows. They were all locked. As he went back to the front of the house, his sister arrived home from her piano lesson. "Sarah, do you have your house key with you?" Kendall asked eagerly. "I forgot mine."

Sarah shook her head. "I lost mine last week, remember? I don't have a new one yet. Isn't Mom home?"

"Do you see her car?" asked Kendall with a sigh. "Come on. Let's check the first floor windows. I'll boost you up so you can reach them." He locked his hands together. "Here," he said. "This will make a step for you. Try it." So Sarah put her foot in Kenny's hands, but when she tried to step up, his hands gave way and they both fell. Sarah plunged headfirst into a bush and Kendall fell flat on his stomach in the mud.

Just then, Mom's car pulled into the driveway, but Mom didn't get out. It was Raul, the mechanic from Bob's Car Repair Center. Kendall and Sarah watched as Raul knocked on the front door. To their surprise, Mom opened it. She had been in the house the whole time! "Thanks, Raul," she said. "You seem to have a way with that car."

As Raul left, Mom spied the children. "What happened to you two?" she asked.

Kendall and Sarah looked at one another and began to laugh when they realized how ridiculous they looked. "This reminds me of my Bible verse, 'Knock and the door will be opened to you,'" said Kendall. "Why didn't we just think to knock?" *JJL*

HOW ABOUT YOU?

Have you "thought to knock"? Perhaps there's something you need help with, someone you're concerned about, some problem at school or with a friend. Have you prayed about it? Jesus invites you to talk with him about it.

ASK GOD FOR HELP

MEMORIZE:

"You do not have, because you do not ask God. When you ask, you do not receive, because you ask with wrong motives." James 4:2-3, NIV

SEPTEMBER
2

MISSED BY A HAIR
(Read Ephesians 2:4-10)

Amy dashed out the door and ran down the lane toward the bus stop. She hurried faster when she heard a long blast on a horn. The bus was there! But as she approached the bus stop, huffing and puffing, she saw the bus going on down the road. There was nothing she could do but run back home. "We missed the bus," she told her sister, Connie, who was just coming out the door.

"This is the third time this month you've missed the bus," scolded Mom as she drove them to school a little later. "From now on, please be ready on time!"

"Well, I was way ahead of Connie," Amy said. "I just missed the bus by a hair."

"Well, you still missed it," Connie retorted, "same as me."

"Sometimes being close doesn't help a bit," agreed Mom. She was thoughtful as she drove on. "What happened this morning reminds me of something others might miss," she said after a moment. "You missed a bus, but there are people who are going to miss heaven. When they attend church faithfully and try to be good, they may seem to be closer to God than other people do, but unless they accept Jesus as Savior, they'll miss going to heaven just the same."

"Hmmm," murmured Amy, "sounds like my friend Jana. Some of the girls at school use bad language and disobey the teacher. Jana doesn't do those things, so she thinks she's a lot better than they are."

"Maybe she *is* better in some ways," said Mom. "But make sure she knows that only those who have trusted in Jesus as Savior will go to heaven."

Amy nodded. "Maybe missing the bus was a good thing," she suggested, "because now I have something to tell Jana." Seeing the look on her mother's face, she quickly added, "But of course, that's no excuse for being late any other day!" *MRP*

HOW ABOUT YOU?
Do you think you'll go to heaven because you act better than many other people do? Being better isn't good enough. And missing heaven "by a hair" is no comfort—it's still missing it! You need to accept what Jesus did for you.

MEMORIZE:
"He saved us, not because of the good things we did, but because of his mercy." Titus 3:5

"ALMOST SAVED" IS LOST

WHO'S THE THIEF?

(Read Ephesians 4:25-32)

"Mom, guess what happened in school today!" cried Elaine, flinging her bag onto the kitchen table.

"What happened, honey?" asked Mom, giving Elaine a hug.

"Some felt pens got stolen from our teacher," said Elaine. "And I'm sure Katherine's the thief!"

"Elaine! You've no right to say that unless you have proof," said Mom at once.

"It must be her," insisted Elaine. "She stole my felt pens once, remember?"

"Yes, but she told you she was sorry and returned them to you," argued Mom. "Anyway, just because she did that once doesn't mean she'll do it again." Mom looked at Elaine. "You haven't told anyone what you were thinking, have you?"

"She told Noelle . . . I heard her," reported Elaine's brother, who had come in. "And David and Ricky were nearby, so they probably heard her, too."

"Mind your own business, Aaron," grumbled Elaine. She certainly didn't want her mother to know that by afternoon the whole class seemed to have heard the story.

When Elaine and Aaron got home the next day, Elaine crept quietly into the house and tiptoed up to her room. "Elaine, is that you?" called Mom. Elaine sighed and went downstairs. "How was school?" asked Mom.

"Oh, all right," said Elaine listlessly.

"Did your teacher find out who stole her felt pens?" Mom asked.

Elaine nodded. "They weren't stolen," she admitted reluctantly. "We found out this afternoon that another teacher had borrowed them."

"Yeah," Aaron piped up. "But before that, the whole class was calling Katherine a thief because of what Elaine told them. Katherine's eyes were all red with crying."

"Poor Katherine!" exclaimed Mom. She shook her head. "And to think, you're the one who turned out to be a thief rather than Katherine."

"Mom!" gasped Elaine, shocked. "I'm not a thief!"

"I'm afraid you are," said Mom. "You stole Katherine's reputation by spreading that story about her. You need to apologize—both to her and to the Lord." *MTF*

HOW ABOUT YOU?

When you hear something bad about someone else, do you repeat it? If your friends start gossiping, do you join in eagerly, or do you move away? Gossip can destroy a person's reputation.

MEMORIZE:

"Evil words destroy one's friends; wise discernment rescues the godly."
Proverbs 11:9

DON'T GOSSIP

SHARPENED TOOLS

(Read Ephesians 6:13-18)

Melissa could hear her parents talking in the kitchen. "Oh, Frank," complained Mother, "this knife will barely slice butter!"

Dad laughed. "I don't think it can possibly be that bad."

"Well, look!" Mother exclaimed. "I can hardly cut things with it anymore."

"Hmmmm—it is pretty dull," Dad answered. "Put it with my lunch, and I'll sharpen it tomorrow at work."

Later that evening, Melissa approached her father. "Dad, I'm stuck on this math problem. Can you help me?"

"I'll try," agreed Dad, taking her paper and looking it over. "Melissa!" Dad exclaimed. "Don't you know how to use a pencil sharpener? This paper is very hard to read because you're using a dull pencil. How about sharpening it for me?" Melissa quickly sharpened the pencil, and Dad helped her see what she had been doing wrong on the problem.

When the family gathered for devotions, Dad read a few verses from Ephesians. "I chose this Scripture because of the dull knife and dull pencil," he said. Melissa looked at him in surprise. Dad smiled. "Your mother's knives and your pencils become dull and need to be sharpened often," Dad explained, "but God's Word—the 'sword of the Spirit' mentioned in these verses—is never dull. It's always sharp and powerful. Of course, we must get it out and use it. Who knows how we do that?"

"Well . . . I guess we use it when we talk to other people about Jesus," suggested Melissa.

"Yes," said Mother, "and God often uses his Word to speak to us, too. That's one reason it's important for us to read it ourselves."

Dad nodded. "Good. And let's be sure to use the rest of the armor God has given us, too," he added. *REP*

HOW ABOUT YOU?

Are you using your "sword"? Open your Bible and read it daily. You'll find that God has given you everything you need to live daily for him, to defend yourself against temptation, and to win others to Jesus.

MEMORIZE:

"For the word of God is full of living power. It is sharper than the sharpest knife, cutting deep into our innermost thoughts and desires. It exposes us for what we really are." Hebrews 4:12

USE GOD'S WORD

LUMPS OF CLAY

(Read Ephesians 4:17-24)

Katie skipped along beside Mom. They were going to an open house at her sister Jenna's school. "How will we find Jenna?" asked Katie.

"She said she'd be in her pottery class, and here we are," answered Mom.

Katie and her mother soon found the room where Jenna was working, and they sat down quietly at the back of the room. The class instructor was at his potter's wheel, demonstrating how to make a clay vase. The students watched and then began work on their own projects.

"Jenna's good, isn't she?" whispered Katie, watching her big sister at work. "She said she was going to make a flower pot for her Sunday school classroom."

"Yes," agreed Mom, "and that vase she's making will look lovely filled with flowers."

"I wish I could do something like that," said Katie wistfully. "Lisa sings in the choir and Jenna's always making pretty things for church. But . . ." Katie gestured towards the instructor's table. "I'm like one of those ugly lumps over there."

"Katie," said Mom gently, "those ugly lumps are the clay the potter uses to make his pots. That vase Jenna is making was a lump of clay like those. And so was the one the instructor is making."

"Really?" asked Katie, looking at the instructor who was again working at the potter's wheel. A tall vase was taking shape under his skillful fingers. "Imagine one of those ugly lumps ending up like that!"

"Katie, we are all like those lumps of clay," said Mom gently. "But God, our Potter, skillfully molds and shapes us into something of his own design. All he requires of us is that we be pliable and . . ."

"What does plia . . . plia . . . plia—whatever—mean?" Katie asked.

"Pliable! That means being soft and easy to mold," explained Mom. "You see, if the clay is hard, it's also hard to mold, and if we are stubborn and our hearts are hard . . . if we're not willing to do the things that please God . . . he can't shape us into something beautiful." She hugged Katie. "But I think God finds you pliable," she added. *MTF*

HOW ABOUT YOU?

Are you learning—and willing—to do the things that please God? Do you try to please him in your thoughts and words and actions? You don't have to feel inferior even if you can't speak or sing or draw or study as well as your brothers or sisters or friends. The important thing is to be willing to do what God wants you to do.

MEMORIZE:

"Look, you and I are the same before God. I, too, was formed from clay."

Job 33:6

YIELD YOURSELF TO GOD

SEPTEMBER
6

FOR FUTURE USE

(Read Psalm 119:9-16)

"Dad, look!" exclaimed Makia. "A chipmunk!" Dad joined Makia at the window, and they watched the little creature stripping an ear of corn. When the chipmunk scurried over to the woodpile, Dad turned away. "He's back again, Dad," said Makia a moment later. "Look at him peel off that corn! He eats fast!"

"He's not eating it," said Dad. "He's stuffing the kernels into little pouches in his cheeks. Watch what he does with it." Makia watched as the chipmunk ran over to the woodpile and used his hind foot to push the corn out of his cheeks. "He's storing it in spaces between the chunks of wood," explained Dad. "God gives him the ability and instinct to do that so he can take care of himself and prepare for the future." Makia and her father watched for several minutes as the tiny animal dashed back and forth from the ear of corn to the woodpile. In a very short time the little rodent had all the kernels stripped from the cob. "You know, Makia, God has built a storage system into us, too," observed Dad.

"What do you mean, Dad?" asked Makia. "I don't have any pouches in my cheeks to carry food."

Dad grinned at her. "I was thinking of a different kind of food—spiritual food," he said. "You store it in your brain, not in your cheeks."

"Spiritual food?" asked Makia. "Oh, you mean like the memory verses I learn for church?"

"Exactly," agreed Dad. "The Bible calls it hiding God's Word in our heart. We can store it away, and God brings it back to our mind when we need it. It helps us in times of trial or testing, and as we obey what he says, it protects us from sin. It's there for us, just as the corn that little fellow is storing will be there for him whenever he needs it in the future. Don't let that chipmunk be smarter than you," he added. "This would probably be a good time to start working on your memory verse for Sunday." *THB*

HOW ABOUT YOU?

Are you preparing for the days and years ahead by memorizing God's Word? If you store Bible verses in your mind and heart, they will be there for the rest of your life, to be used whenever you need them.

MEMORIZE:

"I have hidden your word in my heart,
that I might not sin against you."
Psalm 119:11

MEMORIZE SCRIPTURE!

THE FAMINE

(Read Genesis 41:46-49, 54)

Mary was sitting at her desk, surrounded by books and papers, when her father walked in. "What are you working so hard on?" he asked.

"I'm doing a project about famine," replied Mary. "My group has to pretend that we're rulers in a country where there's a great famine. We have to decide what to do about it. Any ideas?"

"Not any of my own, but I know what one wise man did," said Dad. "The Bible tells of Joseph, who prepared for a famine in the land of Egypt by storing up food for years beforehand."

"How did he know it was coming?" asked Mary.

"The king of the country had a dream, and God gave Joseph the wisdom to understand that it meant a famine was coming," explained Dad.

Mary sighed. "That doesn't really help me," she said.

"Not with this project," agreed Dad, "but it occurs to me that the idea of storing up could be applied to another kind of famine, too. One that would affect you."

"Like what?" Mary turned from her books to listen.

"Like a famine for the Word of God," said Dad. "It doesn't seem like it now, but actually, it's quite possible that the time will come when it will be hard to get your hands on a Bible. In some countries, it's almost impossible now. How do you think we can prepare for that kind of famine?"

Mary thought. "Well, I guess we could save up a little at a time, like Joseph did," she decided.

Dad nodded. "Right you are!" he said. "In countries where Christians are persecuted, they'll do anything to have a Bible. Some even risk their lives to get it. Wouldn't it be wise to fill your mind with Bible verses and passages now?" *HMT*

HOW ABOUT YOU?

Are you prepared for a famine of the Word of God? It has happened in many countries. If the time comes when you are without a Bible, will you have enough of God's Word hidden in your heart to help you through each day? Take time now to learn all you can—learn a little each day.

MEMORIZE:

"Those who love your law have great peace and do not stumble."
Psalm 119:165

LEARN GOD'S WORD

SEPTEMBER
8

BURST BALLOON

(Read Proverbs 16:2-9, 18-19)

"Dad, you should've seen the play I made!" Jenny burst into the kitchen as she spoke. "I won the soccer game, and the kids gave me a big cheer! Aren't you proud?"

"Yeah, she made a great play," agreed her brother Eric.

"Good," Dad said. "All your practice paid off. That was a good win for the team."

"It's a good win for me," Jenny answered.

For days, all Jenny talked about was her big play in the last game. "Soccer is my favorite game," she told people proudly. "I guess that's why I'm so good at it."

Toward the end of the week, Jenny seemed sad and quiet. "What's the matter, honey?" asked Mom as they finished dinner. "Don't you feel well?"

"I don't think my friends like me anymore," Jenny answered, trying not to cry. "I think they're just jealous because I'm so good at soccer."

"Hardly!" said Eric scornfully. "They don't like your swelled head!"

Dad took a large balloon from a drawer and handed it to Jenny. "Blow it up, Jenny," he suggested. "Make it as big as you can get it."

Jenny was curious, but she started to blow up the balloon. When she stopped for more air, Dad signaled for her to keep blowing. As the balloon got bigger and bigger, Eric put his hands over his ears. Then Dad took over blowing the balloon. BANG! The balloon burst, and pieces flew all over. Jenny looked startled.

"Jenny," Dad said, "I think your pride is like that balloon. It grew and grew. You saw how Eric covered his ears when the balloon was getting bigger. Well, when we become conceited and think we are better than everyone else, those around us sort of 'cover their ears'—they don't like to hear what's coming. Your friends may be tired of hearing how great you think you are. Remember, it's not wrong to be proud of yourself when you do something well. But it is wrong to brag about it." *DK*

HOW ABOUT YOU?

Do you do some things very well? It's OK to celebrate when you do something well. But do you brag about it? How do you think others feel when you act like you're better than they are? Don't brag. Instead, remember that all the abilities you have come from God. Thank him for them.

MEMORIZE:
"Pride goes before destruction, and haughtiness before a fall."
Proverbs 16:18

BE THANKFUL, NOT PROUD

ROSE OF KINDNESS

(Read Ephesians 4:32; 5:1-2)

As soon as Ellen and her friend, Kristen, stopped to smell the beautiful roses near the fence, they knew it was a mistake. "You girls get away from my roses," screeched Mrs. Kramer. "Thought you'd pick 'em, didn't you? Well, I caught you. Now get out of here before I call the police!"

Ellen and Kristen quickly walked away, with Mrs. Kramer watching until they turned the corner. "Boy," breathed Kristen, "what a mean lady she is!"

"You can say that again," agreed Ellen. "She ought to be called 'Mrs. Crabby.'" Giggling over the new name, the girls continued on their way to school.

That evening, Ellen recited her daily memory verse to her dad. "Be ye kind one to another. . . ." she began. Then she paused, remembering the incident with Mrs. Kramer. "She sure wasn't kind," Ellen said, after telling Dad about it. "I ought to tell her this verse. She was so mean that we call her 'Mrs. Crabby' now."

"Hmmm," murmured Dad, "it certainly does sound as if she wasn't very kind. But how about you? Were you kind in giving her a nickname? What do you think?"

Ellen's face turned red. "Why, I . . . I . . . I never thought of that." Dad smiled as she continued, "But I'm never going to call her 'Mrs. Crabby' again! I'll ask Jesus to forgive me, and I'll ask him to give me an opportunity to show kindness to her." *CH*

HOW ABOUT YOU?

Think back over the past week. Were you kind to everyone? Don't excuse any lack of kindness on the grounds that the other person wasn't nice, either. If you're a Christian, God says to you, "Be kind." Ask him to help you show kindness today and every day.

MEMORIZE:

"Be kind to each other, tenderhearted, forgiving one another, just as God through Christ has forgiven you."

Ephesians 4:32

BE KIND

SEPTEMBER
10

THE PERFECT KEY

(Read John 10:1, 7-10)

Tayna ran over to offer help when she saw her neighbor, Mrs. Brown, unloading groceries from her car. "Oh, thank you, Tayna," said Mrs. Brown, looking down at the little girl. She opened her purse and took out a chain full of keys. "Tell you what—you can help by unlocking the door for me while I get some bags from the trunk," she said, handing the keys to Tayna. "Do you think you can do that?"

"Sure," agreed Tayna. She quickly ran to the back door of the house, but she didn't know which key would unlock it. She began trying key after key. She was beginning to think none of them would fit into the lock, but just as Mrs. Brown walked up with a load of groceries, the last key on the chain finally worked. "I sure had a hard time finding the right key," said Tayna. "I tried all of them, and this is the only one that works."

"Oh, dear me!" exclaimed Mrs. Brown. "I should have told you which key to use. I'm glad you found it." She smiled down at Tayna. "You're right," she said. "That's the only key that will open this door." Then she asked, "Have you also found the only key that will open the door to heaven?"

Tayna looked at Mrs. Brown in surprise. "I didn't know you had to have a key to get into heaven," she said. "Where do you get it, Mrs. Brown?"

"Jesus is the key to heaven," Mrs. Brown told her. "The only way you can get through my door is by using just the right key, and the only way to get through heaven's door is by having the perfect key—the Lord Jesus—as your Savior." *DVG*

HOW ABOUT YOU?

Have you thought the "good person key" or the "good deeds key" would unlock heaven's door for you some day? They won't work. Only one key will work in heaven's door, and God offers it to you as a gift. Jesus is that key. Trust him as Savior today!

MEMORIZE:

"Jesus told him, 'I am the way, the truth, and the life. No one can come to the Father except through me.'"
John 14:6

JESUS IS THE ONLY "KEY" TO HEAVEN

ON THE SHELF

(Read Romans 12:6-16a)

When Cathie got home after school, she called a greeting to her mother, grabbed a cookie, and headed for the piano. Mother smiled as Cathie began to practice her lesson. She loved to play and often continued to play the piano long after she was through practicing. When Cathie stopped playing, she came to the kitchen. "Lisa asked some of us over to play games this evening," she said. "May I go?"

"I think so," agreed Mother. "By the way, Mrs. Parker called today. She said she'd like you to play at church next week. I said I'd ask you but that I was sure you would."

"Oh, Mother!" exclaimed Cathie in dismay. "I don't really want to do it! I'll call and tell her tonight." She stomped angrily from the room. Mother sighed. In spite of Cathie's ability and love of music, she objected to playing in public. "I'll play when I'm older," she often said.

When Cathie returned home from Lisa's that evening, she seemed very unhappy. "Didn't you have a good time?" asked Mother.

"Oh, yeah, I guess so," mumbled Cathie, "but do you know what? Some of us were getting a game from Lisa's room, and up on the closet shelf I saw the necklace I gave her for her birthday. It's still in the box! When I gave it to her, she said it was pretty and that she liked it. But then why doesn't she use it? I spent two weeks' allowance to get it for her, and now it just lays there!"

"I'm sorry," sympathized Mother. "Maybe she'll wear it later." She hesitated, then added, "Cathie, are you sure you aren't treating God's gift in the same way?"

"What do you mean?" asked Cathie.

"God has given you a gift in music. He's given you the ability to play the piano. Although you play at home, you seem unwilling to take your gift out and use it."

Cathie was silent for a while. "I guess you're right," she said finally. "I'll tell Mrs. Parker that I'll play for church after all." *HWM*

HOW ABOUT YOU?

What gift has God given you? Do you use it? What good is a voice that isn't used? An idea that is kept to oneself? An ability to draw that isn't shared? A talent for baby-sitting that isn't developed? God has given wonderful gifts. When they're not used, it's like storing them on a shelf. Use your gifts for his glory.

MEMORIZE:

"There are different kinds of service in the church, but it is the same Lord we are serving." 1 Corinthians 12:5

USE YOUR GIFTS

12

A POOR TESTIMONY

(Read Romans 12:17-21)

I wonder what this is, thought Angelica's mother as she emptied Angelica's jeans pockets before tossing them into the washing machine. She looked at the note in her hand. "Ann," she read, "did you ever see anything so ugly as the blouse Jasmine is wearing? I wouldn't wear that to a dogfight! Yuck!" Mother wondered if this was the same Jasmine they were praying for. She also recalled that Angelica had asked them to pray for another friend—Ann. *This Ann?* wondered Mother.

Mother showed the note to Angelica. "I found this today," she said. "Is this the same Jasmine we're praying for?"

Angelica was embarrassed. "Oh, Mom," she said, "one day last week I got so mad at her. I was wearing the new blouse you made me, and Jasmine said, 'You know what? I have a robe and a nightgown made of that same material.' I wanted to hit her."

"You didn't, did you?" asked Mother. "Hit her, I mean?"

"No," said Angelica. "I sure felt like it, but I didn't do anything back to her . . . except write that note."

"I think this was quite enough," Mother said, "especially if you want to talk to her about Jesus. And how about Ann—didn't you ask us to pray for her, too?" Angelica nodded slowly. "Well, writing this note wasn't a very good testimony or a good way to win either one of them, was it?" challenged Mother.

Angelica shook her head. "I guess you should have washed the note along with my jeans," she said with a sigh. "It needs cleaning up."

Mother smiled slightly. "I'd be glad to do it yet if it would help," she said. "But we both know that what you did was wrong, and only God can cleanse your heart and make things right. You need to talk to him about it. And I think you owe some apologies, too." *REP*

HOW ABOUT YOU?

When someone says or does something mean to you, are you eager to get even? That's not the way to let your light shine for Jesus. Ask God to help you offer kindness when possible.

MEMORIZE:

"Don't let evil get the best of you, but conquer evil by doing good."
Romans 12:21

DON'T BE MEAN; BE KIND

CHILD OF THE KING (PART 1)

(Read Psalm 24)

"Stop in at my house and play awhile," Elsa invited Becky as they walked home from school together.

Becky was glad to accept the invitation. After she called her mother to make sure it was all right, the girls had a snack and then went to play in Elsa's room. "Let's pretend we're princesses," suggested Elsa.

"Oh, that would be fun," agreed Becky. And so the time was spent making paper crowns and walking around in their long "princess gowns" (which Elsa's brother, Steve, said looked just like Mother's old dresses). They sat on imaginary golden thrones, while imaginary servants did everything they were told.

At the dinner table that evening, Steve passed the breadbasket to Elsa. "Have a roll, Your Royal Highness," he teased. "Tell me, are you able to butter it yourself? If not, just snap your royal fingers and someone will apply the golden butter with a golden knife."

Elsa made a face at him, and Dad asked, "What is this all about?" When he heard of the afternoon's activities, he surprised Elsa by saying, "Want to know something? I guess we might say you really are a princess—and Steve is a prince."

"But you're not a king!" protested Elsa.

"No," answered Dad, "but since you both accepted Jesus, God is your Father, and he's the King of kings."

"Oh, that's right! I'm going to tell Becky tomorrow," Elsa said eagerly. "Wouldn't it be great if she became a princess, too?" *VJ*

HOW ABOUT YOU?

Are you a child of God, the King of glory? If you have accepted Jesus as Savior, you are. Maybe you don't feel much like a prince or a princess, but think about the fact that God is the King of kings and you are his child.

GOD IS KING

MEMORIZE:
"Who is the King of glory? The Lord Almighty—he is the King of glory."
Psalm 24:10

SEPTEMBER
14

CHILD OF THE KING (PART 2)

(Read 1 John 3:1-3)

Elsa was eager to find Becky at school. "Remember how much fun it was to pretend we were princesses?" she asked eagerly. "Well, guess what? Daddy says I really am one. I'm a child of God, so I'm a child of the King, because he's King of everything!"

"I never heard of that before," said Becky doubtfully.

Elsa nodded. "The Bible says so. Anyone who accepts Jesus is a child of God. You can be one, too."

After school, the girls played again—this time at Becky's home. Elsa's mother had told her to be home by five-thirty. But shortly before five o'clock, the door opened and Elsa burst in. "That Becky!" she exclaimed angrily. "I'm never going to play with her anymore! We played 'princesses' again, and when I got off my throne for just a minute, she took it, and she wouldn't give it back! And she picked the best dresses to wear."

"Dear me!" exclaimed Mother. "And what did you do? Are you sure you weren't trying to get all the best things for yourself, too?"

"But I was company," pouted Elsa. "Besides, I told her that I should have them because I really am a child of the King, but she wouldn't even give my throne back. I fixed her, though! I hit her hard and ran home." Elsa stomped her foot angrily.

Elsa's father came in just in time to hear her last speech. "Elsa," he said quietly, "do you think you acted much like a princess today? The Bible says that when we realize we're God's children—and when we look forward to being with him in heaven—it causes us to 'purify' ourselves. That is, we try to live pure lives, even as Jesus was pure. Do you think your actions today were pure?"

"And do you think that your behavior today will cause Becky to want to become a child of God?" added Mother.

"I . . . I . . . I guess not," Elsa admitted. Then she had an idea. "May I go back right now and apologize, Mother?" she asked. "I'll hurry!"

Mother nodded. "That's what a princess should do." *VJ*

HOW ABOUT YOU?

Did you do something today that was not what a prince or princess would do? Were unkind words spoken? Was there an act of disobedience? If you're a child of God, you need to act as he wants you to. Perhaps there's someone to whom you should apologize. Ask God to forgive you, too, and to make you more like Jesus.

MEMORIZE:

"And all who believe this will keep themselves pure, just as Christ is pure."
1 John 3:3

LIVE A PURE LIFE

NAMES

(Read Psalm 72:17-19)

When Ellen came in after school, she dumped her schoolbooks on the table. "Something wrong?" asked Mother, seeing a scowl on her face.

"Some of the kids were passing around a note making fun of my last name. It said, 'Who'd want a name like Steep? Only Steep the creep!'" replied Ellen angrily. "And then some of them were chanting it after school."

"How did this get started?" asked Mother.

Ellen shrugged. "That same group of kids are a bunch of bullies." She picked up her books and sighed. "Oh, well. It'll blow over, I suppose, but I'd sure like school better without that group."

At supper, Dad listened as Ellen told him about the problem at school. "How did it make you feel to hear your name used that way?" asked Dad.

"Awful," said Ellen. "Mad, and . . . and . . ."

"Hurt?" asked Dad. Ellen nodded. "This reminds me of the plumber who came last week," said Dad. "Mom says the whole time he was here, he was swearing—using the name of Jesus Christ and God. I expect the Lord feels hurt, too, when his name is used wrongly."

"Do you think so?" asked Ellen. "I never thought about that." She felt a little guilty, because hearing God's name used in swearing had never bothered her very much. "I know when the kids chanted and teased me about my name, it made me feel bad. I mean . . . it was really *me* they were making fun of. So I guess when they swear and use God's name, it's really God himself they're speaking against."

"Right." Dad nodded. "I'm sorry about what happened at school, but if it helps you remember the importance of using God's name respectfully, it will be worth it."

"Yeah," agreed Ellen thoughtfully. "And I'm sure it *will* help me remember."

RSS

HOW ABOUT YOU?

Do you use God's name only in respect? How about substitutes for his name such as "gosh" or "gee"? As you want your name respected, respect his.

MEMORIZE:
"Bless his glorious name forever!"
Psalm 72:19

GOD'S NAME IS HOLY

SEPTEMBER
16

RULES

(Read Psalm 119:127-135)

Mary brushed away tears as she hurried into the house. *I never thought obeying rules would make me feel so stupid,* she thought. It seemed that more and more of her friends were rebelling against the things she knew were right. She plopped her books onto the kitchen table and slumped into a chair. "I walked past two girls from my class on the way home," said Mary as Mom took a loaf of bread from the oven. "They were smoking cigarettes behind a tree. They asked me if I wanted to smoke, too."

Mom frowned. "What did you say?" she asked.

"I said no. I told them smoking isn't good for us and that we should take good care of our bodies," replied Mary. "They laughed and said I was a baby and that I was following a lot of old-fashioned rules. They said I should make my own decisions about things instead of listening to other people's rules. They made me feel so silly."

"Listening to people who love you seems like a smart idea to me," said Mom.

Mary shrugged. "Martha says her mom doesn't like to tell her what's right or wrong. She thinks Martha should decide for herself what's right for her. But God doesn't want us to decide *some* things for ourself, does he?"

Mom gave Mary a sympathetic hug. "No," she said. "The Bible clearly states a lot of things we *should* do, as well as many we should *not* do."

"Yeah." Mary sighed. "It seems like life would be simpler if God didn't care what we do."

Mom smiled. "Remember some of the rules I taught you when you were very young?" she asked.

Mary grinned. "Look both ways before you cross the street," she said, mimicking mom's voice. "Wash your hands before you eat."

Mom laughed. "Right. And why did I give you those rules?"

"Well . . . to keep me from getting hurt or sick," said Mary.

Mom nodded. "That's why God gives rules, too," she said. "His laws of right living are like loving arms that keep us safe." *KEC*

HOW ABOUT YOU?

Do you have friends who do not choose to obey God's laws? If so, don't give in to the temptation to join them. Remember, like the rules your parents make, God's rules are for your own protection.

MEMORIZE:

"Open my eyes to see the wonderful truths in your law." Psalm 119:18

GOD'S RULES PROTECT YOU

WRONG "RIGHT" ANSWERS

(Read Psalm 119:41-46)

"All right, students, today we'll begin our study of evolution," announced Miss Pruitt. "Of course, most scientists today consider this to be more fact than theory, and so do I. Yes, Brianna?"

"Miss Pruitt," said Brianna hesitantly, "the Bible says that God created people."

"Young woman," snapped Miss Pruitt, "we are getting our information from scientific literature, not some book of fables. We cannot take the Bible seriously."

That evening, Brianna told her folks about the class. "What am I going to do?" she moaned. "I don't believe in evolution, but Miss Pruneface will never give me a passing grade if I don't write the answers given in my science book."

"Being disrespectful of your teacher won't help," Mother warned. "Call her by her correct name."

"Why don't you go ahead and learn the material," suggested Dad. "When you have written work, give the answer Miss Pruitt wants, but then also put down why you don't believe it. Stand firm for what you believe—but show respect for her and don't argue. We'll pray about it, too—that you'll be a good student in that class."

When Brianna took the final exam on the theory of evolution, each student was asked to explain all the "facts" of evolution. Brianna quickly put down all the "right" answers. Then she added that as far as she was concerned, the "right" answers were all wrong. She briefly explained why she believed the Bible account of creation.

When the tests were returned, Brianna was surprised to see that she had gotten an A for the section. "Brianna, you know what you believe, and I'm sure I can't convince you otherwise," said Miss Pruitt as she gave her the test paper. "You're a good student, and you've certainly studied your material. And that I admire." *PR*

HOW ABOUT YOU?

Are you brave enough to stand up in school for what you believe? To be a good testimony, you may not only need to trust the Lord, but you may have to study harder than ever before. Although it may not be easy, it's worth the effort. You may be laughed at, and as far as you can tell, you may not influence anyone. But stand up for what you believe because it is the right thing to do.

STAND FOR YOUR BELIEFS

MEMORIZE:

"Instead, you must worship Christ as Lord of your life. And if you are asked about your Christian hope, always be ready to explain it." 1 Peter 3:15

SEPTEMBER
18

ACKNOWLEDGE IT

(Read Psalm 14:1-3)

Robin was stunned. Her best friend, Susan, was moving to another country.

"I think we need to talk about Susan's moving," Robin's father said one evening.

Robin shook her head. "No, I don't want to talk about it."

"But, honey," Dad persisted, "we must talk about it. Losing a best friend is hard, and you need to face the fact that Susan will be leaving soon."

"I don't want to face it," Robin snapped back. She knew things without her best friend would never be the same. She just wasn't going to think about it. And that was final! For several days, Robin made all kinds of excuses for not going over to see Susan.

One Sunday morning, the family got into the car and headed for church. "Now," said Mother, "let's talk about things you can do to help you make some new friends when Susan moves."

"No," Robin answered. "I don't want to talk about it!"

"Robin," Mother said sternly, "refusing to talk about it isn't going to keep Susan here. And I think you will feel better once you talk about your feelings."

"Robin, do you remember when you accepted Jesus as your Savior?" Dad asked.

"Yes," sighed Robin.

"What was the first thing you needed to do before you became a Christian?" he asked.

"Tell Jesus that I knew I had done wrong things," replied Robin.

"That's right," agreed Dad. "You had to acknowledge that fact before anything could be changed."

Suddenly Robin saw what her father was trying to tell her. People must accept the fact that they have done wrong before Jesus can take away their sin. And Robin had to accept the fact that her best friend was moving away before she could think about living without Susan nearby. "OK, Mom," she said finally. "Even though it hurts, let's talk about some things I can do." *RIJ*

HOW ABOUT YOU?

Have you asked Jesus to be your Savior? The first thing you need to do is acknowledge that you have a problem with sin. Then talk to a trusted friend or adult to find out more.

MEMORIZE:

"For I recognize my shameful deeds—
they haunt me day and night."
Psalm 51:3

CONFESS AND BELIEVE

THE GAME OF LIFE

(Read Psalm 119:129-135)

"That was a good game this afternoon, Paul," observed Dad as they ate dinner. "You did a good job."

"I thought the most exciting part was when the coaches from the two teams got all hyped up over that one play," said Alyce. "For a minute I thought we were going to have a big fight on our hands."

"I was afraid of that, too," agreed Mother. "They didn't calm down until the referee got out a book and looked something up. What book was that?"

"Beats me," Alyce shrugged.

Paul and Dad laughed. "That was the National Football League Rule Book," said Paul. "When there's a disagreement about something, they can look up the rule about it. Whatever the book says, that's it! No more arguing."

"It's the final authority in the game of football," said Dad. He paused, then added, "God has supplied a book that is the final authority in the game of life, too."

"This is an easy one," said Paul. "The final authority in life is—"

"The Bible," interrupted Alyce.

Dad nodded. "Sometimes our 'coaches' disagree on something," he said. "A preacher says one thing. A well-known Christian leader says another. A parent or teacher says something different still. It can get very confusing. Then we need to turn to the Bible and see what God says."

"But he doesn't talk about some subjects," said Alyce, "like how fast to drive or if it's OK for an eleven-year-old girl to wear makeup." She glanced at Mother.

Dad smiled. "No, but he does say we are to obey our government leaders, so we have to abide by the speed limits they set. And he does say you are to obey your parents, so they'll decide on the makeup issue. God will show us principles to help us in all our decisions. We have to read his Word to know those principles, though." He reached for his Bible. "Let's do that right now." *HWM*

HOW ABOUT YOU?

Do you get confused when there is a disagreement among your parents or Christian leaders as to what is right or wrong? Find out what God says about it. Look for principles in his Word to guide you in knowing the truth.

GOD'S WORD IS RIGHT

MEMORIZE:

"For the word of the Lord holds true, and everything he does is worthy of our trust." Psalm 33:4

SEPTEMBER
20

PASSING THE TEST

(Read Genesis 50:14-21)

"Tests! Tests! Tests!" grumbled Steve and Sheila to Gramps Wilson one day. "We hate tests!"

Gramps smiled. "I reckon we all do," he agreed, "but tests are a part of life. Everybody has 'em."

"*You* don't," protested the children. "You're out of school."

But before long, Steve and Sheila learned that not all tests are on paper, and not all lessons are learned from a book. The next time Gramps saw them they looked very unhappy. He asked what was wrong. "Might as well tell you," mumbled Steve. "Soon it will be all over town. We found out last night our folks are getting a divorce."

"Oh, Gramps, why did this have to happen?" sobbed Sheila. "If they loved us, they wouldn't do this to us."

"Oh, they do love you," Gramps assured her, "but I don't know just why this happened. It's a test life is giving you."

"But why should I have to choose between my mother and dad?" asked Steve.

"There's not always a quick answer to the questions on life's tests," said Gramps.

As the children talked with Gramps, he reminded them of Joseph, who had been sold into slavery by his brothers. Joseph faced many lonely hours and difficult situations, but he didn't become bitter. Although he didn't know why things happened as they did, he realized that God allowed them for a reason. He stayed faithful to God and even forgave his brothers.

"That's what we're going to have to do," Sheila suddenly exclaimed. "We'll have to try to be patient. We don't know why this divorce is happening, but we'll just have to make the best of it."

"Yeah, I guess so," agreed Steve. "Mother and Dad must be pretty unhappy, too."

Gramps nodded. "I'm sure they are," he said. "Try not to be bitter or angry. Look for ways to make things easier for everyone. Ask the Lord to help you 'pass' this test." *BJW*

HOW ABOUT YOU?

Are you facing one of life's tests—a divorce in your family? loss of Dad's job? Mother going to work? Whatever it is, trust the Lord. Wait to see what he is working out for you. Meanwhile, be patient, sweet, and kind. Help those around you pass their tests.

MEMORIZE:

"For when your faith is tested, your endurance has a chance to grow."
James 1:3

BE FAITHFUL
WHEN TESTED

IT HAPPENED TO ME

(Read 2 Corinthians 1:3-7)

Christy was sorry when she heard that Nicole's mother had been in a car accident and was in critical condition in the hospital. Many of the children stared curiously at Nicole but stayed away from her because they didn't know what to say. And most of those who did talk to her felt very awkward about it. Christy didn't know Nicole very well, but she could truly understand how Nicole felt because her own dad had been in a serious accident the year before. There were still some things he couldn't do because of the accident.

At lunchtime, Christy sat next to Nicole. "I know how hard it is," she said softly. "My father was in a car wreck last year."

"Oh," sighed Nicole, "then you understand how I feel!"

"Yes, I do," Christy assured her. "Would you like me to pray for your mother?"

"Oh, would you?" Nicole's face showed her first smile of the day.

When Christy got home from school that afternoon, she told her dad about Nicole's mother. "I told her that knowing the Lord helped me. She listened to what I had to say, Dad, because she knew I understood how she felt."

Dad smiled and nodded. "It often happens like that, Christy," he said. "In fact, the Bible tells us that because God comforts us during the bad times, we can, in turn, comfort others who are going through bad times. One way we can do this is by telling them about Jesus." *LMW*

HOW ABOUT YOU?

Have you experienced some hard times? Maybe your dad or mom has been seriously sick, or maybe someone close to you has died. The Lord tells us that he will comfort us during any situation, and that we, in turn, can comfort others with his love. Even if nothing really bad has happened to you, you can still pray for those who are going through a tough situation. You can still tell them about God's love.

MEMORIZE:

"He comforts us in all our troubles so that we can comfort others. When others are troubled, we will be able to give them the same comfort God has given us." 2 Corinthians 1:4

COMFORT OTHERS WITH GOD'S LOVE

SEPTEMBER
22

DIG DEEP
(Read 1 Corinthians 2:7-12)

Nathan yawned and blinked. Quickly, his eyes scanned the page of his Bible, then with a sigh he closed the book. He set it on the nightstand just as Mother came in to say good night. "Does the *plunk plunk* of the oil well pump ever bother you at night?" she asked as she opened the window a couple of inches.

Nathan shook his head. "No. I guess I'm so used to it, I never hear it. It's been out there behind the barn as long as I can remember."

"But I can remember when it wasn't there," Mother said dreamily. "Before oil was discovered, this farm wasn't worth much. We lived in the old house, and life wasn't nearly as comfortable as it is now. That was when you were a baby." Nathan rearranged the pillow under his head as Mother continued. "Then the oil company asked permission to drill on our land."

"And they struck oil!" Nathan declared. "Not just once but three times!"

"All those years while your grandparents were hardly able to make a living on this farm, there was great wealth under their feet. It wasn't discovered, though, until someone dug deep." Mother emphasized the last two words. "Son, there is also wealth in the Bible, but you will never find it unless you dig deep. You'll never find the riches of God's Word by merely scanning the pages."

She bent over and kissed him lightly on the cheek before leaving the room. *How does Mother know I haven't been reading carefully?* Nathan wondered as the door closed behind her. He sat up in bed, turned on the lamp, and reached for his Bible. Outside, the pump droned on, *plunk-plunk-plunk-plunk. BJW*

HOW ABOUT YOU?
Do you scan your Bible or really think about what you're reading? Read it slowly and carefully. If you're too small to read it by yourself, listen carefully while someone reads to you.

MEMORIZE:
"O Lord, what great miracles you do!
And how deep are your thoughts."
Psalm 92:5

**READ THE BIBLE
THOUGHTFULLY**

TOO MUCH SALT

(Read Matthew 5:13-16)

Jan looked up from her place as she and her family were eating supper. "You know what?" she asked. "Keith sure is stupid. He won't even believe the facts! Since Pastor Hughes talked about witnessing and being the salt of the earth, I decided to witness to Keith. I saw him cheat on a test today. So after school, I told him that God would punish him for cheating and that I wouldn't want to be in his shoes."

"Sounds like you came on a little too strong," said Dad. "What else did you tell him?"

"I invited him to come to church," replied Jan, "but he said he already went. Then I told him his church must not be any good since he wasn't a Christian yet, and he'd better hurry up and get saved before it was too late."

"Why, Jan!" exclaimed Dad. "If you insult the person you're talking to, he'll just get angry."

"I don't see that I did anything wrong," replied Jan. "If Keith won't listen to reason, then that's his own fault." Jan picked up the salt shaker and started to sprinkle salt onto her food. After just a few shakes, the top fell off, and all the salt came pouring out onto her plate.

"Whoops!" cried Mother. "I must not have put the top on tight when I filled the shaker this afternoon!"

"You know, Jan," Dad said, "that's kind of like what you tried to do with Keith. All that salt on your food has spoiled it. And when you hit Keith with all that talk today, you may have spoiled his interest in spiritual things."

Jan looked in dismay at the food on her plate. "I guess you're right, Dad," she admitted. "Keith probably didn't know what I was talking about. I'll apologize tomorrow, and next time I'll try to be more tactful."

"Good," said Mother. "Now I'll get you some more food." *DSM*

HOW ABOUT YOU?

Do you witness to your friends? It's important that you do so. You may be the only Christian they know. It's also important to be careful as to how you go about it. Make sure you don't offend people. They have feelings just like you do. Pray about it, and then trust the Lord to give you the right words.

MEMORIZE:

"Let your conversation be gracious and effective so that you will have the right answer for everyone."
Colossians 4:6

WITNESS TACTFULLY

SEPTEMBER
24

UNDER THE SKIN

(Read Hebrews 12:14-15)

Dawn's tears blurred the beauty of the roses she was clipping. She had been lonely and miserable ever since Amy had moved to town. Before that she and Melody had done everything together, but now Melody always wanted Amy included. "So who cares?" she muttered. "I'll find a new friend. I'll—ouch!" Looking at her thumb, she saw a tiny drop of blood. As she rubbed the injured spot, Dawn could feel the thorn under her skin.

"Dawn!" Mother called. "Telephone for you!"

"Coming!" Dawn picked up the roses and went into the house. "Hello . . . Oh, hi, Melody . . . To your house? Now? Who's there? . . . Just you and Amy? Well, I don't think so. Not today. I'm busy. Maybe some other time. Good-bye." Dawn slammed the receiver onto the hook. "Just Amy and me," she mocked. "It's always 'Amy and me.' Since Amy moved to town . . ."

"Are you going over to Melody's house?" Dawn jumped at the sound of her mother's voice.

"No." As Mother wrinkled her brow, Dawn explained, "Amy's over there. Melody doesn't need me." Then she quickly changed the subject. "Where do you want me to put these roses?"

The next day, Dawn's thumb was very sore. It seemed to throb with every pulse beat. "It's that thorn," she remembered. "I forgot to get it out." She showed it to her mother, and after considerable digging and probing, Mother held up a tiny sliver. Dawn was startled by Mother's comments. "Reminds me of Amy," Mother said. "She's just like a thorn. Seems she has also gotten under your skin. And you know, honey, if you allow the bitterness you feel about Amy to remain, the hurt will become worse. Why not dig it out and ask Jesus to give you kind thoughts about Amy?"

As Dawn went to her room, she rubbed her thumb. "Lord," she whispered, "it may take some digging and probing, and it may hurt for a bit, but I can't stand this ache in my heart any longer. Will you help me?" *BJW*

HOW ABOUT YOU?

Is there something in your heart that causes you to think bitter, hurting thoughts? Does someone get "under your skin"? Is there a relationship in your life that needs healing? Ask the Lord right now to show you how to dig out any resentment and bitterness you feel and to replace those feelings with his love.

MEMORIZE:

"Get rid of all bitterness, rage, anger, harsh words, and slander, as well as all types of malicious behavior."
Ephesians 4:31

DIG OUT BITTERNESS

PART-TIME FRIEND

(Read John 15:8-14)

After school on Monday, Lynn bounced up the bus steps looking for Stacy, her best friend from church. She was thrilled that Stacy was transferring to her school. Of course, Stacy was a grade ahead of her, but she'd still see her at lunch and they would ride the same bus. "When I have a Christian friend at school, I'll witness like I should," Lynn promised herself.

Stacy hadn't been on the bus that morning because her mother had taken her to school to enroll. Somehow Lynn had missed her at lunch, too, so now she was eager to hear about Stacy's day. But Stacy wasn't on the bus yet.

Soon Stacy and a couple of other girls boarded the bus. They were giggling and having a great time. "Stacy, I've saved you a seat by me," said Lynn as she scooted over.

"Oh, thanks, Lynn, but I'm with Beth and Anne. Beth's my cousin."

All the way home Lynn heard the happy chatter of the girls behind her. Tears welled up in her eyes. At her stop, she jumped off the bus and ran home. Once inside the house, she started to cry.

"What's the matter?" Mother held her arms open wide.

Lynn hid her face on Mother's shoulder. "S-S-Stacy already has fr-friends at s-s-school. She's just my friend at ch-church."

"That's too bad," sympathized Mother when she had heard all about it. She sighed softly. "But isn't that just the way you've been treating your Best Friend?"

Lynn shook her head. "I'd never ignore her."

"Not *her,* Lynn—*him,*" Mother corrected. "I mean Jesus." Lynn had talked with her mother about her fear of witnessing.

"Oh!" Lynn gasped. "I never thought of it like that! You're right—I guess I only wanted him for a part-time friend. I ignored him when I was with kids who didn't know him." *BJW*

HOW ABOUT YOU?

Are you a friend Jesus can depend on, or do you act as if you don't know him when you're with people who aren't Christians? Be a true friend to him. Talk to him and talk about him to others.

**BE A TRUE FRIEND
OF JESUS**

WHAT BEAUTIFUL FEET

(Read Romans 10:13-15)

"You'll be late to school if you don't hurry, Anne," warned Mother. Anne gave her hair a final pat, smiled at herself one more time, and reluctantly turned away from the mirror. "OK, Mom, I'm leaving," she said, tucking her comb into her pocket. It was her first year in junior high, and that comb was her constant companion.

"Girls!" muttered her brother Joey.

At dinner that evening, Anne talked excitedly about the harvest party her church was having the next evening. "I'll wear my new blouse," she announced. "It's just the right color for my hair. Gayle and I plan to go to the party together unless she has to baby-sit. Oh, I do hope she can go! I don't know what I'll do otherwise." She sighed dramatically.

"Can't you just go alone and meet everyone there?" asked Mother. "Or maybe you could go with Brittany." Anne made a face. "Just what is that supposed to mean?" Mother wanted to know.

"Oh, Brittany is so . . . uncool, if you know what I mean."

Mother eyed Anne sternly. "I think appearance has become too important to you."

"But Brittany dresses all wrong," protested Anne.

"She looks all right to me," stated Joey.

"And she has beautiful feet," put in Dad. "I know because of how she lives her life in a way that is pleasing to Jesus. And that is the most important kind of beauty." *HWM*

HOW ABOUT YOU?

Do you have beautiful feet? You do if you are witnessing for Jesus. It's interesting to find that the Bible nowhere commends a beautiful face, but it speaks in praise of beautiful feet. And the wonderful part is that we can all have them. Start witnessing today!

MEMORIZE:

"How beautiful are the feet of those who bring good news!" Romans 10:15

WITNESS FOR JESUS

AN EARLY FROST

(Read Isaiah 5:11-15)

"The leaves are so pretty already," exclaimed Rhonda as she and her grandfather walked to church together. She picked up a few leaves.

Grandpa, whom she was visiting for the week, nodded. "Jack Frost arrived a bit early this year," he said. "Some people say that means we're going to have a hard winter." He looked at the house they were passing and added, "This is where the Burmonts live. They're good friends of ours, but their oldest son, Craig, got involved with drugs. He's never gotten over it."

Rhonda remembered Craig—a good-looking boy who liked to draw. So he had used drugs! She felt a little guilty, because she had been wondering about trying some herself. She was in high school, and she was concerned about what kind of impression she would make. She felt she needed some experience to make her more worldly-wise, to give her a bit of color! She had thought using drugs might help her be more popular, too.

"In some ways this early frost we've had reminds me of what happens when young people use drugs," said Grandpa.

"What do you mean?" asked Rhonda.

"The frost resulted in beautiful leaves. And when kids take drugs, they usually feel good about themselves at first," explained Grandpa. "But just as the deadly effects of the frost will soon be seen, the effects of drugs also become apparent. Sometimes drugs actually kill young people. Craig Burmont might have been a great artist if he'd developed his talent through steady practice and study at a good art school. Instead he tried to take a shortcut with drugs. What a shame!"

As Rhonda walked, she kicked some leaves that had already turned brown and dry. She wondered if God had sent this early frost just for her, as a warning. *LBM*

HOW ABOUT YOU?

Have you been tempted to try drugs for the sake of being popular? It's far better to stand alone than to risk your health and your future by taking drugs. Pray that God will help you to resist the temptation.

MEMORIZE:

"There is a path before each person that seems right, but it ends in death." Proverbs 14:12

DON'T TRY DRUGS

SEPTEMBER
28

A HOME FOR CARYN

(Read John 14:1-6)

Caryn gazed longingly at the miniature castle in the Chicago museum. How she wished she had a miniature house of her own to furnish with the little things she'd collected over the years. But she knew they were very expensive and she'd just have to get along with cardboard boxes, as she had in the past.

A couple months later, it was Caryn's birthday, but she didn't even dare to hope for a dollhouse. She expected she'd get something useful just as she had other years. Sure enough, when she opened her package, there was a blouse and a skirt. She was grateful, but she would have liked to have a miniature house.

"Now, close your eyes until I say you may open them," commanded Dad. The "birthday person" always had to close her eyes while the cake was brought in. But this time, when Dad finally said, "You may open your eyes," there stood a beautiful little house with tiny rooms to decorate and furnish.

"Dad! Dad! I love it!" Caryn squealed, throwing herself into her father's arms.

Dad's eyes beamed with pleasure. "I worked on it every night while you were in bed," he told her. "I'm sure I had as much fun building the house as you'll have decorating it. All the time I was working on it, I thought about the wonderful home Jesus is making for those who have believed in him," added Dad. He gave Caryn one more hug. "If you think this is beautiful, just wait till you see what he's preparing. It's going to be perfect, much better than this house I built."

"And best of all, Jesus himself will be there," added Mother. Smiling, Caryn nodded. *CEY*

HOW ABOUT YOU?

Do you enjoy the home God has provided for you here? Do you have good times with your family and friends? That's great, but think about the fact that Jesus is preparing a far more wonderful place for those who love him. There will be no crying, sadness, or sickness in that perfect place. If you're a Christian, you can look forward to your home in heaven.

MEMORIZE:

"There are many rooms in my Father's home, and I am going to prepare a place for you. If this were not so, I would tell you plainly."
John 14:2

HEAVEN IS THE BEST HOME

TORN FRIENDSHIP

(Read John 15:9-17)

"Denny, get away!" stormed Janice as her brother hopped and jumped through the hopscotch squares she and her friend Martha were using. Denny laughed and moved on down the street.

"He's an awful pest, isn't he?" asked Martha. Janice nodded as the girls resumed the game. "I don't know when I've seen such an awful kid," continued Martha.

"He's not all that bad," replied Janice.

"He should have a good whipping," grumbled Martha.

"Oh, he just likes to tease." Janice quickly came to the defense of her brother. "He's a good kid, really. Besides, your brother's no angel, either!"

"Well, Denny's much worse," insisted Martha. When she continued to criticize, Janice decided she'd heard enough. She left the game and went into the house to read.

As Janice opened one of her favorite books, she noticed a torn page. She found some tape and asked Mother to help her mend the page. As they worked, Janice told Mother about Martha's unkind words. "She's obnoxious!" fumed Janice. "She's not my friend anymore."

"Why did you stand up for your brother?" asked Mother. "You often criticize him yourself, you know." When Janice shrugged, Mother continued, "I think it's because you actually do love him." She pointed to the page they had just mended. "See how the tape holds the edges together and covers up the tear, making the paper strong again? Love is something like that. The Bible says it covers a 'multitude of sins.' I'm glad you defended Denny, but don't be too angry with Martha. She's part of your family, too, since you're both Christians. She's your sister in the Lord. That doesn't mean you have to stand around and listen to her criticize your brother, but it does mean you should be patient and willing to overlook some of her faults. Let love mend the tear in your friendship." *HWM*

HOW ABOUT YOU?

Has someone hurt you? God loves you and has graciously forgiven you. Will you love and forgive as he does? Be willing to overlook differences of opinion. Be tolerant of different ways of thinking.

MEMORIZE:

"Most important of all, continue to show deep love for each other, for love covers a multitude of sins."

1 Peter 4:8

LOVE ONE ANOTHER

SEPTEMBER
30

STOP THAT NOISE!

(Read 1 Corinthians 13:1-3)

"Bye, Marie. See you tomorrow," said Paige. "And congratulations for getting the lead in the play." As soon as Marie had gone, Paige mumbled, "What a snob."

"Why, Paige!" exclaimed her mother. "Didn't you tell me you've been witnessing to Marie?"

"I'm trying," retorted Paige. "I did walk home with her, didn't I? I even invited her in for a snack." A horrible clanging noise started coming from her brother's room. "What's that noise?" she asked.

Mother laughed. "Pete borrowed Grandpa's antique dinner gong for his science project about sound."

"That thing!" Paige groaned. Grandpa collected brass antiques. Paige liked most of them, but the gong was ugly. Pete would probably be banging it all evening!

Pete banged the gong right outside Paige's door while she was doing her homework. "Mom!" Paige screamed. "Make him stop!"

Instead of saying anything to Pete, Mother came into Paige's room and sat down. "I don't like that noise any better than you do," she said, "but when I thought of our conversation about Marie this afternoon, I decided to let Pete clang it a little. I thought it might teach you something." She handed Paige an open Bible. "Here, read the first verse of 1 Corinthians 13."

Paige knew that 1 Corinthians 13 was often called the "love chapter," but she didn't know what that had to do with the gong. When she saw the first verse, though, she simply said, "Oh."

"Do you understand?" Mother asked.

Paige nodded slowly. "Yes. Saying that I want Marie to know Jesus and then treating her the way I do is like the sound of that brass gong Pete is clanging. It's just a bunch of noise."

"That's exactly right," her mother agreed. "Now, why don't you think about those verses, and I'll go tell Pete to quit banging that gong!" *LMW*

HOW ABOUT YOU?

Do you pretend to like someone while inside you're really thinking mean thoughts? If there's someone who really bugs you, ask the Lord to help you sincerely care about that boy or girl so that you can show him or her God's love.

MEMORIZE:

"If I could speak in any language in heaven or on earth but didn't love others, I would only be making meaningless noise like a loud gong or a clanging cymbal." 1 Corinthians 13:1

SPEAK AND ACT IN LOVE

NO SHORTCUTS

(Read 2 Corinthians 5:9-10)

Grandpa was coming for a visit, and he had promised to give both Phil and Alice a nice surprise if they could show him they had done their best in the first six weeks of school. "I bet he expects us to get all A's and B's," said Alice, "because he knows we did that well last year."

"No problem," answered Phil, on his way out the door. "I've got all A's so far."

"How do you do it?" asked Alice. "It seems like you hardly ever study."

Phil lowered his voice. "I'll tell you if you promise not to go blabbing it around," he said. Alice promised, and Phil told how he paid Ben, the class "brain," to let him copy answers.

Alice was horrified. "That's cheating!" she protested.

"Just remember, you promised not to tell," Phil retorted when he saw how she felt.

Grandpa's visit began the day report cards came out. Both children proudly showed him their marks along with several of their homework papers. To their surprise, he began to quiz them from the material on their papers. Alice had very little trouble answering her questions, but it soon became apparent that Phil did not know the material on which he was supposed to have done so well. "Could it be that you tried to take a shortcut to good grades and cheated?" asked Grandpa.

Phil glared at his sister. "Alice told you, didn't she?" he asked.

"No, she didn't tell me. You told me yourself—by all the wrong answers to the questions I've been asking," replied Grandpa. "I'm sorry, but I can't give you any reward—there are no shortcuts." Phil looked ashamed as Grandpa continued. "You thought you could just show me your grades and didn't know you would stand before me to give an account of your work. I hope you'll remember that one day you will also stand before God. As a Christian, you will give a report to him. I hope you won't be ashamed then." *HCT*

HOW ABOUT YOU?

Are you a Christian who will be ashamed when you stand before God? Will you have to confess that you were unwilling to work for him? Will he see unkind or dishonest things that you've done? You should live in such a way that you may look forward to receiving a reward and hearing him say, "Well done!"

**YOU WILL STAND
BEFORE GOD**

MEMORIZE:
"For we must all stand before Christ
to be judged." 2 Corinthians 5:10

OCTOBER 2

THE HOOK

(Read Isaiah 8:19; 47:13-14)

Anna and Sue lay on the living-room floor with the newspaper open in front of them. "Mine says, 'This is a good day to start a new venture,'" said Anna with a giggle.

"What are you girls reading?" asked Dad.

"It's the daily horoscope, Dad," replied Anna.

Dad frowned. "That sort of thing could be the first step in getting involved in some bad stuff," he said. "God does not want his people involved in such things."

"Oh, Dad," protested Sue, "it's such a little thing. We just do it for fun."

Before Dad could speak again, Jon came into the room, followed by Scooter, his puppy. "Is it all right if I practice casting with my new fly rod, Dad?" he asked. "I'll do it in the driveway."

"Yes, but you better take the hook off the end of the line," Dad said. The girls got up quietly and left the room before Dad could continue his conversation with them.

In the kitchen, Sue and Anna were having a snack when they heard Scooter yelp. "Oww-oww," howled Scooter. They ran outside. Jon was holding the struggling puppy while Dad tried to remove a fishhook from his ear. "Jon," said Dad when he finally got the hook out, "I told you to take the hook off the line. Scooter had to suffer for your disobedience."

"I'm so sorry," said Jon, picking up his puppy. "Poor Scooter. It was such a little hook, but it hurts 'big,' doesn't it?" He cuddled the whimpering puppy in his arms. "I'll listen to you next time, Dad. I promise."

"Little things are important," said Dad. "They can cause a great deal of pain and sorrow. Right, girls?" Dad looked pointedly at his daughters.

Anna took Scooter from Jon's arms and held him close. "I know what you're saying, Dad," she said. "Reading those horoscopes could be a hook to cause trouble for us later. She turned to her sister. "We won't read them anymore, will we, Sue?" Sue shook her head and held out her arms for her turn at cuddling Scooter. *BK*

HOW ABOUT YOU?

Do you read the horoscopes in the paper? They may seem like a small and harmless thing to you, but God hates all types of fortune-telling. Don't be caught by even a "little" hook of disobedience. It could result in great sorrow.

MEMORIZE:

"Anyone who does these things is an object of horror and disgust to the Lord." Deuteronomy 18:12

DON'T READ HOROSCOPES

MAKING PEARLS

(Read Romans 5:1-5)

"I hate this school," said Judy bitterly. "The kids don't like me, the teachers pick on me, and the work is so different from what we did in my old school. Why does life have to be so tough?" She collapsed wearily onto Dad's armchair. Ben's animal book was lying there, and Judy began flipping through it listlessly. Her father watched in silence. He was just going to speak when Judy pointed to a picture in the book. "Here's an oyster," she said. "That's where we get pearls from." Judy smiled. "I think pearls are so pretty," she said. "I wish I knew how to make them—like an oyster does."

"Do you know how oysters make them?" asked Dad.

"Sure. We studied that in school," replied Judy. "The oysters have a strong, hard shell outside, but they're soft and fleshy on the inside. Sometimes, a grain of sand or something like that gets inside the oyster's shell, and that's quite painful and uncomfortable."

"Right," said Dad, "and what happens next?"

"Then the oyster oozes out a liquid onto the grain of sand. He goes on doing this, layer upon layer, and the liquid hardens. And guess what you get in the end?"

"A pearl," said Dad. Judy nodded. "Something that began with discomfort and pain ends in producing something of great value and beauty," observed Dad. "And honey, we can have the same thing happen in our life."

Judy raised her eyebrows. "I'd love to make pearls, Dad," she said with a grin, "but I'm no oyster!"

Dad laughed. "No, you're not! But when suffering, pain, and unpleasantness creep into your life like irritating grains of sand, you can't always get rid of them. However, if you accept them without bitterness, and ask for God's strength and wisdom to learn from them, you can produce pearls of another kind."

"What do you mean?" asked Judy curiously. "What kind of pearls could I make?"

"Pearls of patience, endurance, trust, faith, and hope—far more precious than the oyster's pearls," replied Dad. *MTF*

HOW ABOUT YOU?

How do you react to difficulties? Do you get angry and bitter? Or do you ask God for his strength and wisdom so that you will learn to use your struggles and trials to produce beautiful pearls in your life—pearls of patience, endurance, trust, faith, and hope?

MAKE PEARLS OUT OF DIFFICULTIES

MEMORIZE:

"Dear brothers and sisters, whenever trouble comes your way, let it be an opportunity for joy. For when your faith is tested, your endurance has a chance to grow." James 1:2-3

OCTOBER
4

APPRECIATION EXPRESSED

(Read Philippians 1:1-5)

Mary was just reaching for a snack when the phone rang. "I've got it, Mom," she called as she picked up the receiver. After talking a few minutes, she hung up and went to find Mother. "Guess what, Mom," she said. "That was Mrs. Chafley, my Sunday school teacher when I was in the primary department. She's in town today and she's calling some of her old students."

Mother smiled. "That's nice of her," she said.

"Mrs. Chafley say she still prays for us each week," Mary said thoughtfully. "I really did like having her for a teacher!"

Taking an apple and her books, Mary headed for her bedroom. Math problems were her first priority, but as she flipped through the pages, she kept thinking of Mrs. Chafley. It was she who had explained so well how Jesus died, rose again, and was now living in heaven. She had shown Mary that all Jesus desired of her was to believe in him and receive what he had done for her.

That night during family devotions, Dad read from Philippians about how Paul was thankful every time he remembered others who loved God and shared that love with him. "Paul's example is a good one for us to follow," Mother said thoughtfully. "Your phone call today, Mary, started me thinking about my former Sunday school teachers. It reminded me that we should be thankful for those who help us learn about God. We should also pray for them and let them know how much we appreciate them."

"How can we do that?" asked Mary.

"For me, one way is to visit Mrs. Palmer," answered Mother. "She's one of my old teachers, and she lives in a nursing home near here. I'll see if I can help her in any way. She helped me so much when I was young."

"And I'll write Mrs. Chafley a note, thanking her for being my teacher," Mary said.

"Good idea," approved Dad. "Give me a minute here—I'm going to think of a way to thank someone, too. I don't want to be left out." He snapped his fingers. "I've got it! I'll invite Mr. Lance, our Sunday school superintendent, out for lunch." *JAG*

HOW ABOUT YOU?

Do you pray for your Sunday school teacher, youth leader, pastor, and friends who are helping you understand God's Word? Have you thanked them for the time they spend in preparation, the effort they give in presenting the Bible message, and the concern they have for you and others? Take time to do that soon.

MEMORIZE:

"I always thank God when I pray for you." Philemon 1:4

GIVE THANKS FOR SPIRITUAL TEACHERS

THE SANDWICH

(Read Philippians 4:11-13)

"Courtney's taking a nap," Whitney told her mother. "Can I ride her new tricycle?"

Mother shook her head. "I think you're too big for it, honey," she said.

Just then the phone rang, and Whitney answered it. She listened for a moment; then, putting her hand over the mouthpiece, she turned to her mother. "Jamie wants to know if I can go to the mall with her. Can I, please?" she asked. Whitney looked at her mother and waited. She had never been allowed to go to the mall with her friends.

"Just the two of you?" Mother asked.

Whitney nodded. "Her mother will take us and pick us up."

"I'm sorry, honey," said Mother. "You're not old enough to do that."

Whitney frowned as she hung up the phone. "You let Hillary go to the mall with her friends, but I can't go with my friends. I'm too little to go to the mall, and I'm too big to ride the tricycle," she complained. "I'm stuck in between." She started to leave.

"Whitney," her mother spoke quietly, "don't leave. It's almost lunchtime—could you make sandwiches for us?"

Whitney walked over to the kitchen cupboard. She pulled a loaf of bread out of the box and banged the peanut butter jar on the counter. She jerked open a drawer. "I hate being in the middle!" she grumbled. "I'm always too little or too big."

Her mother watched her for a moment. "Whitney," she said, "make one sandwich without any filling, please."

"This is good bread," said Whitney, "but it's better with peanut butter and jelly."

"Yes, filling makes it better," her mother agreed. "God gave me Hillary and Courtney for my two special 'pieces of bread.' He gave you to me for my 'filling.' "

Whitney leaned against the counter and thought about what her mother said. Then she covered a piece of bread with peanut butter and jelly. She put a piece of bread on top of the jelly and put the sandwich on a plate. Her mother leaned down and gave her a hug. "Careful, Mom," said Whitney with a grin. "Don't squeeze your 'filling' too hard." *RMH*

HOW ABOUT YOU?

How do you feel about your place in the family? Do you wish you were older or younger? Do you spend time wishing for things that can't be changed? God put you in a place only you can fill.

MEMORIZE:

"For I have learned how to get along happily whether I have much or little."
Philippians 4:11

BE CONTENT

OCTOBER 6

PUNISH OR PROTECT?

(Read Proverbs 6:20-24)

"I still don't see why I can't go," muttered Jeanie sulkily.

Mom sighed. "Jeanie, for one thing, you're too young, even to double-date without a chaperone; and for another, Dad and I just don't think that movie is suitable for you."

Jeanie shoved back her chair violently. "I hate all your rules and regulations," she stormed. "It's mean and unfair not to let me have fun."

"Jeanie . . . ," began Mom sternly, but she was interrupted when the front door banged loudly and Benny limped in.

"Mommy! I hurt my leg," wailed Benny.

"What happened, honey?" asked Mom gently.

"I was playing in that old storage shed near Mrs. Wilson's home, and something pricked my foot and—" Benny broke into sobs— "and it hurts, Mommy!"

"I'm sure it does, but I'll clean you up and put some medicine on it," said Mother soothingly, scooping Benny into her arms.

Jeanie leaned over to hug her little brother. "That place ought to be torn down," she said angrily, following Mother into the bathroom. "It's full of rusty nails and bits of barbed wire; Benny could've gotten badly hurt." She shook her head in disgust. "There's not even a 'danger' sign warning kids to stay away."

"No, but Benny does know he's not allowed to play there, don't you, Ben?" said Mom as she washed Benny's foot. "But obviously, he and the other kids have fun playing there, so maybe we should adjust our rules and not tell him to keep away."

Jeanie stared at Mother in surprise. "He may not like the rule, but after what happened today, he should be able to see that it's for his own good, to prevent him from getting hurt."

Mom nodded. "That's true of all the rules Dad and I make," she told her daughter. "They're not to spoil your fun; we only want to protect you from harm." *MTF*

HOW ABOUT YOU?

Do you grumble about obeying your parents' rules? When they tell you to be home by a certain time, not to watch some program on TV or listen to a particular kind of music, do you accuse them of being cruel or trying to punish you or spoil your fun? It's not always easy to obey, but remember that both God's rules and your parents' rules are intended to protect you—your body, your mind, your heart, and your soul—from harm.

MEMORIZE:

"Children, obey your parents because you belong to the Lord, for this is the right thing to do." Ephesians 6:1

OBEY YOUR PARENTS

TONGUE OF FIRE (PART 1)

(Read Proverbs 29:15-17)

One evening Teresa helped her dad clean the vacant lot behind their house. After raking dry leaves and twigs, she begged to have a bonfire to roast marshmallows. But Dad was firm. "No fire," he said as he went to the house. "It's much too dry and windy."

"I don't see what he's so nervous about," muttered Teresa to herself. "It's not all that windy." She decided to just light a match. She watched the fire burn its way toward her fingers, then blew it out. She lit a second match to see if she could let it burn a little farther down. But this time, she let it go too far, and— ouch! She quickly dropped the match—right into a pile of dry leaves and sticks. Before she knew it, the whole pile was crackling merrily.

Teresa ran to get the hose, hoping to put the fire out before Dad came out again. But when she returned, hose in hand, she saw that the wind had blown bits of burning material around, and other fires were starting as well. She screamed as a large piece was blown toward the garage roof. Mother came to the window, took one look, and ran to call the fire department.

Later that evening, after the excitement had died down, Teresa sat with her parents in the kitchen. "I'm so thankful no serious damage was done," said Dad. "But you have some explaining to do, Teresa."

"I didn't mean to do it," sobbed Teresa, after telling how it had happened. "I'm s-s-sorry!"

"I know," said Dad with a sigh, "but we'll have to punish you for this, you know."

"But, Dad," protested Teresa, "it was an accident."

"Yes," agreed Dad, "but you know you are not to play with matches. If you had obeyed, the accident wouldn't have happened. I hope you've learned a valuable lesson, honey." *BJW*

HOW ABOUT YOU?

Do you think you're punished too much? God has given your parents the responsibility of training you. Part of that training involves punishing you when you do wrong. They don't do it because they want to but because they love you. The next time you are being punished, stop and thank the Lord for giving you parents who care.

MEMORIZE:

"If you refuse to discipline your children, it proves you don't love them; if you love your children, you will be prompt to discipline them."

Proverbs 13:24

DISCIPLINE
SHOWS LOVE

OCTOBER
8

TONGUE OF FIRE (PART 2)

(Read James 3:2-10)

Teresa had so hoped to be the princess in the school play, but Miss Moore was giving Joy Burns the part. "Joy's so braggy about it," grumbled Teresa to her friend Lynn. "With a family like hers, I wouldn't brag so much."

"What's the matter with her family?" Lynn asked eagerly. After a little coaxing, Teresa informed her that Joy's father drank and her mother had a serious mental problem. "Wow!" exclaimed Lynn. "Let's not play with her anymore." Although Teresa knew it was wrong, she agreed. After all, she should have been the princess!

"I heard something very disturbing today," said Teresa's mother a couple of weeks later. "Rumors about the Burns family have apparently been circulating at school, and I heard that the kids have been avoiding Joy. What do you know about this, Teresa?" Teresa just shrugged, but her mother noticed her face turning red. "I think you had better tell us anything you know about this," added Mother. "The story is that Mr. Burns is a drunkard and that Mrs. Burns may have to be sent to a mental institution. You didn't have anything to do with starting these rumors, did you?"

"Uh . . . well, I didn't mean to," stammered Teresa, "but Joy did say her father took a drink at a Christmas party, and that he said her mom was about to . . . I mean . . . he said he didn't know how her mom kept from having a nervous breakdown."

"Teresa, those things should not have been repeated," said Mother sternly. "But those things are entirely different from what's being said now. This just goes to show how gossip grows and spreads."

Dad spoke thoughtfully. "Remember the fire we had last week when you raked leaves? One little match caused so much trouble! And your little tongue has done the same. This fire may be harder to put out than the other."

"Oh, Dad, I'm so sorry," cried Teresa.

"Well, in the morning you'll have to go over to Joy's house to explain and apologize," Dad told her. "And at school, you'll have to straighten out the story with all those you've talked to." *BJW*

HOW ABOUT YOU?

Do you control your tongue? Or does it give you trouble? Whenever you're tempted to tell an unkind thing, remember that what you say could spread like fire. It can cause so much heartache and damage.

MEMORIZE:

"The tongue is a flame of fire. It is full of wickedness that can ruin your whole life." James 3:6

DON'T GOSSIP

THE REAL REASON

(Read Psalm 19:12-14)

"Hi, Mary Beth," crooned Shana into the phone. She was using her sweetest voice. "I was wondering if you'd like to come to my birthday party on Saturday . . . it's at one o'clock. OK, see you there!"

Mother smiled as Shana hung up the phone and headed out the door to play with her friends. But the smile faded when she overheard the conversation that took place between Shana and her friend Sara. "Is she coming?" Sara asked. Shana grinned and nodded. "Good," continued Sara. "When she gives you something as nice as the bracelet she gave me, you'll be glad you invited her even though she is weird. You'll even thank me for telling you about it." Giggling, the girls linked arms and headed for the park.

That evening, Mother sat on the edge of Shana's bed. "Shana, I couldn't help but overhear you and Sara talking this afternoon," she said. "I was sorry to learn that you had an ulterior motive when you invited Mary Beth to your birthday party."

"Ulterior motive? What's that?" Shana wanted to know.

"Well, when you have an ulterior motive, it means you have a reason other than the obvious one for doing something. It looked like you invited Mary Beth to your party because you wanted her to be your friend. However, your real reason was to get a nice gift from her. People may not see the real reason for what you do, but God always does. The Bible says God searches every heart and understands all our motives for doing things."

Shana's face turned red. "I . . . I didn't mean any harm, but I know you're right. I'm sorry," she said. "Should I call her and tell her not to come?"

Mother looked solemn. "How do you think that would make her feel? I think you can find a better solution."

Shana thought about it. "You mean I should be a friend to her all the time," she said at last. Mother nodded. "I'll try." *PR*

HOW ABOUT YOU?

Can you think of a time when you might have had an "ulterior motive"? You always need to look inward to see if your motives please God. In Psalm 139, David prayed, "Point out anything in me that offends you." Will you ask God, as David did, to show you when your motives are wrong?

**GOD KNOWS
YOUR MOTIVES**

MEMORIZE:
"For the Lord sees every heart and understands and knows every plan and thought." 1 Chronicles 28:9

NOT GOOD ENOUGH

(Read Colossians 3:22-24)

"OK, Dad!" Emily exclaimed as she ran into the garage. "I'm ready to help with Ruff's doghouse now."

"You are?" asked Dad. "I thought you had some homework to do for your history class, and we just left the dinner table ten minutes ago. I can't understand how you could do a very good job on your assignment in that amount of time."

Emily picked up a hammer and nail. She placed the nail carefully on the board. "Well, maybe it wasn't the best homework job, but it'll be good enough." She raised the hammer and pounded in the nail. "Perfect! Did you see that, Dad? I drove the nail in perfectly straight." She stepped back to admire her work.

"Yes, that's fine," said Dad. "OK. Let's get it done." He picked up a hammer and carelessly pounded a nail, causing it to bend. "Oops!" he said. "Oh, well. I'll just pound it down into the wood so it doesn't show too much."

"What are you doing?" gasped Emily. "I don't want this doghouse to be just thrown together. I want it done right."

"Well, this should be good enough," said Dad.

"Dad, you're always telling me that when nails go in crooked they will never hold like well-driven nails will," protested Emily.

Dad smiled. "That's true, and I can't blame you for not being pleased with this," he agreed as he began to pry out the nail. "You know," he added. "God isn't pleased when we do a job just 'good enough' to get by, either."

Emily sighed. "You mean my homework, I suppose."

"Well, yes." Dad nodded. "Do you think the homework you did tonight would be a good testimony?"

Emily frowned. "I guess not," she admitted. "OK . . . I'll do it over, and I'll do my best this time. But will you wait till I come back?"

Dad put down his hammer and grinned. "I'll be right here!" he promised. *DA*

HOW ABOUT YOU?

When you dust, do you neglect the corners you think won't be noticed? When you wash dishes, do you wipe the cupboard but leave the stovetop? When you mow the lawn, do you skip the grass close to the bushes? Do you sometimes do work just "good enough" to get by? Do your best.

MEMORIZE:

"Work hard and cheerfully at whatever you do, as though you were working for the Lord rather than for people." Colossians 3:23

DO YOUR BEST FOR GOD

FORBIDDEN SWEETS

(Read Psalm 139:1-6)

"Sarah, it's about time to go pick up Jenny from preschool," called Mom.

"Coming, Mom," responded Sarah. She had a day off from school because of teacher conferences, and she enjoyed these rare opportunities to go along to get her sister from preschool. "Can we go early and watch a little while?" she asked. The preschool was also a training school for early education students at the university, so there was a large, one-way mirrored window. College students and parents could observe the activities through the large window, but the children could not see them.

"OK," agreed Mom, picking up her car keys.

"Can I have a piece of candy, Mom?" asked Sarah.

"No. It's too close to lunchtime," said Mom. "Let's go." But after Mom went out the door, Sarah grabbed a piece of candy and popped it into her mouth. She got into the car, sure that Mom would never know.

When they arrived at the school, they stood at the window and watched. "Jenny gets to do the weather chart today," said Mom as Jenny took the "cloudy" sticker up to the calendar.

"Look at that boy next to the teacher," said Sarah. "He's poking the girl in the pink dress. She looks like she's ready to slug him." She laughed. "If that were Jenny getting poked, she definitely would slug him."

Mom glanced at Sarah. "Why is your tongue green?" asked Mom.

"I . . . I . . ." Sarah didn't know what to say as Mom looked at her sternly. "I had . . . I had a piece of candy," admitted Sarah.

Mom nodded. "And you thought I'd never know, didn't you?" she asked. "Even if I had never found out, you disobeyed me. I may not see everything you do, but God does." She motioned toward the window. "It's like this one-way mirror here," she added. "We can see Jenny and her teacher and the boy poking the little girl, but they can't see us. We can see everything that goes on in that room, good and bad. And God sees all that happens here on earth. We can't hide anything we do from him." *TKM*

HOW ABOUT YOU?

Are you ever tempted to cheat on a test or homework assignment, or to steal a pack of gum from the store when you're sure no one will see? Even if no person ever sees you or catches you, God sees everything you do.

GOD SEES ALL

MEMORIZE:
"You spread out our sins before you—
our secret sins—and you
see them all." Psalm 90:8

THE POWER TO FORGIVE

(Read Romans 7:19-25)

Erin grinned as Mom put a plate of spaghetti in front of the baby. Although little Paul loved to eat with the rest of the family, he always made a mess. "You'll have to wash his hair when he's done," said Erin.

Mom smiled. "I know," she said. "I'll have to put him in the tub, but it's worth it. He loves spaghetti."

Sure enough, when he was finished, Paul was a mess. He had spaghetti in his hair and sauce smeared across his cheeks. Mom picked him up and carried him to the bathtub. After his bath, Mom wrapped him in a fluffy towel. His hair was combed, and it smelled like baby shampoo. Erin kissed his cheek. "You look better now," she said.

Just then the phone rang, and Erin answered it. It was her friend Sandy. Erin frowned. During the soccer game the week before, Sandy had said something that hurt Erin's feelings. Sandy had apologized, but Erin had not been able to forgive her. She tried to be polite as she talked to Sandy on the phone, but she soon made an excuse to hang up.

"Problems?" asked Mom, who couldn't help hearing. "You didn't sound very friendly."

Erin sighed. "I really do wish I could forgive Sandy, but I just can't," she murmured. "I keep telling myself she didn't mean what she said, but I can't seem to get over being mad. Still, holding a grudge makes me feel as grubby inside as . . . as Paul looks after he eats spaghetti."

Mom thought a minute. "If nobody gave Paul a bath, he'd really get to be a mess, wouldn't he?" she said. "He'd always have food on his face and hair, because cleaning up is something he can't do for himself. He needs help. And we need help, too, when we try to clean up our spiritual life. We can't do it on our own."

"You mean . . . God's help?" asked Erin.

Mom nodded. "Ask him to help you in your relationship with Sandy," she suggested. "Ask him to help you truly forgive her. Don't let an ugly, unforgiving spirit remain in you." *KEC*

HOW ABOUT YOU?

Do you wish you could break bad habits, forgive others, or overcome some sin in your life? You can't do it on your own. Ask God to help. With his strength and wisdom, you can find the grace and power you need.

MEMORIZE:

"So let us come boldly to the throne of our gracious God. There we will receive his mercy, and we will find grace to help us when we need it."
Hebrews 4:16

SEEK GOD'S HELP

DISAPPOINTMENTS

(Read Habakkuk 3:17-19)

"But we had everything planned! We were ready to go," wailed LoriAnn. "Why did this have to happen now?" She shoved her suitcase into her closet as she fought back the tears that stung her eyes.

"I'm sorry, honey," said Mom comfortingly, "but it can't be helped."

"It's just not fair!" protested LoriAnn. "We've been planning for months to visit Granny." She held up the calendar with the date circled in red. "See, I marked it on my calendar. I told all my friends that I was going. Besides, we don't even know this lady."

Mom put her arm around LoriAnn and spoke gently. "You may not know Mrs. Taylor, but you know Rick and Jan Miller. She is their grandmother. In fact, she's the one who raised them when their parents died. Now she's very sick, and they asked your dad to come. He's disappointed that we had to postpone our trip, too, but the Miller family needs their pastor with them at the hospital during this time."

"I know, Mom, but Granny and I had a lot of things planned," whined LoriAnn. "Now it will be another month before we can visit her."

Mom walked to the desk in the corner of the room. She picked up a notepad and pencil. "Let's make a list. Name three things you and Granny are going to do when you visit her."

"That's easy," LoriAnn answered. "We're going to bake cookies, go shopping at the mall, and see the new baby giraffe at the zoo."

"Now name three things Rick and Jan are going to get to do when they visit their grandmother," said Mom.

LoriAnn looked surprised, and then ashamed. "Oh, Mom, I was only thinking about how disappointed I was," she admitted. "But I should be thanking God that Granny is healthy." Then LoriAnn looked up. "I'll quit fussing," she promised. "I'll let Rick and Jan know that I'll be praying for their grandmother, too." *LGR*

HOW ABOUT YOU?

When you face disappointments, how do you react? Try looking at the problem from other people's point of view. You may find blessings hidden in your disappointments. Thank the Lord for these blessings. Can you look past your disappointments and find ways to reach out to others?

**LOOK PAST
DISAPPOINTMENTS**

MEMORIZE:
"Yet I will rejoice in the Lord! I will be joyful in the God of my salvation."
Habakkuk 3:18

OCTOBER
14

Sarah was excited! She actually had her own telephone in her own room! Her grandmother had given it to her for her 13th birthday. Immediately Sarah began to call all of her friends. For almost an hour she talked on her new telephone.

"Sarah," Dad called, "I need to use the phone line—now! You've been using it long enough."

Sarah hung up reluctantly. As soon as her father finished his calls, she quickly dialed another number and talked to another friend for more than thirty minutes.

"Hey, Sarah!" her brother shouted. "Quit hogging the line. I need to call one of the guys about practice tonight." Once again Sarah hung up, grumbling as she did so. "What good is a phone if you can't use it when you want?" she said with a sigh.

Early the next morning the telephone rang. Hurriedly Sarah picked up the receiver. "Uncle Arnie!" she squealed when she recognized the voice. "Are you coming to see us?"

"I would have come last night if I could have gotten hold of you," her uncle answered. "I was at the airport, and I had a long layover. I tried to call you, but the line was busy." Suddenly Sarah realized how much time she had spent on the phone. Because she had "hogged" the phone line, she had missed seeing her favorite uncle.

As Sarah listened to the radio later, she heard a song comparing prayer to talking on the telephone. The words of the song pointed out that no one gets a "busy buzz" when calling upon the Lord. "Isn't that great?" said the speaker when the song was finished. "God is always available. But do you know that there is something that could block your 'connection' with God? The Bible says that if you hang onto sins in your heart, God will not hear."

As Sarah listened, she made two decisions. First, she would not spend so much time on the telephone. Second, and even more important, she made up her mind to make sure there was no sin in her life to disrupt the connections in her prayer line to God. *RIJ*

HOW ABOUT YOU?
Sin interferes in the prayer lines between God and his children. Is there any sin in your life that could block the connections? If so, confess it to the Lord. Keep the prayer lines open!

MEMORIZE:
"Your sins have cut you off from God. Because of your sin, he has turned away and will not listen anymore."
Isaiah 59:2

**KEEP PRAYER
LINES OPEN**

UNFAIR!

(Read Isaiah 53:5-7, 12)

"It's not fair!" stormed Karen angrily. "Kim lied, and Mrs. Edwards punished *me!* She made me stay inside during recess, and all the kids laughed at me." Karen spoke rapidly. "I was humiliated!"

"But what happened, Karen?" prodded Mother.

"Kim told Mrs. Edwards that I was the one who scribbled on everyone's test papers. It wasn't me, Mom," cried Karen. "Kim did it because she thought she had failed."

"How do you know Kim did it, honey?" asked Mother.

"I saw her. Mrs. Edwards was on duty on the playground, and I hadn't gone outside yet," Karen explained. "But Mrs. Edwards believed Kim and not me! Why should I be punished for her bad behavior?"

Mother put an arm around Karen and handed her a tissue. "I'm sorry about this, honey." Mother spoke softly. After a moment she added, "When something like this happens to me, it makes me think of Jesus."

"Jesus?" Karen sounded surprised. "Why?"

"Jesus did nothing wrong his entire life," explained Mother, "yet he took the punishment for our sins. How do you suppose he felt?"

Thoughtfully, Karen responded, "A lot like me, maybe?"

"Maybe," said Mother, "but even though he was humiliated and denied justice, he didn't complain. And he forgave those who treated him so badly." Mother hugged Karen. "I've found that when I go through even a little, tiny bit of the kind of treatment Jesus experienced, it helps me understand a little better what he went through. It makes me feel closer to him. Can you understand what I'm saying?"

Karen nodded and attempted a smile. "I feel like getting even with Kim, but I won't," she said. "I'll ask God to help me forgive her, because Jesus forgives me." *CJW*

HOW ABOUT YOU?

Are you ever punished when it's not your fault? Do you try to get even and make the guilty person pay? Next time this happens, pause a moment and think about Jesus. Try to behave the way he would.

MEMORIZE:

"Never pay back evil for evil to anyone. Do things in such a way that everyone can see you are honorable." Romans 12:17a

DON'T TRY TO GET EVEN

OCTOBER
16

FLEA MARKET BARGAIN

(Read Psalm 119:161-168)

Jeanne stood at the entrance to the flea market. "Wow! What a lot of stuff!" she exclaimed, pointing to rows of tables and booths. She ran to catch up with Mother. "What are we looking for?" asked Jeanne.

"A candy dish for Aunt Helen," replied Mother. "She likes old-fashioned things. She says they have character."

"Dad says Aunt Helen is a character," said Jeanne. Mother gave her a stern look, so she changed the subject. "Look," she said, "here are some candy dishes. Maybe Aunt Helen will like one of these."

They stopped to look, and before long Mother had made a purchase and was ready to go. "May I look at those books first?" asked Jeanne, pointing to another booth.

"OK," agreed Mother, "but don't go out of this aisle. I'll look at some other things along here, too."

Jeanne looked at the old books and found one that was in a box. It was a Bible and she could see it looked new. *This looks like it's really in good shape,* she thought. *If it's old, maybe it's worth a lot of money. I wonder if I can afford to buy it.* She took it to a lady behind the table. When she learned that it was only fifty cents, she promptly bought it and went to show Mother.

"Did you check the date to see when it was printed?" asked Mother.

"Oh, I never thought of that," admitted Jeanne. When they checked the date in the front of the Bible, she was disappointed to find that it wasn't very old at all.

That evening, Mother showed Dad the candy dish she had bought. "It looks old, all right," said Dad. "Could be a priceless treasure."

Mother laughed and shook her head. "No, but Jeanne bought a priceless treasure at the flea market today," she said. "Show Dad the book you bought, Jeanne."

Jeanne grinned. "Oh, Mom!" she said. "So I forgot to check the date and see if that Bible was old. You don't need to rub it in!"

Dad smiled. "You bought a Bible?" he asked. "Well, then you sure *did* buy a priceless treasure, whether it's old and worth a lot of money or not. The Word of God is truly priceless." *HAD*

HOW ABOUT YOU?

Do you use your priceless treasure—your Bible? No matter what you paid for your Bible, it is priceless, but you have to read it to find the treasures of God.

MEMORIZE:

"I rejoice in your word like one who finds a great treasure." Psalm 119:162

THE BIBLE IS
TRUE TREASURE

RICH OR POOR

(Read James 2:1-5)

"Mom! Guess what!" asked Jessica excitedly. "We have three new girls in my class. I really like one of them—her name is Cindy. May I invite her to my party?"

"Sure," answered Mom. "But what about the other two? Aren't you inviting all the girls in your class?"

Jessica shrugged. "I don't think they'll fit in with me and my friends," she said. "They dress funny." The doorbell rang and Jessica jumped up to let in Brenda, a neighbor who had come to play.

Later that afternoon, Mother overheard Jessica and Brenda talking about the new girls at school. They agreed that Cindy was "cool," but that the two other girls looked "poor." They hoped to be friends with Cindy—but not with the others. Mother frowned but didn't say anything.

Brenda had been invited to stay for supper. When Mother called them to come and eat, they were surprised to see that she had set up a folding table in the dining room. "Brenda, you may sit here at the dining-room table with the rest of us," said Mother, "and Jessica, your place is at the folding table."

"But, Mom!" exclaimed Jessica in surprise. "I want to sit at the dining-room table with Brenda! There's plenty of room for me."

"Yes . . . but you have blonde hair and the rest of us have brown hair," said Mother. The girls just stared at each other.

"What's that got to do with it?" Jessica protested. "I can't help having blonde hair."

"Well," said Mother, "I bet the two new girls in your class can't help it, either, if they're poor and don't have such nice clothes." Jessica and Brenda looked down, embarrassed. They knew Jessica's mother must have heard what they had said. "How do you think those girls would feel about being left out just because of the clothes they wear, Jessica?" asked Mother.

"I . . . I think they'd all feel really bad," admitted Jessica. "I'll invite them, too." *SKV*

HOW ABOUT YOU?

Are you friendly with everyone, or only with those who are considered "popular"? Do you look down on people who may be poor or don't have clothes as nice as yours? Jesus wants you to love others as yourself.

**DON'T SHOW
FAVORITISM**

MEMORIZE:

"But if you pay special attention to the rich, you are committing a sin, for you are guilty of breaking that law."

James 2:9

OCTOBER
18

"Ooohhh, Mother, isn't he sweet?" Lisa cuddled the puppy in her arms. "Can I keep him? Mrs. Johnson said I could have him—free! Please, Mother?"

Mother looked down at four pleading eyes. "Very well, but remember, he's your responsibility. You'll have to take care of him, and you'll have to use your allowance to buy food and supplies for him."

"Oh, that's OK. Thank you!" Lisa jumped to her feet and held up the puppy. "Give Mother a kiss, Taffy."

Mother laughed and backed away. "No, thank you. I can do without puppy love."

In the following days, Lisa found that she had to quite often give up something she had hoped to buy for herself in order to have money for puppy food, flea powder, a collar, and dog shampoo. Sometimes she had to leave her play or a favorite book to go and care for her dog.

One day when Lisa's friend Denise was visiting, Mother said, "Lisa, don't forget that Taffy needs a bath today."

"Will you give him one, Mother?" pleaded Lisa.

"Oh, I'll help you, Lisa," Denise offered as Mother shook her head. "It'll be fun." Later, Mother heard the girls talking as they worked. "I wish I had a puppy like Taffy. How much did he cost?" Denise asked.

"Oh, he was free," Lisa replied, "but he sure has cost me a lot since we got him. He's lots of work, too. But he's worth it, really. I sure do love him." *BJW*

HOW ABOUT YOU?

Salvation is a free gift from God, but with it comes responsibilities. If you have become a Christian, you have the responsibility of being a witness. Every blessing comes with responsibility attached. Are you using your good mind, your voice, or your ability to make friends for the Lord? Are you giving him your time and your money? Thank God for your blessings, use them for him, and he will continue to bless you.

MEMORIZE:

"My child, never forget the things I have taught you. Store my commands in your heart, for they will give you a long and satisfying life."
Proverbs 3:1-2

USE BLESSINGS
FOR GOD

PRAISE WORKS WONDERS

(Read Philippians 4:4-7)

Beth slammed the door as she came in from school. "What an awful day," she moaned. "Why I was so lucky as to get Mrs. Dodge for two classes a day, I'll never know. She's a grouch! Looks like junior high is going to be awful with Mrs. Dodge!"

"Remember the verse we read this morning?" reminded Mother. "It says to thank God for everything he does. I'm sure the Lord has some lessons to teach you in that class."

"Oh, I'm sure I'll learn lots of lessons before I get out of there," grumbled Beth. "It's 'Sit up straight. No talking during class. Stay in your seats at all times, blah, blah, blah!' I don't see how I can be expected to give thanks because I have the misfortune of being in Mrs. Dodge's class—not just once, but twice a day."

"No matter what circumstances we find ourselves in, we can look for something to be thankful for," explained Mother. "God tells us to pray about what is happening and to include thanksgiving in those prayers."

"Well," snorted Beth, "it sure will be hard to praise the Lord in Mrs. Dodge's classes. Just think! I've got to be in her class two hours a day, five days a week, all year long! Oh, I can't stand it! It's too much!" She clapped her hand to her head and fell into a soft chair.

"Now, Beth, don't get dramatic," said Mother, laughing. "If you have to stand it, you can. You can even win Mrs. Dodge's respect if your attitude is right." *BJW*

HOW ABOUT YOU?

Have you talked to the Lord about the circumstances you face each day? Perhaps there's a teacher, a classmate, or even a parent that you think you cannot stand. Talk to God about it; pray for that person; ask the Lord to give you a proper attitude toward that person. Then thank God for the opportunities and the lessons you can learn.

**HAVE A THANKFUL
ATTITUDE**

MEMORIZE:
"Don't worry about anything; instead, pray about everything. Tell God what you need, and thank him for all he has done." Philippians 4:6

OCTOBER
20

SUBSTITUTE TEACHER

(Read Romans 13:1-5)

Jane walked into the house smiling. "Mom," she called, "we had the best time in school today!"

"What did you do that was so much fun?" asked Mom with a smile. "You're not usually so excited about school!"

"Oh, we had a substitute teacher today. It was so funny!" Jane laughed. "Todd, Mike, and John all switched seats. So all day long she was calling them the wrong names. Then some of the kids told her that our teacher always lets us out for recess early, so we got out fifteen minutes before everyone else! What a dummy!"

Mom frowned. "How was your substitute supposed to know who the kids were?" she asked.

Jane shrugged. "I suppose our teacher left a seating chart for her."

"Well, then, how would she know if the boys were in the right seats or not?" asked Mom. "And how would she know you weren't supposed to be let out early? Has she taught your class before?"

"No," answered Jane. "I guess she couldn't have known, could she?"

"I doubt it," said Mom. "It really wasn't very nice to fool her and laugh at her!"

"Well, she's just a sub," said Jane with a shrug. "It doesn't matter."

"Oh yes, it does matter!" exclaimed Mom. "You are under her authority while she's in your class, and you must respect and obey her. It's not only common courtesy. It's a command from God!"

Jane's eyes widened. "It is? I thought the Bible just said to obey your parents."

"It also tells us to obey anyone who is in authority over us," said Mom, "and that includes substitute teachers."

"I suppose she must have felt really bad," said Jane thoughtfully. Suddenly she had an idea. "Mom, will you drive me back to school? I heard our sub say she'd be correcting papers after school, so she should still be there. I could apologize to her."

"That's a great idea!" said Mom. "Let's go now!" *DSM*

HOW ABOUT YOU?

Have you or any of your classmates ever had a little "fun" with a substitute teacher? Have you played tricks and given the substitute a bad day? Did you think it was funny? God didn't. He tells us that we must not only obey our parents, but we must also respect and obey anyone who has authority over us.

MEMORIZE:

"Obey the government, for God is the one who put it there." Romans 13:1

RESPECT AUTHORITY

ONLY ONE WAY?

(Read John 10:7-10)

"How can you believe that there's only one way to heaven?" Abby asked Carla. "There are lots of good people following different ways to heaven. What's important is just that we make it, one way or another."

Carla spoke firmly. "Jesus says he is the only door to heaven."

Abby shook her head. "My dad says nobody has all the truth, and a person will go to heaven if he does what he sincerely believes is right. Like, some people worship Buddha. Surely if they're sincere, God will let them into heaven."

"Those people may be sincere, but my minister says they're sincerely wrong," Carla answered. "Jesus is the only way."

The girls changed the subject, but Carla kept praying that she could lead Abby to Jesus. A few days later Abby called Carla. "Want to go over to school with me?" she asked. "I left my trumpet there, and I have to get it so I can practice."

"Sure," agreed Carla, "but I doubt if you can get in. I think the whole school will be locked up by now."

When the girls arrived at the school, they first went to the band room door. It was locked. They tried all the other doors, but everything was locked. Just as they were leaving, a janitor saw them and let them in. They got the trumpet and headed for home.

"Hey, Abby," Carla said, "you really thought some of the doors would be open at school, didn't you?"

"Of course I thought they'd be open," answered Abby. "So what?"

"So you sincerely thought you could get in by yourself, but you were sincerely wrong," stated Carla. "In a way, the janitor was 'the door' for you to get into school. It was only when he opened the band room door that you could get in. Does this remind you of anything?"

Abby grinned. "I guess maybe you're right. I'll have to think about what you said the other day. Jesus is the only door, huh?" *REP*

HOW ABOUT YOU?

Do you sincerely believe you can get to heaven by being good? Do you think that people who earnestly do their best will be OK? Jesus says he is the only door. Trust him.

**JESUS IS THE DOOR
TO HEAVEN**

MEMORIZE:
"Yes, I am the gate. Those who come in through me will be saved."
John 10:9

OCTOBER 22

GOD'S TRAINING SCHOOL

(Read Philippians 2:14-18)

"Hi, Mom," Shelly said as she put her books down. "Hi, Gram."

"Hello, Shelly," said Mom. "I was fixing some coffee for Gram and me. Would you like some juice?"

"Sure," answered Shelly. She went to the refrigerator.

"Why are we all dressed up?" asked Grandma.

"We're having dinner with the Hoyles," Mom replied.

"The Hoyles are so nice. I remember when we spent a week with them at the lake. It was so pretty . . ." Grandma's voice trailed off. Shelly slammed down her glass. She must have heard that story a hundred times! Mom shot a warning look at her. Shelly opened a book.

"Why are we all dressed up?" Grandma asked again, and again Mom answered patiently. "The Hoyles are such nice people," said Grandma. Shelly picked up her book and juice and left the room.

"Mom, how can you be so patient?" Shelly asked later.

"I remind myself that Grandma is sick with Alzheimer's disease and she doesn't remember," Mom said. "It's like a short circuit in the brain. She can't help it."

Shelly frowned. "But how come she has to live here? My friends laugh at her."

"I know it isn't easy sometimes," Mom said. "But we love Grandma."

Grandma came in the bedroom door and smiled. "Why are we all dressed up?" she asked.

Shelly sighed as she glanced at her mom. Then she grinned. "We're having dinner with the Hoyles, Gram."

"They're such nice people. I remember the time we were at the lake together," Grandma said cheerily.

"Tell me about it, Grandma," said Shelly. *VLC*

HOW ABOUT YOU?

Do you need extra understanding or patience with a friend or family member? Ask the Lord to help you develop that patience.

MEMORIZE:

"But when the Holy Spirit controls our lives, he will produce this kind of fruit in us: love, joy, peace, patience, kindness, goodness, faithfulness." Galatians 5:22

BE PATIENT

REJECTED!

(Read Matthew 13:54-58)

Tears streamed down Melanie's face as she came in the back door. "Nancy is having a birthday party on Saturday," she cried. "She invited all the girls in our room except me. Mom, why didn't she invite me? It's not fair."

Mother put her arms around Melanie and hugged her tightly. "I'm sorry, honey," she said. "I know rejection hurts. We want our friends and family to accept us. When they don't, our heart aches."

Melanie wiped her eyes and looked at Mother in surprise. "Have you felt rejected?"

"Do you remember when I wanted to work part-time at the school?" asked Mother. "They hired someone with more skills, and I didn't get the job. That was rejection, and it hurt." She smiled. "I got over it, though, and you will, too. Maybe it will help to remember that no one felt unloved more than Jesus did."

"Yeah, but Jesus' friends didn't reject him. It was his enemies who crucified him," Melanie pointed out.

"Let's read something," said Mother, getting a Bible. Together they read about one day when Jesus taught in the synagogue in Nazareth.

"Does this mean Jesus' friends didn't believe him?" Melanie asked.

Mother nodded. "They ridiculed and rejected him," she said. "Remember, it was one of his own disciples who betrayed him. And the others all left him when he was arrested."

"I guess he does know how I feel right now," decided Melanie.

"Yes," Mother assured her, "he understands and cares." *MJS*

HOW ABOUT YOU?

Do you feel rejected when someone says no to you or forgets you? Remember that Jesus knows the pain of rejection. He knows and cares how you feel. Let that comfort you, and then treat those who have hurt you the way you think Jesus would treat them.

MEMORIZE:

"Give all your worries and cares to God, for he cares about what happens to you." 1 Peter 5:7

GOD UNDERSTANDS

THE LAST WORDS

(Read Psalm 19:12-14)

"I hate you!" Julie screamed as she ran out of the house. She was glad to see the school bus coming around the corner. She climbed on quickly before her mother could call her back, but she knew she would have to answer for her words after school.

Later, Julie's anger began to go away, but she didn't want to lose it. When she felt it weakening, she would feed it bitter thoughts. *Why does she always say no? Why can't she be like Connie's mother? Her mom lets her do what she wants to do.*

At lunchtime Julie scowled. Thanking God for her food didn't fit her mood, so she skipped it. Feeling guilty, she pulled her favorite sandwich from her lunchbox. Tucked in the sandwich bag was a note, "Julie, I love you. Mother." Julie felt a bit ashamed, but not too much. *She's just feeling guilty for not letting me go to Lana's party,* she reminded herself.

By the time school was dismissed, Julie had made a long list of complaints to present to her mother. She had to have something to justify her angry words that morning. She was thinking about them when she heard sirens scream and saw a fire engine roar past the bus. The kids watched and talked excitedly as the bus followed slowly. When Julie saw the lights flashing in front of her house, terror gripped her. She stumbled from the bus and ran wildly up the street. Was her house on fire? Where was her mother?

Frantically, she searched the crowd. Oh, there was Mother, standing on the edge of the crowd, watching the firemen pour water onto the burning storage building behind the house. Sobbing, Julie ran into her mother's arms. "Oh, Mama," she whispered, "I'm sorry! I love you!" *BJW*

HOW ABOUT YOU?

Do you ever leave home with sharp words hanging between you and your family? Do you feed those feelings of anger with bitter thoughts? Right now, make up your mind to stop.

MEMORIZE:

"Don't talk too much, for it fosters sin.
Be sensible and turn off the flow!"
Proverbs 10:19

WATCH YOUR WORDS

THE INVITATION

(Read John 14:1-6)

When Ellen returned to school after fall break, it seemed so good to see all her friends again. As they chatted happily together, she noticed that several of them referred to Marilee's party.

Marilee's party? thought Ellen. *That was going to be after fall break.* She vaguely remembered being handed an invitation, but since it wasn't happening right away and she was very busy, she hadn't paid much attention. What had she done with the invitation? She hurried to look in her desk. There it was—a small square envelope sticking out of her math book. She quickly pulled it out and read, "Please come to a party." The details were on the inside. She read only the first line, "We'll look for you on October 20, 7:00 . . ." Oh no! It was October 25! The party *was* after fall break, but it had been last week! Just then two girls came over to her desk. "You really missed it!" exclaimed Sue. "Marilee's dad took us out to her grandparents' place in the country, and we had a real hayride."

"And we pulled taffy afterward," added Brenda. As the two girls walked away singing "Jingle Bells," Ellen bit her lip to keep from crying. But when she told her parents about it that evening, she did shed a few tears. "It sounded like so much fun, and I could have gone," she sniffed. "I was invited, but I didn't read the invitation carefully. Now it's too late. I missed it."

"Oh, I'm sorry," sympathized Mother.

"Yes, it is too bad," agreed Dad. "This reminds me of another invitation that is often ignored. God invites us all to spend eternity in heaven with him, but many people pay no attention. The day will come when it will be too late to accept that invitation, too."

Ellen nodded. "I'm glad I won't miss that," she said. *HWM*

HOW ABOUT YOU?

Have you been careless with God's invitation to heaven? Have you been too busy to think about it? Do you intend to have a look at it later? Accept the invitation, which God is patiently offering now. If you have questions, talk to a trusted friend or adult.

**DON'T IGNORE
GOD'S INVITATION**

MEMORIZE:
"Then the Lord said, 'My Spirit will not put up with humans for such a long time.' " Genesis 6:3

OCTOBER
26

DUMB EXCUSES

(Read John 3:16-21)

Barbi stubbornly shook her head. "My dad and mom are going to the college game on the Saturday of the youth retreat," she said. "I want to go with them."

"But that's just for one day," persisted Molly. "The retreat is for the whole weekend. Why don't you come?"

Barbi shrugged. "I don't have the right clothes for it."

"Oh, honestly!" fumed Molly. "You make up the dumbest excuses."

Barbi grinned. "Besides, it costs too much."

"Barbi Edwards!" exclaimed Molly. "You know that's not true. A couple of families offered to sponsor the group, so it doesn't cost a thing. They've already paid for 20 kids to go, and so far only 14 are going."

But in spite of Molly's best efforts to persuade Barbi to go to the retreat, Barbi refused.

After youth group one Saturday, Barbi was quiet as she and Molly walked home. "I don't get it," she said suddenly. "Miss Ellis is always bugging us to 'be saved from sin.' I don't think I've done anything so bad."

Molly was thoughtful. "Well," she answered slowly, "even though you think you're not so bad, you're not good enough for heaven. No sin at all can enter there, so even the 'little' bad things you've done have to be forgiven."

"Maybe so," said Barbi with a shrug, "but Miss Ellis said that Jesus paid the price for everyone to go to heaven. If that's so, the price is paid for my salvation, right? So I don't need to worry about it."

Molly hesitated. "Remember the retreat?" she asked.

"Retreat?" repeated Barbi. "I didn't go."

"No," said Molly, "but the price was paid for you to go. You just made dumb excuses for not accepting the offer. It's like that with salvation, too. Jesus paid the price for you to go to heaven, but unless you receive the gift God offers, you won't go there. That makes sense, doesn't it?"

Barbi hesitated. "Yes, I guess it does," she admitted. *HWM*

HOW ABOUT YOU?

Have you accepted God's offer of salvation? Perhaps you have questions. Find a trusted adult or friend to talk to.

MEMORIZE:

"But to all who believed him and accepted him, he gave the right to become children of God." John 1:12

GO TO GOD FOR HELP

FRACTURED FRIENDSHIP

(Read Proverbs 27:6-10)

"Mom," called Cathy as she returned from school one day, "can we go get my party invitations?"

Mother shook her head. "I'm sorry, honey, but I promised Mrs. Kettering I'd drive her to the doctor's office this afternoon. Ever since she broke her leg last year, she's had a hard time getting around."

"Well," said Cathy, "we'd better get the invitations soon."

Mother smiled. "Have you decided who you'll invite?" she asked. "Remember, five guests is the limit."

Cathy nodded. "I want to invite Susie, Lori, Lena, Emily, and Joanne."

Mother looked surprised. "What about Pam next door?" she asked. "I thought you two were best friends!"

"Oh, we are," Cathy said, "but I can see her any time. I want someone different for a change. I suppose Pam might be mad about it when she finds out, but she'll get over it."

Mother was quiet for a minute. "I'm thinking of Mrs. Kettering's broken leg," she said. "Even though the fracture did heal, her leg will never be quite the same. Sometimes it hurts, and she has to be careful not to put too much stress on it. She can't trust it fully. It's the same way with friendship."

"Friendship?" asked Cathy. "What do you mean?"

"If you hurt a friend out of selfishness or carelessness, she may be willing to forgive you. But she may never be able to fully trust you again, and your relationship will suffer." Mother sighed. "I learned that lesson the hard way—I once lost a good friend because of a cruel, thoughtless remark I made. Friends are a precious gift from God, Cathy—don't take them for granted."

Cathy looked thoughtful. "I think I'd better go over my guest list again," she decided. "Pam is too important to leave out." *SLK*

HOW ABOUT YOU?

Do you take your friends for granted? Do you assume that they'll always be willing to forgive you, no matter what? Even a strong friendship can be broken, and healing can be difficult. Treat your friends as you want them to treat you—with kindness and respect.

TREAT FRIENDS WITH CARE

MEMORIZE:
"Never abandon a friend—either yours or your father's." Proverbs 27:10

OCTOBER
28

LOVE FOR HATE
(Read Luke 6:27-36)

Shari walked briskly into the house, slamming the door. "I'm never going to talk to Kayla again. Never!"

Her mother put down her sewing. "Never is a long time, honey," she said. "I thought Kayla was your best friend."

"That's right," Shari retorted. "She *was* my best friend, but not anymore. She's been going around telling all kinds of stories about me."

"And are any of them true?" Mother asked.

"No, they're not true!" Shari snapped. "Kayla's just being mean and hateful, that's all. I told her off good, and I'm not going to have anything to do with her ever again!"

"And what about Sunday?" asked Mother. "You girls are in the same Sunday school class, you know."

"I'll sit on the other side of the room." Shari tossed her head.

"Honey," Mother said, "maybe Kayla hurt you by talking the way she did. But you're a Christian, and your reactions must not be unkind. The Bible tells us to be loving and forgiving."

Shari thought about that for a moment. "I can't forgive her," she said at last.

"No, not in your own strength," her mother agreed. "But the Bible tells us that we can do all things through Christ. He gives us the strength to do what's right."

Her mother was right. Shari knew that. She knew what the Bible said about loving and forgiving even your enemies. And Kayla really wasn't an enemy; she was a friend. That was all the more reason to forgive her.

"I'll try," Shari said. "I'll ask Jesus to help me." *RIJ*

HOW ABOUT YOU?

It's easy to be nice to someone who is nice to you, isn't it? The Bible says even sinners do that. But is there someone who has been mean to you? Are you nice to that person, too? If you're a Christian, God says you should show love even to those who are mean to you. When you see that person at school or church this week, give him or her a smile. God will help you.

MEMORIZE:

"But love your enemies, do good, and lend, hoping for nothing in return; and your reward will be great, and you will be sons of the Highest. For He is kind to the unthankful and evil."
Luke 6:35, NKJV

REPAY EVIL WITH GOOD

TRUE LOVE

(Read 1 Corinthians 13:4-7)

Tina sighed happily as she walked into the living room. "I'm in love!" she announced. "Gregg's such a wonderful guy! He's always so nice to me!"

Mother frowned slightly. "I'm glad you and Gregg are friends, but remember, *love* is a pretty strong word."

Tina's brother, Joel, laughed. "Tina thinks that just because she's fifteen, she knows everything about love." He reached down to pat his dog. "Now, me and Ralph here—that's love! He does whatever I tell him, he's always ready to play, and he doesn't talk my ear off like some girl would. That's what I call true love."

Shortly afterward, Tina had a phone call and came back looking upset. "That rotten Gregg!" she said. "He took another girl to the basketball game last night and never even asked me! I'll never speak to him again!"

"Ha, ha!" laughed Joel. "All that true love gone right down the drain!" Joel was laughing so hard that he didn't see Ralph sitting on the floor beside him. He stepped right on the dog's tail, and Ralph nipped him on the leg!

"Ouch! You bad dog!" scolded Joel. "Go away! I don't want you anymore!"

Hearing the commotion, Mother hurried in. "I overheard what you two were talking about. Each of you was certain that you had found 'true love.' What happened?"

"Well, I thought I loved Gregg, until he did something that made me mad," said Tina.

"Yeah, that's how I feel about Ralph," agreed Joel.

"I'm afraid that's the way it goes when we use the word *love* too loosely. Real love is constant. It doesn't change just because our feelings change. What if God stopped loving us just because we disobeyed him?"

"It would be awful!" Tina exclaimed. "I'm glad he never stops loving us. I guess our love wasn't so real after all!" *SLK*

HOW ABOUT YOU?

Do you ever wonder what "true love" is? Some people think that love is a feeling, an emotional "high," something that just happens. But the Bible teaches that loving is something you decide to do. Today's Scripture passage is a good description of love. God commands you to love others. And he'll help you to do it!

LOVE ONE ANOTHER

MEMORIZE:

"So now I am giving you a new commandment: Love each other. Just as I have loved you, you should love each other." John 13:34

OCTOBER
30

GOD AND ME

(Read Isaiah 42:5-12)

"We'll all be late for church if Rachael doesn't hurry up," complained Peter. "She takes forever to fix her hair!"

Finally they were on their way. "Dad!" cried Rachael, "make Peter close his window. The wind makes my hair a mess."

Before going into the church service, Rachael went to comb her hair again. Peter, Mother, and Dad sat down. Mother and Dad frowned as she tiptoed into the pew during the first hymn.

After church that night, Peter got out a magnifying glass. "It's fun to look at stuff under this," he said. "It really makes everything look big."

"Oh, let me see, too," said Rachael, and he shared the magnifying glass with her.

Observing them, Dad wrote something on two small pieces of paper, which he placed on the table with some other things Peter had lined up to look at. He watched as Peter put the first paper under the magnifying glass. Peter looked at it and shrugged. Then Rachael looked. "Why did you write *God* on the paper for us to see?" she asked her father.

"Because God should be magnified," explained Dad. "Whoa, there," he added as Peter picked up the second piece of paper. "Don't put that one under your glass, Son. It's not supposed to be magnified."

Peter read it and handed it to his sister. Written in small letters was the word *me*.

"You see," continued Dad, "sometimes we tend to magnify ourself instead of God. If we do that, we might spend too much time on appearance."

"Yeah," broke in Peter with a grin. "We comb our hair all the time and make everybody late for church."

"On the other hand," said Dad, "when we magnify God instead of ourself, we try to please him in our behavior and we don't point the finger at someone else."
HAD

HOW ABOUT YOU?

Do you spend too much time in front of your mirror? God wants you to look neat, clean, and as attractive as possible, but remember that real beauty is seen in actions more than in appearance.

MEMORIZE:

"Come, let us tell of the Lord's greatness; let us exalt his name together." Psalm 34:3

GLORIFY GOD, NOT SELF

NO MORE SECRETS

(Read Luke 12:1-5)

"Janice," said Mother one Saturday afternoon, "I'm going down to the estate sale at the end of the block. Do you want to come?"

"Sure," Janice replied eagerly. "Is it like a garage sale?"

"In a way," answered Mother, "but in this case, the lady who lived in the house died, and her relatives are having the sale to dispose of all her things."

The two walked down the block to a large brick house where a number of people were milling about, examining furniture, dishes, and other objects. After looking it all over, Mother paid for some glassware she had selected, and they walked out.

Janice was unusually quiet on the way home. "You know, Mom," she said finally, "I'd sure hate to think that someday people might be going through my things, and even taking some of them home."

"That idea does give one a strange feeling," agreed Mother, "and that makes me think of something else." She looked at her daughter seriously. "It's not only our worldly possessions that will be exposed when we die. The Bible says that someday the records in heaven will be opened, and all of our thoughts and actions will be exposed. We won't be able to keep any secrets as we stand before God."

"That makes me want to live as good a life as I can," mused Janice.

"Yes," Mother, nodding, said. "I feel that way, too. I'm so glad that I've accepted Jesus as my Savior. If I hadn't, some day I'd have to stand before God and admit that I refused his salvation. Wouldn't that be dreadful?"

"I never thought of it that way." Janice smiled. "I'm glad I know Jesus as my Savior, too!" *SLK*

HOW ABOUT YOU?

Do you ever wonder what it will be like to meet God someday? That day is going to come, and many of the things that seem important now will be meaningless then. Have you prepared for your eternal future? Be sure you know Jesus Christ as your Savior. If you haven't yet done so, accept him today.

NO MORE SECRETS

MEMORIZE:
"And just as it is destined that each person dies only once and after that comes judgment." Hebrews 9:27

THE JUNGLE KILLER

(Read Psalm 143:8-12)

The Wilsons were missionaries in Africa, where Beth and Sam eagerly helped prepare for an overnight camping trip to a distant village. They loaded the tent, boxes of food, and pots and pans into the back of the jeep.

They had gone quite a distance when the jeep engine made a coughing sound and stopped. Dad tried, but he couldn't start it again. "We're going to need help," he said. "Mr. Jonas, the missionary in the next village, has a radio, but do you think you can walk that far?" He looked anxiously at Mother, who had turned her ankle the previous week.

She shook her head. "You go on," she told him. "The kids and I will be fine waiting for you here." Beth and Sam nodded, so after giving them a few final words of instruction, Dad reluctantly hurried off.

Time passed quickly. Beth and Sam kept busy reading, playing games, and watching for animals. Suddenly, they stopped and looked at each other. The earth was trembling beneath them. "What is that?" gasped Sam. "An earthquake?"

Mother strained to see into the distance. "Something's coming . . . oh, no!" she exclaimed. "It's a herd of elephants! Look! They've stopped, and they're look-ing at us."

"What are we going to do?" whispered Beth. "If they stampede, they'll destroy the jeep and crush us to death."

"Quick! Grab a skillet!" Mother instructed. "Let's all take a couple of pans, and we'll make as much noise as we can. Maybe they'll run away." They put the idea into action, yelling and shouting and clanging and banging the pots and pans. "Look, the elephants are running away. Keep pounding that skillet for all you're worth," encouraged Mother.

When Dad finally returned with some of the villagers, the children had quite a story to tell. "We were so scared! It seemed silly for us to pound on those pans, but it was the only thing we could think of," said Beth.

"I believe the Lord led you to do that," said Dad. "We've asked him to watch over us, you know. And when you're in the will of God, you're safe in the jungles of Africa—even when surrounded by a herd of wild elephants. In fact, you're safer than you would be back home out of the will of God." *HCT*

HOW ABOUT YOU?

Do you worry that God might send you to a dangerous place? Are you afraid of wild animals, snakes, spiders, or perhaps evil men? Remember, the place God wants you is the safest place for you to be.

DO GOD'S WILL

MEMORIZE:
"Show me where to walk."
Psalm 143:8

NOVEMBER
2

IT MADE ME LAUGH

(Read Zechariah 7:9-10; 1 Peter 3:8-12)

After the basketball game, Kelly's mom picked her up. As Kelly and her friend Lynn rode home in the backseat, Lynn laughed heartily. "Didn't that girl with the black pants make you laugh?" she said. "She was so fat she could hardly run!" Kelly just looked out the window. When she didn't join in the laughter, Lynn changed the subject.

At home, Mom began to fix dinner. "I'm proud of you, Kelly," she said as she took out a recipe book. She moved things around on the counter, looking for something. "I'm glad you didn't join Lynn in making fun of the big girl who played on the other team."

"Well, I kind of felt bad for her. Besides, I'm not so skinny myself," Kelly said.

Mom hugged her. "Maybe that helped you to be kind," she said. "I know it's tempting to poke fun at people, but we have to remember that God created every one of us, and he wants us to respect one another. I'm sure he's pleased with the way you acted." She went to a hall table and moved things around. Then she opened a drawer and rummaged through it.

Kelly puckered her brow. "Are you looking for something?" she asked.

Mom nodded. "My glasses," she said. "I can't imagine where I left them."

Kelly looked at Mom and burst out laughing. "Look in the mirror," she suggested. "You pushed them up on top of your head." Suddenly she stopped laughing. "Oh! I didn't mean to make fun of you. I guess I shouldn't laugh, should I?"

Mom nodded. "Yes, you should," she said. "It's OK to laugh if you make sure you're laughing at what a person does and not at the person—and if you're sure that by laughing you won't hurt anyone's feelings. In this case, you're not hurting my feelings at all."

Kelly relaxed. "It did look funny," she said. "It made me laugh." Laughter spilled out again—and Mom's laugh was even louder than Kelly's. *KEC*

HOW ABOUT YOU?

What makes you laugh? Is it hard to know when it's OK to tease? The next time you're tempted to poke fun at someone, put yourself in that person's place and think how it would feel to have others laughing. If it would hurt, don't do it even if others do. Be kind.

MEMORIZE:

"This is what the Lord Almighty says: Judge fairly and honestly, and show mercy and kindness to one another." Zechariah 7:9

DON'T HURT OTHERS BY LAUGHING

THE QUILT

(Read Psalm 37:3-7, 39-40)

Leanne slammed the screen door, threw her schoolbooks on the nearest chair, and slumped down at the kitchen table where her mother was working. "I hate school," she announced as Mother looked up from cutting a long strip of light blue material. "I don't even like recess," Leanne added. Mother raised her eyebrows and quietly continued working. "What are you making with all those tiny pieces?" asked Leanne, pointing to the strips of material laid out all over the table.

"I'm starting a new quilt," replied Mother.

"A quilt? Can I help?" asked Leanne eagerly.

"Sure," agreed Mother as she handed Leanne a piece of material. "This is marked—just cut it on the lines."

Leanne carefully followed the markings on the bright pink material. As she snipped, she thought about her problems. She decided her life was ruined. Nothing seemed to be working out the way she wanted. "Don't you want to hear why I hate school?" she asked, glancing over at Mother. Without waiting for an answer, she frowned and said, "I don't like the dark stuff you're cutting now. Do we have to use it?"

Mother smiled. "It will look good in the quilt," she said. She picked up a picture from the table and held it up. "This is what the quilt will look like when it's finished. See where the dark pieces are used?"

Leanne looked at the picture. "Wow!" she exclaimed. "That's pretty!"

Mother nodded. "When you think about it," she said, "our life is something like a giant quilt. Life is made up of lots of different experiences—some that we like and some that we don't. We only see snips and scraps, and we wonder how everything is going to work out. But God sees the beauty of fitting each piece together. We need to trust him. He knows what he's doing. He knows the beautiful picture he has planned for our life."

Leanne grinned. *I guess my life isn't really ruined,* she thought to herself. *I'll just have to trust God to work it out for me. SEF*

HOW ABOUT YOU?

Do you wonder why God allows your friends to "be mean" to you? Why he lets your parents fight? Why he permits people you love to die? We all have to go through difficult times. Remember that God is still in control. Trust him to use all the experiences you go through to make something beautiful out of your life.

MEMORIZE:

TRUST GOD

"Trust in the Lord with all your heart;
do not depend on your own
understanding." Proverbs 3:5

NOVEMBER 4

A BETTER COMPARISON

(Read 1 Peter 1:13-16)

"Hi, honey." Mom smiled as Yolanda slid into the car and snapped her seat belt in place. "How was school?"

Yolanda looked out the window. "Fine," she said softly.

Mom backed the car out. "Anything interesting happen today?" she asked.

"I got a 73 on my math test." Yolanda forced a smile.

"Seventy-three?" Mom glanced at her. "What happened?"

Yolanda shrugged her shoulders. "I don't know," she said. Then she added, "But that's not such a bad grade compared to a kid who got a 40."

Mom sighed. "I see," she said. "And what was the highest score?"

Yolanda didn't speak for a moment. "One hundred," she said finally.

They rode in silence for a while until Mom spoke. "Well, if you compare your score with a 40, a 73 looks pretty good," she agreed, glancing again at Yolanda. "But, if you compare it with 100, 73 doesn't look so good, does it?"

Yolanda shook her head and stared out the window.

"If 73 is the best you can do, that's fine," said Mom, "but I don't think it is. How about letting me help you with some of the problems you got wrong?"

Yolanda shrugged her shoulders. "OK," she said, "but I still don't think 73 is so bad."

Mom frowned. "You know something, sweetheart," she said at last. "Maybe we can both learn an important lesson about living for Christ from this test you took."

"What do you mean, Mom?" asked Yolanda.

"Well, you think 73 isn't so bad when compared with 40, and it's easy for us to start thinking some wrong things we've done aren't so bad when we compare ourselves with others who use bad language, or steal, or get into fights. When we compare ourselves with the things others do, we might even be tempted to think we don't need to ask God to forgive us for our 'little' sins. But if we compare ourselves to Jesus, who obeyed the Father 100 percent, we can really see how much we need God's forgiveness." *RSM*

HOW ABOUT YOU?

Do you compare yourself with others, thinking, "I'm not as bad as they are"? Remember, all sin is wrong—even those things we call 'little' sins. The wonderful thing is that when you confess your sin to Jesus and ask him to forgive you, he will.

MEMORIZE:
"You must be holy because I am holy." 1 Peter 1:16

COMPARE YOURSELF TO JESUS

THEY'RE PEOPLE, TOO

(Read Ephesians 4:25-32)

"It's not fair!" Shelly complained as she and her mother walked into the super-market. "It's just not fair! When Mr. Benson said we could have free time to study, I opened my history book, and my pencil fell off my desk. I couldn't reach it from where I was sitting, so I stood up to get it, and he yelled at me! He didn't ask why I was standing up or anything—just told me I had to write 'I will not stand up in class' 50 times! It's ridic . . ." Shelly's voice stopped in the middle of the word as she spotted Mr. Benson himself at the produce counter.

The teacher nodded to Shelly and her mother and then looked awkwardly at his cart. "I'm not used to planning meals and doing the grocery shopping," he said, "but my wife is in the hospital for some surgery. Actually, the biggest challenge each day is getting two of my children to the day-care center, and the third to kindergarten." He sighed. "Teaching, parenting, and trying to spend as much time as possible with my wife is not easy!" He turned back to the produce counter.

"I think now you know why Mr. Benson scolded you unfairly today," Shelly's mom said as they drove home. "He looked very tired and worn out."

"I never thought about a teacher having problems before," said Shelly. "I guess teachers are people, too!"

"I've had the same experience you've had," Mother told her gently. "I've felt that someone acted unfairly toward me, only to discover later that a serious personal problem was hurting that person. As Christians, we need to be patient and accept other people. We need to be kind and help them with their difficulties instead of becoming angry."

"I'll ask the Lord to help me be especially nice to Mr. Benson," Shelly said thoughtfully. *LMW*

HOW ABOUT YOU?

Do people sometimes treat you unfairly? It's easy to get angry in such a situation, isn't it? Remember that the Lord tells you to have patience with others and to be forgiving. Perhaps they have a problem that you do not know about. Your friendly attitude could help them feel better.

MEMORIZE:

"Instead, be kind to each other, tenderhearted, forgiving one another, just as God through Christ has forgiven you." Ephesians 4:32

BE UNDERSTANDING

NOVEMBER
6

DISGUISED

(Read Galatians 1:6-10)

"That Chad is the wildest kid I've ever seen," complained Lynn as she sat at the table one evening. "I don't know why Miss King gave him the part of Governor Bradford in our Thanksgiving play."

"Maybe Miss King thought he would act in a responsible manner if he had a responsible part," suggested Mother. "Sometimes kids respond to what's expected of them."

"Well, at first I thought maybe he was getting better," admitted Lynn. "He was actually polite for a day or two. But now he's horrid. Having the part of Governor Bradford really didn't change him at all. He goes around saying he's the governor and we'd better listen to him. What really bugs me is that some kids in our class go along with him. He seems to really have some of the little kids fooled."

"Oh?" asked Dad. "What do you mean?"

"Well, he gets them to think it's OK to do the things he does. Like at recess . . . Chad persuaded some of the kids to walk like old Mr. Cronk, the janitor. He limps," explained Lynn, "and I just know he knew what they were doing."

"You didn't join them, did you?" asked Mother.

Lynn shook her head. "No, but Missy Jones did. When I said something to her about it, she just laughed and said it didn't hurt anybody—that even Governor Bradford—meaning Chad—walked that way."

Dad shook his head. "As you pointed out, wearing the costume obviously didn't change Chad's character," he said. "You know, this reminds me of the greatest deceiver of all. The Bible says that Satan himself masquerades as an angel of light. But no matter what disguise he wears, his intent is always evil. We need to continually be on our guard against him."

"I will be," promised Lynn, "and I'm going to be on my guard against 'Governor Bradford,' too." *HWM*

HOW ABOUT YOU?

Do you feel it's OK to sneak some cookies as long as you plan to share them with someone else? Or to cheat on schoolwork in order to help someone else get the right answer, too? Or maybe to tell a lie to keep a friend out of trouble? Be careful. Satan is putting a nice disguise on something that is really wrong. Don't do the things you know are wrong, no matter how good they may seem at the time.

MEMORIZE:

"Even Satan can disguise himself as an angel of light." 2 Corinthians 11:14

WRONG IS NEVER RIGHT

THE YARDSTICK

(Read 2 Corinthians 10:12-13, 17-18)

Marissa slammed her books amid the craft supplies on the table. "Miss Rogers is on the warpath," she stormed, "just because some kids cheated a little when she left the room. Now we all have to take another test."

Mother frowned. "Did you cheat, Marissa?"

"Well . . . on one question," admitted Marissa. "Everyone else did, too—even Tonya, and you know what a good Christian everyone says she is." After trying to justify her actions, Marissa quickly changed the subject. "What are you making? May I help?"

"I'm getting the materials ready for our craft class at the nursing home," answered Mother. "You may cut this ribbon into one yard lengths. I need twenty strips, each just a yard long. Here's the yardstick."

For several minutes, only Marissa's quiet counting broke the silence. "Did you say you need twenty?" Marissa asked. Mother nodded. "But there's not enough ribbon!" Marissa exclaimed. "I have nineteen with only a little piece left."

Mother looked at the ribbons. "These are not all the same length," she observed. "How did you measure them?"

"As I cut each one, I used it to measure the next ribbon," Marissa explained.

"Oh, I see." Mother nodded. "I'm afraid you've been using the wrong measure more than once today." Marissa looked at her curiously. "When you measure one ribbon by another, it's just natural to cut each one a little bit longer than the one before it, so they get longer and longer. If you had used the yardstick, you would have had an accurate measure for each one," explained Mother. "And just as you shouldn't measure ribbon by ribbon, you shouldn't measure yourself by other people. You thought it was OK for you to cheat because Tonya cheated, and she's a 'good Christian.'" Marissa blushed. She knew the scolding she deserved was coming. "The apostle Paul said we are not wise if we measure ourselves by others," Mother told her solemnly. "Jesus Christ is our example. We should always measure our actions by him." *BJW*

HOW ABOUT YOU?

Do you determine whether or not your actions are right by comparing them to what others are doing? That's the wrong measure, and using it will get you into trouble. When you're in doubt about what to do, ask yourself, "What would Jesus do?" Follow his example. Ask him to help you measure up to his standards.

MEMORIZE:

"This suffering is all part of what God has called you to. Christ, who suffered for you, is your example. Follow in his steps." 1 Peter 2:21

**MEASURE YOUR
LIFE BY JESUS**

HEATHER'S NEW FACE

(Read 1 Timothy 6:6-10)

Heather watched her brother tie his new shoes and then smooth his shirt. "Pretty neat, huh, Heather?" Tom asked with a grin. "Everybody's wearing this kind of shoes and shirt."

Heather nodded. Then she ran upstairs to her grandmother, who was staying with them for a couple of months. Perched on the arm of Grandma's chair, she hugged her. "What do you want this time, Heather?" asked Grandma knowingly.

"Oh, Grandma, you always say that," pouted Heather. She squirmed. "Would you buy me a new pair of shoes and a shirt? Everybody wears this one kind. Tommy's got . . ."

". . . what Tommy needed," Grandma finished. She shook her head. "If it would make you happy for even a few months, I might buy you an outfit, but I know you wouldn't be content for a week. Besides, you have plenty of clothes."

"They're old," whined Heather, stomping her foot.

Grandma frowned. "Oh, I doubt that," she said, "but even the latest fashions wouldn't look good on you today."

"What do you mean?" exclaimed Heather, startled.

"Pouting, frowning, and proud looks are never attractive," Grandma told her. "You're a Christian, honey, and you need to learn to be thankful for all God has given you. The best fashion designers can't make a grouch look attractive."

Heather scowled and shrugged. "Oh, well," she said, "I bet Mom would scold you if you bought me anything more anyway. She says you spoil us." Suddenly she grinned at Grandma and gave her a hug.

"Ah! Now I see a truly pretty girl!" exclaimed Grandma. "Try to remember that a smile is always 'in.'" *AGL*

HOW ABOUT YOU?

Are you concerned only about the style of the clothes you're wearing and not the expression on your face? Your attitude reveals the quality of person you are, and fine clothing cannot hide it. The Bible says to be content with the things you have. A thankful heart and an attitude of contentment make a person most attractive.

MEMORIZE:

"I am overwhelmed with joy in the Lord my God! For he has dressed me with the clothing of salvation and draped me in a robe of righteousness." Isaiah 61:10

SMILES ARE ALWAYS "IN"

LYNN'S VISIT

(Read John 14:16-20, 25-28)

"I wish I'd been alive 2000 years ago," said Julie. "Jesus was living on earth then, and I'd have been able to see him and talk to him, but now he's left us and gone to heaven." As she spoke, the phone rang. Julie ran to the hall to answer it. When she returned, she greeted Mother excitedly. "That was Melissa, and guess what? She said Lynn VanDyke is going to be in town and give a concert next week! Can I go? Ple-e-e-ese?"

Mother smiled. "I don't know why not," she said.

"All right!" exclaimed Julie. "Imagine being able to see Lynn VanDyke—live! I can't think of anything better than having her in our own town and seeing her concert."

Mom smiled. "I can," she said. Julie looked at her in disbelief. "How about having her stay with us?" continued Mom.

Julie's mouth fell open. "Here? In our house?" she asked.

"I told you that Lynn and I were in school together, remember?" asked Mom. "When I heard she was going to be in town, I invited her to spend a week with us."

"And she said yes? She's actually going to stay with us? In our own home? Oh, wow!" Julie danced up and down in delight.

"That reminds me of what you were saying earlier," said Mom thoughtfully.

"About what?" asked Julie.

"You were wishing you'd been living when Jesus was on earth," Mom reminded her. "That would be even better than seeing Lynn VanDyke, but I think we've been forgetting something important."

"Like what?" asked Julie.

"Well, Jesus promised that when he left, he would send the Holy Spirit to us," said Mom. "The Holy Spirit lives, not just in our town, not just with us, but within the hearts of those who have trusted in Jesus. I know it's hard to understand, especially at your age, but that's even better than having your favorite singer here." *MTF*

HOW ABOUT YOU?

Do you, too, wish you'd been alive when Jesus was here on earth? Don't forget that when Jesus left this earth, he promised to send the Holy Spirit. Jesus paid a brief "visit" to this world and lived with the people for a short while, but the Holy Spirit is not just with us, he lives in us.

MEMORIZE:

"Or don't you know that your body is the temple of the Holy Spirit, who lives in you and was given to you by God?" 1 Corinthians 6:19

THE HOLY SPIRIT LIVES WITHIN CHRISTIANS

NOVEMBER
10

CHECK IT OUT
(Read 2 Peter 3:14-18)

Bethany ran up the stairs and into the church foyer. "Dad!" she called as she marched toward her father and thrust her Bible into his hands. "Look at this. Noah didn't just take two of every kind of animal on the ark. He took seven of some! Did you know that?"

Dad nodded. "But I didn't know it when I was your age," he added. "In fact I was sixteen, and I learned it the hard way." He smiled sheepishly. "I was sitting in the back of a small country church," he said, "and the pastor said that Noah led in two of some kinds of animals and seven of others. I actually stood up and corrected him."

Bethany's eyes grew wide. "You didn't," she gasped. "What did he say?"

"He was very gracious," said Dad. "He smiled and thanked me for pointing out what a lot of people were probably thinking. Then he asked everyone to turn with him to Genesis chapter 7, and of course I quickly saw that I was wrong."

"How embarrassing!" Bethany giggled.

"Yes," agreed Dad, "but it was a valuable lesson. I hope you can learn from it, too, instead of embarrassing yourself, like I did—or worse."

"What could be worse than that?" asked Bethany.

"Believing a lie," Dad answered, and his face became serious. "A lot of people preach things that the Bible really doesn't say, and they're not going to remind you to check it out. That's how cults get started and how people get led away from the truth. That's why you always need to check things out with the Bible. Even when the pastor is preaching."

"But our pastor would never mislead us," protested Bethany.

"No," Dad agreed, "I don't believe he would. But if he did, would you know?"

Bethany took her Bible back from Dad as they walked into the service together. "I will now," she said, sitting down. "I'll follow along when Pastor Hunt reads and preaches from the Bible." *HMT*

HOW ABOUT YOU?

Do you take your Bible to church? Do you follow along with the pastor's message? When you hear something new, do you check it out? Most pastors know the Bible well, but they can make mistakes. Others will intentionally lead you astray. If you are fortunate enough to have a Bible, use it!

MEMORIZE:

"Make me walk along the path of your commands, for that is where my happiness is found." Psalm 119:35

FIND OUT WHAT THE BIBLE SAYS

CHOCOLATE WITHOUT SUGAR

(Read 1 Corinthians 13:1-3)

"Do you know what Lori did to me?" Marcie asked her friend Kim. "She totally ignored me at the basketball game. She didn't say one word to me, and I was sitting right in front of her. When I said hi, she didn't even answer. What a snob!"

"Yeah," agreed Kim. "Lots of times she won't say hi to me, either—especially when she's with some of her popular friends. She's so two-faced! But who needs Miss Stuck-Up anyway?" Kim glanced at her watch. "Oh, it's getting late . . . I'd better go. See you tomorrow."

After Kim left, Marcie went into the kitchen where her mother was working. "Ooooh! Are you making brownies?" asked Marcie.

"Yes, I am," Mom answered as she stirred melted chocolate. Then she began measuring sugar.

"Yum." Marcie wiped a drop of chocolate off the counter with her finger. Then she licked her finger.

"I wouldn't do that if . . . ," began Mom, but she was too late. Marcie's finger was already in her mouth.

"Oh, yuck!" Marcie groaned and made a face. "This is awful!" She ran to get a drink. "Mom, why did that taste so horrible?" she asked when she finally got the taste out of her mouth. "It looked like regular chocolate, but it sure didn't taste like it."

"That's unsweetened chocolate. It doesn't have sugar in it yet. That's why it tastes so bitter," explained Mom. Thoughtfully, she added, "That chocolate reminds me of your conversation with Kim. I couldn't help overhearing it."

"Why would it remind you of our conversation?" asked Marcie.

"Well, just like the chocolate was without sugar, sometimes we do things without love," said Mom. "Like talking about someone without love."

"Oh! But all we said is that Lori is stuck-up, and she is," protested Marcie. "We didn't say anything so bad."

"The things we say might not seem too bad to us, but they might be bitter to someone else," replied Mom. "This chocolate needs to be sweetened with sugar, and God wants us to 'sweeten' our life and our conversation with love." *ICS*

HOW ABOUT YOU?

Do you remember to do things with love? Today's memory verse is very short, but if you do as it says, it will make a big difference in your life.

DO THINGS WITH LOVE

MEMORIZE:
"Let love be your highest goal." 1 Corinthians 14:1

DEAD BREAD

(Read James 2:14-18)

"And please help the people at Westside Mission to find enough workers for the Thanksgiving dinner," prayed Sherry. "Amen."

"Amen," said Dad. Family devotions were over, and Sherry started clearing the supper dishes from the table.

"I was thinking," said Mom, "that maybe our family could volunteer to help at Westside Mission this Thanksgiving."

"What!" exclaimed Sherry. She looked up from loading the dishwasher. "I don't want to spend my Thanksgiving there! What about our own turkey dinner?"

"Well, I think we could work that in, too," said Mom. "Let's think about it."

"I think it's a rotten idea," muttered Sherry. She cranked the dishwasher knob to "Start," then did her last chore—putting ingredients into the bread machine to make a loaf of bread for breakfast the next day.

The next morning, Sherry woke to the delicious smell of fresh-baked bread. Her mouth watered as she thought of warm bread with butter melting into it. But when she saw the loaf on the cooling rack, she frowned. The loaf was tiny, and when Sherry picked it up, she found that it was heavy and hard, like a brick. "What happened?" she asked Mom, who was getting breakfast.

"I think you forgot the yeast," said Mom.

"Oh, no," groaned Sherry. "We can't eat this."

"No," agreed Mom, "but I kept it because it reminded me of you."

"Me!" exclaimed Sherry. "Why?"

"Well, yeast is what brings about 'action' in the dough—it causes it to rise," said Mom. "So bread without yeast reminded me of your attitude toward helping out at the mission. You prayed for helpers, but you're not willing to mix actions with your words. An ingredient is missing. The Bible tells us that faith without action to back it up is as useless as this loaf of bread without yeast." *VEN*

HOW ABOUT YOU?

Do you have good intentions but find it hard to put actions to them? Helping others may be inconvenient, but God wants to use your hands and feet to show his love. Don't just talk about God's love to others; show it.

MEMORIZE:

"Remember, it is sin to know what you ought to do and then not do it." James 4:17

SHOW FAITH BY ACTIONS

HOLY SPIRIT FEET (PART 1)

(Read Romans 8:1-2, 9-11)

"Wow! Look at all the shoes," Carrie exclaimed. "How am I ever going to choose one pair?"

"How about clogs?" asked her sister, Glenna.

"These canvas shoes would be good for school," suggested Mom.

Carrie tried on several different kinds of shoes and finally decided on the denim clogs.

After dinner that night, Dad read some verses about the Holy Spirit. "I really don't understand much about the Holy Spirit," said Glenna.

"Carrie's feet are like the Holy Spirit," Mom replied.

"Huh?" exclaimed Glenna and Carrie in unison.

Mom grinned. "Remember all those shoes at the store today?" she asked. "Did you see them skipping around or jumping from one display to another?"

"Of course not," said Carrie. "That's silly."

"Yes, it is," agreed Mom. "They don't have any life in them. They are dead." She smiled. "That's just the way people are without God the Holy Spirit living in them. They're dead to spiritual things. They can't understand them. And they won't be able to live in heaven with God."

"Aha!" exclaimed Dad. "I see what you're getting at. Mom's right. We all were dead in sin, but when Christ came to dwell in our heart through the Holy Spirit, he made us alive spiritually—just like when Carrie put on her clogs, the clogs began to move around. Carrie's feet put life inside of them."

"And just as there are many different colors and styles of shoes, there are many different colors and types of people," added Mom. "But no shoe will jump and play without someone's feet living in them. And no person will have new life without God's Holy Spirit living in him." *LJR*

HOW ABOUT YOU?

Do you have God's Holy Spirit living within you? When you ask Jesus to forgive your sins and to be your Savior, he gives you new life through his Holy Spirit. The Holy Spirit helps you to learn how to live in a way that pleases God. He comforts you when you're sad. And he helps you to know when you do wrong.

MEMORIZE:

"The Spirit of God, who raised Jesus from the dead, lives in you. And just as he raised Christ from the dead, he will give life to your mortal body by this same Spirit living within you." Romans 8:11

THE SPIRIT GIVES NEW LIFE

HOLY SPIRIT FEET (PART 2)

(Read Ephesians 4:29–5:2)

Clip-clop! Clip-clop! "These new clogs take some getting used to," said Carrie, stumbling for the third time while walking to school.

"There's Mrs. Clark peeking through her curtains," said Glenna as the girls passed the Clarks' house. "She's so nosy! Whenever something happens, she's the first one there. She says she wants to help, but what she's really doing is trying to find some juicy gossip she can spread."

"Look at her yard," added Carrie. "She should spend time taking care of it instead of putting her nose in other people's business."

"Candice Clark is as bad as her mother," replied Glenna. "Look at her up ahead with Marcia and Alex. Did you see how she came flying out her front door, half ready for school, just so she could walk with them?"

Carrie laughed. "Her hair's a mess, and she always wears a ripped jacket. And I bet her shoes are untied, too . . . OUCH!" Carrie stumbled over some crumbling concrete in the walk. "My toe!" She took off one clog and found a bloodied, throbbing toe. "Oh, it hurts really bad. I'm going home to let Mom fix it up."

"OK," said Glenna. "I'll see you later."

Carrie limped home, wincing painfully with every step on her left foot. "What happened?" Mom asked, seeing Carrie's agonizing limp.

"Glenna and I were talking about Candice Clark when I tripped and hurt my toe," Carrie explained.

"You weren't running down the Clarks, were you?" Mom asked, knowingly, as she opened the medicine cabinet.

"Uh . . . kind of," confessed Carrie.

Mom shook her head. "Remember your 'Holy Spirit feet'?" she asked. "You hurt your toe when you weren't careful about walking, and you can hurt the Holy Spirit when you're not careful about your talking." *LJR*

HOW ABOUT YOU?

Are there times you have grieved the Holy Spirit by the mean things you have said about others? Or the unkind ways you have acted? If you've done such things, ask God's forgiveness.

MEMORIZE:

"And do not bring sorrow to God's Holy Spirit by the way you live. Remember, he is the one who has identified you as his own, guaranteeing that you will be saved on the day of redemption."
Ephesians 4:30

**WATCH YOUR TALK
AND YOUR WALK**

LEGS ON HER PRAYERS

(Read Romans 15:1-7)

Kaley winced when her friends made cutting remarks about Michelle, another classmate. Michelle's clothes were often dirty and mismatched. Her skin and hair didn't look clean, either. Many of the girls at school teased her, but Kaley had never joined in.

After school, Kaley told her mother about Michelle. "I've prayed about it— I've asked God to make the teasing stop, but it doesn't seem to do any good," said Kaley. "I feel so sorry for Michelle."

"Well, maybe you need to put 'legs' on your prayers," suggested Mother. "Are you willing to be her friend?" Kaley thought about it and then nodded slowly. She would do it.

Kaley began by saying a few friendly words to Michelle whenever they met in the hall. Next, she invited Michelle to sit with her at lunchtime. A few weeks later, Kaley asked her friends, including Michelle, to spend the night at her house.

Kaley was glad to see that Michelle was wearing a clean shirt when she arrived at her home. During the evening the girls talked about hair styles, choosing suitable clothes, cleanliness, and other good grooming habits. Michelle listened intently. After a bit, she asked, "Will you help me fix my hair so it looks better?" Soon the girls were all giggling together as they tried fixing Michelle's hair different ways.

After that evening, Michelle's appearance slowly improved. She was clean and neat, and as the others teased her less, she lost some of her shyness. She also went to church with Kaley.

Kaley was delighted. God had answered her prayer—using Kaley herself to bring about the changes. She was glad she had pleased the Lord and brought glory to him by being kind to Michelle. *CEY*

HOW ABOUT YOU?

Do you refuse to join in teasing others? That's good, but sometimes there's even more you can do. Are you willing to help someone who has a problem? Start out with just a friendly word or two. As time goes by, you may have a chance to do other things. Be ready to help in any way God shows you.

MEMORIZE:

"So accept each other just as Christ has accepted you; then God will be glorified." Romans 15:7

REACH OUT TO OTHERS

ROTTEN TEETH

(Read Psalm 50:16-23; Ecclesiastes 8:11)

"I had two cavities!" exclaimed Andrea as she and Dad drove home from the dentist's office. "I can't believe it! I didn't think I'd have any at all!"

"Too many sweets, I guess," suggested Dad.

"Well . . . maybe. I do like candy," said Andrea, "and cookies and ice cream and . . ."

"And cavities?" asked Dad.

"No, not cavities," said Andrea. She sighed. "How can teeth rot like that, and you never even feel it?" she grumbled.

Dad shook his head. "I don't know," he said, "but I once heard someone compare that to sin. Sometimes we lie, steal, or cheat, and when we seem to get away with it, we continue to do wrong. Like with eating too many sweets, we often don't reap the consequence until much later."

"Like me," said Andrea. "Since I didn't get cavities right away, I thought I was getting away with eating all that good-tasting stuff."

"Right," said Dad. "But every action—good or bad—will bring a consequence, no matter how long it takes to show up."

"Well, I think I'll give up sweet stuff for good," declared Andrea.

Dad smiled. "Oh, I don't think you need to give it up completely," he said, "but when you do have sweets—or anything else for that matter—maybe you can brush a little more often and more carefully."

"Oh, yeah," agreed Andrea. "I could do that."

"And when it comes to sin in our life," continued Dad, "we do need to give that up completely. But when we sin, there's cleansing for that, too. We need to repent and confess our sins. We need to ask God to 'cleanse' our life and then make up our mind to please him in our actions." *GDM*

HOW ABOUT YOU?

If you receive no immediate consequence or punishment for wrong actions, such as gossiping, cheating, or stealing, do you think you're getting away with it? No one gets away with doing wrong.

MEMORIZE:

"But if you do what is wrong, you will be paid back for the wrong you have done. For God has no favorites who can get away with evil."
Colossians 3:25

ALL THINGS HAVE CONSEQUENCES

BEEPER CALL

(Read 1 Samuel 3:1-10)

Boomp, boomp, boomp! Katelyn broke away with the basketball and headed down the court. A second later a big Royals guard blocked her way. Katelyn picked up the ball, ducked left . . . right . . . then aimed and let it fly. The ball arched through the air and descended perfectly through the hoop, whooshing past the net.

The crowd went wild. Katelyn grinned and glanced up at the bleachers where Mom and Dad were sitting. But then her shoulders sagged. Her dad was walking to the exit. He had missed seeing Katelyn make her basket. *I suppose the hospital called him again,* thought Katelyn.

After the game Katelyn's friend Becky approached her. "Want to shoot some baskets with me tomorrow night?" Becky asked.

"Thanks, but I can't," said Katelyn, remembering she had a youth group meeting at church. *Ask Becky to come along,* a little voice seemed to whisper. Katelyn had felt before that she should invite Becky to join her at some church activity. But like all the other times, she said nothing. *After all,* she thought, *if Becky wants to go to church she'll go on her own.*

When Dad came home later that night, Katelyn was still sulking. "You missed the basket I made, and most of my game, too," she told Dad.

"I know, and I'm sorry," said Dad, "but tonight I had more than a medical emergency to deal with. I had a beeper call from both the hospital and from the Lord. I was able to talk to a lady about Jesus before she died."

Suddenly Katelyn didn't feel angry at Dad anymore. She felt proud of her father and ashamed that she had been so selfish. She also felt a little uneasy. She remembered feeling that she should invite Becky to youth group. *Maybe that was God's beeper call to me,* she thought, *and I just ignored it. But maybe it's not too late! I can talk to Becky tomorrow and ask her to come to youth group with me.* VEN

HOW ABOUT YOU?

Are you on call for Jesus? Can he count on you to hear his voice and do what he asks you to? It may not always be convenient or easy, but your obedience is important.

MEMORIZE:

"Then I heard the Lord asking, 'Whom should I send as a messenger to my people? Who will go for us?' And I said, 'Lord, I'll go! Send me.'" Isaiah 6:8

BE ON CALL FOR JESUS

NOVEMBER 18

THE BIKE ACCIDENT

(Read Matthew 10:29-31)

Amy could hardly sit still as she and Mom drove to the bike shop. She had been saving money and now had a total of $165. She hoped it would be enough for a new bike. When they arrived at the shop, Amy saw several bikes she liked, including a nice red one on sale for $169. Amy looked up at Mom, and she smiled. "I'll chip in the rest of the money," she said. "You can buy it."

The next day as Amy was riding her bike down a steep hill, she started going faster and faster. Suddenly the bike veered wildly out of control! Before she knew what had happened, Amy found herself lying on the pavement beside her bike. She felt pain on her knee and looked down to see blood and dirt covering a scrape as big as a silver dollar. She stumbled to her feet and half ran and half limped as she headed straight for home, pushing her bike along. When she got near the house she began to cry loudly. "Ooohhhh! Oh, Mom," she wailed, "help me!" She sobbed as she limped through the door.

Mom came quickly and gently began to fix Amy's knee. "Why did God let me fall?" Amy whimpered. "Doesn't he care if I get hurt?"

Mother smiled. "He cares for you even more than I do," she assured Amy. "Remember last spring when the baby birds fell out of the tree? God says that not one sparrow can fall on the ground without his knowing it. He also says we are more important to him than many sparrows. He didn't have anything to do with your fall, but he knew that you would fall. And he cares about that." Mom hugged her, and then Amy walked back outside, quite pleased with the huge bandage. *CLG*

HOW ABOUT YOU?

When you fall, or even get hurt in your heart, do you know God cares? Do you "run" straight to him in prayer like Amy ran to Mom? Do you tell God how much you hurt and give him a chance to help you and show you how much he cares? If you feel hurt or sad right now—for any reason—pray and ask God to help you.

MEMORIZE:

"Not even a sparrow, worth only half a penny, can fall to the ground without your Father knowing it."
Matthew 10:29

GOD CARES FOR YOU

WHAT WE HAVE

(Read 1 Timothy 6:6-12)

Maria sighed as she pushed the door open, pulled the key out, and put it in her pocket. She swung the door shut and locked it. "Ashley's lucky—her mom is home baking cookies, but I have to peel potatoes and put the meatloaf in the oven," she said out loud. She talked to herself a lot when she was alone. That way the apartment didn't seem so empty. "I wish I had a pet."

Maria continued to mumble as she did her chores. Soon she heard her mother at the door. "Hi, honey, how was school?"

"OK." Maria didn't look up.

"Thanks for putting the meatloaf in the oven. It sure smells good." She looked at Maria closely. "Is something wrong?" she asked.

"No."

"Are you sure?" Mom paused on her way toward the stove. "I can tell something's bothering you. Let's talk about it." She put down a dish and hugged Maria. Soon Maria was telling her mother all her troubles, especially how she hated coming home to an empty house.

Mom sighed. "We talked about this before, and you know I have to work," she said. "I'd rather be home, but I have no choice. I wish you could have a pet, but the landlord won't allow that." Her shoulders slumped. Then she sat up straight. "Maria, you have something many of your friends don't have—you have Jesus," Mom reminded her. "That's more important than anything else in the world. When we have to do without things we want, I think it helps to remind ourselves of what we do have. Let's make a list. I'll start." Mom picked up a pen and paper. "We have a place to live."

"And clothes," Maria added.

Mom wrote it down. "You can go to school, and I have a job," she said. "What else?"

"Friends." Maria started to smile.

"We have a church where we can worship God."

Maria sniffed the air. "And we have meatloaf." *VLC*

HOW ABOUT YOU?

Do your friends have something you wish you had? Instead of thinking of those things, make a list of what you do have. Learn to be content in your circumstances.

MEMORIZE:

"No matter what happens, always be thankful, for this is God's will for you who belong to Christ Jesus."

1 Thessalonians 5:18

COUNT YOUR BLESSINGS

IT OUGHT TO HURT

(Read Psalm 51:1-12)

Jon and Wendy were hungry, but Mother was gone to the store. "Hey, there's candy up in the cupboard," said Wendy. "Let's sneak some. Mother will never know."

Jon looked uncertain. "Doesn't that make you feel guilty?" he asked.

Wendy shook her head. "Nah. At first I felt guilty, but it doesn't bother me anymore."

Jon still hesitated, but when he saw his sister eating a chocolate bar, he just couldn't resist. The two finished their candy, carefully threw away the wrappers, and went outside to play in the snow.

After a while their feet were wet and cold, but they wanted to finish the snow fort they were building. They refused to give in and go back indoors. For some time they kept on working. When Mother arrived home, she called them inside. She was shocked when she saw how wet and cold their feet were. "Why didn't you come inside when your feet got cold?" she scolded.

"We wanted to finish our fort," Wendy replied. "Besides, they didn't feel so cold after a while, Mom!"

Mother looked grim. "That sensation of cold was meant to be a warning to you. If you had stayed out much longer, you might have gotten frostbite. The most dangerous time is not when your feet get cold, but when you stop feeling it." She rubbed their feet gently and added, "The cold is like our conscience. Like the cold was a warning to come inside, our conscience is a warning to stay away from doing wrong. We're in danger if our conscience stops bothering us when we do something wrong."

When Mother left the room, the children looked at each other, remembering the candy they had eaten.

"I sure feel my feet now," commented Jon. "Now that they're getting warmed up, they hurt. And my conscience hurts, too."

"Mine, too," agreed Wendy. "And it's going to hurt more when we tell Mother about the candy we took. But I'm sure we'll feel better afterward!" *SLK*

HOW ABOUT YOU?

Are there habits or activities in your life that made you feel guilty in the past but not anymore? You may have changed, but God's standards of right and wrong haven't. Confess your sin, and be willing to follow your conscience and the Holy Spirit. Don't let yourself become "numb" to sin!

MEMORIZE:

"Create in me a clean heart, O God.
Renew a right spirit within me."
Psalm 51:10

DON'T GET USED TO SIN

WORTH LISTENING

(Read Proverbs 1:7-9)

"I'm the only girl in my class who has to ride a bicycle!" Kim stormed as she picked up her library book. "The other girls' parents take them whenever they have to go somewhere! And the other girls get to date, too."

Mother looked up. "Kim, we've been through all this before. Why don't you sit down and let's talk about it."

But Kim headed for the door. "I have to get to the library," she grumbled. She went out to the garage, slamming the door behind her.

Mother sighed. "Well, we might as well enjoy a few minutes of quiet," she said. "Jason's taking a nap."

Dad nodded. "Might be a good time to clean the garage," he suggested, and the two of them got busy.

For an hour they worked in companionable silence. Then, just as a fuming Kim rode her bike into the garage, a voice rang out from the house. "Mommie?"

"Peace and quiet just went out the door." Mother grinned at Dad. She lifted her voice. "Jason, we're—"

"MOMMIE!" The little boy's scream drowned out her words.

Mother tried again. "Jason," she called, "we're in—"

"MOMMIE!" a terrified wail split the air. Mother and Dad, followed by Kim, flew into the house. Jason, looking wild-eyed, was standing in the kitchen. "I thought you left me," he sobbed.

"If you'd listened a minute, you could have heard Mother," Kim scolded crossly.

Dad nodded. "That's true, Kim. Looks like we have two children not listening to their parents." Kim blushed. "We ask the Lord daily to help us make the right decisions concerning you, Kim," Dad continued, "and I think we all need to do a better listening job. Why don't we start practicing our listening skills by talking about this dating thing. " *BJW*

HOW ABOUT YOU?

Do you feel that your parents don't understand you? Have you tried to understand them? Have you really listened to what they have to say? God has given them the responsibility of using their wisdom in guiding you. He has given you the responsibility of listening to them and obeying them. They're worth listening to.

LISTEN TO YOUR PARENTS

MEMORIZE:

"Listen, my child, to what your father teaches you. Don't neglect your mother's teaching." Proverbs 1:8

NOVEMBER
22

JUST LIKE DORCAS

(Read Acts 9:36-43)

"What are you making, Mom?" Jody asked as she looked up from her book.

"I'm making a baby sweater for one of the ladies at church," answered Mom. "Mrs. Pauley is having a baby next month."

"How come you do so many things like that for other people?" Jody asked.

"I enjoy making things, and I enjoy giving them away." Mother smiled. "When you make something special at school, you enjoy bringing it home to me, don't you?"

Jody nodded. "Sure, but that seems a little different," she said. "I mean, you're my mom! But you do a lot of things for people you hardly know."

"Not as much as Dorcas did," Mother answered.

"Dorcas?" Jody asked. "Who's she?"

"The book of Acts tells about Dorcas," explained Mother. "She was probably one of the first women inspired by Christ to be active in works of love. She knew how to sew, and she devoted time to making clothes for widows and poor people. She was also their friend and listened to them."

"Oh, I remember hearing about her in church," Jody said thoughtfully.

Mother smiled. "When Dorcas died, everyone was very sad. Do you remember what happened then?"

Jody thought for a moment, then her face brightened. "Was she raised from the dead?"

"That's right," said Mother. "The apostle Peter was in town at the time, and when he was told about it, he prayed, and God used him to raise her to life."

"When I get older I'm going to do things for other people, too—like Dorcas and you," Jody decided.

"You don't have to wait that long," said Mom. "Let's think of something you can do for others right now." *VLC*

HOW ABOUT YOU?

What can you do for someone? Could you draw a picture, or make a small gift, and give it to your grandparents? Help them by dusting or cleaning? Help your mother make cookies for someone who is sick? Make a card for a shut-in? Mow the lawn for an elderly neighbor? When you help others, you please the Lord, too.

MEMORIZE:

"She extends a helping hand to the poor and opens her arms to the needy."
Proverbs 31:20

HELP OTHERS

IN SHAPE

(Read Luke 9:23-26)

Donna had never been so glad to see the end of a week. Band camp had been hard work! There had been fun times like the huge pillow fight the other night, but for the most part, this long weekend of camp had been too much work. What a way to spend Thanksgiving vacation!

On Saturday, Donna had played her trumpet so long and so hard that she'd split her lip, and the nurse had given her ointment to soothe it. She had to admit, though, that after all the hours of practice, her lips were stronger.

It wasn't just her lips that had been put to the test. Every morning the band had gotten up and done exercises at six o'clock. They had also marched two hours each day. After the first day, Donna's legs had been so sore she felt like she never wanted to walk again! But her legs felt really strong and tough now that the weekend was over.

The very first day back at school, Donna turned her ankle in gym and had to stay off it for several days. She was almost glad. At least she didn't have to march with the band! They were preparing for a long parade, and Mr. Artz, the band director, was really making them work hard.

Then just as Donna was getting ready to rejoin the band, she got the flu. Now she began to get worried. She *did* want to march in that parade. She hoped nothing else would happen to her!

And nothing did. On the day of the parade she was feeling fine. Mr. Artz wasn't quite sure that Donna would be up to marching, but he gave in to Donna's pleas. Off Donna marched with the band. She couldn't believe how tired it made her!

At church the next day, Pastor Steward talked about being spiritually strong. "Our spiritual lives are like our physical lives," concluded the pastor. "We don't have to do anything to get *out* of shape, but we must exercise daily to stay *in* shape."

Donna knew exactly what the pastor meant, and she knew that she had allowed herself to get out of shape spiritually, too. She asked the Lord to help her get her spiritual body back in shape and keep it that way. *REP*

HOW ABOUT YOU?

Is your spirit out of shape from lack of exercise? Doing nothing will get you out of shape very quickly, so discipline yourself to read the Bible, pray, and live for Jesus every day.

**GET DAILY
SPIRITUAL EXERCISE**

MEMORIZE:
"Because of this, I always try to maintain a clear conscience before God and everyone else." Acts 24:16

PRETTY PACKAGE

(Read Matthew 7:1-5, 12)

When Dottie came into the kitchen, sleepily rubbing her eyes, she found the rest of her family there ahead of her. "Happy Birthday!" they shouted. A big smile spread across Dottie's face as she saw gifts piled beside her plate. There was one all done up in rainbow colors, with long, curly streamers. Another had a teddy bear trinket on top. And then there was a plain white envelope. "We thought we'd let you open presents now," said Mother with a smile.

Eagerly, Dottie reached for the package with the teddy bear on top. Inside she found a cute little notepad and pen. She was surprised to see that it was from her brother. "Thanks, Ned," she said. "I love it." Next, she opened the "rainbow" package. It was from her sister, and it contained a new coloring book and magic markers. "Oh, good!" she exclaimed. "Half of my old markers won't even write anymore." Finally, she reached for the uninteresting white envelope and slowly slit it open. But when she saw what was inside, her eyes widened. "Oh," she squealed, "a kitty? I'm going to get a kitty?" She held out a certificate that read, "Good for one small kitten. With much love, Mom and Dad."

"You and Mom can pick it up after school," said Dad, smiling.

"Oh, thank you! This is the best present I ever had!"

As they went to get the kitten after school, Dottie told her mother all about her day. "We have a new girl in our class," she said, "but she looks kind of messy. She could use some new clothes. She combs her hair funny, too."

"Be careful. Man looks on the outward appearance, but the Lord looks on the heart," Mother reminded her. "You can't tell what's in a package by the wrappings, you know." As they pulled up in front of the pet store, Dottie had to agree. She remembered the plain white envelope. *HWM*

HOW ABOUT YOU?

Do you make quick judgments when you meet new kids? Do you decide whether you like them by what they wear rather than by what they are? That's not God's way. He judges others—and you—by what he sees inside. Don't judge people just by the way they look. Ask the Lord to help you love them as he does.

MEMORIZE:

"People judge by outward appearance, but the Lord looks at a person's thoughts and intentions."
1 Samuel 16:7

**DON'T JUDGE BY
APPEARANCE ONLY**

THANK YOU

(Read Psalm 136:1-9, 23-26)

"I'm full!" declared Cassie, pushing away from the table.

"Me too," agreed Jacob. "That turkey was yummy!"

"Would you all like pie now?" asked Mother. "Or would you rather wait till later?"

"Later!" chorused everyone.

Mother began to clear the table, and everybody pitched in to help. "Let me pull the rest of the meat off the turkey bones," offered Grandma when the table was empty.

"Thanks. That will be a big help," said Mother. "I'll put the leftovers away, and you kids can load the dishwasher. I think you'd better scrape the plates first today."

Cassie sighed. "Jacob, you scrape, and I'll rinse," she said quickly, and they got to work. "Oh, Mom," wailed Cassie after a bit, "there are so *many* dishes to do today."

"Oh, that's not so bad," said Grandma. "At least you have a dishwasher and don't have to do them all by hand."

"Yes," agreed Mother. "That's definitely something to be thankful for!"

"I still hate dirty dishes," insisted Cassie stubbornly.

"*You* hate them!" said Jacob. "*I* absolutely despise this job! I think doing dishes should still be girls' work."

"Hmmm," murmured Mother. "A long time ago I read a little poem that has always stuck with me. I tried to find out who wrote it, but I never did. It goes like this: 'Thank God for dirty dishes . . . they have a tale to tell. While other folks go hungry, we're eating very well. With health and home and happiness, we should not fret or fuss. For by this stack of evidence, God's very good to us.' "

"Oh, that's good!" exclaimed Grandma. *HWM*

HOW ABOUT YOU?

Have you ever thanked God for dirty dishes? How about dirty clothes? Maybe you can think of other things that seem like a trial but really are a blessing. All that God gives you is good, and he gives so much! Be sure to thank him for all things—things both big and small.

REMEMBER TO THANK GOD

MEMORIZE:

"Give thanks to the Lord, for he is good! His faithful love endures forever." Psalm 136:1

NOVEMBER 26

GOD'S PATCHWORK QUILT

(Read 1 Corinthians 12:20-27)

Janet's mother was sewing, and Janet was looking through a box of material scraps. "Mother!" she exclaimed. "Look at this gorgeous blue satin! Can you make me a dress out of this?"

"It *is* pretty," Mother agreed, "but there's not enough to make a dress, or even a blouse." Sadly, Janet laid it back in the box.

Several weeks later when Janet came home from school, she found a large gift-wrapped bundle lying on her bed. When she tore off the wrappings, she found a pretty, handmade, patchwork quilt. It was made with many different colors and designs. Janet squealed with delight. "What a surprise!" she said. "And the border—it's made of that pretty blue satin I liked!"

"It would have been a shame not to be able to use that material for some-thing," said Mother, "so I thought of making a quilt! And while I was sewing it together, do you know what I was thinking?"

"What?" asked Janet.

"God has a patchwork quilt, too—the church!" replied Mother. "Some Chris-tians are young, some are old; some are rich, and some are poor. There are those with many talents and others with just a few. But all of them are necessary in God's church. Together they make a beautiful, finished product, just like this quilt."

"It is beautiful," Janet agreed. "None of the pieces would be as beautiful by themselves."

"No, they wouldn't," answered Mother. "But together they make something beautiful and useful. Christians need one another."

Janet's eyes twinkled. "The next time I feel like a small, unimportant scrap," she said, "I'll just remember that I'm an important part of God's patchwork quilt!" *SLK*

HOW ABOUT YOU?

If you are a Christian, you are an important part of Christ's body, the church. That means you need to serve him, and serve others, the best way you can. You also need the help that other Christians can give you. Go to a church where there are Christians and where the Bible is taught. Get involved!

MEMORIZE:

"Now all of you together are Christ's body, and each one of you is a separate and necessary part of it."
1 Corinthians 12:27

GO TO CHURCH

THE KIWI

(Read 1 Peter 3:3-4)

Lindsey frowned as she looked at herself in the full length mirror. "I'm ugly," she sighed sadly. "Everyone laughs at me because I'm short and chubby. My eyes are too small and my nose is too big. My nails aren't pretty, either, and my teeth are crooked. I'm ugly, and that's it."

"That's nonsense," Mother said. She had noticed that Lindsey often walked around with slumped shoulders lately and was not her usual friendly, cheerful self. "You're changing," Mother continued, "but you are definitely not ugly. Come on, let's go to the store."

At the store, Mother asked, "Would you get two kiwi for me, please?" She pointed toward the strange, brown fruit.

"I've never seen kiwi before," said Lindsey. "Are you sure you want these funny-looking things?" Mother smiled and nodded as she added some bananas to the basket.

After dinner that evening, Mother set out a colorful bowl of fruit for dessert. "What a pretty green this fruit is, Mom," observed Lindsey, pointing to one of the pieces. She took a bite. "Oh, and it's so good! What is it?"

"It's kiwi," Mom informed her, smiling.

"You're kidding!" Lindsey gulped. "You mean that ugly, fuzzy, brown thing we bought?"

"That's right," said Mom. "You know, honey, you've been putting too much value on the way things look lately. You've been especially hard on yourself. Just like with the kiwi, it's what's inside that counts. Keep working on that. Look your best, and then be content with the way you're made. Ever since you've become so concerned about your looks, all your inside sweetness has been covered up. And I really miss my old Lindsey."

"I think I like the old Lindsey better, too," Lindsey said. She grinned at her mother. *SLN*

HOW ABOUT YOU?

Are you unhappy with the way you look? Learn to accept the way God made you, and be content. Most of all, work at becoming a beautiful person inside by living the way God's Word tells you to live.

BE CONTENT WITH YOUR LOOKS

MEMORIZE:
"Charm is deceptive, and beauty does not last; but a woman who fears the Lord will be greatly praised."
Proverbs 31:30

NOVEMBER
28

BACK TO THE BEGINNING

(Read Matthew 5:23-24)

"I can't! I just can't do it!" Diana cried out. She wadded up the paper and burst into tears.

"What can't you do?" Dad looked up from his paper.

"I can't get these figures to balance," sniffed Diana. "Tomorrow when I turn in our club treasurer's report, everyone will think I'm dumb. And Janet will gloat!"

Dad looked at Diana's report. "Speaking of Janet, I haven't seen her lately. I thought she was your best friend. Why would she be happy if you make a mistake on your report?"

Diana hesitated. "Well, we both wanted to be treasurer and we quarreled. I got elected, but she still tried to tell me how to do the job. I finally informed her that I'd do things my own way. Since then we haven't been speaking," Diana said sadly.

"I'm sorry to hear that," began Dad. Suddenly he pointed to some of the figures on the report. "Say, Diana, go back to the beginning and add up your figures one by one."

Diana tried it, and it worked. "I found my mistake, Dad!" she exclaimed. "In the beginning I multiplied by four instead of adding it. Now it's right."

"It usually helps to go back to the beginning," Dad said. "You know, Diana, I think it would be a good idea to go back to the beginning of your quarrel with Janet, too."

"What do you mean?" asked Diana.

"It sounds like both of you wanted your own way in the beginning. That was selfish. Then you hurt each other by using cutting words," Dad explained. "How about going to Janet and apologizing for wanting your own way? Listen to what she has to say. I'm sure she has some good ideas."

Diana sighed. "OK, Dad." *JLH*

HOW ABOUT YOU?

Is there someone with whom you've had a disagreement? Are you sure it was all that person's fault? Ask God to show you what you might have done wrong. Confess your sin to God; then go to the other person and apologize. A restored friendship will make you both happy. Don't carry old grudges into the new year.

MEMORIZE:

"Now it is time to forgive him and comfort him. Otherwise he may become so discouraged that he won't be able to recover." 2 Corinthians 2:7

RESTORE FRIENDSHIPS

ORDINARY BUT PRETTY

(Read Ephesians 4:7-12)

"I still wish I could sing or act in the Christmas play," Angela sighed. "It would be so nice to be important once in a while—to really be needed instead of just pressing dumb old costumes."

"I've told you—you are important. You are needed," replied Mother patiently. "But you seem determined not to believe that. Well, I'd better get supper ready."

Angela nodded. "I'll set the table," she offered, going to the cupboard. "Mom, can we use the good crystal goblets tonight? They're so pretty!"

"I don't see why not," said Mother. "But before we eat, I want you to take this casserole to old Mrs. Jenkins. Visit with her a little while, too. She's lonely. Tell you what—I'll set the table tonight. Just be back at 5:30 for supper."

When Angela returned home, the family was just sitting down to eat. She slipped into her place and looked at the table in surprise. There were at least three crystal goblets at each place, but no plates. Dad said, "Let's thank the Lord for our food," so she quickly closed her eyes.

When Dad said "Amen," Mother picked up a casserole dish and handed it to Angela. "Help yourself," she invited.

Angela held the casserole uncertainly. "What am I supposed to do with it?" she asked. "Where are the regular plates?"

"Oh," said Mother, "the goblets are so pretty, I thought we'd just use them."

"But we can't use them for this kind of food," protested Angela. "What's going on here?"

"So you admit that we need different 'vessels' for different jobs," said Mother. "That's what I was trying to tell you earlier this afternoon. You see, it's that way in God's kingdom, too. He needs some 'vessels'—some people—to sing, some to preach, some to visit lonely folks. Some jobs appear to us to be 'prettier' than others, but each is as important as the next."

Angela laughed. "OK, I get the point," she said. "But right now ordinary plates sound mighty 'pretty' to me." *HWM*

HOW ABOUT YOU?

Do you feel that the things you're asked to do for the Lord are unimportant? That's not true. There is no such thing as an unimportant task when it's done for Jesus.

YOU'RE IMPORTANT

MEMORIZE:

"Your life will be clean, and you will be ready for the Master to use you for every good work." 2 Timothy 2:21

LITTLE BY LITTLE

(Read Ephesians 4:17-24)

"Ugh! Mom, the smell in that house is horrible!" said Misty as she and her mother got into the car. "How does Mrs. Brown stand it?"

"Honey, she probably doesn't even smell it; she's so used to it," said Mom as they drove away. They had been visiting an elderly lady from their church who was homebound. She had several cats and a dog living in her house with her.

"Now I know why you make me change Feisty's litter box so often," said Misty. "I'm sure glad our house doesn't smell like that! I could never get used to it."

"Don't be so sure," said Mom. "Remember when we went to visit Aunt Allie on her farm? We thought we'd never be able to stay three days with her, because the smell from the cattle barn across the road was so bad. But after several hours we hardly noticed the smell anymore."

"That's right, I remember. The smell was awful at first. Aunt Allie said it was because the wind was blowing from that direction. I thought the wind must have changed before we left, but Aunt Allie said it hadn't," mused Misty. "You know, Mom, that's like my Sunday school lesson last week. It was about our consciences being seared. My teacher says it means that, little by little, we get used to things that are wrong. Then before we realize it, our consciences don't bother us at all, and we don't even think of our sin as wrong anymore. That's worse than Mrs. Brown and Aunt Allie getting used to those awful smells, isn't it?" *KRL*

HOW ABOUT YOU?

Are you growing used to the sin in your life that once bothered you? Confess it today, and ask the Lord to keep your conscience alert and sensitive to sin. Ask him to remind you of things that are wrong and then to help you live a life pleasing to him.

MEMORIZE:

"I will maintain my innocence without wavering. My conscience is clear for as long as I live." Job 27:6

DON'T GET USED TO SIN

THE CLAY POTS

(Read 1 Corinthians 4:6-7; Isaiah 29:16)

"I'm prettier than Lisette," said Rachel, tossing her head, "and Sally says she's never seen such glossy hair as mine!" Rachel began to flatten a stick of red modeling clay. "And I can sing better than anyone in my class," she announced proudly.

"God has certainly given you a talent for singing," said Mom mildly.

"And boasting!" muttered Brian as he heaved a loud sigh.

Rachel scowled at her brother and started fashioning a slender vase. "I'm smarter than you are, Brian," she said loftily, "even though you're older than me." Brian clicked his tongue impatiently, walked out of the room, and slammed the door. Rachel's lips curved into a smile. "Mrs. White said mine was the best essay in our writing class," she said loudly as she stood back to admire her handiwork.

Mother looked over her shoulder. "Isn't that blue bowl you made yesterday a clever little thing!" exclaimed Mother. "And that red clay vase looks really intelligent, too. I can see that both those pottery pieces are very smart—they're so nicely made."

"What do you mean? Things aren't smart," said Rachel, frowning. "I was the one who made them."

"Oh, but they're so smart to turn out so pretty and neat," said Mom.

Rachel looked puzzled. "Mom, I don't get it," she said. "Those were just sticks of clay. I'm the one who made them turn out that way."

"That's true," said Mom softly, "and here's something else to think about. You may be pretty and smart, and you may sing well . . . but who made you that way?"

Rachel shuffled her feet uneasily. "God did," she mumbled at last.

"So who gets the credit for all of that?" asked Mom.

"God, I guess," replied Rachel.

"So," said Mom, "there's nothing for you to boast about, right?"

Rachel sighed. "Right, Mom," she admitted. *MTF*

HOW ABOUT YOU?

Are you pretty? Clever? Do you sing well, draw well, or speak well? God gave you whatever talents or gifts you have. And while it is OK to be happy and pleased about things God helps you do well, it is not OK to brag.

MEMORIZE:

"What makes you better than anyone else? What do you have that God hasn't given you? And if all you have is from God, why boast as though you have accomplished something on your own?" 1 Corinthians 4:7

DON'T BRAG

DECEMBER
2

THE BLANK TAPE

(Read Psalm 51:1-2, 7-10)

"Give me my red sweater!" shouted Carrie as she chased her twin down the stairs.

"It's not your sweater. It's mine. Yours is in the wash," Shelly answered. She ran around the kitchen table, holding the sweater tightly.

"You're always taking my things," pouted Carrie.

"Am not," said Shelly. "You're the one who's always starting trouble." She appealed to her mother. "Carrie wouldn't walk home with me, Mom," she said. "She told the girls I was a wimp."

Mom held up a hand to stop Carrie's angry retort. "Girls," she said, "I know you love each other, but lately you seem to be quarreling all the time. Would you like to hear what you sound like?" The twins looked at each other. They weren't sure what Mom had in mind. "Your father's tape recorder is here on the kitchen counter," continued Mom. "I turned it on when I heard you come quarreling down the stairs." She pushed a couple of buttons, and in a moment the twins heard their own voices yelling at each other. "It's not very nice to listen to, is it?" asked Mom. "I can get rid of it by unplugging the microphone and pressing this button. Then the tape will be blank again. Shall I do it?" The twins nodded.

While the tape was being erased, Mom spoke. "Girls," she said, "God hears every word we say. He even knows our thoughts." The girls looked at each other. "He made a way in which our wrongdoing can be forgotten. If we're truly sorry, he is willing to forgive and forget. Our record can be erased like this tape. Do you want to ask God to forgive your quarreling and to help you be more loving to one another?"

Both girls nodded. "I'm sorry," they said at the same time. After Mother prayed with them, they went off to do their homework together. *BK*

HOW ABOUT YOU?

Would you like something erased from your record? Did you start a quarrel today or tell a lie or cheat at school? Are you sorry? If so, tell God. He'll forgive you and give you a fresh start—sort of like a blank tape. Fill your life with good words and thoughts.

MEMORIZE:

"I will never again remember their sins and lawless deeds." Hebrews 10:17

LET JESUS ERASE YOUR SIN

JUST LIKE OUR BABY!

(Read Philippians 2:5-11)

"Isn't he sweet!" whispered Shawna, gazing at her brand new brother, Samuel.
Mom smiled. "Yes, he is!" she agreed.

Shawna continued watching the baby while Mom did the ironing. Samuel stirred and opened his eyes. He waved chubby little arms in the air. "He's so tiny!" breathed Shawna in awe. Suddenly the baby began to cry. "Mom! Come quick!" yelled Shawna. "He's crying!"

Mother came and leaned over the side of the crib. She turned Samuel on his side and gently patted his back.

The baby stopped crying. "He must have felt uncomfortable," said Mom. "Time for a change of position."

"Why didn't he turn over?" asked Shawna.

"Well, he's still so tiny, he can't coordinate his movements very well," explained Mom, "and he hasn't developed his muscles. He needs to become stronger before he'll be able to turn over by himself."

"Oh," said Shawna thoughtfully. "He's a pretty helpless baby, isn't he, Mom?"

Mom nodded. "Yes, he is; all new babies are," she said. "About all they do is sleep and eat." She smiled. "He'll soon be stronger and will learn to do other things," she added, "but for a while, he's going to be almost totally dependent on his family."

A little later, Samuel began to cry again. "Now what's he crying for?" demanded Shawna.

Mom smiled. "I think perhaps he's hungry," she said. "Time for him to eat." She went to pick him up.

Soon after the baby was fed, he was again fast asleep in his crib. Shawna had a question for her mother. "Mom, when Jesus was born, was he helpless and dependent, too, just like our baby?"

Mom nodded. "Yes, he was, Shawna. You know, he could have come as a fully-grown man or even as a mighty king if he wanted. But he didn't—he chose to be born as a helpless baby, dependent on his family to take care of him. That's what the Bible means when it says that 'He made himself nothing; he took the humble position of a slave and appeared in human form.' He did that for us, because he loves us so much. *MTF*

HOW ABOUT YOU?

Do you realize how much Jesus humbled himself by becoming a helpless baby? As his follower, do you try to boss others? Or do you try to imitate Jesus by being humble?

MEMORIZE:

"Your attitude should be the same that Christ Jesus had. . . . He obediently humbled himself."

Philippians 2:5, 8

BE HUMBLE LIKE JESUS

DECEMBER
4

FOOTSTEPS IN THE SNOW

(Read 1 Corinthians 8:9-13)

"Oh, I know some rough kids hang out at Hamburger Haven," admitted Leah, "but my friends and I just drink pop and talk. We won't do anything wrong."

Mother sighed. "You may be influenced more than you think," she said. "Besides, even if you don't do anything bad, you may influence younger Christians to go there—like your friend Heidi, for example. She's just a new Christian and may not be able to resist the temptation to do wrong."

"Well, OK," grumbled Leah. "But I don't see why I have to be responsible for the actions of others." She put on her boots and coat. "I'm going to see if the ice is hard on the pond."

When Leah reached the pond, she tested the ice with her foot, and it cracked. No skating yet. She headed home, taking the back way. As she reached the house, her mother was just coming out. "Melissa was playing out here, but I don't see her anywhere," Mother said with a worried look.

Leah stood still as a thought struck her. *The pond! She knows she's not allowed to go there alone, but maybe she followed me.* Leah ran and looked at the place where she had left the yard to go to the pond. Seeing not only her own footprints in the snow, but also a set of tiny ones, she scurried down the hill as fast as she could. As she approached the pond, she saw the little girl step out onto the ice. It seemed to be holding, and Melissa took another step. Just as Leah snatched her up, the ice broke and one foot went into the freezing water.

Melissa's teeth chattered as Leah carried her home. "I just wanted to be with you," said Melissa. "I didn't know it would break."

Back home, Leah was quiet and thoughtful. "I see what you were talking about now, Mom," she said finally. "I knew I shouldn't step on the ice, but Melissa didn't. And as an older Christian, I know the danger in certain situations, but younger Christians might not. I'll be more careful where my footsteps lead from now on." *MRP*

HOW ABOUT YOU?

Are you setting a good example for others, especially those who have not been Christians very long? Could they easily go wrong if they follow your footsteps? Be sure that nothing you do causes others to sin.

MEMORIZE:

"Don't let anyone think less of you because you are young. Be an example to all believers in what you teach, in the way you live, in your love, your faith, and your purity."
1 Timothy 4:12

SET A GOOD EXAMPLE

A CALL FROM GOD

(Read 1 Samuel 3:1-10)

Lisa raced through her breakfast. "Gotta go, OK?" she said, pushing away from the table. "I told Mrs. Hart I'd come early to help paint scenery for the drama our youth group is doing. Mrs. Hart says it's an important ministry because someone might accept the Lord after hearing the play."

When Lisa came home at suppertime, Mom met her at the door. "I'm glad you're home," said Mom. "Your friend Amy has been calling all day. She asked if you would call her when you got home. It sounded important."

Lisa frowned. "I know she wants help with her homework," she said, "and I don't have time for that. I've got to finish working on some posters."

"Couldn't you give Amy a little of your time?" asked Mom.

"Do I have to?" asked Lisa. "I want to get these done for Mrs. Hart."

Mother looked thoughtful. "Lisa, suppose Mrs. Hart had asked you to wash and iron costumes instead of painting scenery today. I know you hate ironing . . . would you have done it?"

Lisa shrugged. "Sure."

"So you're willing to do whatever job Mrs. Hart gives you," observed Mom. "How about God? Have you asked what he wants you to do?"

"God?" asked Lisa. "Well . . . Mrs. Hart says all this work is really for him."

"And I know God is happy to have such a willing servant," agreed Mom, "but what if he needs you to do something else? For example, when someone needs you badly enough to phone four times, it just might be a call from God, too."

Lisa looked at the poster board and paints she had brought home. "I suppose I could do these after I help Amy," she admitted. Then her eyes lit up. "And maybe Amy could help me . . . and then I could invite her to the play!"

"Now that's the servant I love." Mom smiled and handed Lisa the phone. *HMT*

HOW ABOUT YOU?

Do you know where God wants you to help? Have you ever asked what he wants you to do—and then listened for the answer? It's wonderful to get involved in Christian ministry of all types, but sometimes God needs us to do something extra-special.

LISTEN TO GOD'S INSTRUCTIONS

MEMORIZE:
"Yes, Lord, your servant is listening."
1 Samuel 3:9

DECEMBER
6

I DESERVE . . .

(Read Psalm 103:8-11)

"It's not fair," said Kate as she stormed up to her teacher's desk. "I don't have any wrong answers on these word problems, but you still gave me a B instead of an A."

"But you didn't show your work," Mrs. Anderson replied patiently. "I told you that you needed to show me how you got your answers or you would not receive full credit."

"But on my last assignment I didn't show my work, either, and you didn't lower that grade," complained Kate.

"That's true, but I can't continue to be that lenient," replied Mrs. Anderson. "I warned you about that."

"But I deserve . . . ," Kate began. The school bell interrupted her.

"You'd better hurry, or you'll be late for your next class," said Mrs. Anderson.

That night at dinner, Kate told her parents about her talk with Mrs. Anderson. She ended her story by saying, "But I deserved to get an A just like on my other paper."

"I disagree, honey," said Mom gently. "You knew the penalty for failing to show your work. What you really deserved was to lose points on both assignments. You should be grateful that Mrs. Anderson went easy on you the first time."

During family devotion time that evening, Dad read a few verses from Psalm 103. When he was finished, he said, "This reminds me of Kate's problem with Mrs. Anderson."

"What do you mean, Dad?" Kate asked.

"The Bible clearly says that all people are sinners, and no one deserves heaven. But listen to verse ten again. 'He does not treat us as our sins deserve.' As Christians, we will go to heaven, not because we deserve to, but because of God's mercy." He closed his Bible. "Let's pray and thank God for his gift of salvation," Dad suggested. *PJA*

HOW ABOUT YOU?

Do you think you "deserve" to go to heaven? Remember that God's Word says we deserve death. If you trust Christ as your Savior, God will show mercy and give you eternal life. Don't ask God for what you deserve. You don't really want it.

MEMORIZE:

"God saved you by his special favor when you believed. And you can't take credit for this; it is a gift from God." Ephesians 2:8

GOD OFFERS MERCY

CABBAGE PATCH WHAT?

(Read Isaiah 51:4-6)

Aneca, who had been exploring in her aunt's attic, stooped to go out through the little attic doorway. "Look what I found," she said, holding out a doll. "Was it yours?"

Aunt Twila's face broke into a big grin, causing her large dark eyes to smile. "Oh, you've found my Cabbage Patch doll—little Rosie May. I used to play with her all the time when I was your age." Aunt Twila held out her arms for the doll.

Aneca wrinkled her nose. "What's a Cabbage Patch doll?" she asked.

Aunt Twila settled the soft body of the doll into the crook of her arm like a real baby. Its round, brown face smiled up at her. "Haven't you seen them in the stores?" she asked. Aneca shook her head. "Well, they're dolls that were very popular some years ago," explained Aunt Twila. "They came with birth certificates, and we were crazy about them. One year they were almost impossible to find at Christmastime, so Mama bought Rosie May for my birthday in April." She looked at the doll thoughtfully. "You know," she said, "I remember a message our pastor gave the Christmas before I got Rosie May. He referred to the fact that, although these dolls would lose their popularity in a year or two, people were still willing to stand in line and pay big money to get them. He pointed out that material things can never bring lasting joy, but Jesus does."

Aunt Twila handed the doll back to Aneca. "Pastor Smith was right! Although you can still buy Cabbage Patch dolls in the stores today, people don't seem to get all excited about them anymore. But I still get excited when I think about Jesus!"

Aneca looked at the doll. "Rosie May is nice," she said, "but I can't believe you and your friends got that excited over a doll."

Aunt Twila's eyes twinkled as she quickly stepped into her bedroom and came back out with a hand behind her back. "Then you won't be interested in this," she said, holding out her hand.

"A Beanie Baby!" Aneca exclaimed. "I guess I'm a lot like you after all!"

Aunt Twila laughed. "Well, one thing's for sure: Dolls and toys may have changed, but Jesus is still the same. He's the one to really get excited about!" *AJS*

HOW ABOUT YOU?

Do you stand in long lines to get certain things? Are there some things your friends have that you'd give almost anything to have? Don't forget that the greatest gift of all is the salvation Jesus offers. It's absolutely free!

MEMORIZE:

"For the wages of sin is death, but the free gift of God is eternal life through Christ Jesus our Lord." Romans 6:23

JESUS' GIFT IS FREE

STORMY WEATHER

(Read Psalm 91:1-4, 9-10)

Josie put down her book and stared out the window at the trees and fence posts whizzing by. The drive home from Grandma and Grandpa's was a long one, and she wished they were home.

As the road climbed into the mountains, the sky grew dark. It began to rain, and tree branches and grass waved in the wind. Then the raindrops changed to snowflakes. It was toasty warm in the van, and Josie was glad she was not outside.

Soon the snow was making a dizzying design outside the window. The windshield wipers swung frantically back and forth to keep the windshield clear. "It's getting hard to see," said Dad, peering out the window. He cautiously slowed the car to a crawl. Soon he stopped behind a string of red car lights.

"Why are we stopping?" asked Josie's brother, Timothy.

"I don't know," said Dad. "Maybe there's an accident up ahead."

"I'm scared," whimpered Josie.

"Not me," said Timothy. "What's to be scared of? Just be glad you're in this nice warm van instead of out there in the cold and snow!"

Mom smiled. "That reminds me of some verses from Psalm 91," she said. "They point out that we have an even better refuge than this van." She quoted the verses. "Those who live in the shelter of the Most High will find rest in the shadow of the Almighty. . . . He will shield you with his wings. He will shelter you with his feathers."

Dad nodded. "That means that God promises to be with us and protect us just like a baby bird is protected under its mother's wings," he added as the line of lights began moving. Dad eased the car forward.

"I was thinking of those verses as we were leaving Grandpa and Grandma's house," added Mom. "They've been through a lot of difficult experiences, but the Lord has cared for them in each one. I wouldn't want to be in this storm outside the van, and neither would I want to be in life's storms out of God's shelter." *VEN*

HOW ABOUT YOU?

Is life sometimes "stormy" for you? Are you ever afraid? Remember that God is with you when you are sick or in danger. He has promised you his shelter when life seems scary.

MEMORIZE:

"When they call on me, I will answer; I will be with them in trouble. I will rescue them and honor them."
Psalm 91:15

TRUST IN GOD'S PROTECTION

A GOOD IDEA

(Read Titus 3:8-9, 14)

Amy wasn't too surprised when she got the chicken pox. Lots of children in her school had them. She was glad she wasn't very sick—she didn't even itch too badly—but she sure was bored! Mother had bought some cross-stitch work for her to do, but she soon tired of that, too.

"What can I do?" she called out several times during the day. Finally, Mother brought in a paper with a list of names on it. Still bored and unhappy, Amy looked briefly at the list. "What am I supposed to do with this?" she snapped.

"I thought you might like to go through this list of our church missionaries and pick out the names of some of the children," suggested Mother. "You could write them letters."

"But I don't even know them," Amy retorted.

Mother smiled. "All the more reason for writing and introducing yourself," she said.

Amy picked up the list again. She remembered some of the names from the missionary conference at church. She had met some of the girls, too. Maybe it wouldn't be such a bad idea to write to them. At least it would give her something to do.

So Amy wrote—telling who she was, where she lived and went to church, that she was a Christian, and that she had the chicken pox. Before she knew it, she had written three letters. It would be fun to get answers from these girls. Maybe they would tell her about themselves and what it was like to live on a mission field.

When Amy's mother brought in her lunch, Amy not only thanked the Lord for the food, but she prayed for the three girls and asked the Lord to bless them, too.

"Writing missionary kids was a good idea, Mom! I'm going to write to more of the kids on the list—it's really fun," she said. "And it will remind me to pray for them, too." *RIJ*

HOW ABOUT YOU?

Have you written to any missionary kids? A letter would probably make their day a little brighter. And then when they return to your town, it will be nice for them to feel like they already have at least one friend there. Remember to pray for them, too.

ACTION CURES BOREDOM

MEMORIZE:

"And God will generously provide all you need. Then you will always have everything you need and plenty left over to share with others."
2 Corinthians 9:8

DECEMBER
10

WRITTEN DOWN

(Read Proverbs 2:1-6)

When Jayla got home, her mother fixed some hot chocolate for them to drink while they talked. "How did the baby-sitting job go?" Mother asked.

"Good. I like the boys," Jayla answered. "Mrs. Randall said she was pleased with my work and asked me to baby-sit again next week. But this time it will be for a much longer time. Do you think I can do it?"

"I don't know why not," said Mother.

"Mrs. Randall makes baby-sitting easy," said Jayla. "She writes down the instructions and leaves a phone number so I can reach her if I have a problem."

"That's a good idea." Mother smiled. "And now you need to get to bed."

Jayla called Mrs. Randall the next morning and agreed to baby-sit Saturday evening. But in the afternoon, Jayla's friend Marsha invited her to a party on Saturday night. Jayla wanted to go to that, too. She asked her mother for advice.

"I can understand your problem," sympathized Mother. "The party sounds like fun. But just this morning, Mrs. Randall mentioned how glad she was that you were the one who would be baby-sitting Saturday. Seems you made quite an impression! I'll tell you what—why don't you look up 1 Corinthians 4:2."

Jayla ran to get her Bible and quickly found the place. "It says, 'Now, a person who is put in charge as a manager must be faithful,'" she read slowly.

"As Christ's servants," replied Mother, "we're to be faithful, not only to other people, but to God."

"And I wouldn't be a very good servant if I didn't keep my promise, would I?" Jayla asked with a sigh. Then she smiled. "I was just thinking about Mrs. Randall writing down instructions for me to follow," she said. "God did that, too, didn't he? He wrote them down in the Bible." *JLH*

HOW ABOUT YOU?

Do you ever wonder what is the right thing to do when problems come up? God has given instructions in the Bible to guide you. He doesn't always give specific instructions for each particular problem, but he has written down principles for you to follow. Read his Word, pray, and trust him to show you what to do. Then do it.

MEMORIZE:

"I will guide you along the best pathway for your life. I will advise you and watch over you." Psalm 32:8

FOLLOW GOD'S INSTRUCTIONS

BORROWED THINGS

(Read Exodus 22:10-15)

"Dana," called Leah to her older sister. "Will you let me wear your practice mesh shirt to the basketball game tonight?"

"No, Leah, you're not wearing it," Dana answered firmly.

"Aw, please," begged Leah. "All the other players are letting their younger sisters wear their shirts. Why can't I wear yours?"

"Because you'd ruin it. I can just see you snagging it on something and making a wreck of it. I said no, and that's final." Dana hurriedly left to catch her school bus.

"Oh, Mom," wailed Leah, "why can't Dana do like the other girls on the team? I'll be the only one without a practice shirt tonight."

"You know why Dana won't let you wear it, Leah," said Mother. "You have no one but yourself to blame."

"But I'd be careful with it," protested Leah. "Honest!"

"Dana has no reason to believe that," Mother pointed out. "She's responsible for her uniforms and doesn't want them to look ragged. She has loaned you things before, and you were careless with them."

"Well, when Dana borrowed my bike, she got it all muddy, and I didn't get mad," murmured Leah.

"But she hosed it off and shined it up before she put it away, didn't she?" asked Mother. Reluctantly, Leah nodded. "You need to learn to show respect for other people's things," continued Mother. "You really should be extra careful of anything you borrow."

Leah was silent. "Mom," she said at last, "I heard somebody say we're all living on 'borrowed time.' Does that mean we need to be extra careful with our time, too?"

"Wow!" said Mother. "I never really thought about that before. But I think that's right. Our time on earth really belongs to the Lord—he just allows us to live here for a while. As you suggested, we *should* be careful with it. We should use it in ways that bring glory to our God—and one of those ways is being careful with things we borrow!" *AGL*

HOW ABOUT YOU?

Are you careful of other people's property? Be sure to follow God's principles regarding borrowed things. Respecting what belongs to someone else shows respect for that person, too, and it's important to your testimony for the Lord. Take good care of the things you borrow. And make very good use of the time the Lord gives you!

TAKE GOOD CARE OF BORROWED THINGS

MEMORIZE:
"The wicked borrow and never repay, but the godly are generous givers."
Psalm 37:21

DECEMBER
12

THE RIGHT REPAIRMAN

(Read Psalm 37:3-7)

"Hey, Mom, look!" exclaimed Kylie. She held up a carton of milk. "Noah and I were going to have a glass of milk, but it's frozen!"

Mother frowned. "That's odd," she said. She bent down and peered inside the refrigerator. She checked some of the other items there. "Uh-oh!" she said. "We have a problem. Other things are frozen, too."

"Shall we move the refrigerator out from the wall?" asked Noah. "If I look at the back, maybe I can tell what's wrong."

Kylie laughed. "I doubt that," she said. "You don't know a thing about refrigerators and what makes them run."

Mother smiled. "I think we should call a repairman," she said. "Someone who knows exactly how to fix broken refrigerators."

When Kylie got home from school the following day, she opened the refrigerator and pulled out the carton of milk. She shook it. "The repairman must have been here," she said as she found a glass. "I'm glad we called an expert and didn't try to fix it ourselves." She sighed. "I wish I knew an expert I could call to fix a problem I'm having at school. I try so hard to get along with both Molly and Sara, but they don't like each other and they want me to take sides. Sometimes I don't know how to handle it."

"I know an expert who can help you," said Mother.

Kylie was surprised. "You do? Who?" she asked.

"God," replied Mother. "He's the best 'repairman' we could ever call on. Sometimes when we have problems we try to fix them ourselves, but calling on God to help us is always the best way."

"Does it mean that my problem will go away if I just pray about it?" asked Kylie.

Mother smiled. "No," she said, "though God does sometimes change the circumstances that are troubling us. Other times he shows us the way to handle them and gives us strength to do so. Sometimes he uses teachers or parents or a Bible verse to show us what to do. Sometimes he apparently wants us to use good common sense and to simply do our best and trust him to work things out."
WEB

HOW ABOUT YOU?

When you have a problem, do you remember to call on God, the greatest "repairman"? Trust him to show you how to take care of your problems.

MEMORIZE:

"Trust in the Lord with all your heart; do not depend on your own understanding." Proverbs 3:5

LET GOD HELP WITH PROBLEMS

SNOWBALLING

(Read Romans 12:18-21)

"Allison! Wait!" called Heather. "I want to tell you . . ." Heather could hardly believe it when her friend looked her way, frowned, and then got in the car. "She just left," Heather told her mother as they shopped. "She must be mad at me."

The next morning Heather was late for Sunday school. Allison always saved her a seat, but this morning there was a stranger sitting next to Allison. *She must really be mad at me,* Heather thought.

Heather and Allison usually walked to school together, but the next day Heather had to go early to take a makeup test. She forgot to call Allison.

So it went all week. The girls, usually such good friends, hardly saw each other. Each thought the other was angry. Both had a miserable week.

Sunday morning, Mr. Stone, their Sunday school teacher, surprised his class by showing them a huge snowball just outside their window. "How many of you think you could lift that snowball?" he asked. A few of the boys raised their hands.

"Pooh!" scoffed Heather. "I bet you can't. I bet even Mr. Stone can't lift it."

"Heavy? Everyone knows snowflakes aren't heavy," Mr. Stone teased.

"Packed like that they are," insisted Heather.

Mr. Stone nodded. "You're absolutely right," he said. "Snowballs remind me of misunderstandings. They start little, but they often grow and grow. They can destroy friendships." Heather looked across the room at Allison as Mr. Stone continued. "Have you had a misunderstanding with someone? If so, clear it up before it gets any bigger."

After class the girls met in the hall. "Why are you mad at me?" each asked at once.

"Why didn't you speak to me last Saturday? And why didn't you save me a seat last Sunday?" asked Heather.

"I didn't have my contacts in last Saturday because I lost one," explained Allison. "I couldn't see anybody. On Sunday Mr. Stone told a visitor to sit by me. Why didn't you meet me Monday morning?"

"I had a makeup test and had to go early," said Heather. She giggled. "Oh, Allison, we were so silly. We've had a terrible week because of a little misunderstanding!" *BJW*

HOW ABOUT YOU?

Has someone been acting differently toward you, and you don't know why? Why not ask? It could be a tiny misunderstanding. Stop it before it "snowballs."

**CLEAR UP
MISUNDERSTANDINGS**

MEMORIZE:
"A wise person is hungry for truth." Proverbs 15:14

DECEMBER
14

BLESSED AND A BLESSING

(Read Psalm 92:12-15)

As Janet walked into the nursing home with her mother, she wrinkled her nose. "What's that awful smell?" she asked. She had not really wanted to come here in the first place, and the smell of medication and illness didn't do anything to change her mind!

"These people are old and sick," Mother replied, "and a sickroom often has an unpleasant odor. But I think you'll be glad you came after you've visited Grandma Harper and some of the other people here. They're always such a blessing to me."

Janet could not imagine getting a blessing from being around these people. But she had promised to give a report next Sunday on her nursing home visit, so she just sighed and followed her mother down the hall.

They had hardly entered the room when Grandma Harper called out cheerily, "Oh, you brought your precious daughter!" Then she turned to Janet. "Honey, you'll have to forgive that outburst, but around here we seldom see such young and beautiful girls. Most of us have so many wrinkles we've forgotten what it was like to be young." She laughed pleasantly as she spoke, and Janet began to smile, too. Before long, she was telling the elderly woman about her school activities, her Sunday school class, and even about her birthday party. By this time there were several other people in the room, and at their urging, she sang a song for them. When they asked for another, Mother suggested that she sing an old, familiar one. Janet did, and soon several quavering, old voices joined the clear, young one in some well-loved hymns.

When they were ready to leave, Janet promised to bring other members of her class with her the next time. "You should hear them sing," she said, smiling.

Back in the car, Janet turned to her mother. "You were right, Mom," she said, "I'm the one who got the blessing." *RIJ*

HOW ABOUT YOU?

Are there some elderly people in your hometown who would enjoy a visit from a group of young people? Many of the sick and elderly are not able to go to church. Will you visit them and share some of God's blessings with them?

MEMORIZE:
"It is more blessed to give than to receive." Acts 20:35

VISIT THE ELDERLY

EXPERIENCED COMFORTER

(Read 2 Corinthians 1:3-7)

"Mama!" called Janice loudly. "Kendall isn't helping me. Why should I have to pick up all the toys by myself?"

Mother found Kendall sitting on the floor, breathing hard. "Why, Janice—look at your brother! The dust must have triggered his asthma," Mother said with concern. "Go lie down, Ken, and I'll give you your medicine."

"Oh, Mom," complained Janice, "Kendall always gets out of everything just because he has asthma. It's not fair!"

Mother gave Janice a hug. "I know it seems that way at times," she said, "but it isn't his fault. I'm sure he would get rid of his asthma in a minute if he could."

"I'm not so sure," grumbled Janice.

A few days later, Janice developed a bad cough. Because she also had a high fever, Mother took her to the doctor. "It's bronchitis," he said. "I'll prescribe some medicine, and you'll need lots of rest for the next week or two, Janice."

Janice stayed inside for four days. She didn't like the medicine, and she missed playing with her friends. Worst of all, it was hard for her to breathe. She had to sleep propped up on pillows, the way Kendall slept sometimes. *Imagine feeling like this as often as he does,* Janice thought. Right then, she bowed her head and prayed—for herself, and especially for Kendall.

Finally, Janice was able to go back to school. Right after school, she hurried home and entered the kitchen with a big smile. "It's so neat to be feeling good again," she told Mother.

"I imagine you're eager to go out and play with your friends, too," said Mother, grinning.

But Janice hung up her coat instead. "I think I'll go play a game with Kendall," she said. "I noticed that he acts tired lately, so I thought I'd try to cheer him up awhile. I now know what it feels like to be sick." *SLK*

HOW ABOUT YOU?

Are you as sympathetic with others as you should be? Do you sincerely pray for them? Think of times you've been sick or have had problems. Try to remember little things people did for you which you liked. Give others the same kind of help you experienced.

MEMORIZE:

"He comforts us in all our troubles so that we can comfort others. When others are troubled, we will be able to give them the same comfort God has given us." 2 Corinthians 1:4

BE A COMFORTER

DECEMBER
16

MAKE UP YOUR MIND

(Read Acts 24:24-27; 26:1, 27-29)

On the way to church, Anita hummed along as the voices of a choir came over the car radio. "I have decided to follow Jesus. . . ." She considered the words. *I guess I don't really follow Jesus,* she thought. *Actually, I'm not sure I'm saved.*

Her sister, Joni, interrupted her thoughts. "Look at the big sale sign in the store window!" All Anita could think about then was the clothes she wanted to buy.

In Sunday school class, Mrs. Tomkins spoke about Paul's experiences with Felix and King Agrippa. "Both men heard the gospel," she said, "but neither made up his mind to accept Christ. I hope none of you put off making such an important decision." Anita decided to talk to Mrs. Tomkins after class and ask her about being saved. But when class was dismissed, she spotted Becky at the door. She hurried over and began to chat.

After dinner that day, Anita put the few leftovers in her dog's dish. She opened the back door and called, "Come, Spunky. I've got something good for you." Spunky looked up. He romped toward the door. Then he hesitated as a bird caught his attention. "Forget the bird. Come on," Anita yelled. Spunky came closer. He put his paw on the threshold. Another dog barked. Spunky was off running around the yard. Anita was frustrated. "Spunky, come on! Aren't you hungry? What are you waiting for?" Spunky sniffed the grass. "Make up your mind," Anita shouted. "Either come in or stay out!"

Suddenly it dawned on Anita that she had been acting just like Spunky. She allowed all sorts of things to take her attention away from the most important decision she had to make. And that was what she would do with Jesus. *JLH*

HOW ABOUT YOU?

Have you made up your mind to accept Jesus as your Savior? If not, talk to a trusted friend or adult to find out more.

MEMORIZE:

"Look! Here I stand at the door and knock. If you hear me calling and open the door, I will come in, and we will share a meal as friends."
Revelation 3:20

ACCEPT JESUS TODAY

GOOD NEWS! (PART 1)

(Read Matthew 28:18-20)

"If I watch anything as violent as that, Daddy, you make me turn the TV off," observed Jill as her father was watching the evening news.

"You're right," he agreed, and he snapped off the set. "I do like to keep up on what's happening in the world, but frankly, I think it would be better if they wouldn't show some of those pictures. Maybe I should rely more heavily on my newspaper."

"Did I hear someone say they want a newspaper?" asked Andrea as she came in the back door. "Well, now, I just happen to have one for you. Here you are, sir." She handed her dad a paper. "I just finished my paper route," she said. "Seems like everybody I saw remarked about the number of articles on crime these days. I felt like the bearer of bad news!"

"Well, *I'm* the bearer of good news—dinner's ready!" announced Mother as she joined them. Laughing, they trooped to the table and together thanked God for the food they were about to eat. "Ummmm, this lasagna sure is good news," commented Andrea as she took a large portion. "Too bad I can't tell my customers about this."

Dad looked at her thoughtfully. "There is some good news that all of us should be telling," he said. "Who knows what it is?"

Jill and Andrea looked puzzled. "I'll give you a clue," said Dad. "It's found in the Bible."

"Oh, I know—it's the good news of Jesus!" exclaimed Jill. "We're supposed to tell everybody about him."

"Right," agreed Dad. "We are to tell others the gospel message. 'Gospel' means 'good news.' Perhaps there's so much bad news in the world today because not enough people know the good news of the gospel. Let's all make an effort to tell it to at least one person this month." *HWM*

HOW ABOUT YOU?

When was the last time you shared the good news of Jesus with someone? If you are a Christian, why not tell others that Jesus died on the cross for our sins, that he was buried, and that he rose again? Invite your friends to trust in Jesus.

MEMORIZE:

"And then he told them, 'Go into all the world and preach the Good News to everyone, everywhere.'"

Mark 16:15

SHARE THE GOSPEL

DECEMBER
18

GOOD NEWS! (PART 2)
(Read 1 Corinthians 15:1-4)

As Andrea delivered her papers, she thought of what Dad had said about telling the good news of Jesus to someone. Andrea really meant to do it. Just as she was placing a paper on Mr. Watkins's steps, the door opened, and there was Mr. Watkins himself.

"Saw you coming," he greeted Andrea. "I suppose you're bringing me gloomy news again tonight." He accepted the paper from Andrea's hand.

"Evening, sir," said Andrea, and she began to move away.

But Mr. Watkins was still talking. "Sure would be nice if you'd bring me some good news for a change."

Andrea gulped. Here was her chance to tell the good news! If only Mr. Watkins would go in . . . but he seemed to be waiting for a reply. "Why, uh, actually, I do know some good news . . . ," Andrea began fearfully.

"You do? What's that?" questioned Mr. Watkins.

Andrea didn't know how to proceed. "Well, it's found in the Bible. Jesus died for you and me."

Mr. Watkins looked surprised. "He did, eh? Well, that doesn't sound like such good news to me—another death."

"He paid the price for your sins. And . . . and he didn't stay dead. He rose again, and lots of people saw him. If you'll believe in him, you'll go to live with him in heaven someday," said Andrea.

To Andrea's surprise, Mr. Watkins was listening carefully. "Well, now, young lady, I suppose I've not always done the right thing, but I'm not so bad," he argued. "I don't think it was necessary for anybody to die for me."

"You have to believe the gospel if you want to go to heaven," Andrea told him firmly.

Mr. Watkins smiled. "You're a very persuasive young lady," he said. "I learned about Jesus when I was a boy, but I never did anything about it. I'm going to think about this a lot more. Thanks for reminding me." Andrea hurried home with a smile on her face. *HWM*

HOW ABOUT YOU?
Perhaps you've heard the Good News many times, but have you ever done anything about it? Have you accepted what Jesus did for you? If you have questions, talk to a trusted friend or adult.

MEMORIZE:
"'At last the time has come!' he announced. 'The Kingdom of God is near! Turn from your sins and believe this Good News!'" Mark 1:15

BELIEVE THE GOSPEL

THE SAMPLE

(Read 1 Thessalonians 1:5-9)

"Can I go to the store with you, Mom?" asked Laura. "You need me along to make sure you get the right cereal."

Mother laughed. "Come along," she agreed.

Shortly after arriving at the store, they met Chandra, a classmate of Laura's. "Hey, Laura," called Chandra, "my mom says I can go to church with you tomorrow."

"Oh, great!" exclaimed Laura. "It starts at eight o'clock."

"I'll be there. Want to know why?" Without waiting for an answer, Chandra rushed on, her words tumbling over each other. "I know I've teased you about being a goody two-shoes because you go to church. But these last few weeks—well, what can I say? You helped me with my homework when I was sick, and you stood up for me when the other girls gave me a rough time about my new hair-cut the other day. Anyway, if it's Jesus who makes you be this way, I want to know more about him." Chandra looked embarrassed after her long speech. "Gotta go," she mumbled, heading for the door.

As Laura and her mother turned down another aisle, they saw a lady handing out samples of ice cream bars. "Yummy!" exclaimed Laura, taking a bite of the sample. "Let's get some of these, Mom."

"It is good," agreed Mother.

"How can the store afford to give away so much ice cream?" asked Laura as they approached the checkout counter. "Look at all the people getting samples now."

Mother smiled. "The samples cause people to want the product, and the store will sell lots of ice cream bars," she explained. "You know, Laura, this reminds me of you."

"Me?" asked Laura. "What do you mean?"

"You've been a 'sample' Christian," said Mother. "Do you remember what Chandra said when we met her? Your life gave Chandra a taste of what it means to be a Christian, and now she's wanting more. You've been a good example." *GW*

HOW ABOUT YOU?

Do you know that you, too, can be a "sample" for Jesus? People around you need to know what a real Christian is like. They need to see Jesus in you. Your words and actions should cause them to want to know him. Be the kind of person that Jesus wants you to be.

LET JESUS BE SEEN IN YOU

MEMORIZE:

"In everything set them an example by doing what is good." Titus 2:7, NIV

DECEMBER
20

SNOWFLAKES AND PEOPLE

(Read Acts 10:25-28)

Jessica and her friend Jason shouted with glee as they stood back to admire the snowman they were making. As they began to fashion some arms, a classmate, Aiko, came along. She grinned and stopped to help. "Go away," said Jessica with a scowl. "This is our snowman." Aiko's grin faded, and she slowly left. "She'd have wanted to give him slanting eyes," Jessica said loudly enough for Aiko to hear. At the window Jessica's mother frowned.

A little later Jefferson, another classmate, stopped to help, and he, too, was soon sent on his way. "You'd probably want to cover his face with mud and make him all black," Jessica laughed.

"Oh, who wants to help you anyway, Whitey?" Jefferson retorted.

Jessica angrily stomped her foot. "You stop calling us names!" she shouted. Still watching, Mother went to call Jessica in.

"Oh, Mother! Did you see our snowman?" Jessica asked as she came in the door. "We call him Mr. Snowflake!"

Mother smiled. "Really?" she asked. "Did you know there was once a man who was called 'The Snowflake Man'? Why don't you look him up in the encyclopedia? His name was Wilson Bentley."

Interested, Jessica hurried to see what she could find. Soon she returned to report to her mother. "I found him," she said. "He lived in Vermont, and his hobby was studying snowflakes. He found that each one was a perfect crystal and no two were ever alike. But they were all beautiful!"

Mother nodded. "Kind of like people," she said. "They have different kinds of hair and eyes and skin. But they're all made by the great artist—God—and in his sight, each one is beautiful."

Jessica was quiet for a time. "Mother," she said finally, "may I have some kids over after school tomorrow? I need to apologize to Aiko and Jefferson, and I'd like to ask them to come help me build another snowman." *HWM*

HOW ABOUT YOU?

Do you think you're better than people who look different from you, are poorer, or don't seem as smart? God made everyone according to his own special plan. And all people are beautiful to him.

MEMORIZE:

"From one man he created all the nations throughout the whole earth." Acts 17:26

GOD MADE EVERYONE BEAUTIFUL

IS THAT ME?

(Read 1 Corinthians 3:1-5)

"I didn't really understand the pastor's message," said Kayla one Sunday afternoon. "He said the people in the church at Corinth were babies. Weren't there any adults?"

"I have something that might help you understand," Mom said, smiling. "I came across a cassette tape this week that you might like to hear." She put a tape in the player and turned it on.

Kayla heard some giggles, and then Dad started talking. "Welcome to the Browns. It's September 16, and Kayla is three years old. She's going to tell us what she did in church today."

Kayla heard more giggles and then, "I builded with blocks, and . . . and we sanged, and I sanged loud, and my teacher told a story."

"Is that really me talking?" Kayla laughed as the babyish voice went on to recite the ABCs. "I sound so little!"

"You *were* little, Kayla," agreed Mother.

"That's a funny tape," Kayla said when it had stopped. "But what does that have to do with the pastor's message?"

"Well, Kayla," said Mom, "it would be silly if you talked that way now, wouldn't it?"

"Sure." She grinned. "I've grown up since then."

"That's right," Mom agreed. "And now you talk and act differently from when you were little. You see, Kayla, many of the people in Corinth had been Christians for a long time, but they still were acting like babies, spiritually. They had accepted Christ as Savior, but instead of studying the Scripture, they were arguing over whether Paul or Apollos was the better preacher. You see, just as it's important to grow physically, it is also important to grow spiritually." *LMW*

HOW ABOUT YOU?

Have you been a Christian very long? Have you been growing spiritually or do you still act like a baby in the Lord? You should know more about the Bible this year than you did last year. Spiritual growth comes by talking to God, reading your Bible, and serving the Lord. Make sure these things are part of your life.

MEMORIZE:

"You must crave pure spiritual milk so that you can grow into the fullness of your salvation." 1 Peter 2:2

GROW SPIRITUALLY

WELL-PROTECTED

(Read Psalm 91:4, 9-10)

"Ooooh! I don't feel good," moaned Shelly as she came to the breakfast table. "Can't I just stay home today?" She sat down and clutched her stomach.

"I don't believe you have a fever," said Mother as she felt her daughter's forehead, "but if you really don't feel well, I suppose you could stay home."

Later that morning Mother was making cookies, and Shelly joined her in the kitchen. "Oh, let me help!" she exclaimed. Putting on one of Mother's aprons, Shelly squealed as one of the eggs broke and slid down her arm and onto the floor. "Oh, I never will learn to do this right! It's a good thing I have a big apron on."

"It certainly is!" agreed Mother, laughing as she helped clean up the mess. Looking at Shelly thoughtfully, she said, "The stomachache seems to have disappeared." As Shelly nodded, Mother continued, "Do you think you really were sick, honey, or were you just nervous about going to a new school?"

"Oh, Mother," burst out Shelly, "I wish we had never moved! I feel so strange in this school, and I don't have any friends. I don't know *anybody*."

"It will get better," Mother assured her. "You know, it's a good thing you had the protection of that apron as we made cookies. But are you aware that you also have protection as you go to school?" Shelly looked surprised as Mother continued. "You're a Christian, a child of God, and he is your protection. Verse 4 of Psalm 40 says, 'Oh, the joys of those who trust the Lord.' God will take care of you, even in a new school and among many new faces. And while he doesn't promise to protect us from all hurtful or hard things, he does promise to go through those things with us." *HWM*

HOW ABOUT YOU?

What are you afraid of? A new school? A difficult class? A school bully? The dark? If you're a Christian, God is with you in whatever situation you face. Trust him.

MEMORIZE:

"The Lord is my light and my salvation—so why should I be afraid? The Lord protects me from danger— so why should I tremble?" Psalm 27:1

GOD WILL TAKE CARE OF YOU

THE STRANGE BIRD

(Read Daniel 1:1-6, 8)

"Hi, Mom," said Rita as she hung up her jacket. "We had fun at Girl Scouts today. We're working on our nature badge. Did you know that a mockingbird has been known to change its tune 87 times in seven minutes? What a strange bird!"

"That's amazing," agreed Mother. "Amazing and rather wonderful."

The next day Mother overheard two conversations while waiting for Rita after her basketball game. Jamie, one of Rita's teammates, approached her. "Hey, Rita, I stole a pack of my dad's cigarettes," said Jamie. "Wanna meet me at that old empty warehouse near my place for an after-dinner smoke?"

"Sounds like fun," said Rita, "but I can't. I have to go someplace." Jamie ran off to find someone else to join her.

As Rita turned, she bumped into Tina, a girl from her Sunday school class. "Hey, Rita," said Tina, "you wanna hear something? Jamie stole a pack of her dad's cigarettes."

"I know," interrupted Rita. "And they call that fun?"

On the way home in the car, Mother asked, "How is my 'strange bird' doing today?"

"What do you mean?" Rita looked confused.

"You know—my mockingbird," said Mother. Then she explained. "I'm really pleased that you didn't agree to meet Jamie tonight, but I did hear a 'little bird' I know change her tune pretty quickly this afternoon. 'Sounds like fun,' she said one minute, and the next minute she said, 'They call that fun?' "

"Oh, that," replied Rita sheepishly as she slid down in her seat a little. She knew she should have told Jamie right out why she wouldn't come. She sat up straighter as they neared home. "I'm gonna tell Jamie the real reason I wouldn't join her," she said firmly. "I'll call her as soon as we get home." And she did. *PR*

HOW ABOUT YOU?

Do you change your tune like a mockingbird, depending on what other "birds" you are near? It's difficult to take a stand for what you really believe to be right when your friends don't agree, but with God's help, it is possible. Daniel did it. You can, too!

**ALWAYS STAND
FOR RIGHT**

MEMORIZE:
"But Daniel made up his mind not to defile himself by eating the food and wine given to them by the king."
Daniel 1:8

DECEMBER
24

THE REAL GIFT

(Read Matthew 1:18-23)

After supper on Christmas Eve, little Anna climbed into Mother's lap as Grandpa reached for the family Bible and began to read the familiar Scriptures about the birth of Jesus. Marsha's mind wandered as Grandpa read of the angels, shepherds, and wise men. This would be little Anna's first Christmas, and Marsha could hardly wait to see her excitement as she opened her presents. She just knew Anna would love the little baby doll she and Ted had bought for her!

When Grandpa finished reading, Dad prayed, thanking God for Jesus who came to give them eternal life. Then Marsha and Ted passed out the presents. "Open them, Anna," said Ted.

Anna grinned, but she didn't seem to know what to do. She just looked at the bright wrappings. "Here, open them like this," said Marsha as she pulled off a bow. Anna grabbed the ribbon and put it in her mouth.

"At this rate it will take her all night," Ted muttered.

"Help her a bit," suggested Grandma, and both Ted and Marsha began removing the gift wrappings.

Marsha put the baby doll in Anna's lap. "Baby," said Marsha. "Pretty baby."

Anna looked at the doll. Then she flung it aside and reached for the wrapping paper. She laughed as she crinkled the paper in her fingers and draped the ribbons over her head.

"What a disappointment!" Ted exclaimed. "We give her a really neat gift, and she ignores it! She'd rather play with the wrappings than the doll!"

"Right now, I think the bright trimmings have distracted her," said Mother.

"And most Christians at Christmastime," commented Grandpa.

"What do you mean?" Ted asked in surprise.

"God sent Jesus to save us from our sins," Grandpa explained. "He's the real gift of Christmas, but too many people ignore him. They get distracted by the trimmings of Christmas—the presents, lights, gifts, trees, and carols—and they ignore Jesus completely." *JLH*

HOW ABOUT YOU?

What does Christmas mean to you? Do you worship Christ at Christmas time, or do you get caught up in the "trimmings"? Christ is the perfect gift. He gives meaning to life.

MEMORIZE:

"Thank God for his Son—a gift too wonderful for words!"
2 Corinthians 9:15

HONOR THE REAL GIFT

THE CHRISTMAS WATCH (PART 1)

(Read John 3:1-7)

Ten-year-old Gloria could hardly wait for Christmas morning! She had to admit that she usually didn't pay too much attention while Dad read the beautiful story of Jesus' birth, because she was thinking about what came next—the opening of all the Christmas presents!

At last it was time, and the family gathered around the Christmas tree. Gloria's little brother, Roberto, was elected to pass out the gifts. Finally, he handed her the one she had been waiting for—a great big box from Mom and Dad. Gloria soon found that her parents had decided to fool her, because inside the big box was one just a bit smaller, and inside that one was one smaller yet! Her eyes got bigger and bigger as she finally unwrapped the last box and found it was—a watch! Not a make-believe one either, but a real watch! She let out a loud squeal of delight and gave Mom and Dad each a big hug and kiss.

"Do you like it, honey?" asked Dad.

"Like it? Why, I just love it!" exclaimed Gloria.

"That watch reminds me of you, Gloria," said Dad. "Tell me . . . what do you see when you look at your watch?"

"The hands and the face," said Gloria, "and the pretty gold case and band."

"Right." Dad nodded. "But there's an important part of your watch that you can't see, too. It's what's on the inside—it's the part that makes your watch run."

"But how does the watch remind you of me?" Gloria asked, puzzled.

"There's a part of you that can't be seen either," explained Dad. "That part is your soul! Your body is like the case of your watch. It may live 60, 70, or even 80 years. But your soul will live forever! If you've trusted Jesus as your Savior, your soul will live with him in heaven. That's why it's so important that you take time to think about your soul as well as about your body!" *CVm*

HOW ABOUT YOU?

Did you know that your soul is the most important part of you? Nobody can see your soul, but it will live forever! Have you trusted Christ as your Savior? If not, you should ask him to come in right now!

LIVE FOREVER IN HEAVEN

MEMORIZE:
"I assure you, unless you are born again, you can never see the Kingdom of God." John 3:3

DECEMBER
26

THE CHRISTMAS WATCH (PART 2)

(Read Psalm 119:97-104)

"Gloria!" Roberto called. "Hey, Gloria!"

"What is it, Roberto?" Gloria asked rather impatiently.

"You left your watch on the edge of the bathtub," Roberto told her. "I didn't see it, and I knocked it into the water. If I get a watch for Christmas when I'm ten years old, I'll sure take better care of it than that!"

"Cool it, little brother," retorted Gloria. "I just forgot. You're not perfect, either." She took her watch from Roberto's hand and put it on. She looked to see what time it was. "Oh, no!" she moaned. "It's not running!"

Just then Dad came out of the family room. "Let me take a look at it," he said. After checking it, Dad shook his head. "Get me a hair dryer," he said. "I'll take the back off, and we'll see if we can dry it out." He worked on the watch for a while, and to Gloria's great relief, it did start running again. "You know, Gloria, your watch is reminding me of you again," Dad said as he handed it to her.

Gloria laughed. "Here we go," she said. "What do you mean this time?"

"Well, if we hadn't gotten this watch dried out, it probably would have gotten rusty inside," Dad said. "That could happen to you, too."

Gloria grinned. "I could get rusty inside?" she asked. "How would that happen? And how would you dry me out?"

Dad smiled. "Well, I guess my object lesson breaks down when it comes to the drying out part," he admitted. "But, yep! In a way, you could get rusty inside. You see, since you've accepted Christ as your Savior, you need to guard against getting rusty spiritually."

"And I bet I do that by going to church?" asked Gloria.

Dad nodded. "Right," he said, "and it's also important to have a time each day when you read your Bible and pray. Church is important, but daily devotions are, too. After this, take care that the inside of your watch doesn't get rusty, and that the inside of you—your soul—doesn't get rusty, either!" *CVm*

HOW ABOUT YOU?

Do you let several days go by without reading God's Word? How about talking to the Lord in prayer? Don't get "rusty" spiritually. Spend time with God on a regular basis.

MEMORIZE:

"Oh, how I love your law! I think about it all day long." Psalm 119:97

READ THE BIBLE AND PRAY

THE CHRISTMAS WATCH (PART 3)

(Read Psalm 51:1-4, 10-12)

Gloria wore her watch every day. It helped her get places on time, and since it had a calendar built in, it even told her what day it was. But after several months, it stopped running. "Dad, something must really be wrong with my watch this time," she said with a worried frown on her face.

"Well, then I guess we'd better take it back to the store where I bought it," said Dad. "Maybe the jeweler can solve the problem. Let's take a walk up there."

After taking the watch apart, the jeweler nodded. "There's quite a lot of dirt in here," he said.

"Mom had me digging in the garden this week," said Gloria. "She told me I probably should take my watch off, but I didn't want to be bothered."

"Well, a good cleaning should take care of it," said the jeweler. "I'll have it ready for you in about a week." He gave Gloria a claim ticket, and she and Dad headed for home.

"Hey, Dad!" Gloria exclaimed with a twinkle in her eye. "You remember those lessons you taught me about myself last Christmas when you gave me my watch? Like how it has an important part that can't be seen, just like my soul can't be seen? And how it's important that I don't get rusty spiritually, just like it's important to keep my watch dry so it doesn't get rusty?"

"Sure, I remember," said Dad. "Have you thought of a new lesson by yourself?"

"Yep," said Gloria with a smile. "I was just thinking that when my watch got dirty, it was a good thing to take it back to the jeweler so it could be cleaned. Well, when I do something that's wrong, it's important that I go to the Lord and ask him to clean me up."

Dad smiled. "Mighty good thinking," he said. *CVm*

HOW ABOUT YOU?

Do you sometimes say things you shouldn't say? Look at things you shouldn't see? Do things you shouldn't do? You need to go to the Lord, confess your sin, and ask him to clean you up.

**KEEP YOUR
HEART CLEAN**

MEMORIZE:
"Wash me clean from my guilt. Purify me from my sin." Psalm 51:2

DECEMBER
28

THE RIGHT TIME

(Read Genesis 2:18-25)

Note to parents: The following story may not be appropriate for very young children.

Mary looked up as her mother came into the room. "How about going shopping with me?" asked Mother.

Mary shook her head. "I'll stay home and wrap gifts."

After Mother was gone, Mary began her task. When she looked in Kathleen's room to see if the box of ribbons was there, she saw a package with her name on it. "Ohhh!" she breathed. "Maybe if I'm careful, I can take a peek, and no one will know the difference." Carefully she untied the ribbon and picked at the tape. A small box slid out, and inside it she found a beautiful necklace. Mary swiftly rewrapped the gift. She felt guilty, but she was right about one thing—nobody else knew the difference.

Soon it was Christmas. When Mary opened her package from Kathleen, she tried to act surprised, but it was hard. Having opened it ahead of time spoiled the fun of getting it now. She felt guilty, and she knew Kathleen expected her to be more excited than she was sounding. She was relieved when the phone rang, and she scurried to answer it. But when Mary returned, she was upset. "What's wrong?" asked Mother.

"Patty called," answered Mary. "She says Jane won't be returning to school after Christmas. She's pregnant! She's going to live with an aunt until the baby is born and adopted."

"How sad," Mother said. "You know, Mary, sexual intimacy between a man and woman is a wonderful gift, but God knew what he was doing when he planned it for marriage. Taking that gift ahead of time has resulted in much unhappiness."

Mary thought about her Christmas gift from Kathleen. It had been wrong to open it ahead of time, and she knew she had to confess what she had done. She thought about Jane, who hadn't waited until marriage to enjoy the gift of intimacy. Mary didn't want to make that mistake. She wanted to follow God's plan. *JLH*

HOW ABOUT YOU?

Television programs, books, and even friends often imply that if you feel like having an intimate sexual relationship, you should do so. That's wrong! God's Word says to wait until marriage or you'll spoil the beauty of it. Wait!

MEMORIZE:

"Run from anything that stimulates youthful lust. Follow anything that makes you want to do right. Pursue faith and love and peace, and enjoy the companionship of those who call on the Lord with pure hearts." 2 Timothy 2:22

KEEP YOUR BODY PURE

JUST A BABY

(Read Hebrews 6:9-12)

Tami's little brother spied a glittering piece of broken glass on the ground. He picked it up and was about to put it into his mouth when Tami stopped him. Immediately young Troy let out a loud scream that brought Mother out to see what was happening. "I just took this piece of glass away from him," Tami explained.

Mother picked up the little boy. "I'm glad you were watching him," she said to Tami. "You probably saved him from being cut very badly."

Tami shrugged her shoulders. "Yeah, but Troy sure didn't appreciate it. He thought I was being mean."

"That's because he's just a baby," Mother explained, "and babies don't always understand that you're helping them."

Later Tami talked to her mother about a friend. "Karry is mad at me," she said. "At first she was mad because her mom won't let her watch some of the TV shows they used to watch before they were Christians. I agreed with her mom, so now Karry's mad at me, too."

"That's too bad," sympathized Mother. "Try to be patient with her. She's only a baby Christian, you know, and sometimes baby Christians react exactly as Troy did when you took the broken glass away. When someone tries to help them and protect them from dangerous things, they resist and act up because they are not being allowed to live as they want. They often argue and resent guidance from older Christians."

When Tami thought about it, she knew she had been like that, too. She had often thought she knew how to live the Christian life without interference from others, especially from her parents. She hoped she didn't still act that way! She determined in her heart to be more patient with Karry and not to resist or resent the help that older Christians offered to her. *RIJ*

HOW ABOUT YOU?

Do you accept the advice and help that is offered to you by your parents? Your pastor? Your Sunday school teacher? They are more experienced in life and know more than you do about the dangers and tricks of Satan. Be open to their guidance.

**ACCEPT
CHRISTIAN ADVICE**

MEMORIZE:
"Follow the example of those who are going to inherit God's promises because of their faith and patience."
Hebrews 6:12

DECEMBER
30

A GOOD HABIT

(Read 1 Timothy 2:1-8)

Donna really meant it when she promised to pray every day during the next year for a missionary. She had made the same pledge during last year's missionary conference, but she had failed miserably in keeping that promise. She started out well, but before long she forgot all about it. Now she had made the promise again. "I don't know what to do to remind myself," Donna confided to her mother.

Mother was thoughtfully quiet. Finally she spoke. "If you pray for your missionary before you do anything else each day, you might remember better," she suggested.

"Last year I did pray the first thing in the morning," Donna said, "at least to begin with. But sometimes there just didn't seem to be enough time before school."

"Did you give thanks before you ate?" her mother asked.

"Of course," said Donna, a little surprised that her mother would ask that. At their home, prayer was as much a part of the meal as the food itself.

"Why do you suppose you had time to thank God for your food but didn't have time to pray for your missionary?" Mother asked.

"Why, I don't know." Donna hadn't thought about that before. "We just always do it, that's all."

"Exactly!" Mother nodded. "It's a habit, isn't it? I trust it's not just a habit, but that you sincerely thank God for the food he has provided. Still, it is a habit—and a very good one, too. I think you need to work harder at establishing a habit of spending time with God daily. Since you've tried doing this in the morning, and it didn't seem to work, maybe you should try it before bedtime or after school. If you miss a day or two, don't quit. Start over."

"OK," agreed Donna. She opened a drawer and took out a blank piece of paper. "Maybe it will help if I make a chart and check off the times I remember. You can ask me about it once or twice a week, too—OK, Mom? I intend to keep my promise this time!" *RIJ*

HOW ABOUT YOU?

Do you have a regular time to read the Bible and pray? This should be a natural, everyday event. If you find yourself forgetting or getting out of the habit, ask someone to check up on you. Check up on yourself, too, by keeping a chart. Daily prayer time should be as much a habit as giving thanks at mealtime.

MEMORIZE:

"Lord, teach us to pray." Luke 11:1

PRAY REGULARLY

FOLLOW THE LEADER

(Read 1 Timothy 4:11-16)

Stephanie often was impatient with her little sister, Karen, because she followed Stephanie wherever she went. Karen loved to copy whatever Stephanie did.

One day Mother sent Stephanie to Grandpa Wells with some freshly baked cinnamon rolls. Grandpa was happy to see her. As they sat down at the kitchen table to visit and enjoy one of the rolls, there was a knock at the door. "More company?" wondered Grandpa.

"Karen!" exclaimed Stephanie as the door opened. "Mother is going to be mad at you!" Stephanie turned to Grandpa. "Karen thinks she has to go everywhere I go and do everything I do," she complained.

"I reckon that's the highest compliment she could pay you," Grandpa told Stephanie. "Karen looks up to you. You are her example. Where you lead, she will follow."

Stephanie sighed. "She looks up to me all right. And she follows me like a shadow. Every time I sigh, she sighs and says, 'Me, too.'"

"Then you had better be careful how you sigh," laughed Grandpa.

"Me, too," announced Karen.

Stephanie laughed. "Oh, come on, little 'Me, Too.' We've got to get home. Bye, Grandpa. We'll be back soon."

Stephanie glanced at Karen. Stephanie remembered Grandpa's words about being an example. Stephanie had often complained about the way Karen followed her, but she had never realized what a responsibility that put on her. Stephanie determined to be the best example for her little sister that she could be. Stephanie would need the Lord's help for that. *BJW*

HOW ABOUT YOU?

Real life is a little bit like the game "Follow the Leader." Everyone is both a follower and a leader. You follow someone and someone follows you. That gives you a double responsibility. First, be sure you are following the right leader—the Lord Jesus. Second, be sure you are setting a good example for those who look up to you.

MEMORIZE:

"Be an example to all believers in what you teach, in the way you live, in your love, your faith, and your purity." 1 Timothy 4:12

BE A GOOD EXAMPLE

INDEX OF TOPICS

INDEX OF SCRIPTURE READINGS

INDEX OF MEMORY VERSES

Proverbs 13:24 *October 7*
Proverbs 14:12 *September 27*
Proverbs 14:23 *April 18*
Proverbs 15:14 *December 13*
Proverbs 16:18 *September 8*
Proverbs 17:9 *May 27*
Proverbs 17:17 *September 25*
Proverbs 18:24 *May 7*
Proverbs 22:1 *January 13*
Proverbs 25:25 *February 22*
Proverbs 26:20 *June 28*
Proverbs 27:10 *October 27*
Proverbs 28:1 *July 27*
Proverbs 31:20 *November 22*
Proverbs 31:30 *May 8, November 27*
Ecclesiastes 12:1 *June 30*
Isaiah 5:20 *May 19*
Isaiah 6:8 *November 17*
Isaiah 26:3 *July 23*
Isaiah 43:2 *January 27*
Isaiah 45:22 *July 25*
Isaiah 55:7 *April 12*
Isaiah 55:11 *June 19*
Isaiah 57:15 *January 28*
Isaiah 59:2 *October 14*
Isaiah 61:1 *August 14*
Isaiah 61:10 *November 8*
Isaiah 64:6 *January 2*
Isaiah 64:8 *June 20, August 5*
Jeremiah 1:5 *January 30*
Jeremiah 17:7 *July 2*
Jeremiah 29:11 *March 14*
Jeremiah 31:12 *May 28*
Jeremiah 32:19 *January 20*
Lamentations 3:22-23 *June 25*
Ezekiel 34:16 *May 31*
Daniel 1:8 *December 23*
Habakkuk 3:18 *October 13*
Zechariah 7:9 *November 2*
Matthew 5:8 *March 10*
Matthew 5:45 *June 14*

Matthew 6:2 *April 10*
Matthew 7:12 *June 18*
Matthew 10:29 *November 18*
Matthew 19:6 *June 12*
Matthew 24:44 *January 26*
Matthew 25:21 *March 1*
Mark 1:15 *December 18*
Mark 8:36 *January 7*
Mark 16:15 *December 17*
Luke 6:31 *March 18*
Luke 6:35 *October 28*
Luke 10:20 *January 12*
Luke 10:27 *March 8*
Luke 11:1 *December 30*
Luke 12:15 *July 8*
Luke 18:13 *August 13*
Luke 18:16 *August 7*
Luke 21:15 *May 18*
John 1:3 *January 24*
John 1:12 *January 6, June 9, October 26*
John 3:3 *December 25*
John 3:16 *July 6*
John 7:24 *May 30*
John 10:9 *October 21*
John 13:15 *February 13*
John 13:34 *May 23, October 29*
John 14:2 *April 5, September 28*
John 14:6 *September 10*
John 14:15 *April 21*
John 14:26 *August 3*
John 15:12 *August 22*
John 15:13 *May 9*
John 15:5 *April 2*
John 20:29 *August 26*
Acts 5:42 *February 8*
Acts 11:26 *January 21*
Acts 17:25 *January 29*
Acts 17:26 *December 20*
Acts 20:35 *December 14*
Acts 24:16 *July 12, November 23*
Romans 1:16 *February 10*

Romans 1:20 *February 17*
Romans 3:12 *June 6*
Romans 5:3 *April 30*
Romans 5:8 *January 1, March 31,*
  April 20
Romans 6:23 *May 24, December 7*
Romans 8:11 *November 13*
Romans 8:28 *April 8, June 21, July 9*
Romans 10:15 *September 26*
Romans 12:17a *October 15*
Romans 12:21 *September 12*
Romans 13:1 *October 20*
Romans 15:1 *February 27*
Romans 15:2 *May 29*
Romans 15:7 *November 15*
1 Corinthians 1:18 *May 16*
1 Corinthians 3:6 *July 26*
1 Corinthians 3:7 *May 26*
1 Corinthians 3:16 *July 16*
1 Corinthians 4:7 *December 1*
1 Corinthians 6:19 *July 20, November 9*
1 Corinthians 6:19-20 *August 31*
1 Corinthians 6:20 *April 11, August 16*
1 Corinthians 9:22 *January 15*
1 Corinthians 10:13 *February 23*
1 Corinthians 10:31 *April 15, May 10*
1 Corinthians 11:26 *March 29*
1 Corinthians 12:5 *September 11*
1 Corinthians 12:27 *November 26*
1 Corinthians 13:1 *September 30*
1 Corinthians 13:4 *February 28, May 14*
1 Corinthians 14:1 *November 11*
1 Corinthians 14:20 *January 8*
1 Corinthians 15:42-44 *May 5*
1 Corinthians 15:43 *July 30*
1 Corinthians 15:52 *June 27*
1 Corinthians 16:15 *March 12*
2 Corinthians 1:4 *March 24,*
  September 21, December 15
2 Corinthians 1:21-22 *July 18*
2 Corinthians 2:7 *November 28*

2 Corinthians 3:3 *August 9*
2 Corinthians 3:18 *August 27*
2 Corinthians 4:7 *May 6*
2 Corinthians 4:17 *April 9*
2 Corinthians 5:8 *March 22*
2 Corinthians 5:10 *October 1*
2 Corinthians 5:17 *January 3, April 14,*
  May 2
2 Corinthians 6:14 *May 4*
2 Corinthians 6:17 *April 19*
2 Corinthians 8:5 *April 16*
2 Corinthians 9:7 *January 4, March 23*
2 Corinthians 9:8 *December 9*
2 Corinthians 9:15 *December 24*
2 Corinthians 11:14 *July 5, November 6*
Galatians 2:20 *March 30*
Galatians 5:22 *May 17, October 22*
Galatians 6:10 *January 14*
Ephesians 1:13 *May 25*
Ephesians 2:8 *December 6*
Ephesians 2:8-9 *July 21*
Ephesians 2:10 *April 4*
Ephesians 4:3 *March 2*
Ephesians 4:15 *June 1*
Ephesians 4:30 *April 17, November 14*
Ephesians 4:31 *July 28, September 24*
Ephesians 4:32 *March 19, September 9,*
  November 5
Ephesians 5:1-2 *August 17*
Ephesians 6:1 *October 6*
Philippians 1:6 *August 25*
Philippians 1:21 *January 16, March 27*
Philippians 1:26 *April 13*
Philippians 2:5, 8 *December 3*
Philippians 2:14 *June 4*
Philippians 4:6 *October 19*
Philippians 4:11 *July 22, October 5*
Philippians 4:13 *March 26*
Colossians 1:13-14 *August 12*
Colossians 2:7 *February 15*
Colossians 3:2 *August 21*